D1568380

DESIGN FOR FLOODING

DESIGN FOR FLOODING

Architecture, Landscape, and Urban Design for Resilience to Flooding and Climate Change

Donald Watson, FAIA, and

Michele Adams, P.E.

JOHN WILEY & SONS, INC.

For general information about our other products and services, please contact our Customer Care Department within the United States at (800) 762-2974, outside the United States at (317) 572-3993 or fax (317) 572-4002.

Wiley also publishes its books in a variety of electronic formats. Some content that appears in print may not be available in electronic books. For more information about Wiley products, visit our web site at www.wiley.com.

Library of Congress Cataloging-in-Publication Data:

Watson, Donald, 1937-
     Design for flooding : architecture, landscape and urban design for resilience to flooding and climate change / Donald Watson and Michele Adams.
          p.   cm.
     Includes index.
     ISBN 978-0-470-47564-5 (cloth : alk. paper);
     ISBN 978-0-470-89000-4 (ebk); ISBN 978-0-470-89001-1 (ebk); ISBN 978-0-470-89002-8 (ebk);
     ISBN 978-0-470-95031-9 (ebk); ISBN 978-0-470-95056-2 (ebk);
          1. Architecture and climate.   2. Flood damage prevention.   3. City planning—Environmental aspects.   4. Environmental management.   5. Climatic changes.   I. Adams, Michele (Michele C.), 1961-   II. Title.   III. Title: Architecture, landscape and urban design for resilience to flooding and climate change.
     NA2541.W38 2011
     720'.47—dc22
                                                                                        2010016472

Printed in the United States of America

10 9 8 7 6 5 4 3 2 1

CONTENTS

Preface and Acknowledgments   *vii*
Foreword by Carol Franklin,
RLA, FASLA   *ix*
Foreword by Daniel E. Williams, FAIA   *xi*
Introduction   *xv*

PART I: NATURE OF WATER   1

Chapter 1: Weather   3
1.1   Sun and Earth   3
1.2   The Atmosphere   6
1.3   Weather   17

Chapter 2: Land and Water   31
2.1   Water and Carbon Cycles   31
2.2   Biodiversity and the Landscape   36
2.3   Follow the Water: The Opportunity
       for Watershed Planning   43

Chapter 3: Flooding   49
3.1   Flooding from Increased
       Precipitation   49
3.2   Flooding from Severe Storms   54
3.3   Economic and Social Costs of
       Water-Related Natural Disasters   61

PART II: DESIGN WITH WATER   67

Chapter 4: The Natural Landscape   71
4.1   Understanding the Natural
       Water Balance   71
4.2   When the Water Balance Is Altered   74
4.3   Soils and Vegetation   78
4.4   Subsurface Water Movement   83
4.5   Stream Systems, Wetlands, Riparian
       Zones, and Floodplains   84

Chapter 5: The Altered Landscape   91
5.1   When the Landscape Is Altered   91
5.2   Altered Stream Systems and
       Increased Flood Damage   95
5.3   Why Detention Does Not Solve
       Flooding   98
5.4   Summary: The Natural Landscape
       as a Model for Resilient Design   99

Chapter 6: Design for Inland Flooding 103
6.1   Resilient Design for Inland Flooding 103
6.2   Tools for Watershed Protection   125
6.3   Communities and Buildings in
       Floodplains   129

PART III: FLOOD-RESISTANT DESIGN 131

Chapter 7: Flood Design Analysis   135
7.1   Definition of Terms   135
7.2   Flood Elevation: Base Flood and Design Flood   143

Chapter 8: The Coast   151
8.1   Coastal Processes   151
8.2   Shoreline Protection   160
8.3   Flood Barriers and Floodgates   164
8.4   Summary of Coastal Protection Measures   164

Chapter 9: Flood Design Practices for Buildings   169
9.1   Overview of Flood Design   169
9.2   Flood Design at the Building Scale   176

PART IV: DESIGN FOR RESILIENCE 197

Chapter 10: Flood-Resistant Design for Sites and Communities   199
10.1   Coastal Communities   199

10.2   Comprehensive Planning for Resilient Communities   207
10.3   Local Actions to Build Community Resilience   210

Chapter 11: Sea Level Rise   219
11.1   Sea Level Rise: The Issues   220
11.2   Sea Level Rise: Design Responses   223

Chapter 12: Design for Resilience   257
12.1   The Wave of the Future   257
12.2   Models for National and International Action   259
12.3   Design Resolution   268

Epilogue   271
Glossary   273
Index   295

PREFACE AND ACKNOWLEDGMENTS

The ideas presented in this book combine many voices, over many years of conversation and professional endeavor. The concept of resilience has emerged in the past decade in both international and national responses to severe climatic impacts. The fact that those climatic impacts are in part explained by how we build on the land—the enterprise of the design and construction professions—reverses what many of us spend careers in teaching and practicing: to *design with climate*, building informed by bioclimatic design principles. This conception has been part of architecture writing and theory since Vitruvius wrote of climate, Sun, and wind influences within the art and science of "building well." In early twentieth century, Frank Lloyd Wright promoted a poetic and philosophic conception of "organic architecture" in recognition of the inspiration of nature in his work. The "green thread" continued to be expressed in the 1920s and 1930s work of Bauhaus architects, Finnish master architect Alvar Aalto, and American works of Mary Colter, Richard Neutra, the Keck Brothers, and the collaboration of Maria Telkes and Eleanor Raymond, among many others.

Now *climate* is influenced by *design*, a reversal of the vector of influence. As viewed in this book, every building project, large or small, contributes to climatic moderation or extremity in some way as part of a watershed, floodplain, or coastal environment. The line that the designer draws has global consequence.

This book thus follows an evolving approach to architecture that the Olgyay brothers defined in the 1950s as "bioclimatic design," subsequently defined by Ian McHarg as "environmental design," by Malcomb Wells as "gentle architecture," followed by "passive solar design" in the 1970s, "regenerative design" by landscape architect John T. Lyle, and "sustainable design" after the Rio Earth Summit in the early 1990s. Each of these terms and their variations attempt some nuance to a deeply felt response of architecture and landscape architecture to the world.

This book grows out of these conversations. The challenge to define a comprehensive vision of sustainable communities evolves from formative discussions of the AIA Committee on the Environment with Bob Berkebile, Randolph Croxton, Susan Maxman, Bill McDonough, Gail Lindsay, Richard Rittelmann, Carol and Colin Franklin, Harry Gordon, Sharon Sutton, and Pliny Fisk and Gail Vittori, to name only a brief few. The preeminence of water as formative element in design was the focus of a "watershed" symposium, Water + Design, sponsored by EPA/AIA in 2006, led by Daniel Williams and Vivian Loftness. The symposium brought together international experts around the topic of water. It demonstrated the power of collaboration of disparate fields from conservation biology sciences to civil engineering design integrated into community, landscape and building design, adding the "blue stream" to the green thread. This collaboration is central to the agenda for resilient design.

Collaboration made this book possible. The authors are indebted to chapter reviews by Carl McDaniel, David Borton, and Tavis Dockwiller. Kate McElwain, Petrik Watson, Kimberly Ann Watson, Brittany Adams, and Linda Thomas prepared artwork and photographs. The notes to each chapter acknowledge additional contribu-tions, all gratefully received, including examples of world-rank photographers, cited in captions and credits.

The technical review of Christopher Jones, P.E., is responsible for much of what is correct in the representa-tion of FEMA requirements and details of best practices of flood-resistant design. The authors alone are responsible for errors that linger.

FOREWORD

Carol Franklin, RLA, FASLA

The Earth is the water planet, and the only water planet we currently know.

Human beings have become one of the most significant forces misusing water. The premise of this wonderful book is that water is a resource and not a problem and that many small, distributed projects are always better than one big, concentrated solution.

Design for Flooding gives the reader both an understanding of "why to" and a very thorough grasp of "how to" design with this critical resource. It begins with a clear picture of water as a series of interrelated systems that include the atmosphere, the oceans, and the land. The book takes the reader from a broad planetary view to an eagle's-eye focus on the smallest details and the problems of the design and construction of water management systems.

A gold mine of the latest and best information, this book could be considered one of the first survival guides for the global climate change era. It emphasizes that traditional threats to water resources will be exaggerated by global climate change, with severe impacts on our cities and natural lands. As climate experts have predicted (and as we have recently seen in New Orleans), one of the most visible and immediate effects of climate change will be the increasing severity of storms, resulting in greater river and coastal flooding. *Design for Flooding* illustrates how these more intense storms will strain the capacity of our already inadequate stormwater management infrastructure and how the impermeable surfaces of our ever-expanding cities have taken away the capacity of the landscape to absorb this water.

One of the newest goals of "green building" strategies is to slow or prevent the present effects of building and site development on climate change. One of the coauthors, Don Watson, a leader in the Green Building Movement, wrote *Climatic Design* in 1984. That book became a standard reference for architects, detailing how climate can and should influence design in modern building. Twenty-five years later, *Design for Flooding* focuses on water issues. It provides both an in-depth understanding of the processes that created these problems and design solutions that allow buildings and landscapes to be more "resilient" to storms and flooding.

The conventional wisdom for dealing with water has turned around 180 degrees in the last 30 years. As an engineer in Houston once said in exasperation to one of my colleagues, "All my career I have been trying to get water off a site and you are telling me to keep it on." Slapping his head, he said, "I must call my boss."

Many important figures—including the hydrologist Luna Leopold and the landscape architect and regional planner Ian McHarg, among others—laid the foundations for this new paradigm and for the material in this book. Subsequently, civil engineers, such as Tom Cahill, father of Michele Adams, introduced a wider world to the concept of a "water balance" (the flow of water in and out of a watershed). He showed us that the predevelopment water balance was the key to ensuring water in our streams when it is not raining. Tom was not afraid to reach across the aisle to the more "ignorant" design professions to correct our misunderstandings and to convey the basic ways that the water system worked. The solutions that Tom urged on us are now required "best practices" (in more enlightened jurisdictions).

My firm, Andropogon, has worked with Tom and Michele since the beginning of our practice, pioneering imaginative and innovative ways to preserve, restore, or maintain a healthy water balance. Michele now leads the charge that her father started. I have this vivid memory of Michele, 40 years ago, on the site of our first porous paving parking lot. She was carrying big buckets of crushed stone meant for the recharge basin underneath and patiently explaining to the burly construction workers what materials were or were not up to specifications. Both authors bring this combination of solid theory and careful attention to detail, which is one of the delights of this book.

Design for Flooding should be a major tool for public agencies, for the design professions, and for civic activists—indeed, for everyone who wishes to bring a genuinely "intelligent" design for water to their communities. It is a call to action and demonstrates that we have the knowledge, the tools, and the capability to better manage the water system on which we depend.

Carol Franklin, a founding principal of Andropogon Associates, is a registered landscape architect and a Fellow of the American Society of Landscape Architects. She is a nationally recognized expert in sustainable design and in applied ecological restoration.

FOREWORD

DANIEL E. WILLIAMS, FAIA

Over the 6,000-year history of human settlements, the forms and patterns of buildings, cities, and regions have been a response to the social, economic, ecological, and climatic conditions of the time. Science is now telling us that the climate is changing. Cities and regions, especially along coastlines, will be changed from bottom to top. Our response must change as well. The underground infrastructure for water, sewer, communication lines, transportation, and power will be impacted. The structural capacity of the geology and soil will change, as will city boundaries due to sea level rising, changing the terrestrial footprint. These are not "the-sky-is-falling" scenarios. Change has always been part of the planet. The most frequent forcing function of migration and a city's demise is water—too much or too little. The remarkable and real difference now is that we are, for the first time in history, aware of it while it is happening. As we have a hand in the risks created, we have a hand in the solutions to affect the rate and magnitude of change and disruption.

It can be said that we have learned very little from recent history. We have not left the floodplains, but instead expand within them, removing natural areas or functions that protect us from natural hazards. We live on earthquake faults and in paths of hurricanes and tsunamis. We have not been respectful of the ecological benefits of coastal zone ecologies that support all life. We have rejected opportunities to guide growth and development. Instead, we plan by default, often unconscionable and inefficient land use patterns. We have sent our wastes into the very water

reservoirs that provide our children's water supply—all acts detrimental to the planet, the economy, and our families.

But this time we know more and can do better. We are better at understanding the big picture. We are technically savvy in mapping and data resource analysis, in some cases with real-time satellite monitoring of weather patterns, allowing preparation for some (but not all) extreme weather events. With the unique gift of the creative spirit, we are interested in the challenges of the unknown.

To help prepare for the known unknown, authors Watson and Adams have given us an important and timely guidebook. Important because the science tells us that changes are imminent—and this book explains those changes that impact flooding in straightforward and clearly defined terms—and timely because "sea changes" are already being measured—and this book lays out design projects, programs, and policies by which to address those changes.

Architects and planners are a hybrid of knowledge silos—part scientist, part engineer, part artist, and sometimes visionary—but able to be informed by the knowledge relevant to the time and mindful of the past. Whether it is energy efficiency, flooding, or climate change, knowledge is the foundation of our present agenda. The research, references, and compilation of design principles and practices in *Design for Flooding* provide that foundation. The chapters on natural landscape offer a detailed and engaging account of the natural systems from regional watersheds, to vernal ponds, to micropores in soils that rely on the water balance and often the planning decision simply to be left alone to provide nature's free ecosystem services. The chapters on coast flood design provide a clear and comprehensive guide to the complex design and engineering requirements and regulations of flood-resistant design, bringing together dozens of source materials. These chapters, highlighting the most up-to-date recommendations for coastal design professionals, are essential reading for architects, planners, and others working with communities in preparing for flooding or in hurricane disaster remediation. Terms are defined and illustrated to provide the language of multidisciplinary design. *Design for Flooding* defines the need and opportunity for planners, architects, landscape architects, engineers, and conservation biologists to work together to develop the mix of inland and coastal flooding solutions required for a comprehensive response to climate change. The Glossary alone provides a lexicon of terms that design professionals should know to participate in the challenges of environmental renovation and retrofit and, as the authors express it in their summary chapter, in "the *resolution* to design for resilience."

What a remarkable time to be living, a time when we are rethinking what we do, imagining cities as living structures, capable of creating and cycling their own energy and materials, and designing whole regions planned as watersheds that provide a sustainable supply of water, food, and jobs all within a livable-walkable urban patterns.

Illustrative examples in *Design for Flooding* show the way in projects and programs at local, community and national, even international, scale.

If the future of these patterns is to adapt and change—to be resilient—what are the new challenges that we must be aware of and react to? What are the possible opportunities before us for better cities and regions? Watson and Adams give us an overview of these challenges and opportunities with great depth and detail to inform our design and planning and adapt our solutions to flooding. The book *Design for Flooding* is required reading and viewing—the myriad photographs and illustrations tell a rich story of their own—for any and all involved in the challenges of designing and building a more sustainable future, with and without the flood.

Daniel E. Williams, FAIA, is principal of Daniel Williams Architect in Seattle, with specialization in sustainable architecture and planning. He was 2006 chair of the AIA Sustainability Task Group and is a member of the U.S. EPA National Advisory Council for Environmental Policy and Technology. He currently serves on the Clinton Foundation Climate Change Initiative expert panel. His book *Sustainable Design: Ecology, Architecture, and Planning*, published by John Wiley & Sons, was selected among the top 10 books of 2008 in urban planning by Planetizen.com.

Atlantic coastal estuary of the Webhannet River, Wells, Maine. Design for resilience improves water resources and the communities that increasingly rely on them for a sustainable future.

(PHOTO: © Robert Perron)

INTRODUCTION

Design for Flooding turns flood threat into opportunity to improve water resources and community resilience at regional, community, and building scales.

These are the only genuine ideas, the ideas of the shipwrecked.

—José Ortega y Gassett, 1930

Design for Flooding builds on the emerging concept of *resilience* and considers flooding as a natural process. Addressing flooding as a given natural process of weather and water leads to imaginative and comprehensive approaches to resilient design, applicable at regional, community, and building scale.

Resilience is the capacity of a system, community, or society potentially exposed to hazards to adapt, by resisting or changing, in order to reach and maintain an acceptable level of functioning and structure. This is determined by the degree to which the social system is capable of organizing itself to increase its capacity for learning from past disasters for better future protection and to improve risk reduction measures.

—"International Strategy for Disaster Reduction" ISDR Secretariat. 2009
www.unisdr.org/eng/library/lib-terminology-eng home.htm.

Floods are the most frequent natural disaster in the United States. One in three federal disaster declarations are related to flooding, many as a result of hurricanes affecting heavily populated U.S. coastlines. Inland flooding and heavy debris flows follow intense winter storms and spring rainy seasons. Effects attributed to climate change are evidenced in increasingly severe storm events and the prospect of sea level rise.[1]

Flooding is not new. Some flooding is part of the natural hydrologic cycle and the sustenance it brings to life on Earth. Flooding is natural. It is a disaster because of the way we have built upon areas susceptible to flooding.

Because flooding is little understood and appreciated as a natural system in conventional land development, it arrives with unwelcomed and unanticipated intensity. Precipitation patterns are changing, in some areas increasing in annual rainfall, while other areas are experiencing longer and more extensive drought. Across the nation, the severity of rainfall and storm events is increasing. At the same time, land development, agriculture, and urban sprawl take up more of the natural landscape that previously helped to mitigate and diffuse storm and flood intensity.

Natural benefits of flooding become threats of flooding when not considered in community planning and building design. Lack of proper planning and design results in flooding that is a fearful threat to the life and property of individuals and communities in its path.

THE CHALLENGE

Extreme weather events, flooding, drought, and environmental stresses impose new demands on design of buildings and communities and our natural land and water resources. These stresses are impelled by climate change but also by the way we have built on the land and our coastal areas. Sprawl and insensitive land development practices continue to remove the natural resources and their functions from the landscape, thereby increasing environmental stresses.

THE OPPORTUNITY

Design and enhancement of the water balance and resources of watersheds, aquifers, floodplains, and built infrastructure can mitigate and help to prepare for severe weather and climate change.

Flooding can benefit a region if it is anticipated. Rain collection from both intermittent and storm flooding of natural areas serves to replenish and stabilize the vegetative soil layer, and cleanses areas susceptible to salinity. Plentiful rain moving across the land and stored in groundwater aquifers provides inland waterways for wildlife habitat and for countless human purposes, including food, fire safety, recreation, and freshwater essential to all of life.

Design for Flooding presents a new approach to design buildings and communities with five defining concepts.

Design for Resilience

Resilient design prepares for extreme storms and flooding of inland watersheds and coastal areas to provide resiliency and emergency preparedness for natural disaster. The concept of resiliency applies lessons from natural systems to design for extreme conditions using strategies of buffering,

zone separation, redundancy, rapid feedback, and decentralization. Resilient design presents a new paradigm for design and building professionals to create buildings, communities, and regions that restore and improve our water resources and that mitigate threats of extreme weather and climate change.

Protect and Extend Ecosystem Services

The concept of *ecosystem services* recognizes and helps to credit the economic, health, and social benefits derived from functioning natural environments, land, vegetation, water, and living organisms. Natural landscapes provide clean air, fresh water storage, diversity of plants and wildlife, crop pollination, groundwater recharge, waste decomposition, and recycling of nutrients. Forests provide greenhouse gas mitigation and regenerative response to fire, drought, flooding, and climate change. Wetlands control erosion and flooding, remove pollutants from water, and recharge the groundwater reservoirs that we all rely on for our water supply. Coastal marshes, wetlands, and mangroves provide important buffers to coastal storms and storm surge.

Create Watershed Plans and Sustainable Stormwater Systems

Watershed planning is a multidisciplinary approach to water as a valued resource considered at each phase of its flow and use within natural defined by specific geological and climatic conditions. This concept focuses on water flows within the natural systems of regions, including restoration of the subsurface aquifers and integration of water and Green infrastructure in urban development. *Sustainable stormwater design* is an approach that reduces disturbance, protects and restores natural features, and uses soil and vegetation to manage stormwater. The focus of this concept is on designs that improve the local and regional water balance as a resource and principal of flood control engineering.

Implement Floodplain Management and Flood Resistant Design

Floodplain management is a correlate and extension of watershed planning adopted into practice, focusing on the impacts of flooding. It includes land use policies and regulations for development in flood-prone areas, restoration and protection of natural resources and functions of floodplains and contributing watersheds, and flood-resistant design. New "smart grid" techniques allow automatic monitoring and rapid response to river flooding as well as monitoring dykes and other flood-control measures. *Flood-resistant design* includes avoidance by relocating buildings and infrastructure out of harm's way, along with flood protection and mitigation measures: raising buildings above code-mandated flood levels, engineering buildings for severe wind and wave impacts, and using materials that are waterproof or otherwise impermeable to water damage.

Practice the Precautionary Principle

Designing to code minimum is not sufficient as a professional and due diligent response to flooding and the other increasingly severe impacts of extreme weather and climate change. The way we have built on the land—meeting only the minimal regulatory requirements under present law—has made things worse. Following current planning to code minimums in many cases aggravates flooding beyond the project boundaries by fragmenting natural areas, increasing hardscape that increases stormwater overflows, and eliminating open space and vegetation that historically have served as natural filters and buffers. At the same time, increasingly severe weather events are exceeding guidelines and regulatory minimums represented in codes, which are slow to respond to new information and need for higher standards.

The design of buildings, especially in areas exposed to flooding, involves risk assessment by designers and building owners. Risk assessment requires decisions that must somehow mediate between options, some riskier than others, some costlier than others, some more difficult to implement. Design is a response to risk in its charge to provide shelter and habitable spaces and livable communities, fulfilling the broadly define obligation to the public to protect life, safety, and welfare.

The *precautionary principle* considers that if an action or policy might cause severe or irreversible harm to public health or the environment, restraint is called for, and, in the absence of verifiable documentation that harm will not result, either to not undertake the action or to require consideration of all feasible and less risky alternatives.

The precautionary approach is defined in 1992 Rio Earth Summit Declaration:

> In order to protect the environment, the precautionary approach shall be widely applied by States according to their capabilities. Where there are threats of serious or irreversible damage, lack of full scientific certainty shall not be used as a reason for postponing cost-effective measures to prevent environmental degradation.

The precautionary principle is a response to risk of possible or probable harm to health or environment, even if the extent of harm is not yet fully established or documented. It is an ethical principle. When adopted as guideline for public policy and where there is credible evidence of potential harm if an action is taken, then immediate steps must be considered to mitigate, reduce, or eliminate that threat while also pursuing risk assessment studies. The precautionary principle is properly applied to actions that are potentially irreversible, such as planning where biodiversity and ecological services may be irretrievably lost or reduced. The principle suggests that "interventions must be reversible and flexible. Any mistakes must be correctible."[2]

The strong argument for adopting precautionary measures in environmental matters is that, if a practice or action turns out to cause irreversible harm, the finding of harm may come too little and too late to reverse or repair it.

WATER AS A FOCUS OF RESILIENT DESIGN

Water has a direct physical impact evident at every scale of the natural and built environment of regions, communities, and buildings. Climate change has increased severe storms as well as droughts, with threats to water resources impacting both the natural and built environment.

Water is a renewable but limited resource. Water conservation can effectively double water availability but has not yet been adopted to the scale of its potential. Throughout the United States and world, urban development is demanding more water at a greater rate than available either from regional rains or reservoirs in local aquifers.

Unless this is reversed, freshwater can no longer be considered a renewable resource.

Aggressive water well pumping is drawing down deepwater reservoirs and aquifers that accumulated over millennia. Once depleted, these reservoirs are essentially gone forever. We currently use and abuse water in ways that are not sustainable. Once a free gift of nature, water is now a costly commodity. We are throwing away the very elixir of life.

Flooding and extreme weather events are part of natural climate and weather-driven processes. If prepared for, these events can be benefits to long-term environmental health, replenishing aquifers, shredding overgrowth, and transporting nutrients. Resilient design can turn threat into opportunity.

The key to opportunity is how we design and manage the natural landscape, its geography and aquifers, and the complex of engineered waterways, reservoirs, and built environment of water transport, buildings, and sewer systems.

OUTLINE OF THIS BOOK

Part I reviews the basics of weather and water-related events that lead to flooding and other natural disaster risk to buildings and communities. Weather carries water throughout the globe. The land receives and stores water available as the water balance to support natural vegetation, agriculture, and communities. Understanding the life of even small and ephemeral bodies of water helps to deepen the importance of landscape and building designs at the local microclimate scale. Flooding is described within the context of U.S. storm patterns and impact on social and economic communities. Coastal development is long established—essentially embodying the historic and cultural development of each coastal region of the United States, its cities, and maritime heritage. Coastal development is growing in population and value of investment. These two factors—the rich maritime past and an attractive market future—create the opportunity of turning the threat of flooding into the opportunity for resilient design of our buildings and communities.

Part II presents the concept of water balance as part of the natural and sustainable patterns of regional and local water resources. The focus is on landforms and vegetation as a watershed, in which rain and snow are part of the natural cycle of hydrology, including inland and riverine flooding. Watershed design and management is required to create, preserve, and protect the water balance of the region. In this view, all parts of the natural landscape and built environment are intrinsic to the ecology of land, vegetation, and water. Measures of resilient design for inland flooding protect and improve the capacity of communities to be sustained within their regional water balance. In this view, every building design and site is part of either the problem or the solution to regional water sustainability and security.

Part III focuses on designing buildings to avoid or resist flood hazards by meeting and exceeding code-specified levels in both riverine and coastal zones. The most severe risks relate to storm surge and wave effects, so that the principal focus of flood-resistant design is upon coastal zones. Similar measures address flood-resistant design for all floodplains, to meet the standards and model regulations of the Federal Emergency Management Authority. The chapters in Part III emphasize recommendations to go beyond code minimum, to decrease risk and improve quality of communities in flood-prone areas.

Part IV takes up the question of sea level rise. The discussion includes design proposals being developed in the United States and elsewhere that show ways to anticipate and adapt to its impacts. The prospect of rising seas as a result of climate change is daunting and a topic that no one would normally wish to consider. Sea level rise is a prospect and possibility that is now part of established consensus among a majority of climate and ocean scientists. Differences revolve around how much and when rather than if. The implications of sea level rise and the increasingly extreme weather events that climate change impacts are now part of planning and managing any coastal community designed for the long term.

The concluding chapter builds on national and international programs that respond to flood risk in an agenda for resilient design, combining the principles and practices of watershed, floodplain, and coastal area planning and design. An agenda and call for "resolution" for the design and building professions comes out of climate change threat to create opportunity to improve the natural resources and the communities that increasingly rely on resilient design for a sustainable future.

Climate Change and Water, a report prepared for the Intergovernmental Panel on Climate Change (IPCC) in 2008, summarizes impacts of climate change on the world's water resources.

- Climate change has resulted in changing precipitation, intensity and extremes, reduced snow cover and ice melt, changes in soils and runoff.

- By mid-twenty-first century, annual average river runoff and water availability are expected to increase at high latitudes and in some wet tropical areas, while water resources will decrease in some dry regions at mid-latitudes such as western United States and the dry tropics.

- Increased precipitation intensity and variability will increase risk of rain-generated flooding. At the same time, there will be increase extreme drought and aridity in continental interiors, especially the sub-tropics.

- Water supplies stored in glaciers and snow cover are projected to decline, resulting in water shortages, low flows and aridity during warm and dry periods. The hydric regimes of mountain ranges—where more than one-sixth of world's population live—are at risk

- High temperatures and extremes, including floods and droughts, will affect water quality and add to water pollution from sediments, nutrients, dissolved organic carbon, pathogens, pesticides and salt as well as thermal pollution. This will impact ecosystems, human health, and water system reliability and costs, including agriculture and food security.

- Sea level rise is projected to extend areas of salinization of groundwater and estuaries, resulting in a decrease of freshwater availability for humans and ecosystems in coastal areas.

- Negative impacts of climate change impacts on freshwater systems will outweigh benefits. Although increased annual runoff in some areas is projected to lead to increases in total water supply to those areas, in many regions, this benefit is likely to be counterbalanced by the negative effects of increased variability of precipitation and seasonal runoff shifts in water supply, water quality, and flood risks.

- Climate change affects the function of existing water infrastructure, including hydropower, flood defenses, drainage, and irrigation at the same time that water demand will increase, due to population growth and development accompanied by increasing demand for irrigation water.

- Climate change may alter the reliability of current water management systems and water-related infrastructure. Although quantitative projections of changes in precipitation, river flows, and water levels at the river-basin scale are uncertain, it is likely that hydrological characteristics will change in the future.

- Adaptation options require integrated demand-side as well as supply-side strategies. The former improve water-use efficiency, that is, by recycling water. An expanded use of economic incentives, including metering and pricing, to encourage water conservation and development of water markets. Supply-side strategies generally involve increases in storage capacity, abstraction from watercourses, and water transfers.

Source: WMO and UNEP, *Climate Change and Water*. Technical Papers of the Intergovernmental Panel on Climate Change, ed. B.C. Bates, Z.W. Kundzewicz, S. Wu, and J.P. Palutikof (Geneva: IPCC Secretariat, 2008). www.ipcc.ch/pdf/technical-papers/climate-change-water-en.pdf

THESIS OF DESIGN FOR FLOODING

Risk and Opportunity

Climate, weather, and flooding are influenced by the way that communities and urban infrastructure are designed and built.

1. COASTAL AND WATER-EDGE PROPERTIES HAVE HIGH POPULATION DENSITY AND PROPERTY VALUES

- Fifty percent of the U.S. population resides in coastal counties and waterways.

- Population growth of these coastal counties continues to increase, due to their market attractiveness and lifestyle choice of affluent and retirement segment of the housing market.

- Coastal communities along the East Coast and the Great Lakes represent the colonial and nineteenth-century maritime history of the nation. Some are cities with long-established infrastructure of ports, harbors, railway, truck and car access, roads, and bridges.

- Property values and investments in coastal communities and cities remain high, due to their desirable coastal locations, businesses, and lifestyles associated with maritime commerce and seaside recreation.

- Portions of these coastal city waterfronts are abandoned as maritime commerce has moved elsewhere, and they remain in deteriorated condition, awaiting reinvestment and renovation to adaptive uses.

2. INCREASED FLOODING IS IN PART AN UNINTENDED CONSEQUENCE AND RESULT OF INTENSIVE DEVELOPMENT OF FLOODPLAIN AND COASTAL AREAS

Some portions of coastal community sites and building stock were built after World War II in informal plots and without overall community planning, rapidly constructed and without regulation, often for only seasonal rental uses. Much of that building stock is now used year-round, with and without upgrading, and is most at risk to hurricane and other severe storms.

The sprawl of coastal development has impinged on, eliminated, or otherwise compromised natural areas of coastal forest, wetland, and marshes—as well as barrier strands—that have developed over millennia to absorb flooding and storm impacts. The way that buildings and communities were built thus increased risk above and beyond preexisting natural conditions.

As a result of development that did not protect or improve natural site protection, coastal flooding and extreme storm damage has resulted, not because of their coastal location but as a result of the way buildings and communities were designed and built.

Due to the loss of coastal seabeds and the viability of the freshwater estuaries and rivers that serve them, commercial fishing, shellfish, and related enterprises that traditionally flourished in healthy coastal waters are now closed or severely impacted to minimal operations.

3. CLIMATE CHANGE HAS DISRUPTED GLOBAL PRECIPITATION PATTERNS AND RESULTED IN MORE SEVERE STORMS

Climate change has resulted in more severe storm impacts and more precipitation in small and peak events, increasing flooding events and resulting damage.

Although scientific evidence of the rate and schedule of sea level rise is still a matter of debate that is whether sea levels will rise quickly or slowly, in decades or in centuries, it is seen as a realistic possibility within the life of structures and communities being planned and constructed today. Due diligence and precaution requires that the "upper limit" of sea level rise be considered in design.

In some cases, sea level rise will require removal of buildings and infrastructure, essentially moved to high ground. Other areas can be cordoned off with dikes and protective barriers and at the same time improved, as in polder communities in Netherlands, below sea level but with a water balance maintained by normal precipitation and flooding.

Even slight sea level rise will change the nature of inundation of fresh- and salt water through the natural systems of coastal marshes, beach strands, and seabeds that remain. In some areas, such as southeast Florida, very slight rises in sea level will increase saltwater intrusion into the porous limestone aquifers that currently stores freshwater, such that salt water will percolate upwards into shallow freshwater aquifers. For these systems, dikes and levees are ineffective.

4. RESPONSE TO THREAT CAN BECOME AN OPPORTUNITY TO REBUILD OUR NATURAL CLIMATIC DEFENSES AND REVITALIZE COMMUNITIES

Our floodplains and coastal communities are a "new frontier" of development. Stream and river systems previously channeled to divert floodwaters elsewhere and covered over with historic and modern urbanization are opportunities for daylighting along with adding greening and recreational amenities for community revitalization. Coastal areas that were previously abused and polluted by waterfront industries are opportunities for new development that will revitalize coastal communities while restoring the natural flood control services and marine-based aquaculture of coastal ecologies. The agenda of resilient design offers strategies designed for each place, suited to its exposure to risk and opportunities for protection, adaptation, and revitalization.

NOTES
INTRODUCTION

NOTE: Web sites listed in text and notes were accessed in May 2010.

1. WMO and UNEP, *Climate Change and Water.* Technical Papers of the Intergovernmental Panel on Climate Change, ed. B.C. Bates, Z.W. Kundzewicz, S. Wu, and J.P. Palutikof (Geneva: IPCC Secretariat, 2008). www.ipcc.ch/pdf/technical-papers/climate-change-water-en.pdf.

2. Joel Ticknor, Carolyn Raffensperger, and Nancy Myers. *The Precautionary Principle in Action: A Handbook.* Science and Environmental Health Network, 1997.

PART I

NATURE OF WATER

Watershed design and floodplain management are based on the physics of water at all scales of the hydrologic cycle.

We are tied to the ocean ... and when we go back to the sea, whether it is to sail or to watch, we are going back from whence we came.

—John F. Kennedy, 1962

CHAPTER 1 Weather

CHAPTER 2 Land and Water

CHAPTER 3 Flooding

Figure 1.1 *Self-regulating climate*: Clouds form as moisture in thermals updrafts condenses upon meeting cooler air aloft, shading the land and limiting further warming. Gulf of Carpentaria, Northern Australia.

(PHOTO: © Reg Morrison)

Source: Reg Morrison, *The Climate Debate*, 2009, <homepage.mac.com/gregalchin/rm/pdfs/climate%20debate.pdf> .

CHAPTER 1

WEATHER

1.1 SUN AND EARTH

The thin line of life that surrounds the globe is defined by the precise juxtaposition of Earth's orbit around the Sun, its orientation in its orbital eccentricity, and Moon's gravitational balance. Earth's geological history, atmosphere of oxygen and water, and magnetic field contribute to the conditions that created and sustain our biological life. Earth's axial tilt and annual rotation around the Sun define our climates and seasons. The Sun's radiant energy and thermal flux of lands and oceans drive the daily progression of water within the atmosphere and regions of the globe.

Earth has just the right mass, chemical composition, and distance from the Sun to permit water to exist as a liquid, solid, or gas, freely changing its state as it is transported through our atmosphere. Not a drop of liquid water has been found elsewhere in the solar system. This was not always so. Channels on Mars suggest that early in its history, its climate was warmer and it too had free-flowing water.

To understand flooding, one must understand water. To understand water, one must understand climate and weather. Variations that we experience on Earth in climate, weather, and water begin with Sun–Earth geometry. Viewed from a hypothetical position above the North Pole, the Earth orbits the Sun counterclockwise in an elliptical orbit, close to a perfect circle. The average distance to the Sun is 93 million miles (150 million km). This distance is called 1 *astronomical unit of length* (AU), defined by the International Astronomical Union as the mean distance between the Earth and Sun over 1 orbit of the Earth. (Figure 1.2.)

Earth's axis is tilted 23.4° with respect to its orbital plane, defined by the line between the Sun and Earth. The *angle of incidence* is the angle formed between the Sun's parallel rays and earth's surface. This angle is known to designers familiar with requirements for window shading and solar control: For any building at any latitude, the range of solar altitude in degree angles is 23.4° + 23.4° = 46.8°.

Due to the Earth's axial tilt, the amount of sunlight reaching the surface of Earth varies over the course of the year, and heat imbalance is created between the poles, generating conditions for global thermal flows in atmosphere and oceans. By convention, the seasons of the calendar are determined by the *summer and winter solstice*—when the tilt of Earth's axis is most inclined toward or away from the Sun—and the *vernal* and *autumnal equinox*, when the angle of the tilt is perpendicular to the Sun–Earth line and the Sun directly overhead along the equator.

The average distance between Earth and Moon is approximately 240,000 miles (386,000 km) or, for purposes of visualization, approximately 30 times Earth's diameter. Earth is held in orbit by the gravitational force of the Sun. Earth and Moon are influenced by mutual gravitation that counteracts their centrifugal forces. The world's ocean mass is pulled by lunar gravity that influences tides more than the Sun's gravitation field. (Figures 1.3 and 1.4.)

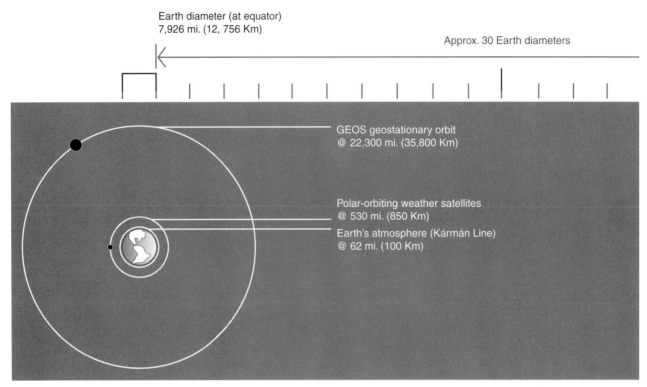

Earth diameter (at equator)
7,926 mi. (12, 756 Km)

Approx. 30 Earth diameters

GEOS geostationary orbit
@ 22,300 mi. (35,800 Km)

Polar-orbiting weather satellites
@ 530 mi. (850 Km)

Earth's atmosphere (Kármán Line)
@ 62 mi. (100 Km)

Figure 1.2   *Earth, Moon, and Sun* shown in scale of size and distance.

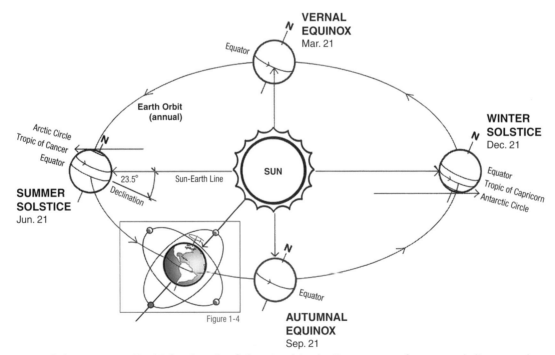

VERNAL EQUINOX Mar. 21

Equator

Earth Orbit (annual)

Arctic Circle
Tropic of Cancer
Equator

23.5°
Declination

Sun-Earth Line

SUN

SUMMER SOLSTICE Jun. 21

WINTER SOLSTICE Dec. 21

Equator
Tropic of Capricorn
Antarctic Circle

Figure 1-4

Equator

AUTUMNAL EQUINOX Sep. 21

Figure 1.3a   *Solar geometry:* Earth's fixed angle of tilt as it orbits the Sun accounts for seasonal climate and weather.

Scaled to this illustration, the sun is represented by a 48 in. ball (122 cm) placed 400 ft. away (122 m).

238,600 mi (384,400 Km)

Perigee   Mean   Apogee

Figure 1.3b *Midnight Sun:* Time lapse of the Sun tracing a line just above the horizon, defining the Arctic Circle, Summer Solstice.

(PHOTO: © J. Farley)

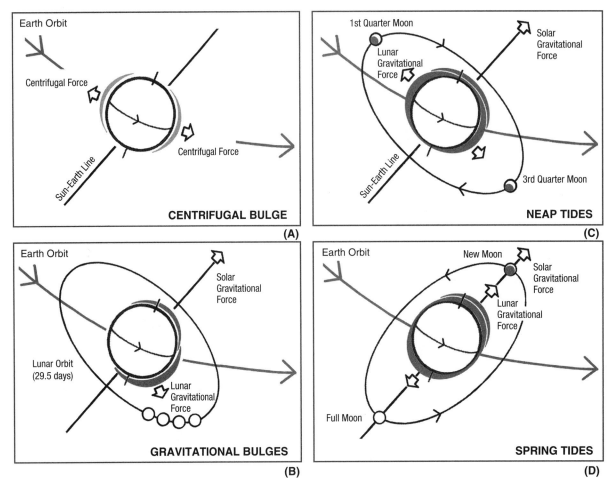

Figure 1.4 *Tides and time:* The ebb and flow of tides result from the 19-year *metonic cycle* of solar and lunar gravitational forces.

1.2 THE ATMOSPHERE

Earth is enveloped by an atmosphere comprised of gases, water, and fine dust retained by gravity and characterized by different layers of distinct temperature and composition. The atmosphere is captured by the gravitational force of its mass and density. The chemical composition of our atmosphere has been created over geologic time by compounds outgassed from Earth's crust, or possibly from impacts of volatile compounds from comets. The atmosphere is composed of 78% nitrogen, 21% oxygen, and small amounts of carbon dioxide, argon, and other gases and an average of 1% water vapor. The oxygen is the product of organic plant growth. (Table 1.1.)

The atmosphere expands and contracts as a function of season and magnetic and solar fluxes. It constantly loses molecules of lighter gases, such as helium and hydrogen. The outer limit has no clear boundary because the layer becomes increasingly thinner with altitude until it merges with outer space. (Figure 1.5 and Table 1.2.)

TABLE 1.1 EARTH ATMOSPHERE AIR COMPOSITION BY VOLUME	
Nitrogen	78.08%
Oxygen	20.95%
Argon	0.93%
Carbon dioxide	0.03%

Traces: neon: 0.0012%; krypton: 0.00005%; xenon: 0.000006%; helium: 0.0003%; also nitrous oxide, methane, and carbon monoxide.

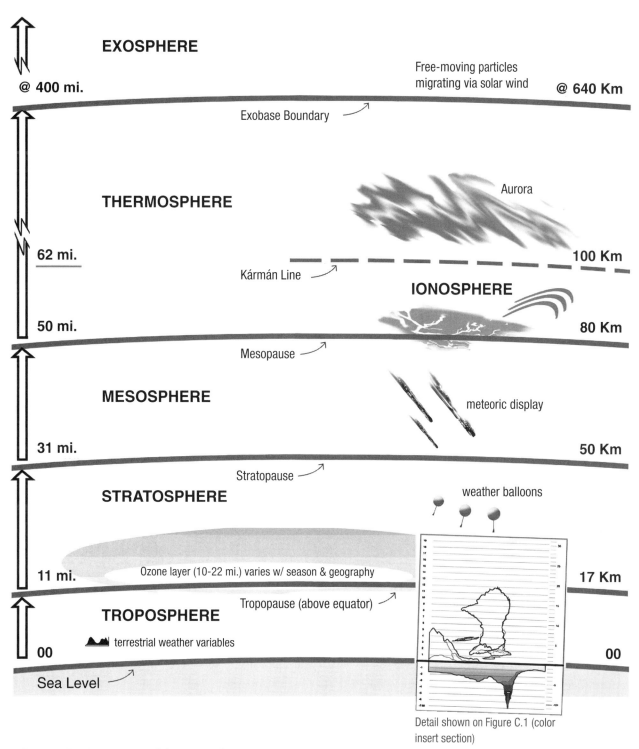

EXOSPHERE

@ 400 mi.

Free-moving particles
migrating via solar wind   @ 640 Km

Exobase Boundary

THERMOSPHERE

Aurora

62 mi.   100 Km

Kármán Line

IONOSPHERE

50 mi.   80 Km

Mesopause

MESOSPHERE

meteoric display

31 mi.   50 Km

Stratopause

STRATOSPHERE

weather balloons

Ozone layer (10-22 mi.) varies w/ season & geography
11 mi.   17 Km

Tropopause (above equator)

TROPOSPHERE

terrestrial weather variables

00   00

Sea Level

Detail shown on Figure C.1 (color
insert section)

Figure 1.5   *Dimensions of the atmosphere.*

TABLE 1.2   EARTH'S ATMOSPHERIC LAYERS

Layer	Height	Temperature Range	
		Fahrenheit	Celsius
Exosphere	440–625 miles	3600°F	< 2000°C
Thermosphere	50–440 miles	−100°F–3,600°F	38°C–2000°C
Mesosphere	31–50 miles	32°F– −100°F	0°C–38°C
Stratosphere	7.5–31 miles	−75°F–32°F	−59°C–0°C
Troposphere	Up to 7.5 miles	65°F– −75°F	18°C–24°C

Exosphere. The outermost layer of the atmosphere in which gases get thinner and thinner and drift off into space.

Thermosphere. Temperatures generally increase with altitude, influenced by solar radiation. The gases of the thermosphere are thin but sufficient to absorb ultraviolet light from the Sun. Within the thermosphere, the *ionosphere* contains gas particles that are electrically charged by the Sun's ultraviolet rays and bounce radio signals transmitted from Earth.

Mesosphere. Temperatures generally decrease with height because thinning gases do not absorb much of the Sun's heat. The air density is sufficient to slow down meteorites hurtling into the atmosphere.

Stratosphere. Freezing temperatures gradually increase with height to about 32°F (0°C). The stratosphere contains 19% of the atmosphere's gases, which move slowly and contain little moisture, so that clouds rarely form. Within the stratosphere is the *ozone layer*, a band of ozone gas that absorbs the Sun's harmful ultraviolet rays.

Troposphere. Lowest major atmospheric layer, containing 75% of the atmospheric mass and 99% of water vapor and aerosols. Named after the Greek *tropos*, meaning "mixing," it is turbulent and influenced by the surface of the Earth. The height of the troposphere varies with latitude, ranging between 5 miles (8 km) at the poles to 10.5 miles (17 km) at the equator.

The *Kármán line* is the adopted reference for the boundary between atmosphere and space, defined by the International Federation of Aeronautics as the "edge of space" at an altitude of 62 miles (100 km) above Earth's surface.

All of Earth's weather occurs in the troposphere. Energy from the Sun heats this layer and the land and oceans below, causing expansion of the air. This lower-density air then rises and is replaced by cooler, higher-density air. The resulting atmospheric circulation drives the weather through redistribution of heat energy and water in all its forms.

Earth's surface has altered the troposphere through interactive processes of weather, water, dust, and oxygen. Photosynthesis evolved 2.7 billion years ago, creating the primarily nitrogen-oxygen atmosphere that exists today. This enabled the proliferation of aerobic organisms as well as the formation of the ozone layer that, together with Earth's magnetic field, blocks ultraviolet solar radiation, which permits life to exist.

Greenhouse Effect

In the 1820s, French scientist J. J. Fourier recognized the atmosphere's role in maintaining climate conditions livable for humans. Without this heat-retention effect, the average surface temperature would be 0°F (−18°C), much colder and essentially a frozen planet compared to actual temperature of 59°F (15°C). Swedish chemist S. Arrhenius published a "hot-house theory" in the early twentieth century, which became known as the greenhouse effect.

About 80% to 90% of Earth's natural greenhouse gas (GHG) effect is due to water vapor (H_2O). The remainder is due to trace molecules of carbon dioxide (CO_2), methane (CH_4), nitrous oxide (N_2O), and a few other minor gases. Carbon dioxide is the greenhouse gas climate experts are most concerned about because the increase in human-related CO_2 emissions since the Industrial Revolution is now linked to the current global warming trend.

These trace molecules are transparent to light and shortwave solar rays but opaque to longer-wave thermal heat rays. They capture thermal energy emitted from the ground, raising the average air temperature and retarding the radiation of heat from the Earth back to space.

Carbon dioxide concentrations are increasing in the atmosphere due to fossil fuel combustion as well as rain forest burning. These concentrations represent an anthropogenic (human-made) contribution to greenhouse gas concentrations, believed to be responsible for accelerated global warming of the last 150 years. Additionally, the atmospheric concentration of methane has increased in recent decades. Reasons are uncertain, but may be ascribable to deforestation and agriculture and also to releases from deep ocean deposits and disintegration of marine and tundra hydrates.

Biosphere and Hydrosphere

The planet's life-forms sometimes are said to exist within and thus define the *biosphere*, a term originally used in geology in early nineteenth century. *Biosphere* was the title of a 1926 book by Russian Geologist V. I. Vernadsky, who defined ecology as the science of the biosphere, encompassing the life and earth sciences.

Earth is the only place in the universe where life is known to exist, which is believed to have begun to evolve about 3.5 billion years ago. The biosphere is divided into a number of biomes, inhabited by broadly similar plants and animals. Terrestrial biomes lying within arctic and polar regions or at high altitudes are relatively barren of plant and animal life. The greatest species diversity is found in tropical zones along the equator.

Bacteria play a major role in the biosphere including formation of rain-bearing clouds. Water droplets that form clouds require a nucleus where water vapor can condense and accumulate. The land supplies these nuclei in the form of dust and the bacteria that escape from plants. The ocean provides nuclei for rain in the form of dimethyl sulfide vapor (DMS) produced by photosynthesis of marine plankton. Such bacteria are a major component of the organisms that drift within the biosphere as aerial plankton.[1]

The term *hydrosphere* refers to the realm of water in all its forms on Earth. It can be said to coincide generally with the biospheric realm of living organisms sustained by water. The hydrosphere consists chiefly of the oceans but technically includes the troposphere and all water surfaces in the world, including lakes, rivers, and underground waters down to a depth of about 6,560 feet (2,000 m). The heat capacity of the oceans buffers Earth's surface from large temperature changes such as those that occur on the Moon.

Climate and Weather

Climate refers to the characterization of long-term temperature of air and ground, humidity, wind, rain, and other meteorological statistics of regions of the earth. *Weather* defines short-term variations, typically one day to several weeks. Climate and its seasons are determined by the position of the globe in its annual migration around the Sun and resulting global and continental patterns of wind and moisture transport. *Microclimate*, of direct relevance to environmental design, landscape design, and architecture, is essentially climate near the ground within 3 feet (1 m), with minute variations influenced by soil, vegetation, and moisture. Weather is determined by tropospheric conditions at regional and microclimatic scales.

Ocean currents, elevation, and latitude influence climate and weather, along with global and regional patterns of winds and storms. Masses of air and weather patterns on the surface of the Earth experience the *Coriolis effect*. The Coriolis effect—named after Gaspard-Gustave Coriolis, a French scientist who gave the force a mathematical expression in 1835—is evident in both water and air masses. At the global atmospheric scale, the Coriolis effect creates the rotation of large cyclones, appearing to veer to the right in the northern hemisphere and to the left in the southern hemisphere. At the equator, wind flow tracks east or west, with a polar tendency. As a result, tropical cyclones, typhoons, and hurricanes never cross the equator. (Figures 1.6 and 1.7.)

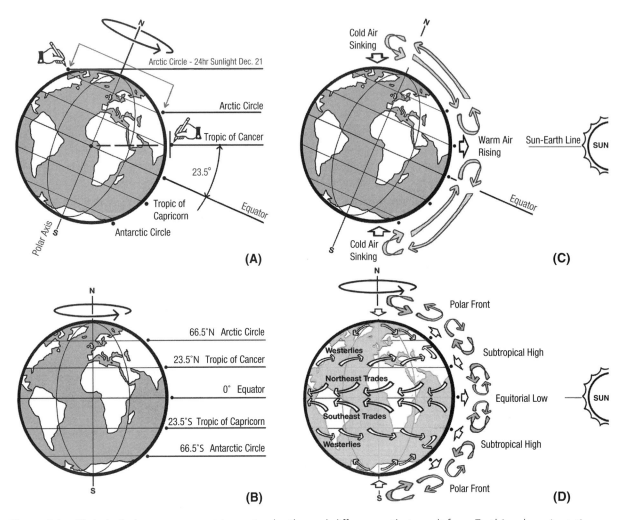

Figure 1.6   *Global wind patterns* are set in motion by thermal differences that result from Earth's solar orientation, rotation, and the *Coriolis effect*.

Meteorology

Meteorology is the study of the changes in temperature, air pressure, moisture, and wind direction in the troposphere. Meteorology addresses both description of weather and prediction of weather events.

Like all indigenous peoples, Native Americans were astute observers of the sky, climate, and weather. The first systematic weather observation beginning in the colonial era in the United States is credited to the Reverend J. Campanius Holm in 1644 in Wilmington, Delaware. Benjamin Franklin, George Washington, James Madison, and Thomas Jefferson were also keen weather observers and kept personal weather diaries. In 1814 a network of

weather observations was established at army posts across the country. By 1848 Joseph Henry, considered the "father" of the U.S. Weather Service, established a meteorological program at the Smithsonian Institution calling for "a system of extended meteorological observations for solving the problem of American storms." He employed the newly developed telegraph and hundreds of volunteer weather observers located through North America, Mexico, and the Caribbean. The volunteer program was taken over by the U.S. Army Signal Service in 1874 and then transferred in 1881 to the newly established U.S. Weather Bureau, establishing the weather data network supported by governments across the globe.[2]

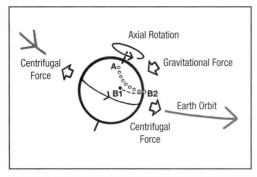
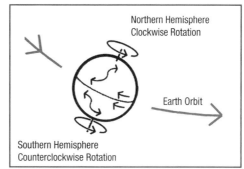

CORIOLIS EFFECT AT HEMISPHERIC SCALE   **DIRECTION OF HEMISPHERIC WINDS**

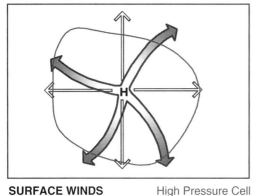
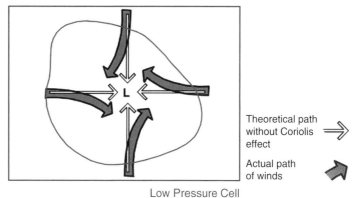

SURFACE WINDS   High Pressure Cell   Low Pressure Cell

Figure 1.7   *The Coriolis effect* creates the rotation and direction of prevailing winds at continental and regional scales.

Weather satellite digital instrumentation records visible, infrared, and microwave radiation. There are two types of weather satellites, defined by their orbits. Geostationary orbiting satellites (GEOS) are placed in orbit at 22,236 miles (35,786 km) directly over the equator. At this altitude, the satellites orbit Earth once in 24 hours following the planet's rotation rate, so that the satellite appears to be fixed over a single spot; thus the word *geosynchronous* or *geostationary*, meaning "motionless in the sky if viewed from Earth." (Figures 1.8 and 1.9.)

Polar-orbiting satellites are placed in a low-altitude orbits about 500 miles (805 km) near the North Pole and the South Pole. Unlike the geostationary orbit, the polar orbit allows complete coverage as Earth rotates beneath.

Weather measurements are also recorded twice each day by radio transmission from weather balloons. Launched each day at the same time, balloon flights transmit data to the National Centers for Environmental Prediction (NCEP) in Washington, DC, creating a global picture of weather every 12 hours. Additional measurements are

recorded at surface stations. All measurements are transmitted to different weather modeling centers throughout the world to produce projected weather patterns. The resulting data are provided to weather forecasters for interpretation and broadcast.

Cloud Formation

Water vapor is water in its gaseous state, typically of minute size and totally invisible. Water vapor is transported by circulatory patterns in the atmosphere in the form of clouds, mist, and precipitation distributed by global weather.

Clouds form when convective condensation reacts with rising air. When air over the warmest part of the land rises and meets cooler air, the water vapor it contains condenses into cloud droplets. The congealing air mass will continue to rise as long as its temperature is higher than the air around it. For both ancient seafarers and modern meteorologists, cloud formations have signaled weather conditions developing on the horizon. (Figure 1.10.)

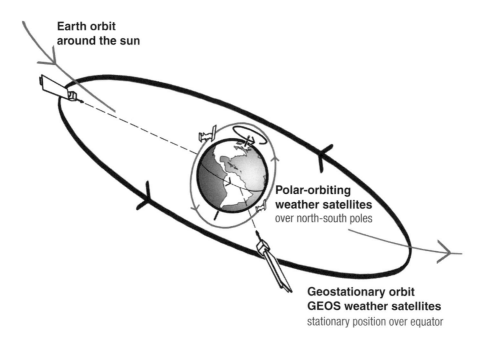

Earth orbit around the sun

Polar-orbiting weather satellites over north-south poles

Geostationary orbit GEOS weather satellites stationary position over equator

Figure 1.8   *Weather satellites* enable real-time tracking of global weather.

Figure 1.9   *Images from space:* Images constructed from digitized data from GEOS satellites depict global moisture, clouds, and temperatures.

Source: NASA Earth Satellite Office, <www.ghcc.msfc.nasa.gov/GOES/>; also NEODAAS Dundee Satellite Receiving Station. <www.sat.dundee.ac.uk>.

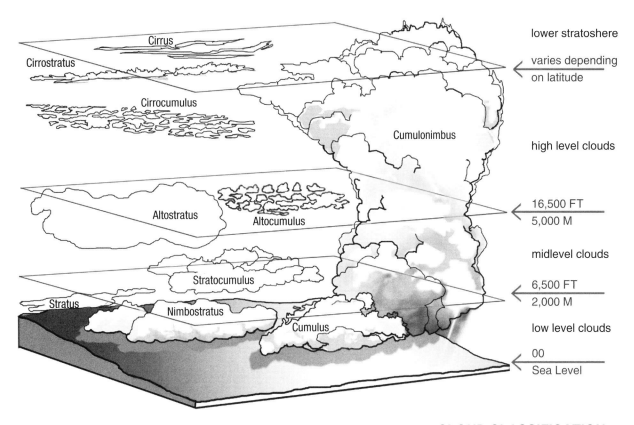

lower stratoshere

varies depending
on latitude

Cirrus

Cirrostratus

Cirrocumulus

Cumulonimbus

high level clouds

Altostratus

Altocumulus

16,500 FT
5,000 M

midlevel clouds

Stratocumulus

6,500 FT
2,000 M

Stratus

Nimbostratus

Cumulus

low level clouds

00
Sea Level

CLOUD CLASSIFICATION

Figure 1.10   *Cloud formations* are defined by their altitude and influence on regional and local weather patterns.

Source: Illustration adapted from Bruce Buckley, Edward J. Hopkins, and Richard Whitaker, *Weather: A Visual Guide* Buffalo (New York: Firefly Books, 2008).

Basic Cloud Types

Alto. Derived from the word "high," but in meteorology used to refer to middle-level clouds.

Cirrus. Meaning "filament of hair" and used to identify high-level clouds.

Cumulus. From a term meaning "pile" or "heap," used to refer to a "tall" cloud or great height.

Nimbus. Meaning "rain," so used to refer to rain-bearing clouds. Commonly used as a suffix.

Stratus. Derived from *stratum*, or layer, used to refer to low-level clouds; also used as a suffix for a set of cloud types that have a layered appearance.

Specific Cloud Types

Cirrostratus. Combination of *cirrus* and *stratus*. Cirrostratus clouds are generally recognizable by a transparent white sheet or veil of ice crystals forming high-level clouds that appear as layered streamers.

Cirrocumulus. Combination of *cirrus* and *cumulus*. High-level ice-crystal clouds consisting of a layer of small white puffs or ripples.

Altostratus. Stratiform clouds with the "alto-" prefix indicate middle-level altitude. Altostratus clouds consist primarily of water droplets that appear as a relatively uniform white or gray layered sheet.

Altocumulus. A middle-level cloud type that has some vertical development indicated by the suffix "-cumulus." Altocumulus clouds have a layered appearance but also consist of white to gray puffs.

Stratocumulus. Low-level layer clouds, as suggested by the prefix "strato-," but having some vertical development, indicated by the suffix "-cumulus." Stratocumulus clouds consist of a layer of large rolls or merged puffs.

Cumulonimbus. Vertically developed clouds (indicated by the "cumulo-" prefix) that are rain producers (indicated by the "-nimbus" suffix). These "tall" high clouds usually extend to the troposphere and have a puffy lower portion and flattened anvil-shape top. These clouds may produce heavy rain or hail.

Nimbostratus. Rain-producing ("nimbus-") layered ("-stratus") clouds. Nimbostratus are low- to mid-level clouds that give the appearance of a uniform gray cloud.

Weather on the Ground

Winds and precipitation are the principal features of weather systems that affect both land and sea. Most weather of consequence occurs in storms, in which the key ingredient is water in any of its forms: ice, liquid, or vapor. (Figure 1.11.)

Ocean currents contribute to global climate and weather, particularly *thermohaline circulation* (*THC*). Also called the global conveyor belt, it is a global circulation pattern that distributes heat energy from the equatorial oceans to the polar regions. The circulation is driven by thermal and saline density gradients in ocean surface currents and deep oceanic "submarine rivers."[3] Cold, salty water sinks into the deep ocean in the north Atlantic, flows south and then east across the south Pacific to resurface as it is warmed in the Indian and north Pacific oceans. Surface currents carry warmer water back through the Pacific and south Atlantic, eventually to return to polar deep water via the Atlantic Gulf Stream. The round trips take between 500 and 2,000 years. (Figure 1.12.)

The primary atmospheric winds consist of the *trade winds* in the equatorial region below 30° latitude and the *westerlies* between 30° and 60° latitudes. The three general conditions in an atmospheric system that lead to widespread participation are described as *convectional, cyclonic,* and *orographic.*

Convectional precipitation usually is associated with thunderstorms. Warm, moist air rises as an unstable air mass and cools adiabatically. The rising parcel is commonly called a thermal. As it reaches cooler air and lower pressure, condensation creates precipitation. The updrafts of wind recirculate, and wind flow on the ground may be turbulent and violent. Convective thunderstorms are the most common type of atmospheric instability that produces lightning followed by thunder. (Figure 1.13.)

Mid-latitude cyclones develop when polar air moves largely within the 30° to 60° latitude range; thus they are referred to as *tropical cyclones.* Lows develop and compete with highs as both types of systems are moved by jet streams and other global patterns of wind and water transport. Development typically follows successive stages beginning with advance of an Arctic cold front into cooler air (to the south in the northern hemisphere). These massive storms may be characterized as tropical disturbances, typhoons, or hurricanes that affect Europe and Asia, North America, and to a lesser extent the southern continents.

Orographic precipitation results from moisture-laden wind as it ascends mountain elevations, such as the West Coast, interior West, and the flanks of the Appalachian Range. The moist air is cooled and precipitation ensues, typically as thunderstorms in summer or as snowstorms in winter. This mass moves down the opposite slope as dry and then warmer air, described as a rain shadow. (Figure 1.14.)

Rainfall amount is recorded as the amount of water captured by a rain gauge at an observing station during a

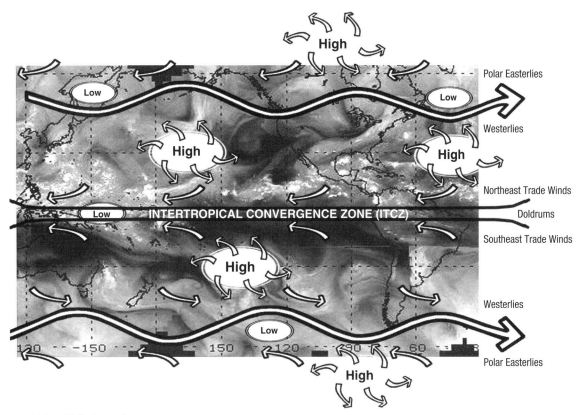

Figure 1.11   *Global weather patterns.*

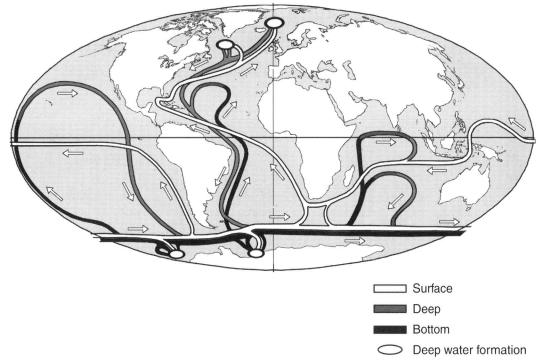

Figure 1.12   *Thermohaline circulation*: Variability in the strength of the global conveyor belt impacts global oceans and climate change.

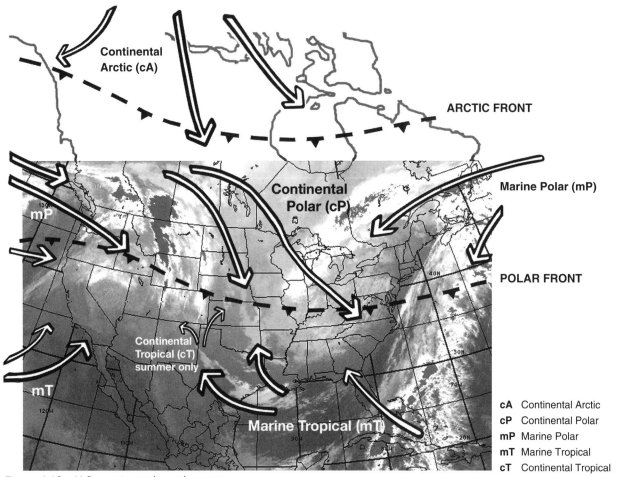

Figure 1.13   *U.S. continental weather patterns.*

cA   Continental Arctic
cP   Continental Polar
mP   Marine Polar
mT   Marine Tropical
cT   Continental Tropical

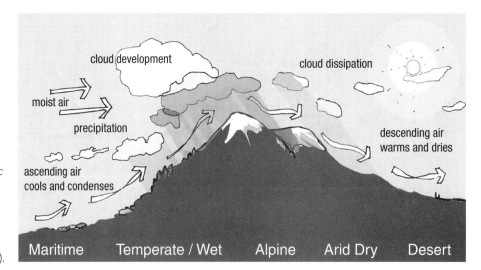

Figure 1.14   *Orthographic
precipitation* creates
contrasting microclimates
in mountain regions, most
evident in windward (wet)
and leeward elevations (arid).

	TABLE 1.3	TYPES OF PRECIPITATION	
Type	Size	State	Characteristics
Mist	0.005–0.05 mm	Liquid	Droplet large enough to be felt on the face when air is moving 1 meter/second. Associated with stratus clouds.
Drizzle	Less than 0.5 mm	Liquid	Small uniform drops that fall from stratus clouds, generally for several hours.
Rain	0.5–5 mm	Liquid	Generally produced by nimbostratus or cumulonimbus clouds. When heavy, size can be highly variable from one place to another.
Sleet	0.5–5 mm	Solid	Small, spherical to lumpy ice particles that form when raindrops freeze while falling through a layer of subfreezing air. Because the ice particles are small, damage is generally minor. Sleet can make travel hazardous.
Glaze	Layers 1 mm–2 cm thick	Solid	Produced when supercooled raindrops freeze on contact with solid objects. Glaze can form a thick coating of ice having sufficient weight to seriously damage trees and power lines.
Rime	Variable accumulations	Solid	Deposits usually consisting of ice feathers that point into the wind. These delicate frostlike accumulations form as a supercooled cloud of fog droplets encounter objects and freeze on contact.
Snow	1 mm–2 cm	Solid	The crystalline nature of snow allows it to assume many shapes, including six-sided crystals, plates, and needles. Snow is produced in supercooled clouds where water vapor is deposited as ice crystals that remain frozen during their descent.
Hail	5 mm–10 cm or larger	Solid	Precipitation in the form of hard rounded pellets or irregular lumps of ice. Produced in large cumulonimbus clouds, where frozen ice particles and supercooled water coexist.
Graupel	2 mm–5 mm	Solid	Sometimes called soft hail, graupel forms as rime collects on snow crystals to produce irregular masses of "soft" ice. Because these particles are softer than hailstones, they normally flatten on impact.

24-hour period. Rainfall rate may be used to describe a heavy rainstorm—for example, "two inches per hour." The hourly rate data typically are identified by Doppler radar, then calculated to predict how much precipitation a storm might produce if stalled. Upper and lower atmosphere temperatures are contingent factors in predicting the anticipated form of precipitation. (Table 1.3.)

1.3 WEATHER

High- and Low-Pressure Areas

Atmospheric pressure results from the total weight of air above any point of measurement, decreasing with height, measured by a barometer. Natural variations in barometric pressure occur at any one altitude as a consequence of weather. Atmospheric pressure differences are an indication of weather trends useful for forecasting.

Highs are high-pressure cells with more atmospheric pressure above their mass at ground level. Highs initiate airflow downward and outward due to higher internal density, inducing cooler and drier air to descend from higher altitudes, clearing the skies above. Due to the Coriolis effect, airflow around a high is clockwise in the northern hemisphere.

Lows are low-pressure cells characterized by less atmospheric mass above, resulting in converging airflow at the ground surface to rise. Air moving upward in a low may condense and initiate clouds and precipitation. Due to the Coriolis effect, airflow around the low is counterclockwise in the northern hemisphere.

An *occluded front* typically forms when a faster-moving cold front catches up to a slower-moving warm front. When the air behind the cold front is colder than the air ahead of the warm front, the occluded front will behave like a cold front, with brief, heavy rainfall and a wind shift to the west or northwest. When the air behind the cold front is not as cold as the air ahead of the warm front, lighter but more prolonged precipitation can be expected, similar to the overrunning precipitation produced by warm fronts. (Figure 1.15.)

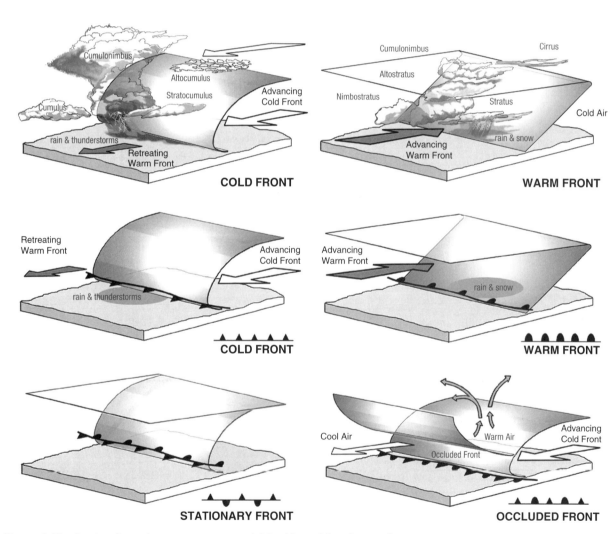

Figure 1.15   *Regional weather patterns* are established by cold and warm fronts.

Wind

Winds accompany most precipitation and storm events, described in weather forecasts in terms of origin, direction, and scale. In building and landscape design, prevailing winds may provide criteria for building form and landscape that deflect winter and storm winds or accommodate summer cooling breezes. For storm protection and hurricane-resistant design, wind design is among the most critical engineering determinants, governed by building codes and subject to professional judgment in assessing additional safety factors.

The *Beaufort Scale* has been developed based on empirical observation of winds and storms. It was first defined by British Navy administrator Admiral Francis Beaufort in 1806 and used as a reference in ship's logs. Its modern version is applicable to description of storms and anticipated risks to safety and property damage. (Table 1.4.)

TABLE 1.4 MODERN BEAUFORT SCALE

Beaufort		Speed				
Force	Description	Knots	km/h	mph	Appearance on Water	Appearance on Land
0	Calm	Less than 1	Less than 1	Less than 1	Sea like a mirror.	Smoke rises vertically.
1	Very light	1–3	1–5	1–3	Ripples with appearance of scales, no foam crests	Direction of wind shown by smoke drift but not by wind vanes.
2	Light breeze	4–6	6–11	4–7	Wavelets, small but pronounced. Crests with glassy appearance but do not break.	Wind felt on face, leaves rustle, ordinary wind vane moved by wind.
3	Gentle breeze	7–10	12–19	8–12	Large wavelets, crests begin to break. Glassy-looking foam, occasional whitecaps	Leaves and small twigs in constant motion, wind extends white flag.
4	Moderate breeze	11–16	20–29	13–18	Small waves becoming longer, frequent white horses.	Wind raises dust and loose paper, small branches move.
5	Fresh breeze	17–21	30–39	19–24	Moderate waves of pronounced long form. Many whitecaps, some spray.	Small trees in leaf start to sway crested wavelets on inland waters.
6	Strong breeze	22–27	40–50	25–31	Some large waves, extensive white foam crests, some spray.	Large branches in motion, umbrellas used with difficulty.
7	Near gale	28–33	51–61	32–38	Sea heaped up, white foam from breaking waves blowing in streaks with the wind.	Whole trees in motion, difficult to walk against wind.

(continued)

TABLE 1.4 (CONTINUED)						
Beaufort		Speed				
Force	Description	Knots	km/h	mph	Appearance on Water	Appearance on Land
8	Gale	34–40	62–74	39–46	Moderately high and long waves. Crests break into spin drift, blowing foam in well marked streaks.	Twigs break from trees, difficult to walk.
9	Strong gale	41–47	75–87	47–54	High waves; dense foam streaks in wind; wave crests topple, tumble, and roll over. Spray reduces visibility.	Slight structural damage occurs, chimney pots and slates removed.
10	Storm	48–55	88–101	55–63	Very high waves with long overhanging crests. Dense blowing foam, sea surface appears white. Heavy tumbling of sea, shocklike, poor visibility.	Trees uprooted, considerable structural damage occurs.
11	Violent storm	56–63	102–117	64–73	Exceptionally high waves, sometimes concealing small and medium-size ships. Sea completely covered with long white patches of foam. Wave crest edges blow into froth. Poor visibility.	Widespread damage.
12	Hurricane	> 64	> 119	> 74	Air filled with foam and spray, sea white with driving spray, very poor visibility	Widespread damage.

Cyclogenesis

Cyclogenesis is an umbrella term for several weather processes that result in the development of some sort of cyclone. In regions outside of the tropics, cyclones may be initiated as waves along weather fronts before developing (occluding) as cold core cyclones, typical of winter storms. (Figure 1.16.)

Thunderstorms

Thunderstorms are formed as cumulus clouds that accumulate and extend throughout the troposphere, forming mountains of moisture that can reach altitudes up to 50,000 feet (1.5 km). The wedge of cold air associated with the advancing cold front drives under the existing air mass, producing

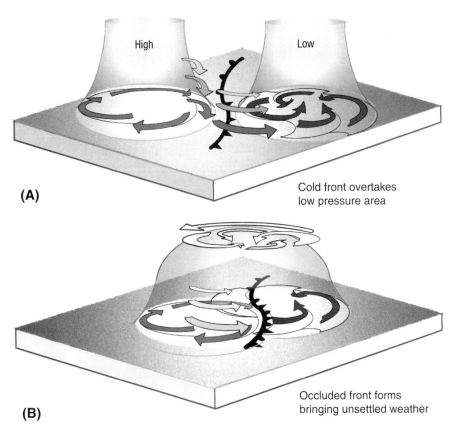

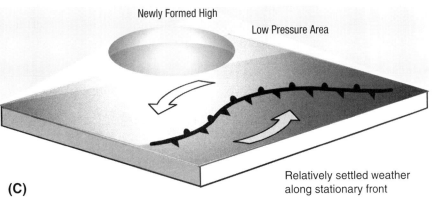

CYCLOGENESIS

Figure 1.16 *Cyclogenesis*— interacting high- and low-pressure systems—initiates formation of mid-latitude cyclonic storms.

an upward motion in the air. As the thunderstorm develops, updrafts and downdrafts form. The cloud flattens as it reaches the top of the troposphere. Very often the higher levels of the clouds are formed into an anvil shape. Blasts of air that reach the ground from thunderstorm downdrafts gust in excess of 100 miles per hour [mph] (160 km/h). (Figure 1.17.)

Tropical Storms

A *tropical cyclone* is a storm system that originates in the tropics and is characterized by a large low-pressure center ("warm core") and thunderstorms, strong winds, and heavy rain, with counterclockwise rotation in the northern hemisphere and clockwise rotation in the southern hemisphere. The terms used for tropical cyclones differ from one region

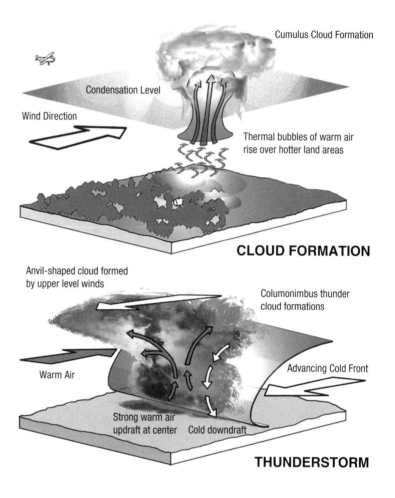

Cumulus Cloud Formation

Condensation Level

Wind Direction

Thermal bubbles of warm air
rise over hotter land areas

CLOUD FORMATION

Anvil-shaped cloud formed
by upper level winds

Columonimbus thunder
cloud formations

Warm Air

Advancing Cold Front

Strong warm air
updraft at center   Cold downdraft

THUNDERSTORM

Overshooting Bulge   Stratosphere

Anvil Head
Cloud

Mammatus
Clouds

Shelf Cloud

Thermal Updraft

TORNADO FORMATION

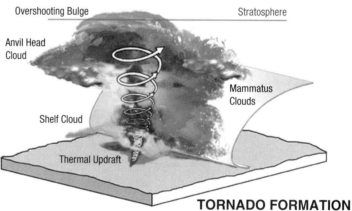

Figure 1.17 *Cloud and storm formations.*

Source: Illustration adapted from Buckley,
Hopkins, and Whitaker, *A Visual Guide.*

to another globally. For most ocean basins, the average wind speed is used to determine the tropical cyclone category. A storm of any intensity can inflict damage and threat to life. Depending on location and strength, a tropical cyclone is referred to by names such as *hurricane, typhoon, tropical storm, cyclonic storm, tropical depression*, or, simply, *cyclone*.

Hailstorms

Hailstorms develop from severe thunderstorms, most typically in summertime, forming in rising air currents that carry water droplets high into a thunderstorm. There they freeze and grow as other drops collide with them. Hailstones grow until they are too large for the storm

CLASSIFICATION OF TROPICAL CYCLONES

Tropical disturbance, tropical wave. Unorganized mass of thunderstorms with very little, if any, organized wind circulation.

Tropical depression. Evidence of closed wind circulation around a center organized system of clouds and thunderstorms with maximum sustained winds* of 38 mph (33 kt) or less.

Tropical storm. An organized system of strong thunderstorms with a defined surface circulation and maximum sustained winds of 39 to 73 mph (34–63 kt). A storm is named once it reaches tropical storm strength.

Hurricane. An intense tropical weather system of strong thunderstorms with a well-defined surface circulation and maximum sustained winds of 74 mph (64 kt) or higher.

Source: NOAA, "Hurricane Basics," <www.nhc.noaa.gov/HAW2/english/basics.shtml>.
* Sustained winds are defined as a 1-minute average wind measured at about 33 ft (10 m) above the surface.

---

updrafts to hold them aloft; then they fall to the ground. Hailstones can fall at speeds well over 100 mph (87 kt).

Hailstorms generate balls or lumps of ice capable of damaging agricultural crops, buildings, and vehicles. Severe hailstorms can damage roofing shingles and tiles, metal roofs, roof sheeting, skylights, glazing, and other building components. Accumulation of hail on flat or low-sloped roofs can lead to significant vertical loads.

Northeaster

A *northeaster*—colloquially called a nor'easter—is an intense low-pressure area that forms in the winter along the East Coast of the United States, producing strong northeasterly winds and often heavy snowfall and rainfall. These storms often travel northward along the coast, eventually affecting the entire eastern seaboard. Persistent strong winds associated with these storms can cause beach erosion and damage to houses along the coast from large waves and high water levels that result from the ocean water being piled up against the coast by the wind. A northeaster typically is followed by unusually cold weather as the cold high-pressure area that created the strong winds moves into the region. (Table 1.5.)

Ice Storm

An *ice storm* is generated when rain falls from or into a layer of air that is above freezing. This can cause pellets of ice to form as sleet or glaze, which is capable of covering outdoor surfaces and tree branches with a layer of ice. Electric power and wire communication disruptions are common effects of ice storms. (Table 1.6.)

Tornadoes

A *tornado* is a rapidly rotating funnel of air that extends to the ground from a cumulonimbus cloud. Tornadoes are characterized by powerful updrafts that may extend to the top of the cloud, producing a bulge in an anvil shape, called an *overshoot*. Tornadoes are the most intense of all atmospheric storms, spawned by severe thunderstorms and hurricanes. Tornadoes often form in the right forward quadrant of a hurricane, far from the hurricane eye. The strength and number of tornadoes are not related to the strength of the hurricane that generates them. The weakest hurricanes often produce the most tornadoes.

Most tornadoes last from 5 to 10 minutes, although they can exist for as few as several seconds to more than an hour. Approximately 75% of tornadoes are classified as weak and only 1% as violent in the extreme. But this 1% is responsible for the greatest percentage of deaths from any storm events, including earthquakes.

The Fujita scale was developed by T. Theodore Fujita in the early 1970s. The scale was enhanced in 2007, defined by rankings EF-0 to EF-5 (Enhanced Fujita). (Table 1.7.) The scale is a set of wind estimates that may have been reached in a tornado, based on forensic observation of postevent damage rather than actual wind measurements which would be practically impossible to record during the actual event.

TABLE 1.5 CLASSIFICATION FOR NORTHEASTERS

Storm Class	Storm Description	Storm Duration	Storm Impacts on Beaches and Dunes	Property Damage
1	Weak	1 tidal cycle	Minor beach erosion.	Little or none.
2	Moderate	2–3 tidal cycles	Moderate beach erosion; dune scarping begins; minor flooding and shallow overwash in low areas, especially street ends.	Undermining of seaward ends of dune walkovers; undermining of slab foundations on or near the active beach; some damage to erosion control structures.
3	Significant	3–4 tidal cycles	Significant beach erosion; dune scarping with complete loss of small dunes; increased depth of flooding and overwash in low areas.	Widespread damage to dune walkovers and boardwalks; increased damage to erosion control structures; undermining of beachfront slab foundations and shallow post or pile foundations; burial of roads and inland property by overwash.
4	Severe	4–5 tidal cycles	Severe beach erosion and dune scarping; widespread dune breaching in vulnerable areas; coalescing of overwash fans; occasional inlet formation.	Damage to poorly sited, elevated, or constructed coastal buildings is common; frequent damage to erosion control structures; flood-borne debris loads increase; overwash burial depths increase.
5	Extreme	> 5 tidal cycles	Widespread and severe beach erosion and dune loss; widespread flooding of low-lying areas; massive overwash; inlet formation is common.	Widespread damage to buildings with inadequate elevations or foundations, and to buildings with inadequate setbacks from the shoreline or inlets; widespread damage to low-lying roads and infrastructure.

Source: FEMA, *Coastal Construction Manual: Principles and Practices of Planning, Siting, Designing, Constructing, and Maintaining Residential Buildings in Coastal Areas* (FEMA 55) (August 2005), <www.fema.gov/rebuild/mat/fema55.shtm>.

Design for tornadoes is beyond the scope of this book, except to include tornadoes as a design consideration along with hurricane and related storm events. Given the extreme force of tornado wind and wind-driven precipitation, it is considered practically impossible to provide property protection in the direct path of a tornado. Precautionary measures focus on life safety; advance warning and evacuation; and when evacuation is not possible, the provision of tornado safe rooms and community shelters.[5]

TABLE 1.6   SPERRY-PILTZ ICE STORM INDEX

Ice Index	Radial Ice Amount (inches)	Wind (mph)	Damage and Impact Descriptions
1	< 0.25 0.25–0.50	15–25 < 10	Some localized utility interruptions possible, typically lasting 1 or 2 hours maximum.
2	< 0.25 0.25–0.50 0.50–1.00	> = 25 15–25 < 10	Scattered utility interruptions expected, typically lasting less than 8 to 12 hours maximum.
3	0.25–0.50 0.50–0.75 0.75–1.00	> = 25 15–25 < 10	Numerous utility interruptions, with some damage to main feeder lines expected, with outages lasting from 1 to 5 days.
4	0.50–0.75 0.75–1.00 1.00–1.50	> = 25 15–25 > 10	Prolonged and widespread utility interruptions, with extensive damage to main distribution feeder lines and possibly some high-voltage transmission lines. Outages lasting 5 to 10 days.
5	0.75–1.00 1.00–1.50 > 1.50	> = 25 15–25 < 10	Catastrophic damage to entire utility systems, including both distribution and transmission. Outages may last from 1 to several weeks in some areas. Shelters needed.

Source: S. F. McManus et al., "Development and Testing of an Ice Accumulation Algorithm," *Oklahoma Climatological Survey* (Norman, OK: University of Oklahoma Press, 2008).

TABLE 1.7   ENHANCED FUJITA SCALE

Scale	Wind mph	Knots (kt)	Damage
EF-0	65–85	57–74	Causes some damage to siding and shingles.
EF-1	86–110	75–95	Considerable roof damage. Winds can uproot trees and overturn singlewide mobile homes. Flagpoles bend.
EF-2	111–135	96–117	Most singlewide mobile homes destroyed. Permanent homes can shift off foundations.
EF-3	136–165	118–143	Hardwood trees debarked. All but small portions of houses destroyed.
EF-4	166–200	144–174	Complete destruction of well-built residences, large sections of school buildings.
EF-5	Above 200	Above 174	Significant structural deformation of mid- and high-rise buildings.

Source: NOAA Storm Prediction Center, <www.nhc.noaa.gov/>.

Hurricanes

A *hurricane* is a type of tropical cyclone, which is a generic term for a low-pressure system that generally forms in the tropics. Hurricanes are one of the ways that Earth's atmosphere keeps its heat budget balanced: by moving excess heat from the tropics to the middle latitudes. Hurricanes convert the warmth of the tropical oceans and atmosphere into wind and waves. Hurricanes also distribute rain and moisture throughout the eastern continental landmass of North America.

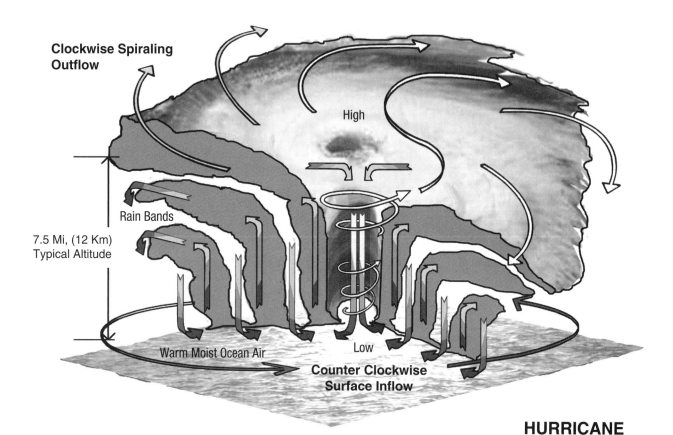

Clockwise Spiraling Outflow

High

7.5 Mi, (12 Km) Typical Altitude

Rain Bands

Warm Moist Ocean Air

Low

Counter Clockwise Surface Inflow

HURRICANE

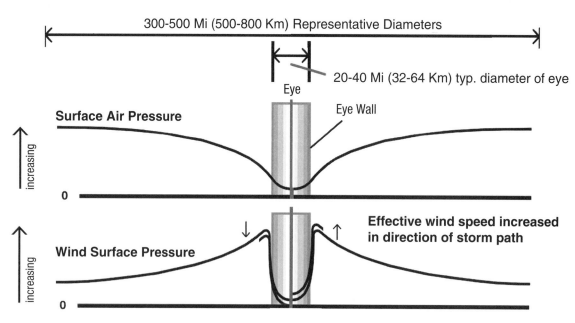

300-500 Mi (500-800 Km) Representative Diameters

20-40 Mi (32-64 Km) typ. diameter of eye

Eye

Eye Wall

Surface Air Pressure

increasing

0

Wind Surface Pressure

increasing

0

Effective wind speed increased in direction of storm path

Figure 1.18 *Hurricane formation.*

Hurricanes are a more extreme development of a tropical disturbances. They begin as atmospheric depressions in the tropics, growing and gaining strength as warm humid air near the ocean's surface rises through cooler air above, generating spiraling convection currents in the atmosphere. The warm and saturated air mass spirals (counterclockwise in the northern hemisphere and clockwise in the southern hemisphere) into the center, or eye, of the developing hurricane, accelerating as it develops. The air mass spirals upward as torrential rain, producing an eyewall cloud that surrounds the eye of the storm. In the upper levels, the air spirals outward away from the center. (Figure 1.18.)

SAFFIR-SIMPSON HURRICANE WIND SCALE (EXPERIMENTAL)

The Saffir-Simpson Hurricane Wind Scale is a 1 to 5 categorization based on the hurricane's estimated intensity. It is called experimental because it is newly published in its present form, eliminating estimates of storm surge that were included in prior versions. Storm surge is the most dangerous component of a hurricane. Storm surge is not always correlated with the category or severity of a hurricane because other factors determine the extent of the storm surge, including surge elevations, such as forward speed of the storm, tide cycle, and shore profile. A tropical storm or moderate hurricane may be accompanied by extreme and dangerous surge.

In general, damage risk rises by about a factor of 4 for every category increase. The damage descriptions are generalized and subject to variables of local topography, building structures, age of buildings, and extent of enforcement of flood regulations.[6] Category numbers are assigned soon after a storm becomes a hurricane, almost always based on data gathered by specially equipped NOAA "Hurricane Hunter" aircraft. (Table 1.8.)

TABLE 1.8 SAFFIR-SIMPSON HURRICANE WIND SCALE (EXPERIMENTAL) MILES PER HOUR (MPH) AND KNOTS (KT)			
Category	Sustained Winds	Damage	Description
1	74–95 mph (64–82 kt or 119–153 km/hr)	Damaging winds are expected.	Some damage to building structures could occur, primarily to unanchored mobile homes (mainly pre-1994 construction). Some damage is likely to poorly constructed signs. Loose outdoor items will become projectiles, causing additional damage. Persons struck by windborne debris risk injury and possible death. Numerous large branches of healthy trees will snap. Some trees will be uprooted, especially where the ground is saturated. Many areas will experience power outages with some downed power poles.
2	96–110 mph (83–95 kt or 154–177 km/hr)	Very strong winds will produce widespread damage.	Some roofing material, door, and window damage of buildings will occur. Considerable damage to mobile homes (mainly pre-1994 construction) and poorly constructed signs is likely. A number of glass windows in high-rise buildings will be dislodged and become airborne. Loose outdoor items will become projectiles, causing additional damage. Persons struck by windborne debris risk injury and possible death. Numerous large branches will break. Many trees will be uprooted or snapped. Extensive damage to power lines and poles will likely result in widespread power outages that could last a few to several days.

(continued)

TABLE 1.8 (CONTINUED)

Category	Sustained Winds	Damage	Description
3	111–130 mph (96–113 kt or 178–209 km/hr)	Dangerous winds will cause extensive damage.	Some structural damage to houses and buildings will occur with a minor amount of wall failures. Mobile homes (mainly pre-1994 construction) and poorly constructed signs are destroyed. Many windows in high-rise buildings will be dislodged and become airborne. Persons struck by windborne debris risk injury and possible death. Many trees will be snapped or uprooted and block numerous roads. Near-total power loss is expected with outages that could last from several days to weeks.
4	131–155 mph (114–135 kt or 210–249 km/hr)	Extremely dangerous winds causing devastating damage are expected.	Some wall failures with some complete roof structure failures on houses will occur. All signs are blown down. Complete destruction of mobile homes (primarily pre-1994 construction). Extensive damage to doors and windows is likely. Numerous windows in high-rise buildings will be dislodged and become airborne. Windborne debris will cause extensive damage, and persons struck by the wind-blown debris will be injured or killed. Most trees will be snapped or uprooted. Fallen trees could cut off residential areas for days to weeks. Electricity will be unavailable for weeks after the hurricane passes.
5	Greater than 155 mph (135 kt or 249 km/hr).	Catastrophic damage is expected.	Complete roof failure on many residences and industrial buildings will occur. Some complete building failures with small buildings blown over or away are likely. All signs blown down. Complete destruction of mobile homes (built in any year). Severe and extensive window and door damage will occur. Nearly all windows in high-rise buildings will be dislodged and become airborne. Severe injury or death is likely for persons struck by wind-blown debris. Nearly all trees will be snapped or uprooted and power poles downed. Fallen trees and power poles will isolate residential areas. Power outages will last for weeks to possibly months.

Source: National Weather Service, "The Saffir-Simpson Hurricane Wind Scale (Experimental)," 2009, <www.nhc.noaa.gov/aboutsshs.shtml>.

UNIT CONVERSIONS

1 kilometer (km):
   0.62 mile
   0.54 nautical mile

1 mile (m):
   1.61 kilometer
   0.87 nautical mile

1 nautical Mile (nm):
   1/60 degree latitude
   1.85 kilometer
   1.15 mile

1 knot (kt):
   1 nautical mile per hour
   1.85 km per hour
   1.15 mile per hour (mph)

Notes

1. Reg Morrison, The Climate Debate, 2009, homepage.mac.com/gregalchin/rm/pdfs/climate%20debate.pdf.

2. Frank Rivers Millikan, "Joseph Henry's Grand Meteorological Crusade," Weatherwise 50 (October/November 1997).

3. Stefan Rahmstorf, "Thermohaline Circulation: The Current Climate," *Nature* 421 (February 2003).

4. NOAA, "Hurricane Basics," www.nhc.noaa.gov/HAW2/english/basics.shtml.

5. FEMA, "Taking Shelter from the Storm: Building a Safe Room for Your Home or Small Business," FEMA Report 320, 2008, www.fema.gov/plan/prevent/saferoom/fema320.shtm.

6. National Weather Service, "The Saffir-Simpson Hurricane Wind Scale (Experimental)," 2009, www.nhc.noaa.gov/aboutsshws.shtml.

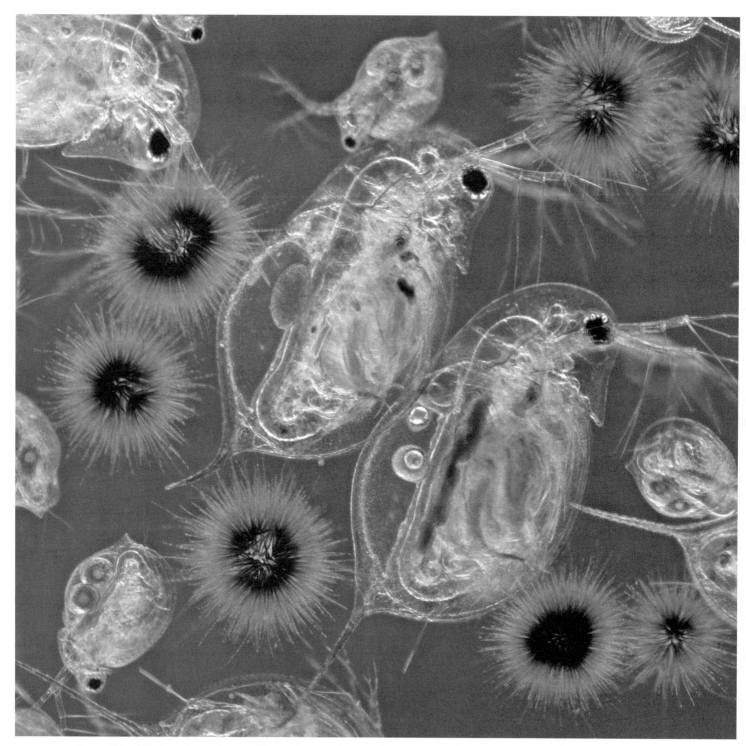

Figure 2.1 *Life in a drop of water*: Photomicrography reveals plankton within one water drop from a local reservoir.
(PHOTO: © Spike M. I. Walker)

Source: Photo courtesy of Spike M. I. Walker, Photomicrographer and zoologist.

CHAPTER 2

LAND AND WATER

Water is one of the most common elements of the planet. One molecule of water consists of 2 atoms of hydrogen and 1 atom of oxygen. These produce mutually attractive forces between water molecules known as a hydrogen bond that give water flexibility. The range of surface temperatures and pressures in the biosphere permit water to exist in three states: solid (ice), liquid (water), and gas (water vapor).

Approximately 71% of the surface of Earth is covered by water. The remaining 29% is land that has formed and reformed over geologic time. Throughout the past 2 billion years, continents have doubled in land surface. At one period in the Earth's geologic history, the land mass was a single continent that broke apart and drifted as continental plates across early oceans. Fractures and collisions of the plates left the valley rifts and mountain ranges of our current geography. (Figure C.2.)

Over millennia, the processes of glaciation, volcanic eruptions, and meteoric impacts have shaped the modern landscape. Surface features continue to weather from precipitation, thermal cycles, and chemical effects. Water shapes the surface of the land as precipitation falls and finds its way to the sea. (Figure 2.2.)

As water progresses through the land and sea, organisms take in water through their bodies as part of the biological process. Water supports the soil, vegetation, and ecosystems that create biodiversity and sustain all living species.

Design for resilience recognizes the natural processes of the hydrologic cycle and the role of soil, plants, and reservoirs in holding and using water. This is a defining concept behind enhancement of the landscape as we find it, design it, and remediate it to limit and mitigate flooding.

The opportunity of resilient design is to reestablish the functioning of watersheds in how we build, where we build, in order to preserve regional water balance and water supply to sustain our regions and communities.

2.1 WATER AND CARBON CYCLES

Water Cycle

The freshwater budget is a balance of evaporation, atmospheric transport, precipitation, runoff, and storage processes. Water evaporates from the surface of Earth, pumping water vapor back into the atmosphere. Rain and snow continually form within clouds and fall back to the surface, completing one link of the hydrologic cycle. Most freshwater exists in the form of ice caps. Smaller amounts are in underground reservoirs (aquifers) and in freshwater lakes and rivers. (Figure 2.3.)

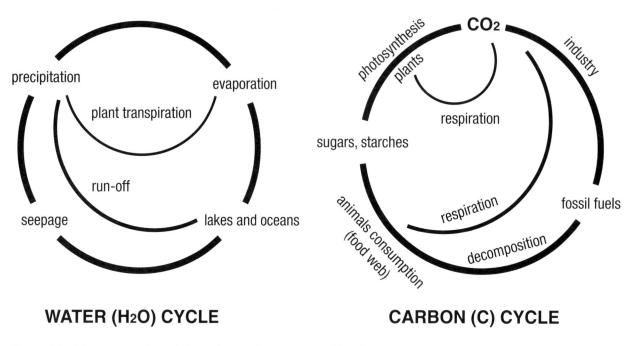

WATER (H₂O) CYCLE   **CARBON (C) CYCLE**

Figure 2.2   *The water cycle and the carbon cycle* are impacted by changes in the land.

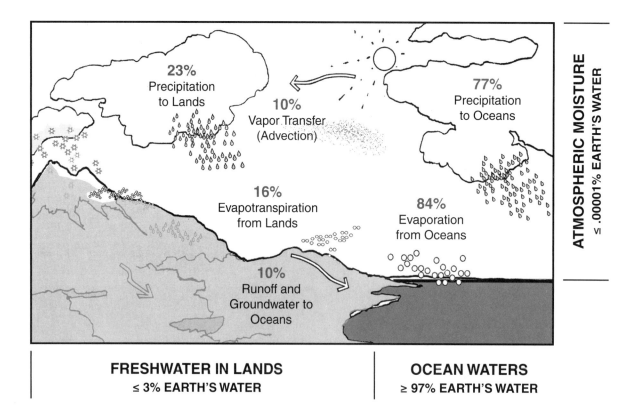

FRESHWATER IN LANDS   **OCEAN WATERS**
≤ 3% EARTH'S WATER   ≥ 97% EARTH'S WATER

Figure 2.3   *The hydrologic cycle at global scale:* Averaged over the globe, evaporation equals precipitation.

Oceans heat and cool more slowly than land and moderate temperature changes on land. The oceanic conveyor belt circles the globe, transporting warm and cold water. The high heat capacity of ocean waters buffers the biosphere from wide temperature swings.

The latent heat of condensation, absorbed when water evaporated, is released back to the atmosphere when the water vapor condenses back into cloud water or ice. This latent heat helps drive clouds and other weather systems. Evaporation from the ocean surface is the primary source of energy for hurricanes.

Water in the global water cycle is renewed on average every 16 days. Subject to region, soil moisture is replaced approximately every year. Waters in wetlands are replaced about every 5 years. The residence time of lake water is about 17 years. In areas of little human development, groundwater can reside more than 1,000 years. The amount and rate of water distribution over the globe over time and location varies greatly, accounting for floods in one location and droughts in another, unpredictable in occurrence from months to years.[1] (Figure 2.4.)

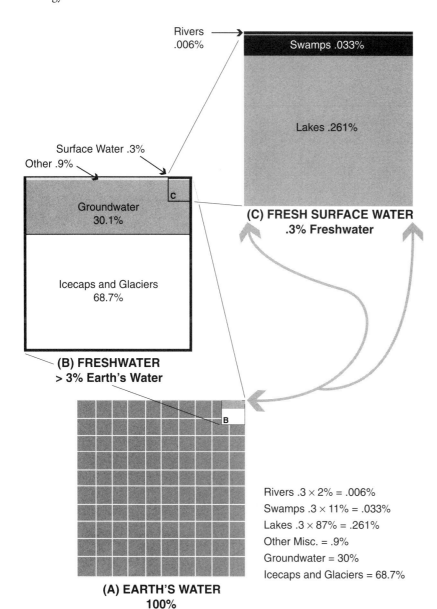

Rivers .3 × 2% = .006%
Swamps .3 × 11% = .033%
Lakes .3 × 87% = .261%
Other Misc. = .9%
Groundwater = 30%
Icecaps and Glaciers = 68.7%

Figure 2.4 *Global water resources.*

Sources: P. H. Gleick, "Water Resources," in *Encyclopedia of Climate and Weather*, ed. S. H. Schneider, vol. 2 (New York: Oxford University Press, 1996) http://ga.water.usgs.gov/edu/watercyclehi.html.

Carbon Cycle

Carbon is the fourth most abundant element in the universe and the building block for all living organisms. The movement of carbon in its many forms among atmosphere, oceans, and land is described by the *carbon cycle*. There is a fixed amount of carbon in the world, which has not been completely accounted for in current research.[2] Carbon is found in the atmosphere, dissolved in ocean water, in tissues of living organisms, and locked in limestone deposits lining the ocean floor. The conversion of carbon dioxide (CO_2) into living matter and back is the main pathway of the carbon cycle. (Figure 2.5.)

Plants absorb CO_2 from the atmosphere during photosynthesis and release CO_2 back to the atmosphere during respiration. A further major exchange of CO_2 occurs between the oceans and the atmosphere. Dissolved CO_2 in the oceans is used by marine biota during photosynthesis. Two other important processes are determined by human action: fossil fuel burning and changing land use. In fossil fuel burning, coal, oil, natural gas, and gasoline are consumed by industry, power plants, and motor vehicles and other combustion engines.

Changing land use is a broad term that encompasses a host of essentially human activities, including agriculture, deforestation, and reforestation. The surface of Earth wherein freshwater and life is sustained is now subject as much to human design and management as to natural processes. Close to 40% of Earth's land surface currently is used for cropland and pasture. (Table 2.1.)

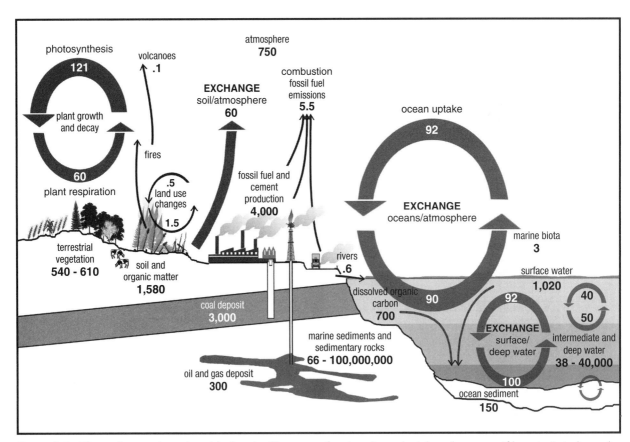

Figure 2.5 *The carbon cycle* at the global scale. The mass of carbon in each sink and process, if known, is indicated in gigatons of carbon (Gt C).

Compiled from multiple sources: Center for Climate Research University of Wisconsin at Madison; Department of Geography, Okangan University College, Canada; *World Watch* (November-December) 1998; UNEP/GRID-Arendal 2005; and University of New Hampshire Globe Carbon Cycle 2007, www.globe.gov/projects/carbon.

TABLE 2.1 LAND USE ON A GLOBAL SCALE

LAND USE	% of TOTAL
Urban areas	1.5%
Permanent crops	4.71%
Arable land	13.13%
Permanent pastures	26.0%
Forests and woodland	32.0%

Source: *Encyclopedia Earth*, <www.statemaster.com/encyclopedia/Earth>.

Carbon Sequestration

The global biosphere absorbs roughly 2 billion tons of carbon annually, an amount equal to roughly one-third of all global carbon emissions from human activity. The remaining two-thirds impact the atmosphere and account for global warming. Carbon sequestration is one of the measures that can help redress the balance.

Terrestrial carbon sequestration is the process through which CO_2 from the atmosphere is absorbed by trees, plants, and crops through photosynthesis and stored as carbon in biomass (tree trunks, branches, foliage, and roots) and soils. The term *carbon sink* also is used to refer to the capacity to sequester carbon of forests, croplands, and grazing lands and other types of landscapes.

Forests cover approximately one-third of Earth's total land surface. Trees can act as a carbon sink by removing carbon from the atmosphere and storing it underground. Trees absorb CO_2 from the atmosphere for photosynthesis and thus help to regulate the natural greenhouse effect. Significant amounts of this carbon remain stored in the roots of certain plants and in the soil.

Trees also act as a *carbon source* after reaching full growth and begin to decompose as bacteria break down dead trees and leaf litter, a process that generally takes years but can be accelerated to hours when they are burned. Deforestation removes a potential sink for the CO_2 humans are pumping into the atmosphere. After fossil fuel combustion, deforestation is the second most significant cause of greenhouse gas emissions.

The forested landscape of the United States currently acts as a net carbon sink—it sequesters more carbon than it emits by natural processes. This is estimated to offset some 15% of total U.S. CO_2 emissions produced by the energy, transportation, building, and other sectors. However, overall forest sequestration levels in the United States have been declining

and are expected to continue to decline due to increasing harvests, maturing forests, and land-use changes.[3]

The capacity for carbon sequestration varies by ecosystem, tree species, soil type, regional climate, topography, and management practice. Carbon accumulation in forests and soils eventually reaches a saturation point beyond which additional sequestration is no longer possible. This occurs when trees reach maturity or when the organic matter in soils builds back to its original levels. Among ecosystem types, peat bogs, wetlands, and forests have the greatest capacity for storage of carbon in soils and plants. (Figure 2.6.)

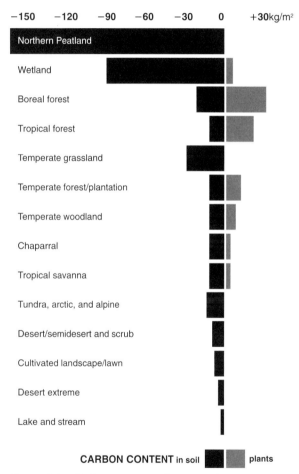

CARBON CONTENT in soil ▓▓ plants

Figure 2.6 *Carbon content of terrestrial ecosystems:* Carbon sequestration is a critical ecosystem service provided by wetlands, forests, and other soil/plant communities.

Source: Jeffrey S. Amthor et al., "Terrestrial Ecosystem Responses to Global Changes: A Research Strategy," ORNL/TM/27 Environmental Sciences Division. Pub. No. 4821, 2010. www.ornl.gov/~webworks/cpr/rpt/1001.pdf.

2.2 BIODIVERSITY AND THE LANDSCAPE

Biodiversity is a measure of the variation of life-forms within a given environmental community, biome, or the entire biosphere. Biodiversity offers lessons for resilient design: The more complex an ecosystem or community, the more likely it is to survive for a long period of time and the less vulnerable it is to damage.

Biodiversity is a defining character of viable natural and human communities, including improved health and resistance to disease.

Biodiversity is a also measure of health and disease protection. With greater biodiversity, there are more natural biological controls of the insect-borne disease vectors that increase when predator-prey balance is disrupted. Biodiversity in wildlife populations helps to reduce disease vectors that affect humans. For example, raptors help control the populations of mice that carry deer ticks. Bats and birds help control mosquito populations.

Disease vectors are paths of disease transmission that may carry bacteria, protozoa, and viruses via parasite hosts to subsequent hosts. Insects such as mosquitoes, flies, ticks, lice, and fleas form a major group of disease vectors that transmit diseases to humans. Wildlife population diversity helps provide natural control of these disease vectors in the environment.

Many factors impact the biodiversity of terrestrial ecosystems. Biodiversity "drivers of change"—threats to the health of the biodiversity of the environment—include global warming, biotic exchange and plant decomposition, forest deforestation, and fossil fuel combustion. Human activity has doubled the rate of nitrogen deposition that is dispersed as runoff to streams, groundwater, and coastal waters and ends in lake and ocean aquatic dead zones.[4] Of these factors, *change in land use* is the most critical. Ecology research studies led by O. E. Sala of Brown University estimate that land-use changes—resulting from human interventions—could have as great an impact on biodiversity over the next century as the combined influence of increased CO_2 and climate change.[5] (Figure 2.7.)

Life of the Forest Floor

The world of biodiversity can be seen at one's feet in a forested landscape. Forests and fields provide natural resources, cleanse water and air, and moderate climate. Fields and woodlots as small as a few acres help support a biotic community, what biologist E. O. Wilson describes as "the ancient miniature wilderness that thrives at ground level."[6]

A cubic foot of soil in a natural landscape teems with hundreds, even thousands, of microscopic organisms—as well as fungi, insects, grubs, worms, leaves, water, and the soil itself. It provides food, decomposes into organic matter, and releases nutrients to the soil. It is an essential building block of the carbon cycle of life. Invertebrate communities—insects, worms, and slugs—thrive in decaying trees. Lichens, mosses,

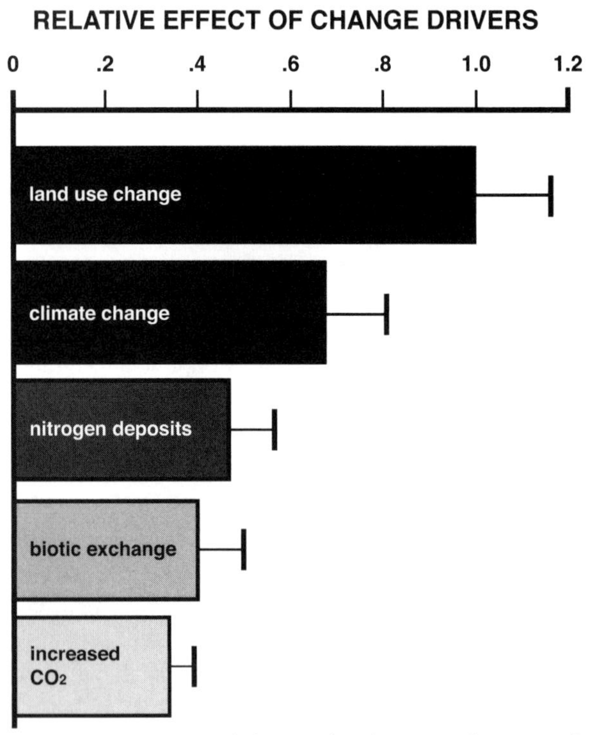

RELATIVE EFFECT OF CHANGE DRIVERS

Figure 2.7   *Drivers of change:* biodiversity of terrestrial and freshwater ecosystems. Land-use change has the greatest impact on biodiversity.

Source: O. E. Sala et al., "Global Biodiversity Scenarios for 2100," *Science* 287 (March 2000): 1770–1774.

and fungi grow within the soil, and decaying trees. They aid in decomposition and return of nutrients to the soil and serve as food sources for wildlife. (Figure 2.8.)

Watershed

A *watershed* is a drainage basin in which rain and snowmelt drains downhill into a shared body of water, such as a river, lake, reservoir, wetland, or ocean. The basin includes the streams and rivers that convey the water as well as the land surfaces that serve those watercourses. Watersheds are separated from adjacent basins by a *drainage divide.* (Figure 2.9.)

John Wesley Powell, the nineteenth-century western explorer and geographer, defined the term *watershed* as "*That area of land, a bounded hydrologic system, within which all living things are inextricably linked by their common water course and where, as humans settled, simple logic demanded that they become part of a community.*"[7]

Figure 2.8 *Primordial life on the forest floor:* Lichen, moss, ferns, and leafy plants represent the stages of primary succession.

(PHOTO: Donald Watson)

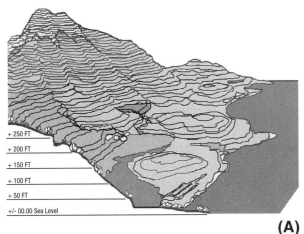

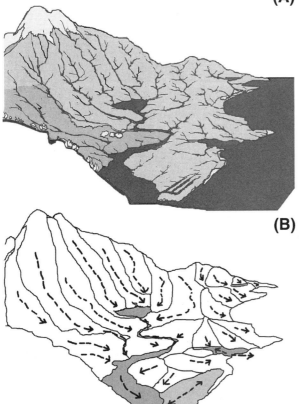

Figure 2.9 *Watershed* (A) defined by contours, (B) dendric pattern of streams and rivers, and (C) drainage divides.

Watercourses are appropriately managed by regulation of the *riparian zone* along the edge of streams and water bodies, typically extending from the edge of the water to a clear change in land conditions, usually based on vegetation, slope, and soil moisture. There is no clear, uniformly accepted definition of a riparian zone. The term is loosely used to describe this transition zone.

Wetlands

Wetlands are a broad category of ecosystems that are supported by water for all or part of the year. They include vernal pools, swamps, and fresh- and saltwater marshes. Water can be freshwater, salt water, or brackish. Brackish waters typically characterize a shoreline where there is a saline gradient resulting from location between land and sea, where freshwater seeps and rivers refresh estuaries and coastal waters. Wetlands are a natural habitat for plant and animal life that in turn support the healthy functioning and renewal of the wetland systems. Wetlands are essential ecosystems for control of flooding.

Permanent wetlands are saturated year-round with a stable vegetation community and often a stable water level. Seasonal wetlands fluctuate and may dry out periodically. All wetlands are inundated frequently enough that the root systems of vegetation experience anaerobic (no-oxygen) conditions.

Wetlands are subject to regulation throughout the United States. In the Clean Water Act and federal code, wetlands are defined as "*those areas that are inundated or saturated by surface or groundwater at a frequency and duration sufficient to support, and that under normal circumstances do support, a prevalence of vegetation typically adapted for life in saturated soil conditions.*"[8]

Table 2.2 outlines the wetland classification system adopted by the U.S. Fish and Wildlife Service, based on dominant plants or substrates. The classification is used for mapping and for federal and state wetland inventories.[9]

Vernal Pool

Vernal pools—also called vernal ponds or ephemeral pools—are shallow depressions that normally contain water for only part of the year. A small depression in a hillside or forest vale may be large enough to become a vernal pool. Vernal pools may fill during the fall and winter as the groundwater table rises. Rain and melting snow contribute water during the spring. Vernal pools typically dry out by mid- to late summer.

Species that must have access to vernal pools in order to survive and reproduce are known as *obligate vernal pool species*. Depending on region, obligate vernal pool species

TABLE 2.2 CLASSES AND SUBCLASSES OF WETLANDS AND DEEPWATER HABITATS

Class	Brief Description	Subclasses
Rock bottom	Generally permanently flooded areas with bottom substrates consisting of at least 75% stones and boulders and less than 30% vegetative cover.	Bedrock; rubble
Unconsolidated bottom	Generally permanently flooded areas with bottom substrates consisting of at least 25% particles smaller than stones and less than 30% vegetative cover.	Cobble-gravel; sand; mud; organic
Aquatic bed	Generally permanently flooded areas that are vegetated by plants growing principally on or below the water surface.	Algal; aquatic; rooted vascular and floating vascular vegetation
Reef	Characterized by elevations above the surrounding substrate and interference with normal wave flow; they are primarily subtidal.	Coral; mollusk; worm
Streambed	Channel whose bottom is completely dewatered at low water periods.	Bedrock; rubble; cobble-gravel; sand; mud; organic; vegetated
Rocky shore	Wetlands characterized by bedrock stones or boulder with areal coverage of 75% or more and with less than 30% coverage by vegetation.	Bedrock; rubble
Unconsolidated shore	Wetlands having unconsolidated substrates with less than 75% coverage by stones, boulders, and bedrock and less than 30% native vegetative cover.	Cobble-gravel; sand; mud; organic; vegetated
Moss-lichen wetland	Wetlands dominated by mosses or lichens where other plans have less than 30% coverage.	Moss; lichen
Emergent wetland	Wetlands dominated by erect, rooted, herbaceous hydrophytes.	Persistent; nonpersistent
Scrub-shrub wetland	Wetlands dominated by woody vegetation less than 20 feet (6 m) tall.	Deciduous; evergreen; dead woody plants
Forested wetland	Wetlands dominated by woody vegetation 20 feet (6 m) or taller.	Deciduous; evergreen; dead woody plants.

Source: L.M. Cowardin et al., "Classification of Wetlands and Deepwater Habitats of the United States," U.S. Fish and Wildlife Service Report FWS/OBS-79/31, 1979.

may include wood frogs, salamanders, and fairy shrimp. Obligate species that define a wetland as a vernal pool may also be called *indicator species*.

Other animals that are found in vernal pools but do not depend on them for successful reproduction are called *facultative species*; they include green frogs, spring peepers, and turtles. (Figure 2.10.)

Freshwater Pond

A *pond* is a small shallow body of water in which sunlight reaches the deepest points sufficient for growth of rooted plant life. Ponds may be spring fed or created by stream or seep inflow. Aquatic plants have developed strategies such as leaves that float on the pond's surface or stems or flowers that extend above the water. Plants such as hornwort and

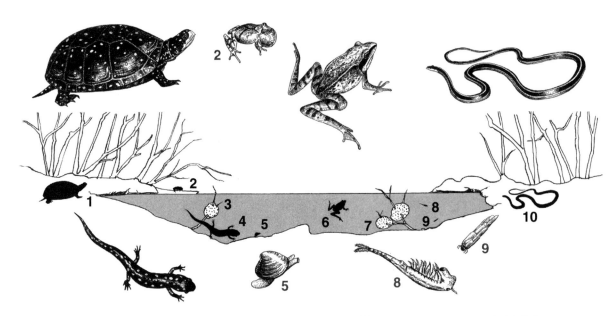

Figure 2.10   *Vernal pool.*

(© Linda Thomas, artist)

1. Spotted turtle
2. Spring peeper
3. Spotted salamander eggs
4. Spotted salamander
5. Fingernail clam
6. Wood frog
7. Wood frog eggs
8. Fairy shrimp
9. Caddisfly larva
10. Eastern ribbon snake

water milfoil grow completely submerged with leaves that are thin and sensitive enough to draw in gases and nutrients dissolved in the water. The bottom layer of a pond consists of sediments that build up over time. If subject to continuing sedimentation, a pond will gradually fill in to become a swamp, bog, or marsh. (Figure 2.11.)

Swamp

A *swamp* is a wetland with large areas that are temporarily or permanently flooded by shallow and slowly moving water flows, within which there are typically woody vegetation (in North America) and dry-land protrusions or *hummocks*. Water in a swamp may be freshwater, brackish, or salt water. Due to their relative inaccessibility, swamps may serve as biodiversity preserves that support rare and endangered trees, plants, orchids, and wildlife. (Figure 2.12.)

Estuary

An *estuary* is a partially enclosed body of water where two different bodies of water meet and mix. An estuary is most typically a tidal zone of a coastline, such as mouth of a river, with a brackish water mix with more salinity than freshwater but less than sea water. An estuary may also be called a bay, inlet, harbor, lagoon, slough, or sound. Salinity and freshwater mix along a *gradient* that changes its location and composition subject to rainfall, tide, normal weather, and storm events. Estuaries provide unique and essential habitat for marine species of fish that breed in freshwater and related plant zones. (Figure 2.13.)

Salt Marsh

Salt marshes develop on coasts, shorelines, bays, and estuaries where wave action is relatively gentle and sheltered from extreme erosion. The biologically productive ecosystem rivals the rain forest in biodiversity. Plant species must be tolerant of salt spray and/or salt water, partial or complete inundation, and anoxic (low-oxygen) mud substrate. Daily tides and flows from uplands continually replenish nutrients for microorganisms and marine and animal life. The young of many species, such as the blue crab, white shrimp, and spot tail bass, utilize the salt marsh as a nursery. Salt marsh grasses and shellfish filter and clean water. Salt marshes serve as a critical barrier and protection for coastal flooding. (Figure 2.14.)

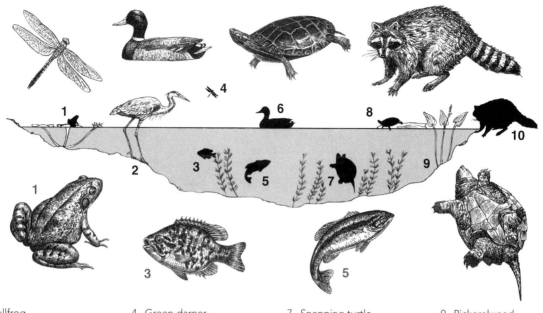

1. Bullfrog
2. Great blue heron
3. Pumpkinseed

4. Green darner
5. Largemouth bass
6. Mallard

7. Snapping turtle
8. Eastern painted turtle

9. Pickerelweed
10. Raccoon

Figure 2.11   *Pond.*

(© Linda Thomas, artist)

1. Tussock sedge
2. Pileated woodpecker
3. Broad-leaved cattail

4. Green frog
5. Red-winged blackbird
6. Wood duck

7. Moose
8. American beaver

9. Eastern screech-owl
10. Northern water snake

Figure 2.12   *Swamp.*

(© Linda Thomas, artist)

1. Wood turtle
2. Belted kingfisher
3. Lizard's tail
4. Ring-billed gull
5. Chain pickerel
6. Curly pondweed
7. Spottail shiner
8. Double-crested
   cormorant
9. Alewife
10. American eel

Figure 2.13   *Estuary.*

(© Linda Thomas, artist)

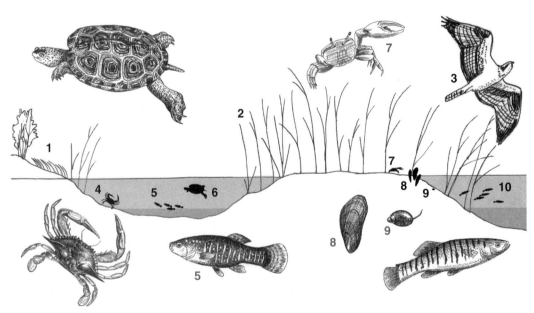

1. Salt hay grass
2. Smooth cordgrass
3. Osprey
4. Blue crab
5. Mummichog
6. Northern diamondback
   terrapin
7. Fiddler crab
8. Ribbed mussel
9. Mud snail
10. Striped killifish

Figure 2.14   *Salt marsh.*

(© Linda Thomas, artist)

Beach

Beaches and sandy shores are dynamic environments subject to extremes of wave and water forces. As a result, sandy shores are typified by a hardy and resilient ecology. An intertidal zone of sandy shores is described by ecological gradients in three directions: vertical and horizontal transects and depth below water, sand, and soil. Organisms on sandy shores can live both on the surface of the substratum and in burrows in the sand. The intertidal zone of sandy shores provides a rich zone for birds and other animals that opportunistically feed on many species that subsist within mud and sand and are revealed in the wash of wave action. (Figure 2.15.)

Rocky Cliffs

A *rocky coastal cliff* is defined as a steep slope rising from the ocean and consisting of bare rock or deposited stone, sand, and silt, often with a rich mix of accumulating marine vegetation and shell life. The nature of the cliff depends on location and exposure, geology (strength, weaknesses in the rock and bedding planes), and coastal protection measures.

Rocky coastal cliffs are a unique ecological setting for birds, shellfish, and other marine life. Ocean cliffs combine proximity and access to marine food sources protected by stable ledges and niches relatively free of human access or predator disturbance. Microhabitats are found in ledges, crevices, and caves, exposed to waves and water above, below, or at the level of sea. Rocky cliffs have been difficult to classify as separate ecosystems but are critical in providing unique habitat and coastline protection.[10] (Figures 2.16 and 2.17.)

2.3 FOLLOW THE WATER: THE OPPORTUNITY FOR WATERSHED PLANNING

The water cycle and the carbon cycle are linked processes balanced and sustained by functioning watersheds. Enhancement of the natural values of landscape, reforestation, and carbon sequestration are allied with flood control strategies.

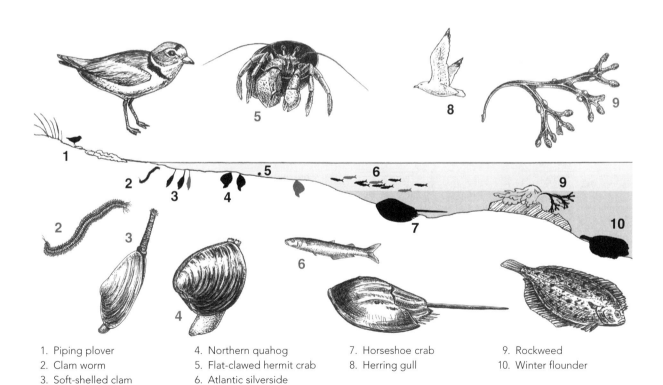

1. Piping plover
2. Clam worm
3. Soft-shelled clam
4. Northern quahog
5. Flat-clawed hermit crab
6. Atlantic silverside
7. Horseshoe crab
8. Herring gull
9. Rockweed
10. Winter flounder

Figure 2.15   *Beach.*

(© Linda Thomas, artist)

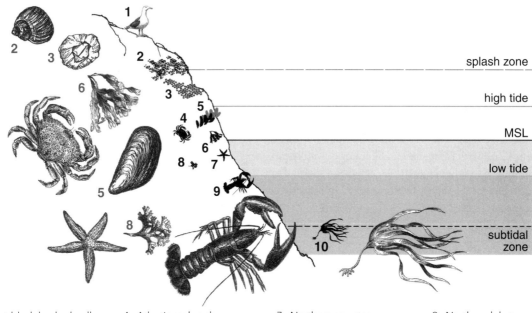

1. Great black-backed gull
2. Rough periwinkle
3. Northern rock barnacle
4. Atlantic rock crab
5. Blue mussel
6. Spiral wrack
7. Northern sea star
8. Irish moss
9. Northern lobster
10. Horsetail kelp

Figure 2.16   *Rocky coast northeast coast.*

(© Linda Thomas, artist)

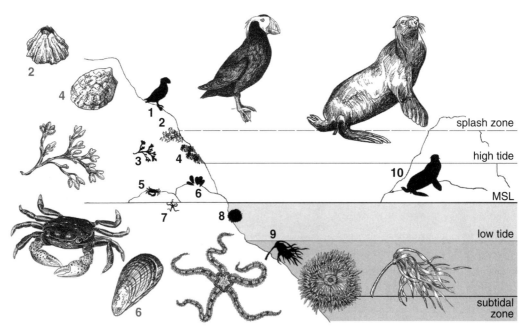

1. Tufted puffin
2. Ribbed limpet
3. Rockweed
4. Acorn barnacle
5. Purple shore crab
6. California mussel
7. Daisy brittle star
8. Giant green anemone
9. Bull kelp
10. California sea lion

Figure 2.17   *Rocky coast west.*

(© Linda Thomas, artist)

Water Supply

Global hydrological cycle supplies and distributes water with great variation, subject to region, climate, and seasonal weather patterns. Arid regions are experiencing water shortages, relying on increasingly costly sources of water of importation, well digging deeper into once-plentiful but now-diminished aquifers, and desalinization. In other regions, water shortages are created when the storage capacities of the surface freshwater streams, landscape, reservoirs, and aquifer are shortcircuited, neglected, or removed.

ANNUAL RAINFALL   Annual rainfall of a region determines its water income or budget of water balance that, with watershed design and management, could become available to support natural landscape and human requirements. Given cyclic periods of drought, watershed planning of reservoir capacity has to extend forward for years and decades.

EXTREME WEATHER EVENTS   Extreme weather events establish the severity and risk from local natural weather hazards. In some regions, hurricanes, storms, and flooding are the foremost natural disaster threats. In other regions, lack of water, drought, and resulting forest fire hazards pose the greatest risk, while flash floods need to be anticipated and mitigated. With the trend toward more severe weather events, regional landscape and infrastructure design needs to anticipate greater peaks and variations and to be made part of every regional and municipal watershed plan.

Water Storage

Either in natural water bodies and available aquifers or structured storage systems, water storage is essential to provide for current and future water needs. Water storage systems in many cities of the United States are inadequate to meet future demands. Techniques for water storage are available for projects at every scale. Implemented together, they can quickly restore and improve the quantity and quality of a community's water independence.

Watershed planning and floodplain management considers water flow as an integrated system. Flood control begins with protection and management of wetlands and the vegetated landscape of riparian buffers along streams, rivers, and water bodies. (Figure 2.18.)

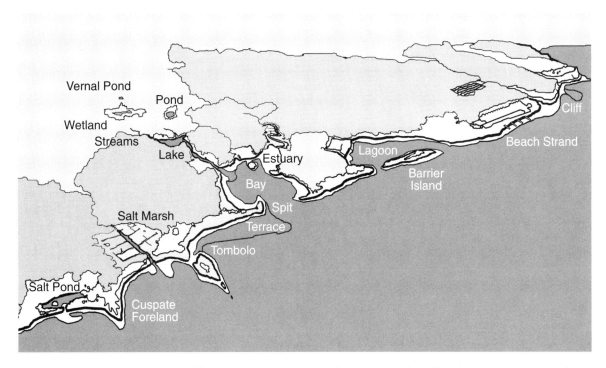

Figure 2.18   *Watershed design and floodplain management* enhance regional and local ecosystem services for resilient design for flood control.

Notes

1. Committee on Earth Science and Applications, National Academy of Sciences, *Earth Science and Applications from Space: National Imperatives for the Next Decade and Beyond* (Washington, DC: National Research Council, 2007).

2. NASA Earth Observatory, "The Carbon Cycle," http://earthobservatory.nasa.gov/Library/CarbonCycle/carbon_cycle4.html.

3. U.S. Environmental Protection Agency, "Carbon Sequestration in Agriculture and Forestry," 2006, http://www.epa.gov/sequestration/faq.html.

4. Peter M. Vitousek et al. 1997. "Human Alteration of the Global Nitrogen Cycle: Causes and Consequences," *Issues in Ecology*, no. 1 (Spring 1997), www.esa.org/science_resources/issues/FileEnglish/issue1.pdf.

5. O. E. Sala et al., "Global Biodiversity Scenarios for 2100," *Science* 287 (March 2000): 1770–1774.

6. Edward O. Wilson, *The Future of Life* (New York: Alfred A. Knopf, 2002).

7. William deBuys, ed., *Seeing Things Whole: The Essential John Wesley Powell* (Washington, DC: Island Press, 2002).

8. Environmental Protection Agency, *Clean Water Act, Guidelines to Regulations Title 40 Protection of the Environment*, Code of Federal Regulations (CFR) Part 230.3, 2009, www.wetlands.com/epa/epa230pa.htm.

9. Ralph W. Tiner, "Technical Aspects of Wetlands: Wetland Definitions and Classifications in the United States," U.S. Geological Survey, Water Supply Paper 2425, n.d., http://water.usgs.gov/nwsum/WSP2425/definitions.html.

10. Douglas W. Larson, Uta Matthes, and Peter E. Kelly, *Cliff Ecology: Pattern and Process in Cliff Ecosystems* (Cambridge: Cambridge University Press, 2000).

Figure 3.1 *Nor'easter winds and waves* at St. Joseph, Lake Michigan, represent the power released when water meets the land.

(PHOTO: © Robb Quinn)

CHAPTER 3

FLOODING

Floods were the most devastating natural disaster in the United States of the twentieth century, in both damage and loss of life. Inland floods are the result of stormwater runoff that exceeds the capacity of their stream and river systems. Contingent factors that increase the extent and severity of inland flooding include frozen ground, ice jams, wind, icing, landslides and mudflow, dam and levee failure, and debris flow. While often seasonal due to spring melt or other seasonal weather patterns, flooding may occur at any time of year and in any location. (Figure 3.2 and Table 3.1.)

Increased flooding can be ascribed to a combination of two factors: changes in land use and increased precipitation. The ecosystem services provided by the natural landscape described in Chapter 2 are part of the "flood design challenge" that is impacted by human alteration of land use. Alternations in land use have reduced the functioning and extent of the natural landscape, soils, and small water systems within watersheds, which are further stressed by increased precipitation and severe events. Over half of the world's wetlands were intentionally drained for agriculture by the 1990s. The United States loses approximately 100,000 acres of wetlands to development each year.[1] Many coastal wetlands are lost to development or to storm erosion and destruction in areas where they previously aided in coastal storm mitigation.[2]

This chapter provides an overview of the risks of weather- and water-related events that cause flooding and determine the basis of floodplain and coastal flood management.

3.1 FLOODING FROM INCREASED PRECIPITATION

Total average precipitation across the United States has increased on average over 5% over the past century. Decreases in annual precipitation have occurred in the Southeast except during the fall season and in the Northwest in all seasons except the spring. (Figure 3.3a.)

While variations in annual precipitation are regional, increases in the heaviest downpours are impacting all regions of the United States. In the past half century, the amount of precipitation falling in the heaviest 1% of rain events has increased on average over 20%. (Figure 3.3b.)

The 2009 *Global Climate Change* Report states: "One of the clearest precipitation trends in the United States is the increasing frequency and intensity of heavy downpours."[3] In reviewing current research, the report projects that very heavy precipitation will increase, principally in northeastern United States. A summary of climate model projections

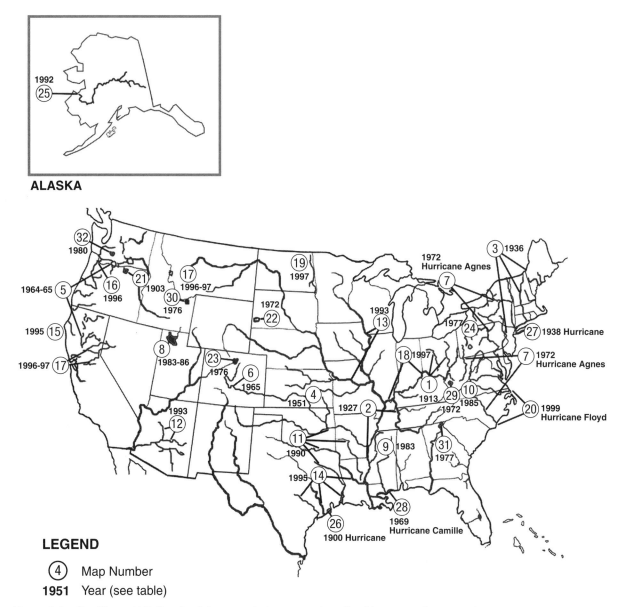

LEGEND

④   Map Number
1951   Year (see table)

Figure 3.2   Significant U.S. floods of the twentieth century described in terms of type and impacts.

indicates that northern areas will become wetter while southern areas will become drier, particularly in the West. The heaviest downpours across the United States are expected to increase, while the lightest precipitation events are projected to decrease.[4] Plans are required to prepare for more extreme flooding as well as for longer periods of drought.

Regional Floods

Some regional floods occur seasonally, when winter or spring rains join with melting snow and inundate river and watershed basins. The ground may be frozen, reducing water infiltration into the soil and thereby increasing runoff.

TABLE 3.1   SIGNIFICANT FLOODS OF THE TWENTIETH CENTURY

Flood Type	Map No.	Date	Area or Stream with Flooding	Reported Deaths	Approximate Cost	Comments
Regional flood	1	Mar.–Apr. 1913	Ohio, statewide	467	$143M	Excessive regional rain
	2	Apr.–May 1927	Mississippi River from Missouri to Louisiana	unknown	$230M	Record discharge downstream from Cairo, Illinois
	3	Mar. 1936	New England	150+	$300M	Excessive rainfall on snow
	4	July 1951	Kansas and Neosho River Basin in Kansas	15	$800M	Excessive regional rain
	5	Dec. 1964–Jan. 1965	Pacific Northwest	47	$430M	Excessive rainfall on snow
	6	June 1965	South Platte and Arkansas rivers in Colorado	24	$570M	14 inches of rain in a few hours in eastern Colorado
	7	June 1972	Northeastern United States	117	$3.2B	Extratropical remnants of Hurricane Agnes
	8	Apr.– June 1983 June 1983–1986	Shoreline of Great Salt Lake, Utah	unknown	$621M	In June 1986, the Great Salt Lake reached its highest elevation and caused $268M more in property damage
	9	May 1983	Central and northeast Mississippi	1	$500M	Excessive regional rain
	10	Nov. 1985	Shenandoah, James, and Roanoke rivers in Virginia and West Virginia	69	$1.25B	Excessive regional rain
	11	Apr. 1990	Trinity, Arkansas, and Red rivers in Texas, Arkansas, and Oklahoma	17	$1B	Recurring intense thunderstorms
	12	Jan. 1993	Gila, Salt, and Santa Cruz rivers in Arizona	unknown	$400M	Persistent winter precipitation
	13	May–Sept. 1993	Mississippi River Basin in central United States	48	$20B	Long period of excessive rainfall
	14	May 1995	South-central United States	32	$5–$6B	Rain from recurring thunderstorms

(continued)

TABLE 3.1 (CONTINUED)

Flood Type	Map No.	Date	Area or Stream with Flooding	Reported Deaths	Approximate Cost	Comments
	15	Jan.–Mar. 1995	California	27	$3B	Frequent winter storms
	16	Feb. 1996	Pacific Northwest and western Montana	9	$1B	Torrential rains and snowmelt
	17	Dec. 1996–Jan. 1997	Pacific Northwest and Montana	36	$2–$3B	Torrential rains and snowmelt
	18	Mar. 1997	Ohio River and tributaries	50+	$500M	Slow moving frontal system
	19	Apr.–May 1997	Red River of the North in North Dakota and Minnesota	8	$2B	Very rapid snowmelt
	20	Sept. 1999	Eastern North Carolina	42	$6B	Slow-moving Hurricane Floyd
Flashflood	21	June 14, 1903	Willow Creek in Oregon	225	unknown	City of Heppner, Oregon, destroyed
	22	June 9–10, 1972	Rapid City, South Dakota	237	$160M	15 inches of rain in 5 hours
	23	July 31, 1976	Big Thompson and Cachela Poudre rivers in Colorado	144	$39M	Flash flood in canyon after excessive rainfall
	24	July 19–20, 1977	Conemaugh River in Pennsylvania	78	$300M	12 inches of rain in 6–8 hours
Ice-jamflood	25	May 1992	Yukon River in Alaska	0	unknown	100-year flood on Yukon River
Storm-surgeflood	26	Sept. 1900	Galveston, Texas	6,000+	unknown	Hurricane
	27	Sept. 1938	Northeast United States	494	$306M	Hurricane
	28	Aug. 1969	Gulf Coast, Mississippi, and Louisiana	259	$1.4B	Hurricane Camille
Dam-failureflood	29	Feb. 2, 1972	Buffalo Creek in West Virginia	125	$60M	Dam failure after excessive rainfall
	30	June 5, 1976	Teton River in Idaho	11	$400M	Earthen dam breached
	31	Nov. 8, 1977	Toccoa Creek in Georgia	39	$2.8B	Dam failure after excessive rainfall
Mudflow flood	32	May 18, 1980	Toule and lower Cowlitz rivers in Washington	60	unknown	Result of eruption of Mt. St. Helens

Source: Charles Perry, *Significant Floods in the United States during the 20th Century: USGS Measures a Century of Floods* (Reston, VA: United States Geological Survey, 2009), <http://ks.water.usgs.gov/pubs/fact-sheets/fs.024-00.html>.

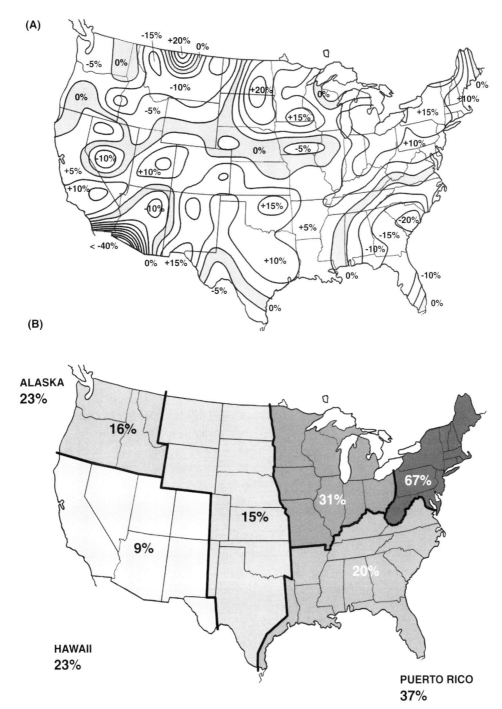

Figure 3.3 (A) *Observed change in annual average precipitation, 1958 to 2008*, has increased about 5% on average, with significant regional variations toward wetter and drier conditions. (B) *Observed change in very heavy precipitation events, 1958 to 2008*, defined as the heaviest 1% of all daily events, has increased in all regions.

Adapted from U.S. Global Change Research Program, *Scientific Assessments: Global Climate Change Impacts in the United States*, "National Climate Change" (2009), <www.globalchange.gov/publications/reports/scientific-assessments/us-impacts/full-report/national-climate-change>.

Extended wet periods during any part of the year can create saturated soil conditions. Any additional rain then runs off and exceeds the capacities of streams and rivers. Regional floods are at times associated with slow-moving, low-pressure or frontal storm systems, including decaying hurricanes or tropical storms. Persistent wet meteorological patterns are usually responsible for very large regional floods, such as the Mississippi River Basin flood during spring and summer of 1993.

Flash Floods

Flash floods can occur with little warning in several seconds to several hours, often originating far from where they may end up coursing. Flash floods can be deadly because they produce rapid rises in water levels and associated debris. Most flood-related deaths are due to flash floods; 50% of such deaths are vehicle related.

Ice-Jam Floods

Ice-jam floods occur on rivers that are totally or partially frozen. Typical of spring melt, a rise in stream stage will break up a totally frozen river and create ice flows that pile up on channel obstructions, such as shallow riffles, log-jams, or bridge piers. The ice creates a dam. The stream can then back up and overflow the channel banks. Floodwater charges downstream when the ice dam fails. The flood can then become a flash flood. The resulting ice-laden floodwater can inflict serious damage on structures.

Landslide and Mudflows

Landslides occur when slopes become unstable and loose material slides or flows under gravity. Landslides are often triggered by erosion at the toe of a steep slope as well as by earthquakes, floods, or heavy rains. Their impacts can be aggravated by destruction or removal of vegetation or uncontrolled vehicular or foot access on steep slopes. They are a hazard along with coastal flooding events on the entire Pacific coast but also on some portions of the Atlantic.

Mudflows are landslides augmented by the speed and weight of hydraulic flow. Heavy rainfall, snowmelt, or high levels of groundwater that flow through cracked bedrock may trigger mudflows. Flooding accompanied by debris and mudflows may also occur when strong rains on hills or mountain terrain causes extensive erosion of tree and supporting vegetation. Terrain previously cleared of vegetation by wildfire is susceptible to flooding, including mudflows.

3.2 FLOODING FROM SEVERE STORMS

Coastal Flooding

Coastal flooding due to seasonal peak tides and average storm events is anticipated in local building and planning and not typically associated with risk. For most coastal communities in the United States, coastal zone regulations and construction practices provide a minimum standard of protection. More serious flooding accompanies severe storms. Property damage and life safety risks result from storm severity, inadequate construction, and the overwhelmed capacity of emergency evacuation provisions in rare but probably severe storms and hurricanes. The 2009 *Global Climate Change* report documents that the force of Atlantic hurricanes has increased in recent decades and that while the total number of storm events has decreased in the eastern Pacific, their intensity has increased.[5]

Climate modeling of global warming indicates that rainfall associated with coastal storms and hurricanes could increase 10% to 31%. Warmer air holds more moisture, so with global warming, rainfall events can be expected to become heavier. Changes in atmospheric circulation patterns cause storms to move more slowly, resulting in more rainfall and flooding in any single area.[6] The U.S. mainland coastlines are characterized by regional variations in geographic and bathymetric profile. (Figure 3.4.)

Tropical Cyclones, Coastal Storms, and Hurricanes

Tropical cyclones and coastal storms include all storms associated with circulation around an area of low atmospheric pressure. Tropical storms, hurricanes, or

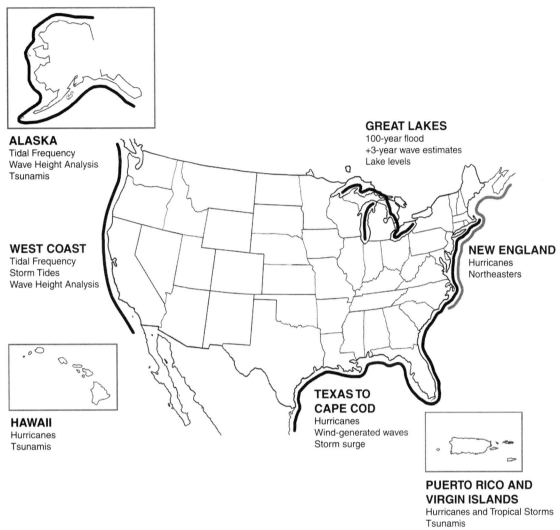

Figure 3.4   *Regional variations in U.S. coastal geography.*

REGIONAL VARIATIONS IN U.S. COASTAL GEOGRAPHY

Atlantic Coast
The *North Atlantic Coast* is glacial in origin, highly irregular, with erosion-resistant rocky headlands, pocket beaches in northern New England, and erodible bluffs and sandy barrier islands in southern New England and Long Island.

The Mid-Atlantic Coast
The coast extends from New Jersey to Virginia. It includes two of the largest U.S. estuaries: Delaware Bay and Chesapeake Bay. The open coast shoreline includes long barrier islands separated by tidal inlets and bay entrances.

The South Atlantic Coast
Three regions characterize the South Atlantic Coast:

1. North Carolina and northern South Carolina shoreline with long barrier and mainland beaches (including the Outer Banks and the South Carolina Grand Strand region).

2. The region extending from Charleston, SC, to the St. Johns River at Jacksonville, Florida, a tide-dominated coast composed of short barrier islands separated by large tidal inlets and wide expanses of tidal marsh.

3. The east coast of Florida composed of barrier and mainland beaches backed by narrow bays and rivers. The *Florida Keys* are a series of low-relief islands formed by limestone and reef rock, with narrow, intermittent carbonate beaches.

Gulf of Mexico Coast
Three regions characterize the Gulf of Mexico coast:

1. *Eastern Gulf Coast* from southwest Florida to Mississippi with low, sandy barrier islands south of Tarpon Springs, Florida, and west of St. Marks, Florida, separated by a marsh-dominated coast in the Big Bend area of Florida.

2. *Mississippi Delta* region with wide, marshy areas and a low-lying coastal plain.

3. *Western Gulf of Mexico Coast*, including the *cheniers* of southwest Louisiana and long, sandy barrier islands of Texas. (*Cheniers* are Mississippi Delta sediments transported westward to form sandy ridges atop mud plains.)

Pacific Coast
The Pacific coast can be divided into two regions:

1. *Southern California reach* with long, sandy beaches and coastal bluffs dominant in this region.

2. *Northern Pacific reach* characterized by rocky cliffs, pocket beaches, and occasional long sandy barriers near river mouths.

Great Lakes
The shorelines of the Great Lakes are highly variable with a combination of wetlands, low and high bluffs, low sandy banks, and lofty sand dunes bluffs (200 feet (60 m) or more above lake level.

Coast of Alaska
The coast of Alaska can be divided into two areas:

1. *Southern Coast*, dominated by steep mountainous islands indented by deep fjords.

2. *Bering Sea and Arctic Coasts*, backed by a coastal plain dotted with lakes and drained by numerous streams and rivers.

The climate of Alaska and action of ice along the shorelines set it apart from most other coast areas of the United States.

Coasts of Hawaii and Pacific Territories
The islands that make up Hawaii are submerged in volcanoes. Rocky cliffs and intermittent sandy beaches form the coast of Hawaii. The coastlines along the Pacific Territories are similar to those of Hawaii. Coastal flooding can be due to storm surges from typhoons and wave run-up from tsunamis.

Coasts of Puerto Rico and U.S. Virgin Islands

Like the Hawaiian Islands and Pacific Territories, the islands of Puerto Rico and the Virgin Islands are the result of ancient volcanic activity. The coastal lowlands of Puerto Rico contain sediment eroded from steep, inland mountains. Ocean currents and wave activity rework the sediments on beaches around each island. Coastal flooding is usually due to hurricanes. Tsunami events have also occurred in the Caribbean.

Source: Federal Emergency Management Agency (FEMA), *Coastal Construction Manual: Principles and Practices of Planning, Siting, Designing, Constructing, and Maintaining Residential Buildings in Coastal Areas*, FEMA 55 (August 2005), <www.fema.gov/rebuild/mat/fema55.shtm>.

typhoons result when the storm origin is tropical and when the circulation is closed. The main hazards associated with tropical cyclones and especially hurricanes are storm surge, high winds, heavy rain, and flooding as well as tornadoes.

The cyclone is accompanied by thunderstorms and, in the northern hemisphere, a counterclockwise circulation of winds near Earth's surface. Hurricanes and coastal storms can generate high winds, coastal flooding, high-velocity flows, damaging waves, significant erosion, and intense rainfall. The low atmospheric pressure at the eye of a hurricane can cause a rise in sea level referred to as a storm surge. When a hurricane makes landfall, the combination of wind, waves, and storm surge can devastate any structure in its path. Lower-category storms are capable of inflicting greater damage than higher-category storms. (Figure 3.5.)

Storm Surge

Intense, low-pressure systems and hurricanes can create storm surges. Storm-surge flooding is a mass of water pushed up onto otherwise dry land by onshore storm winds. Depending on the distance of buildup of offshore water (fetch) and wind velocity, surges can pile water up to heights over 20 feet (6 m). Storm surge does not always correlate with wind speed at landfall. There are recent examples (Hurricanes Ike and Katrina) where pressures rose and wind speeds dropped before landfall, but surges continued the momentum of winds generated offshore. Storm surge is the most dangerous and destructive impact of an ocean storm or hurricane. Nine out of 10 hurricane fatalities are caused by storm surge. Conditions are most aggravated when storm-surge landfall coincides with high tide. Upstream flooding of waterways connected to coastal areas is made worse during the storm surge because of backwater effects.

Other Coastal Storms

Coastal storms occur during winter months and can affect any or all of U.S. coastal areas. Along the Atlantic, these storms are known as extratropical storms or northeasters. Northeasters originate from the northern regions typically in the autumn to spring seasons. The 2009 *Global Climate Change* report states that Atlantic winter storm tracks are shifting northward and are likely to increase in frequency and severity, wind speeds, and wave heights.[7]

Storm patterns along the California Pacific coast are strongly influenced by the *El Niño-Southern Oscillation* (ENSO), a climatic anomaly resulting in above-normal ocean temperatures and elevated sea levels along the coast. El Niño effects can cause increased rainfall and coastal landslides. During El Niño years, sea levels along the Pacific shoreline tend to rise 12 to 18 inches (30–45 cm) above normal, with increased incidence of coastal storms.

Storms on the Great Lakes usually are associated with the passage of low-pressure systems or cold fronts. Storm surges and damaging wave conditions on the Great Lakes are a function of wind speed, direction, duration, and fetch. High winds may occur over a long fetch for more than one hour, resulting in flooding and erosion.

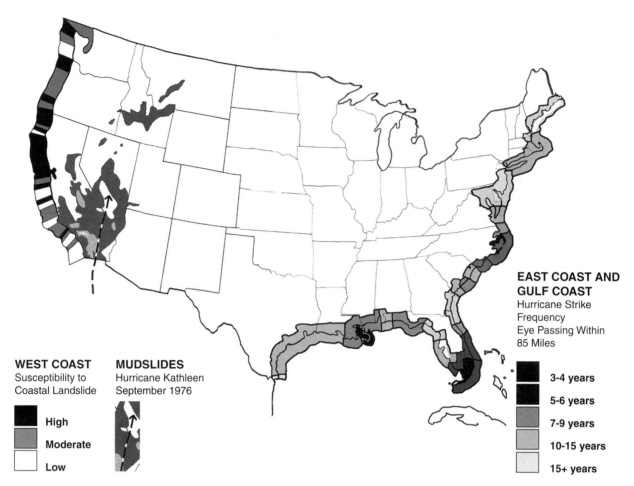

WEST COAST
Susceptibility to
Coastal Landslide

MUDSLIDES
Hurricane Kathleen
September 1976

■ High
▨ Moderate
□ Low

**EAST COAST AND
GULF COAST**
Hurricane Strike
Frequency
Eye Passing Within
85 Miles

■ 3-4 years
■ 5-6 years
▨ 7-9 years
▨ 10-15 years
░ 15+ years

Figure 3.5   *Landfall impacts:* East Coast and Gulf Coast hurricanes and West Coast landslide incidents, 1900 to 2000. In 1976, Tropical Storm Kathleen tracked across northern Mexico and the southwestern United States with lingering rain accompanied by widespread alluvial fan and flash floods in previously unmapped floodplains.

Source: West Coast landslide incidence adapted from FEMA, *Coastal Construction Manual: Principles and Practices of Planning, Siting, Designing, Constructing, and Maintaining Residential Buildings in Coastal Areas* (FEMA 55), Chapter 7, Fig. 7-57, 2005, <www.fema.gov/rebuild/mat/fema55.shtm>. East Coast and Gulf Coast hurricane strike frequency adapted from The Weather Channel, www.weather.com/maps/maptype/severeusnational/hurricanestrikefrequency.

Tsunamis

Tsunamis—in Japanese, meaning "harbor wave"—are long-period water waves generated by undersea shallow-focus earthquakes or by undersea displacements of tectonic plates, landslides, or volcanic activity. Tsunamis can travel great distances, undetected in deep water, but shoaling rapidly in coastal waters. A tsunami's crest will appear as a wall of water up to 50 feet (15 m) high that can travel miles inland with devastating effect. Tsunamis generate a series of large waves capable of destroying harbor facilities, shore protection structures, and upland buildings.

Tsunamis are waves with a very long wavelength in excess of 100 miles (160 km) that travel across the ocean at over 500 mph (700 kph). As they approach shallow water, their wavelength shortens and they become very tall. If the tsunami's trough precedes its crest, the first sign of its approach is a dramatic lowering of sea level, called a *drawback*, in which water recedes and exposes normally submerged portions of the coastline.

The Pacific coast is vulnerable to tsunamis. The coasts of Alaska and the Pacific Islands have the greatest exposure in terms of incidence and height of tsunami wave crest. Tsunamis also occur in the Atlantic Ocean and Caribbean Sea.

Tornadoes

Tornadoes are rotating columns of air of many sizes but in some instances can reach a diameter that may approximate 500 feet (150 m) on average and stay on the ground for 5 miles (8 km). Most tornadoes in the United States develop east of the Rocky Mountains. In a typical year, 500 to 1,000 tornadoes are observed or detected by radar. Many do not touch down. Most tornadoes that do touch down have paths of destruction only a few miles in length (and normally less than a mile in width), but some create paths up to 100 miles (160 km) long.

The vast majority of tornadoes in the United States occur in "tornado alley," although they can occur nearly anywhere in North America. Tornadoes can dislodge or destroy houses and siphon large volumes from bodies of water. (Figure 3.6.)

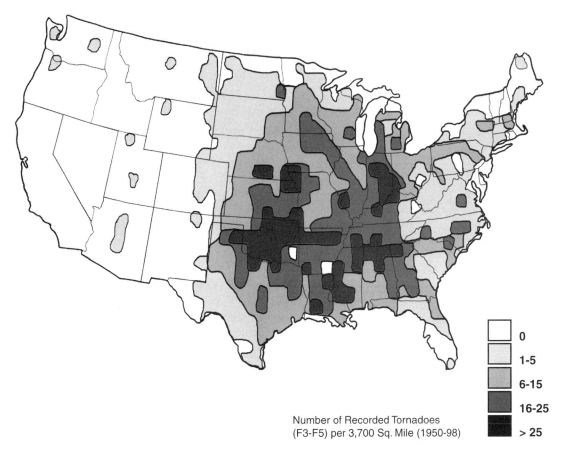

Number of Recorded Tornadoes
(F3-F5) per 3,700 Sq. Mile (1950-98)

☐	0
☐	1-5
☐	6-15
☐	16-25
■	> 25

Figure 3.6   *Frequency of recorded tornadoes*, Fujita Scale F3 to F5, 1950–1998.

Source: FEMA, *Design and Construction Guidance for Community Shelters*, FEMA 361 (July 2008), <www.fema.gov/plan/prevent/saferoom/fema361.shtm>.

Earthquakes

Earthquakes can exist in many areas, including floodplains, in which case buildings must be designed for both flood and earthquake hazards. Earthquake hazards affect coastal areas through surface fault ruptures, liquefaction, and other ground failures. Design in seismic hazard areas must include provisions for two seemingly contradictory requirements:

- The need to elevate buildings above flood hazards and minimize obstructions to flow and waves beneath a structure.
- The need to stabilize or brace the building against violent accelerations and shaking due to earthquakes.

Liquefaction of the supporting soil can be another consequence of ground shaking. In granular soils with high water tables (representative of coastal areas), the ground motion will cause an increase in the pore water pressure, resulting in loss of shear strength that can create a semiliquid state. The soil can temporarily lose its bearing capacity, resulting in settlement and differential movement of roads and buildings.

Subsidence, Uplift, and Ground Failures

Subsidence is a hazard that typically affects areas where:

- Extraction of groundwater or petroleum has occurred due to well pumping on a large scale.
- Organic soils are drained and settlement results.
- Recent sediment deposit over older sediments causes older sediments to compact (e.g., river delta areas).
- Surface sediments collapse in underground voids often associated with mining or groundwater withdrawal.

Differential uplift in the vicinity of the Great Lakes has been shown to increase water levels and flooding.

A *sinkhole* is a form of subsidence, typically very localized. A sinkhole is a natural depression or hole in land caused by water and displacement of soil or bedrock. Size varies but may exceed 650 feet (200 m) in diameter and depth. Sinkholes are common where the subsurface layer is limestone, carbonate rock, or salt beds that can be dissolved naturally by circulating groundwater. Sinkholes also

can be caused by groundwater pumping, construction, and land development when natural water-drainage patterns are changed and new water-diversion systems are developed, such as industrial and runoff-storage ponds.

Coastal Pollution and Hazardous Waste Site Impacts

More than 700 coastal hazardous waste sites have contaminated sediments in U.S. estuaries, reducing the economic and ecological productivity of coastal resources. The number of 2008 closing and advisory days at ocean, bay and Great Lakes beaches topped 20,000 for the fourth consecutive year. United States beaches continue to suffer from serious water pollution that puts swimmers at risk while degrading fishing and aquatic life.[8]

High Winds

Winds accompany weather and storm events. Wind load forces and accompanying damage by wind-borne debris and rain penetration accompany storm and flooding risks, impacting building chimneys, towers, eaves, and openings. Wind-induced property losses annually exceed the sum of all other losses from natural hazards.[9] (Figure 3.7.)

Sea Level Rise

The prospect of rising oceans was raised in the scientific community as a possible result of global climate change in the early 1990s. Research and debate continue in both scientific and policy communities as to the probable extent and rate of sea level rise. The 2009 *Global Climate Change* report [10] documents that over the past 50 years, sea level has increased along most of the U.S. coast. The report concludes: "Sea level rise and storm surge place many U.S. coastal areas at increasing risk of erosion and flooding, especially along the Atlantic and Gulf Coasts, Pacific Islands, and parts of Alaska. Energy and transportation infrastructure and other property in coastal areas are very likely to be adversely affected."

Sea level rise is not yet represented in building codes or coastal management regulations. FEMA requirements and local regulations that add safety factors to minimum requirements do make provision for small increments of sea level rise. Sea level rise as an issue and impact of climate change has been addressed by some planning studies. (Figure 3.8.) Part IV of this book discusses these considerations and the planning and design responses that may result.

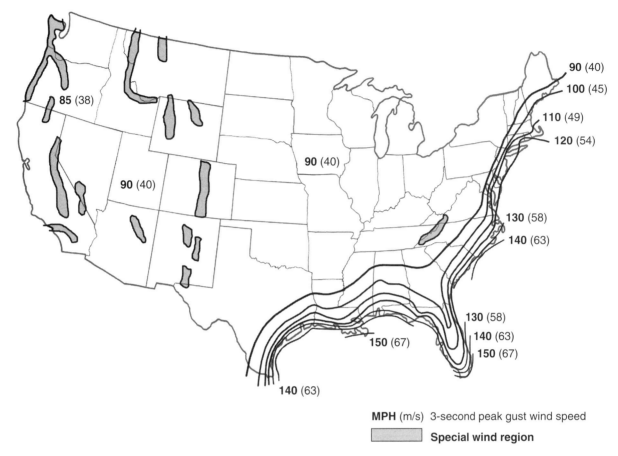

Figure 3.7 *Basic wind speed*: Three-second wind gust speed in mph (m/s). Special wind regions include mountain-ous terrain, ocean promontories, and other conditions to be examined for unusual wind conditions. This map is rep-resentative only and subject to updates by ASCE.

Source: Based on ASCE, *Minimum Design Loads for Buildings and Other Structures.* ASCE/SEI 7-05 (Reston, VA: American Society of Civil Engineers, 2006).

3.3 ECONOMIC AND SOCIAL COSTS OF WATER-RELATED NATURAL DISASTERS

A primary factor contributing to the rise in U.S. disaster losses is the steady increase in the population of flood-prone coastal communities. Coastal zones are the most densely populated and developed areas in the United States. The population in coastal counties represents more than 54% of the total U.S. population but occupies only 26% of the total land area. Ten of the 15 most populous cities in the United States are located in coastal counties. Coastal population and development have grown over the past decades and are expected to increase.[11]

Risks to life safety and property due to severe storms and coastal flooding are defined not by the natural haz-ard but by the decision to locate there and the nature of development that is built. Resulting economic and social risks result from the size and density of population and the infrastructure investment.

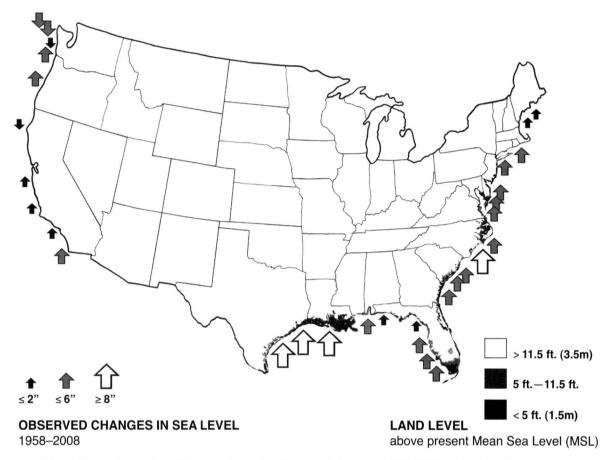

OBSERVED CHANGES IN SEA LEVEL
1958–2008

≤ 2"   ≤ 6"   ≥ 8"

LAND LEVEL
above present Mean Sea Level (MSL)

☐ > 11.5 ft. (3.5m)

■ 5 ft.—11.5 ft.

■ < 5 ft. (1.5m)

Figure 3.8   *U.S. coastline vulnerable to sea level rise:* Observed changes (1958–2008) and vulnerable elevations along the U.S. Atlantic and Gulf coasts.

Source: East Coast elevations susceptible to flooding are adapted from James C. Titus, and Charlie Richman, "Maps of Lands Vulnerable to Sea Level Rise: Modeled Elevations along the U.S. Atlantic and Gulf Coasts," epa.gov/climatechange/effects/coastal/slrmaps_vulnerable.html. Observed changes in sea level (1958–2000) adapted from USGCRP, *Scientific Assessments.*

By 2000, coastal zone counties contained approximately 42% of the nation's total housing supply. Coastal communities—at one time typified by resort and seasonal housing—increasingly support a year-round population. Of 48 million housing units in coastal zone counties, only 3% are classified as seasonal, representing an ongoing conversion of seasonal to year-round occupancy. This trend represents consumer lifestyle choices of both the retirement-age, middle-age, and affluent segments of U.S. population.[12]

Although development is positive for economic growth, poorly considered or unregulated development can reduce, eliminate, or place at risk the natural areas that would otherwise reduce coastal flooding impacts and protect local water resources required to sustain that growth. The nation's coastal counties are losing farmland to urban and other land uses at a faster rate than noncoastal counties are.[13]

This overview of risks and costs of flooding defines the challenge to design buildings, communities, and regions for resilience. The risk is indefinable to the extent that global climate change impacts on weather, severe storms, and sea level rise are based on climate model projects. Current flood regulations are minimum requirements and generally do not reflect climate change impacts. More weight of evidence and broad agreement may be required to increase the required standards in planning policies and regulations.

Coastal communities are increasingly populated in the United States and, as a result, are increasingly vested with financial, social, and political influence. Proposals to revitalize coastal communities and watersheds can rely on this investment in social, political, and economic capital. The fact that flood-prone areas are the most vulnerable to risk means that they can receive the necessary focus for redevelopment and renewal, a project of resilient design.

Inland and coastal flooding impacts are increasingly acknowledged to require integrated watershed and coastal zone management. The need to renew the nation's approach to resilient watershed design gains momentum when the larger issue of water quality and water security is included. A 2009 report sponsored by the National Association of Metropolitan Water Agencies[14] provides a useful summary that indicates the broad sweep of issues of water quality, flood mitigation, and infrastructure renewal.

IMPACTS OF CLIMATE CHANGE ON WATERSHED DESIGN AND MANAGEMENT

Confronting Climate Change: An Early Analysis of Water and Wastewater Adaptation Costs was recently released by the National Association of Metropolitan Water Agencies. The report estimates climate change adaptation issues and costs that the nation's drinking water and wastewater utilities are expected to face in the decades ahead. The climate change effects summarized here impact water and wastewater services.

Impacts Common to All Regions

- Sea level rise and storm surge impacts (except in the Midwest)
- Increased extreme precipitation events
- Anticipated increased regulation for wet-weather management
- Increased disrupted service from flooding
- Declining water quality
- Increased demand for emergency response and recovery
- Increased treatment requirements
- Higher energy demand
- Temperature increase
- Drought, floods, more frequent storms
- Rising sea levels
- Impacts on ecology, agriculture and storm-water

Source Water

- Regional drought
- Intake elevations
- Water quality issues
- Evaporation
- Groundwater depletion
- Seawater intrusion

Water Treatment

- Sedimentation
- Additional treatment requirements
- Siting elevations
- Water quality issues
- Infrastructure flooding

Wastewater

- Siting elevations
- Outfall elevations
- Combined sewer overflow and sanitary sewer overflow frequency
- Temperature-dependent processes
- Infrastructure flooding

Additionally, most regions are expected to have geographically specific impacts.

Northeast

- **Drinking Water Utilities.** Increased storage needs resulting from earlier snowmelt and increased extreme precipitation events

- **Wastewater Utilities.** Increased demand for maintaining quality and quantity of discharges to rivers and streams for environmental purposes

Southeast

- **Drinking Water Utilities.** Greater uncertainty in water supply

- **Wastewater Utilities.** Increased demand for maintaining quality and quantity of discharges to rivers and streams for environmental purposes

Midwest

- **Drinking Water Utilities.** Greater uncertainty in water supply

- **Wastewater Utilities.** Impacts common to all regions

Central Plains

- **Drinking Water Utilities.** Greater uncertainty in water supply

- **Wastewater Utilities.** Impacts common to all regions

Northwest

- **Drinking Water Utilities.** Greater uncertainty in water supply

- **Wastewater Utilities.** Increased demand for maintaining quality and quantity of discharges to rivers and streams for environmental purposes

Southwest

- **Drinking Water Utilities.** Significant reductions in and increased uncertainty in water supply; increased need to optimize water use, conservation, reuse, operations, and storage

- **Wastewater Utilities.** Anticipated increased regulation for many treatment components; increased concentration of sewage, creating odor and treatment process problems; increased demand for maintaining quality and quantity of discharges to rivers and streams for environmental purposes

Alaska

- **Drinking Water Utilities.** Increased storage needs resulting from earlier snowmelt and increased extreme precipitation events

- **Wastewater Utilities.** Impacts common to all regions

Hawaii

- **Drinking Water Utilities.** Impacts common to all regions

- **Wastewater Utilities.** Impacts common to all regions

Puerto Rico

- **Drinking Water Utilities.** Significant reductions in and increased uncertainty in water supply

- **Wastewater Utilities.** Impacts common to all regions.

Source: National Association of Metropolitan Water Agencies and CH2M Hill Inc., "Confronting Climate Change: An Early Analysis of Water and Wastewater Adaption Costs," <www.amwa.net/galleries/climate-change/ConfrontingClimateChangeOct09.pdf>. Reprinted by permission of CH2M Hill Inc.

Notes

1. Thomas E. Dahl and Gregory J. Allord "History of Wetlands in the Conterminous U.S.," *National Water Summary—Wetland Resources Tech nical Aspects*, Water-Supply Paper 2425 (Reston, VA: U.S. Geological Survey, 1999).

2. Louisiana Coastal Wetlands Conservation and Recreation Task Force and Wetlands Conservation and Restoration Authority, *Coast 2050* (Baton Rouge: Louisiana Department of Natural Resources, 1998), www.coast2050.gov/2050reports.htm.

3. U.S. Global Change Research Program (USGCRP), *Scientific Assessments, Global Climate Change Impacts in the United States*, "National Climate Change," 2009, www.globalchange.gov/publications/reports/scientific-assessments/us-impacts/full-report/national-climate-change.

4. K.E. Kunkel et al., "Observed Changes in Weather and Climate Extremes," in T.R. Karl et al., (eds.) *Weather and Climate Extremes in a Changing Climate: Regions of Focus: North America, Hawaii, Caribbean, and U.S. Pacific Islands*, Synthesis and Assessment Product 3.3 (Washington, DC: U.S. Climate Change Science Program, 2008). http://downloads.climatescience.gov/sap/sap3-3/sap3-3-final-all.pdf.

5. USGCRP, *Scientific Assessments*.

6. World Wildlife Federation, "Increasing Vulnerability to Hurricanes: Global Warming's Wake-Up Call for the U.S. Gulf and Atlantic Coasts" (Washington, DC: World Wildlife Federation, 2006), http://cf.nwf.org/extremeweather/pdfs/hurricanes_fnl_lowres.pdf.

7. USGCRP, *Scientific Assessments*.

8. "Testing the Waters 2009: A guide to Water Quality at Vacation Beaches" www.nrdc.org/water/oceans/ttw/titinx.asp.

9. American Society of Civil Engineers, *Minimum Design Loads for Buildings and Other Structures*, ASCE/SEI 7-05 (Reston, VA: Author, 2006).

10. USGCRP, *Scientific Assessments*.

11. National Oceanic and Atmospheric Administration (NOAA), Sandy Ward and Catherine Main, *Population at Risk from Natural Hazards*. NOAA State of the Coast Report (Silver Spring, MD: NOAA, 1998), http://state_of_coast.noaa.gov/bulletins/html/par_02/par.html.

12. NOAA, *Population Trends Along the Coastal United States: 1980–2008* (Silver Spring, MD: Author, 2004), http://marineeconomics.noaa.gov/socioeconomics/assessment/population.html; also NOAA, *Economic Statistics for NOAA*, 6th ed. (Washington, DC: U.S. Department of Commerce, Office of the NOAA Chief Economist, 2008), www.ppi.noaa.gov/PPI…/2008_06_04_EconStatsFinal.pdf; also, NOAA, *Coastal County Snapshots*. http://csc-maps-q.csc.noaa.gov/countysnapshots.

13. U.S. Department of Agriculture, *Census of Agriculture. National Agriculture Statistics*, 2007, www.agcensus.usda.gov/Publications/2007/Full_Report/.

14. CH2M Hill Inc., *Confronting Climate Change: An Early Analysis of Water and Wastewater Adaption Costs*, National Association of Metropolitan Water Agencies, 2009, www.amwa.net/cs/climatechange.

PART II

DESIGN WITH WATER

Michele Adams, P.E., and Donald Watson, FAIA

Natural systems of vegetation, soils, floodplains, and wetlands provide ecosystem services that maintain water balance and mitigate flooding.

I can foretell the way of celestial bodies but can say nothing about the movement of a small drop of water.

—*Galileo Galilei, seventeenth century*

CHAPTER 4   The Natural Landscape

CHAPTER 5   The Altered Landscape

CHAPTER 6   Design for Inland Flooding

IMPACT OF INLAND FLOODING

Damage of Wisconsin Flooding Spring 2008

The severe storms, tornados, and flooding events of late spring and early summer 2008 were preceded by a winter that produced record snowfalls in southern Wisconsin. On March 19, 2008, FEMA [the Federal Emergency Management Association] issued a federal declaration of Snow Emergency in the counties of Dane, Dodge, Green, Jefferson, Kenosha, Milwaukee, Racine, Rock, Walworth, and Washington. The city of Madison set a record snow total of 101.4 inches, breaking the previous record of 76.1 inches in 1978–79. Snow melts in areas already saturated from fall storms resulted in Spring 2008 river levels that were higher than they had been for years. (Figure C-14)

In June and July of 2008, numerous counties in Southern Wisconsin experienced heavy rain, hail, and damaging winds that resulted in record flooding. Supercell thunderstorms and sustained rainfall of two inches per hour in some areas caused flash flooding. Recurring rains over an extended period added more water to already flooded areas causing road closures, mudslides, and washouts. High winds, rotating wall clouds, and tornadoes added to the destruction and damage. Sandbagging held back the water in some areas, but was not enough in others. Evacuations were implemented. When the rains and severe weather finally subsided, five all time river cresting records were set and many others were at or near record levels. . . .

Economic and Business

- $400 million of crop losses with low-lying farm field hardest hit.

- $260 million in unmet business needs estimated for more than 5,200 businesses.

- $7.0 million in damages to Tyson Foods in Jefferson. Forced to cut production, resulting in the loss of 200 permanent positions.

- $1.5 million in damages to Evonik Goldschmidt Corporation. Forced to cease production for nearly a month.

- 1,777 workers laid off in July due to plant closures.

- 71% increase in initial claims for unemployment insurance.

- 75% decline in tourism revenues in certain disaster areas.

- $20 million lost business in Lake Delton, a popular tourist destination, after a breached embankment drained the lake and washed away several houses.

Housing

- Over $92 million unmet housing needs for the almost 41,000 households registered with FEMA.

- $12,189,774 in 1,364 claims filed with the National Flood Insurance Program.

- $36.5 million in SBA loans approved for 1,733 individuals.

- Publicly financed multifamily and elderly affordable housing stock received limited flood damages.

- $46.7 million in housing assistance provided by FEMA.

- $51 million needed to acquire 345 substantially damaged properties in 24 targeted communities.

Infrastructure

- $40.0 million in total unmet infrastructure needs to provide the required state and local match for FEMA's Public Assistance Program.

- 844 local, county, state and private non-profit organizations have applied for the Public Assistance Program.

- WisDOT estimates $30 million in damages to On-System Roads and Bridges.

- $20.5 million in County/Local Routes (non–federal aid roads).

- $5.6 million in claims for municipal buildings have been submitted to the Office of the Insurance Commissioner.

- $17.5 million in damages to publicly owned dams.

- $2.5 million of damages to privately owned dam structures.

- $25 million for municipally owned Water Supply Systems and Wastewater Treatment Plants.

- $3.3 million for the Wisconsin Department of Natural Resources (DNR) owned Natural Resource Facilities (State Parks, trails, and forests, wildlife management areas, marshes, boat access facilities, endangered resource areas, fishery facilities, and restoration projects).

Source: "State of Wisconsin Action Plan for CDBG Disaster Recovery Funds," *Federal Register* 73, no. 177, September 11, 2008, www.commerce.state. wi.us/cd/docs/CD-bcf-drdraft.pdf

Figure 4.1 *Sheet water flow* in the natural landscape resulting from sudden downpour is interrupted and absorbed by ground cover and vegetation.

(PHOTO: Donald Watson)

CHAPTER 4

THE NATURAL LANDSCAPE

Water in all its forms—potable water, stormwater runoff, wastewater, evapotranspiration, groundwater, stream base flow, and water stored in reservoirs, lakes, and glaciers—is a resource that originates as precipitation.

The amount of water within a regional watershed is balanced in a natural cycle of precipitation, vegetation, evaporation, watercourses, and reservoirs. The quality of water in each segment of the water balance defines the local landscape: the type and amount of vegetation, the frequency and type of streams and surface water features, and the groundwater aquifer.

The natural landscape has evolved with the water balance of the region, with soil, aquifer, and vegetation absorbing water where it falls and flows. In each region, natural landscape responds to precipitation patterns to form a sustaining ecosystem that reduces the extremes of drought and destructive flooding. The lessons of the natural landscape provide the basis of resilient design.

4.1 UNDERSTANDING THE NATURAL WATER BALANCE

Precipitation takes many forms as it falls within each region of the globe. Some rainfall or melted snowfall on the land will result in runoff, flowing overland to the nearest swale, wetland, stream, or coastal water. Some rainfall will soak into the soil and from there follow various paths to base flows and aquifers. Snow cover that remains at high elevations is a form of water storage critical for spring thaw and plant growth. (Figure 4.2.)

Water may be returned to the atmosphere through surface evaporation or through respiration of plants (transpiration). The combination of these two pathways is called *evapotranspiration*, the greatest component of the annual water balance in most climates in the United States. Due to the significance of evapotranspiration, the loss of vegetation and the alteration of soils contribute significantly to changes in the water balance and result in increased flooding.

Not all rainfall returns directly to the atmosphere. Some amount of the rainfall that soaks into the soil provides soil moisture and shallow groundwater recharge. This recharge is essential in maintaining a source of steady, clean, and cool water to streams and wetlands. Groundwater aquifers provide the ideal reservoir to preserve the most local water free from pollution and evaporation losses.

A smaller portion of the water that soaks into the soil reaches deeper aquifers. Here it may recharge the groundwater table locally, as in much of the eastern United States. It may provide recharge to an aquifer that extends for many miles, as in the Great Plains region. The ability of natural soils and vegetation to absorb water varies by region. In many natural landscapes, very little runoff occurs until a substantial amount of rain (for that region) has fallen. In a natural system, runoff is a small component of the water balance.

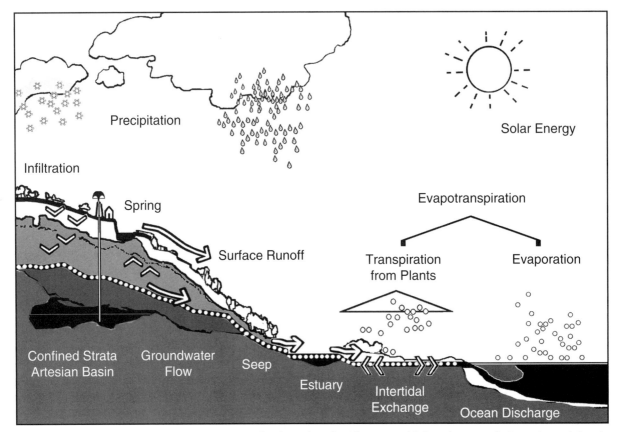

Figure 4.2 *Water balance:* Precipitation as it is distributed in all its forms establishes the water balance in each locale.

The natural hydrologic cycle is altered by human activities, such as agriculture, lawns, and the installation of impervious surfaces of pavement and buildings. While the amount of rainfall may not change, the amount of runoff after a rainfall increases as a result of land use changes. Ground area that previously absorbed and held precipitation becomes a water channel. It may be difficult to appreciate the magnitude of this change on a site-by-site basis in the context of only one site and a single rainfall event. On a cumulative basis, the effects on local water resources of changing land surfaces are significant.

Example of Water Balance Analysis

Watershed and site design for stormwater and flooding is best begun by analyzing the site in context of the water balance or water budget for its region. This is illustrated by examples within the Piedmont region of the eastern United States, which stretches from the Newark Basin in New Jersey south through Atlanta, Georgia.

Along the Piedmont, the average annual rainfall varies from 45 inches per year north of Philadelphia to 51 inches per year in Atlanta. This rainfall is generally dispersed evenly throughout the year, with no months of anticipated drought or flood on an annual basis. The Piedmont region is in this sense "water rich" in terms of rainfall.

Consider a small parcel of land within this region in its natural or undisturbed state and in the context of the rainfall that occurs over an entire year. In Pennsylvania, that natural state is woodlands, suggested by its original name, "Penn's Woods." On an undisturbed wooded site, 45 inches of rainfall occurs in the Philadelphia region. On an annual basis, of this total, approximately 25 inches returns to the atmosphere as evapotranspiration, 12 inches to the groundwater aquifer, and approximately 8 inches of runoff. Woodland soils have a remarkable capacity to

capture and absorb rainfall that is not immediately intercepted by vegetation. The woodland is sustained by and represents the abundance of rainfall in the region. (Figure 4.3.)

Furthering the example, the 12 inches of groundwater
recharge that occurs on a natural landscape of 1 acre in the
Philadelphia region is equivalent to 407,000 gallons per
year, or 1,115 gallons per day. This groundwater recharge
on a single acre of land is more than enough water needed
to supply four Pennsylvania households with all their daily
water needs. For example:

Annual recharge per acre per year
 = 15 inches per year × 43,560 square feet per acre
  ÷ 12 inches per foot
 = 54,450 cubic feet
Average recharge per acre per day
 = 54,450 cubic feet per year ÷ 365 days
 = 149 cubic feet per day
149 cubic feet per day × 7.48 gallons per cubic foot
 = 1,116 gallons per day

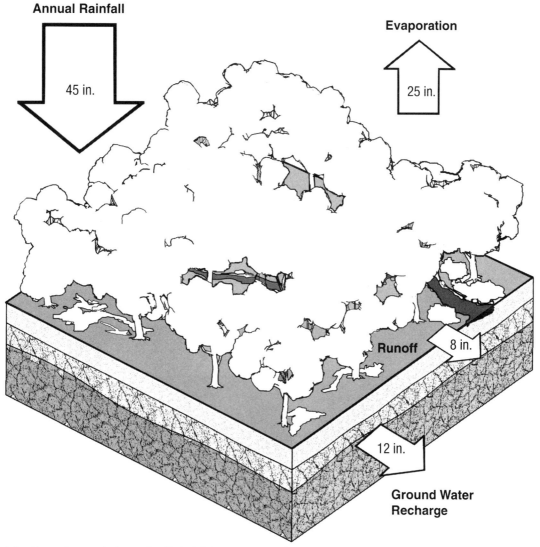

Annual Rainfall

45 in.

Evaporation

25 in.

Runoff   8 in.

12 in.

**Ground Water
Recharge**

Figure 4.3   *Natural water balance for Philadelphia region:* In the natural landscape, most precipitation is returned to
the atmosphere by the evapotranspiration, resulting in very little runoff.

4.2 WHEN THE WATER BALANCE IS ALTERED

As land uses change as they are developed, the natural hydrologic cycle and water balance are altered. Rainfall continues, but where impervious surfaces have replaced woodland, virtually all rainfall is converted to stormwater runoff (on an annual basis). Because more water in the cycle is diverted as runoff, the annual volume of runoff increases dramatically while the annual volume of groundwater recharge and evapotranspiration decreases. The average increase in stormwater runoff from changing land use from woodland to a 1-acre parking lot in the Philadelphia region is 37 inches per year, enough to fill one-and-a-half Olympic-size swimming pools. (Figure 4.4.)

When pervious surfaces are impacted by development, increased runoff due to soil compaction and the loss or change of vegetation will result. The amount of increased runoff depends on the type of land cover and the soil type found under natural conditions. The next discussion outlines the characteristics of the natural landscape that provide the basis of resilient design.

Rainfall Patterns and Why Small Storms Matter

Most rainfall does not occur during extreme events such as the "100-year storm event." On an annual basis, most rainfall occurs in small storms of a 0.5 inch, 1 inch, or maybe 1.5 inches.

Table 4.1 indicates the average annual rainfall for selected cities in different regions of the United States. The total amount of annual precipitation varies significantly by city and region, from as little as 8 inches per year in the dry climate of Phoenix, Arizona, to as much as 60 inches per year or more in Miami, Florida. Although there is considerable variation in total annual precipitation, nearly *all* of the rainfall events in a given location are small storms of less than 1.5 inches total precipitation. At virtually every location in the continental United States, over 90% of the individual rainfall events result in 1.5 inches of rainfall or less. Despite significant variation in annual rainfall and seasonal distribution, in every major city presented except New Orleans, over 70% of rainfall events result in less than 0.5 inches of precipitation—truly small events.

Frequent rainfalls generate little runoff in the natural environment. Water is absorbed by soils and intercepted by vegetation in humid and semihumid climates. In arid climates, shallow dry streambeds quickly "lose" any small flows back to subsurface groundwater. In each region, vegetation and stream systems have evolved as a natural evolutionary response to the distribution of rainfall and the common occurrence of small precipitation events, and most rainfall is captured close to where it falls. A healthy forest or prairie system can absorb well over 1 inch or more of rainfall without generating runoff. Most of the time in the natural landscape, when it rains, it rains a little and generates no runoff. When infrequent larger precipitation events exceed the capacity of the natural systems to absorb water, a second tier of natural components, such as floodplains and wetlands, combine to slow, hold, and buffer the runoff.

In contrast to vegetated landscapes, impervious surfaces generate runoff almost immediately, even during small rainfalls. With as little as 0.1 inches of rainfall, large impervious surfaces will begin to generate runoff as the natural buffering and absorptive capacity of soils and vegetation has been removed. Vegetated landscapes altered by human activity, such as lawns and agricultural fields, are able to absorb some initial rainfall, although generally much less than a naturally vegetated landscape would capture. By comparison, natural woodlands and meadow and prairie systems can abstract well over 1.5 inches before generating any runoff. Comparison values of this capture or interception are provided in Table 4.2.

The functioning of natural and altered landscapes is distinctly different in the amount of water that each generates as runoff early in the storm. During extreme events, most runoff volume occurs during the early portion of the event rather than later. The increased volume of runoff water from altered landscapes must be accommodated by the natural and man-made drainage systems at each site and close to the point of impact to prevent local flooding. The category of storm size will affect the amounts of runoff generated by both natural and altered landscapes.

In the category of rainfall events of less than 0.5 inches, runoff originates primarily from impervious surfaces. Pervious, natural surfaces do not generally generate runoff during these small storms. Small storms represent a significant percentage of annual rainfall events.

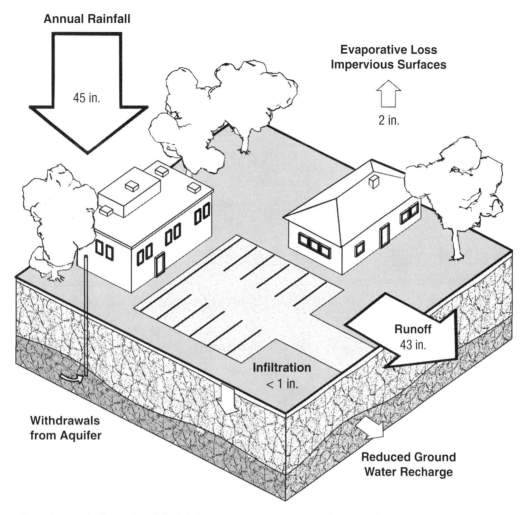

Figure 4.4 *Altered water balance for Philadelphia region:* Impervious surfaces, such as pavements, roofs, and lawns, transform nearly all precipitation into runoff.

Rainfall events in the category of more than 0.5 inches but less than 1.5 inches of precipitation are less frequent but still will generate little runoff in a natural environment. However, runoff will be generated from most surfaces that have been altered by human activities, such as lawns, landscaped areas, and croplands. Although rainfall events in this range are less frequent than the very small 0.5-inch events, they comprise a significant amount of the annual rainfall volume and, correspondingly, a significant amount of the runoff from the altered landscape.

Rainfall events in the next category—greater than 1.5 inches of precipitation but less than 2.5 to 3.5 inches (depending significantly on region)—represent rainfall events in which runoff is generated from a natural landscape but accommodated or slowed in local depressions or wetlands and generally conveyed within stream systems without causing flooding or out-of-bank conditions. These are rainfall events that represent the initiation of runoff from a natural landscape in all but the driest climates.

TABLE 4.1 ANNUAL PRECIPITATION AND PERCENTAGE OF SMALL STORMS FOR VARIOUS U.S. CITIES

City	Annual Precipitation (in)	Percentage of Storms Less than 0.5 (in)	0.5 to 1.5 (in)	More than 1.5 (in)	Total
New England					
Portland, ME	41	72%	23%	5%	95%
Mid-Atlantic/Piedmont					
Atlanta, GA	51	65%	26%	9%	91%
Chapel Hill, NC	46	71%	22%	0%	93%
Philadelphia, PA	45	71%	25%	4%	96%
Southeast					
Miami, FL	60	76%	19%	5%	95%
New Orleans, LA	62	62%	22%	16%	84%
Tampa, FL	48	74%	19%	7%	93%
Great Lakes					
Buffalo, NY	38	80%	16%	4%	96%
Detroit, MI	32	73%	22%	5%	95%
Midwest					
Columbus, OH	38	80%	15%	5%	95%
Rapid City, SD	18	90%	9%	1%	99%
West Lafayette, IN	36	73%	22%	5%	95%
Southeast					
Austin, TX	31	71%	19%	10%	90%
Los Angeles, CA	12	72%	19%	9%	91%
Phoenix, AZ	8	82%	16%	2%	98%
West					
Boise, ID	15	94%	5%	1%	99%
Denver, CO	16	86%	13%	1%	99%
Northwest					
Seattle, WA	37	84%	14%	2%	98%

Sources: National Weather Service data and statistical analysis from historic records of multiple stations. (Compiled by Meliora Environmental Design)

Finally, larger and far less frequent events represent the last category, where even in a natural landscape, runoff and flooding is likely to occur. The natural system components that attenuate the extreme events—such as floodplains, wetlands, and buffers—must be maintained to provide these ecosystem services in extreme events.

Rainfall Intensity

The intensity of a rainfall event usually is measured in inches per hour. Rainfall intensity is increasing due to climate changes. Localized rainfall patterns and intensities also may be altered by local land use changes. An increase in impervious cover in urban areas can increase local heat island effects and possibly the intensified formation of thunderstorms or microbursts of precipitation. The rainfall intensity of these events can increase property damage and overwhelm local drainage systems.

In 2001 the National Oceanographic and Atmospheric Administration (NOAA) began to publish a series of updates to *NOAA Atlas 14 Precipitation-Frequency Atlas of the United States.*[1] *Atlas 14* provides rainfall intensity in inches per hour for various time periods (5–60-minute,

TABLE 4.2 APPROXIMATE MAXIMUM RAINFALL INTERCEPTION BY VEGETATION TYPE

	mm	*inches*
Deciduous forest[a]	35.6	1.40
Big bluestem prairie grass[b]	25.9	1.02
Urban deciduous tree[c]	14.2	0.56
Corn[d]	3	0.12
Turf grass	2	0.08

[a] J. D. Helvey, *Rainfall Interception by Hardwood Forest Litter in the Southern Appalachians* (Ashville, NC: U.S. Department of Agriculture Forest Service, 1964).
[b] C. A. Chant, "Forest and Water Supply," *Journal of the Royal Astronomical Society of Canada* (Toronto, Ontario, 1934).
[c] Qingfu Xiao and E. Gregory McPherson, *Rainfall Interception by Santa Monica's Municipal Urban Forest* (Dordrecht, The Netherlands: Springer, 2002).
[d] M. R. Savabi and D. E. Stott, *Plant Residue Impact on Rainfall Interception. Transactions of the ASAE* 37, no. 4 (1994): 1093–1098.

1–24-hour, and 2-day to 10-day periods) for various frequencies of occurrence or statistical return periods (1 year, 2 year, and so forth).

The updates reflect a more extensive database, better statistical techniques, and better spatial interpretation techniques for data. The precipitation data are important in design to address localized flooding at the site level. Intensity-Duration-Frequency (IDF) curves provide statistical information on rainfall rates in inches per hour for various locations and time periods. (Figure 4.5.)

The most damaging rainfall intensities often occur during brief periods ranging from a few minutes to less than 1 hour, and are usually associated with smaller storms, such as thunderstorms. In coastal areas, extreme events, such as hurricanes, often have periods of intense rainfall. Yet the rainfall intensity in such extreme events is usually much less than the intense frequency of a summer thunderstorm. In both situations, however, the rate of rainfall can quickly overcome local drainage conveyance systems and create localized flooding.

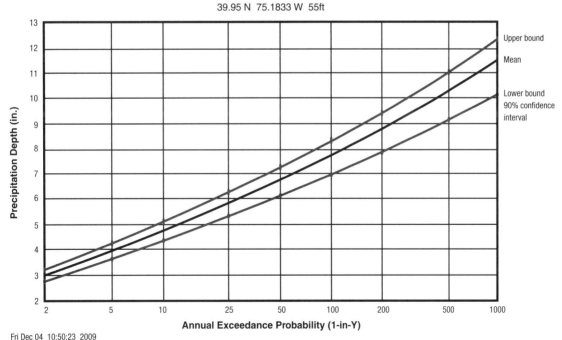

Figure 4.5   *Intensity-Duration-Frequency curve for Philadelphia International Airport* indicates rainfall intensity in inches per hour for different time durations (5 minutes to 9 days). Data are available for various locations and regularly updated at the National Weather Service Atlas 14 Precipitation Frequency Data Server, http://hdsc.nws.noaa.gov/hdsc/pfds/index.html.

Source: NOAA, Office of Hydrologic Development, *Atlas 14*, 2009, http://hdsc.nws.noaa.gov/hdsc/pfds/.

When intense rainfall exceeds the capacity of swales and drainage elements, surface ponding and local flooding will occur. Unintentional surface ponding can damage structures and create safety hazards. By understanding local rainfall amounts and intensities, design of site grading and landscape features can accommodate surface ponding safely and sustainably.

Summary of Rainfall Considerations for Resilient Design for Flooding

Resilient design must evaluate and accommodate rainfall volume using updated rainfall patterns and amounts. A design goal is to capture the first portion of the runoff from large rainfalls and to capture all or most from the small storms. In this way, the volume of water discharged downstream is dramatically reduced, replicating a natural system response to rainfall. Whether implemented at the site scale or the planning scale, the most effective approach to flood reduction is to protect, restore, or replicate the response of a natural system to the small, frequent rainfall events.

- Most rainfall events, regardless of region, result in less than 0.5 inches of precipitation. These small events produce little runoff in a natural landscape.
- In most locations in the continental United States, over 90% of the precipitation events are less than 1.5 inches and, again, produce limited runoff in a natural environment.
- In a natural environment, the "capture" of the smaller rainfalls also serves to reduce the total amount of water that occurs as runoff in larger and extreme rainfalls. Capture of rainfall volume is critical to reducing the damage caused by extreme events.
- The intensity of rainfall may also contribute to damage. However, capture of rainfall during intense rainfall periods will reduce damaging effects at the local level from a sudden surge of water.

The strategies of resilient design are to:

- Capture small rainfalls so that there is little or no runoff volume—no increase in water sent downstream.
- Slow the release of water during modest rainfalls, preferably through retentive grading and local places that are allowed to be "wet" at times.

- Protect and restore the floodplains, wetlands, and buffers that prevent property and human losses and safely convey water so that damage is controlled during extreme events,

This is *not* to say that all systems must be natural; rather, the flood reduction capacity of natural systems can be mimicked to inform design. The intent is to revise the current stormwater design approach of "collect and convey at a controlled rate of flow" to a volume-based approach that captures the small, frequent rainfall events and the first portion of larger events. This "captured rainfall" may be returned to the atmosphere through soils and vegetation, returned to the groundwater, or reused for human needs. Even in highly urbanized environments, measures can be implemented to achieve this capture.

4.3 SOILS AND VEGETATION

The water balance is established by the natural conditions of the site and region. Natural features, such as topography and soils, influence the amount of water that is able to infiltrate through the soil mantle and become groundwater recharge. Precipitation patterns influences the formation of the overlying soils. Both soils and rainfall influence the vegetation that is most successful in a given location. Vegetation will in turn affect soils in an interconnected system that over time co-evolves in achieve a sustaining water balance. (Figure 4.6.)

Vegetation and Evapotranspiration

Evapotranspiration is the return of water to the atmosphere from direct evaporation from the surface or through transpiration of vegetation. Evapotranspiration is the single largest component of the annual water balance, regardless of region or amount of rainfall. Transpiration from vegetation often contributes much of the return of water to the atmosphere. Evaporation occurs directly from land surfaces and open water bodies and from the surface of vegetation and underlying organic material that has intercepted the rainfall. Transpiration and evaporation—combined in the term *evapotranspiration*—often comprise more than half of the annual water balance in a given region.

The leaves of vegetation intercept rainfall, reducing the amount that reaches the ground surface. The branches, stems, and trunks of plants convey some of this water to the ground surface. Root systems convey the water into the

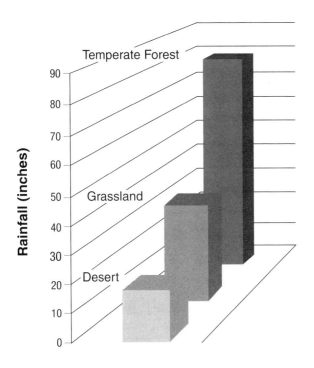

Average Annual Temperature 50°F

Figure 4.6   *Relationship of precipitation and temperature to dominant vegetation type*: Areas with abundant in rainfall tend to support temperate forests.

Source: Meliora Environmental Design.

soil matrix. The physical structure of trees and vegetation serves to:

• Intercept rainfall directly.

• Create an underlying layer of organic material that further captures water.

• Reduce the energy conveyed when rainfall reaches the soil, thereby reducing erosion.

• Convey water down into the soils and create more porous, absorbent soils.

Transpiration is the evaporation of water directly from plants to the atmosphere when the pores of plants and leaves (*stomata*) are open during photosynthesis for the passage of oxygen and carbon dioxide. Up to 90% of a plant's water uptake can be returned to the atmosphere via transpiration. Transpiration is affected by light, temperature, humidity, wind, and especially soil moisture. As soil moisture diminishes, stomata close and transpiration diminishes. If water

is available, transpiration will represent the single largest component of the water balance. An acre of deciduous forest, through interception and evapotranspiration, can account for 20 inches or more of rain absorption during the growing season, equivalent to 540,000 gallons. An acre of prairie or wildflower field (deep grass roots) does nearly as well, absorbing 18 inches or nearly 500,000 gallons. A large oak tree can transpire 40,000 gallons per year.

Vegetation that is native to a region has evolved in response to both the total amount of rainfall and the seasonal rainfall patterns. Temperate broad-leaf forests dominate much of the vegetation native to the contiguous United States east of the Mississippi River because rainfall is in excess of about 30 inches per year and well distributed throughout the year. These areas have few periods of extreme drought or excessive precipitation and moderate average annual temperatures (38° to 66°F). In areas where rainfall distribution is greater in the winter season, such as the Pacific Northwest, temperate forests tend to be dominated by conifers or evergreen species, which lose less water to evapotranspiration in the drier summer months.

As total annual rainfall decreases to less than 30 inches, or is both low and unevenly distributed, forests give way to grasslands and prairies. The grasses and perennials that dominate these systems have both very high rainfall interception capabilities and deep root systems that are able to extend to depths greater than those of many trees. In these areas, grasses can outcompete trees and forests give way to grasslands. With less than 20 inches of rainfall per year, depending on the average temperatures, the landscape begins to shift from grassland to desert.[2]

The movement of water through tree roots from deep soil to the drier surface soil layers is called *hydraulic lift*. In dry periods, trees can redistribute water by drawing water from deep soil to meet the needs of the shallow roots, bringing water into the surface soils. Recent research has documented that during wet periods, the process is reversed as tree roots move excess water to deeper soil layers, providing *hydraulic redistribution*. In saturated surface conditions, trees can actively convey water down to deeper, drier soils, where it can be available for future needs of the tree.[3] Trees actively respond to rainfall, reducing the amount that contributes to runoff and downstream flooding. (Figure 4.7.)

The soil around the root zone of vegetation is called the *rhizosphere*, where plants, microorganisms, water, and nutrients interact. Within the rhizosphere, plants

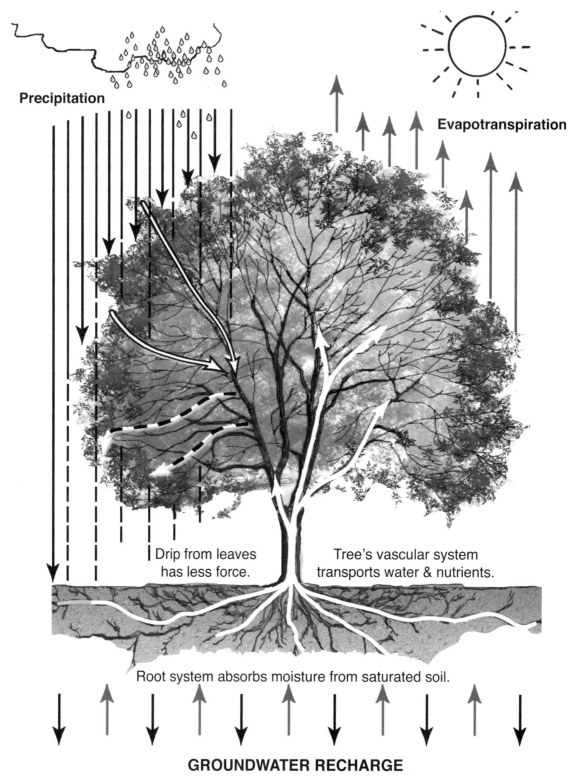

Precipitation

Evapotranspiration

Drip from leaves
has less force.

Tree's vascular system
transports water & nutrients.

Root system absorbs moisture from saturated soil.

GROUNDWATER RECHARGE

Figure 4.7 *Trees as active water pumps:* In response to rainfall, tree roots draw water from deep soils when surface soils are dry and move water down into the soil during excess rainfall.

Source: Viridian Landscape Studio LLC.

release nutrients back into the soil, where they support an extensive community of fungi and bacteria, in turn supporting larger organisms from protozoa to earthworms. Bacteria decompose material, including man-made compounds such as pesticides and pollutants. Certain bacteria also work in partnership with vegetation in obtaining nutrients from the soil. Soils high in organic material have significantly greater capacity to absorb water.

Fungi, estimated to number about 3,000 species, often grow as long threads called *hyphae*. These threads push their way between roots and soil particles and physically bind soil particles together. This creates stable aggregates that increase soil infiltration and holding capacities. *Mycorrhizal fungi* live in symbiotic relationship with roots, helping to process nutrients and bring water to the vegetation. (Figure 4.8.)

Summary of Vegetation Roles for Resilient Design for Flooding

Vegetation returns upward of 50% of the annual rainfall volume back to the atmosphere and serves to:

- Intercept rainfall directly on leaves and stems.
- Reduce the energy of rainfall reaching the soil, thereby reducing soil erosion.
- Create an underlying layer of material that further captures water and protects soils.
- Convey water along stems and trunks to the soils.
- Convey water into deeper soils during times of surface saturation.
- Create more absorbent soils through the addition of organic material.

Figure 4.8 *Soil fungi* help to create a porous and absorbent soil matrix.
(PHOTO: Donald Watson)

- Create more porous soils through the formation of small tunnels (macropores) that convey water into soil.
- Support a healthy microbial community that in turn increases porosity and organic material.
- Pull water from the soil to return water to the atmosphere during photosynthesis (via transpiration).

Soils and Infiltration

Analysis of soils from a water balance perspective requires evaluation beyond the standard classifications of silt, sand, and clay. Healthy soil is a working ecosystem with water and air both entering and leaving the soil. Healthy soil supports a diverse biological community and food web that in turn supports the soil's ability to absorb and move water.

The infiltration rate of soil, often measured in inches or centimeters per hour, represents an attempt to measure how fast water can move into soil under the effects of gravity (i.e., standing water or steady rainfall). Under saturated conditions, the movement of water generally is governed by gravity. Under unsaturated conditions, capillary surface tension forces and adsorptive forces between water and soil particles dominate water movement.

Macropores and *micropores* are small columns or tunnels within the soil formed by vegetation roots, weathering, and soil animals. They provide openings for the movement of water, air, and microorganisms. Macropores are defined as openings that are greater than 1 mm or more in diameter. Micropores are less than 1 mm in diameter. Both macro- and micropores can be limited in length to a few millimeters or extend several meters and through various zones or layers of the soil. The pores are formed by variety of processes, including roots, insects, wetting and drying, and freezing and thawing. Micropores often increase in size due to cycles of wetting and drying and freezing and thawing, becoming macropores. (Figure 4.9.)

The number of macropores is more significant than soil type, in terms of absorption capacity of the soil during rainfall. A clay soil with extensive macropores may have a much higher infiltration rate under saturated conditions than sand that has been disturbed and compacted—as much as three times greater. The passage of heavy construction and lawn mowing equipment compacts the soil and destroys absorption capacity.

The Soil Matrix

The capacity of soil to absorb water is influenced by the *soil matrix*. Soil is generally classified into types according to the percent of sand, silt, or clay, or various mixtures thereof, determined by soil particle size. The U.S. Department of Agriculture (USDA) Soil Triangle Chart indicates various soil descriptions based on the percentage of sand, silt, or clay found in a soil sample. Inconsistencies result, however, because the USDA definitions for sand, silt, and clay are not necessarily consistent with the American Association of State Highway and Transportation Officials (AASHTO) classification. For example, USDA defines silt as a particle between 0.002 and 0.05 mm in diameter; AASHTO defines a silt particle as being between 0.002 and 0.075 mm in diameter. AASHTO has further developed its own soil classification system for soil definition based on sieve analysis, separate from the USDA Soil Triangle. The AASHTO Soil Classification system is more widely used by design professionals, while the USDA classification system is more widely referred to in the agricultural community. The USDA definitions are also used in the design and construction of landscapes.

Textbook values for *soil matrix permeability* are defined as coefficient of permeability, k, estimated in centimeters per second, are based on soil type. These textbook values often are relied on as an estimate of soil infiltration rates. Alternatively, soil samples are collected and analyzed in the laboratory to estimate a site-specific k value. Such assumptions are incorrect when estimating water movement in natural surface soils. Design data for shallow soil infiltration and soil absorption capabilities must be determined by field testing and include both infiltration tests and measurements of soil density.

Summary of Function of Soils for Resilient Design for Flooding

Soils are a component of resilient design for flooding and water resource protection and serve to:

- Actively convey water into deeper soils during times of surface saturation through networks of macropores and micropores.
- Provide an absorptive sponge that captures rainfall and reduces downstream storm flows.
- Move water to deeper layers for groundwater storage and stream base flow.
- Support a healthy microbial and soil fauna community that in turn increases porosity, organic material, and rainfall retention.
- Work in relationship to a vegetative community in a manner that increases rainfall retention.

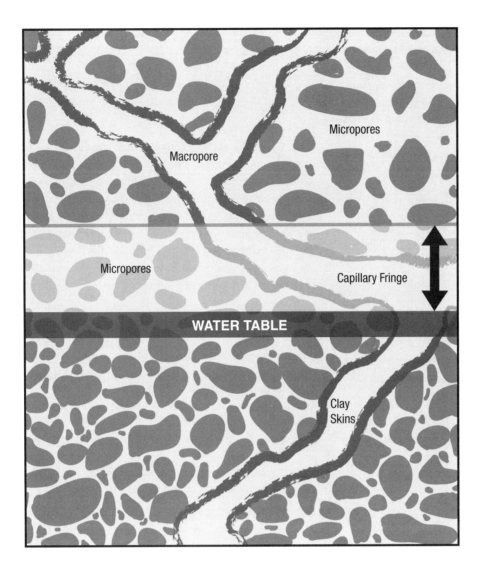

Figure 4.9 *Macropores and micropores* facilitate water movement in uncompacted soil.

4.4 SUBSURFACE WATER MOVEMENT

As it moves into the soil, water moves downward under the force of gravity and laterally toward the downslope groundwater level (base flow) and stream channel. During rainfall periods, as new water enters the soil under saturated conditions, it will "push" water to the base of the slope. This shallow water movement in the surface soils is referred to as *interflow*. In large and extreme events, the horizontal movement of water *through* soils (rather than on the land surface) slows the rate of water flow into the stream system.

Soil interflow maintains soil moisture and the health of vegetation and woodlands.

In moving through the soil, the water quality of the rainfall is altered. The community of fungi and bacteria serve to decompose complex carbon compounds, remove surface bacteria, and capture nutrients to reduce pollutant levels in groundwater. Clays and humic material in the soil have high cation exchange capacity (CEC) and serve to bind with minerals as well as various metals and pollutants. In general, the higher the CEC value, the greater the soil's ability to remove pollutants. (Table 4.3.)

Groundwater and streamflow are intimately related. The natural base flow in a stream often reflects the intersection of the water table and the surface. In areas where the water table drops below the streambed, such as arid climates or areas underlain by barren, rocky ground (*karst*) geology, the stream may serve as a destination for infiltration and is referred to as a "losing" stream. (Figure 4.10.)

Because water that has infiltrated into the soil or underlying geology takes longer to reach the stream than surface runoff, this water does not contribute to the downstream flood volumes in large rainfalls or extreme events. As water travels through the soil and geology at a slower rate, the water temperature adjusts to the average groundwater temperature for that region. The temperature of groundwater may vary by location, but the temperature of discharge to the stream remains constant throughout the year. Steady discharge of groundwater at a constant temperature is critical to the aquatic community of any stream or wetland. (Figure 4.11.)

Summary of Interflow and Groundwater Recharge for Resilient Design for Flooding

Interflow and groundwater recharge serve to:

- Significantly reduce the volume and rate of surface runoff to reduce downstream flooding.
- Maintain base flow in streams and wetlands at a consistent temperature.
- Maintain soil moisture conditions to support vegetation.
- Reduce discharge of pollutants to surface waters and to deeper groundwater resources.
- Recharge groundwater supplies.

TABLE 4.3 CATION EXCHANGE CAPACITY FOR VARIOUS SOIL TYPES

Soil Texture	CEC (meq/100g soil)
Sands (light-colored)	3–5
Sands (dark-colored)	10–20
Loams	10 15
Silt loams	15–25
Clay and clay loams	20–50
Organic soils	50–100

4.5 STREAM SYSTEMS, WETLANDS, RIPARIAN ZONES, AND FLOODPLAINS

Headwater Streams

Surface discharge from groundwater to streams begins in upper headwaters of a stream system at the small seeps, springs, and natural flow paths. This discharge generally continues along the entire reach, unless the stream is a "losing stream," where the water table drops below the stream channel. As small streams join to form larger ones, much like the branches of a tree, the size and flow capacity of the stream increases. Streams were first classified according to their "reach" by Robert Horton, who defined zero- and first-order streams as sources that supply second-order streams, and so on, downstream.[4]

The importance of small streams in reducing the impacts of downstream flooding is often overlooked. Small streams generally are not sufficiently protected by local or state ordinances. The role that zero-order and first-order streams provide in reducing flooding is significant. (Figure 4.12.)

Zero-order streams are small swales, depressions, and hollows in the natural topography that lack natural streambanks but serve as important conduits of water, sediment, nutrients, and other materials during rainfall and snowmelt. In humid and temperate climates, zero-order streams may support wetland plants and marshy meadows. These become important areas for "water storage" during extreme events. (Figure 4.13.)

First-order streams are the smallest distinct channels that flow perennially (year-round), intermittently (several months per year), or ephemerally (periodically after a rain or in the spring). In arid climates, first-order streams may surface and disappear again into the soil.

Second-order streams are formed by two first-order streams combining, and tend to support flow for greater periods of time but may still be intermittent in nature, especially in arid climates. (Figure 4.14.)

Zero-, first-, and second-order streams are referred to as headwater streams. Most zero- and first-order streams do not appear on maps, and second-order streams are often misclassified. Although U.S. Geological Survey maps often serve as the basis of reference for determining whether a flow pathway is a "stream," there are no underlying hydrologic statistics to

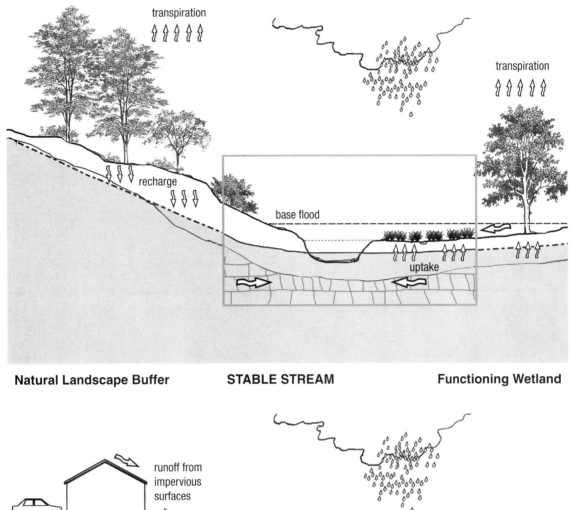

Natural Landscape Buffer   **STABLE STREAM**   **Functioning Wetland**

Altered Landscape   **STREAM EROSION**   **Water-stressed Landscape**

Figure 4.10 *Natural and altered streamflow:* As groundwater levels drop from natural conditions (above), the stream channel may drop below a functional connection to the floodplain (below).

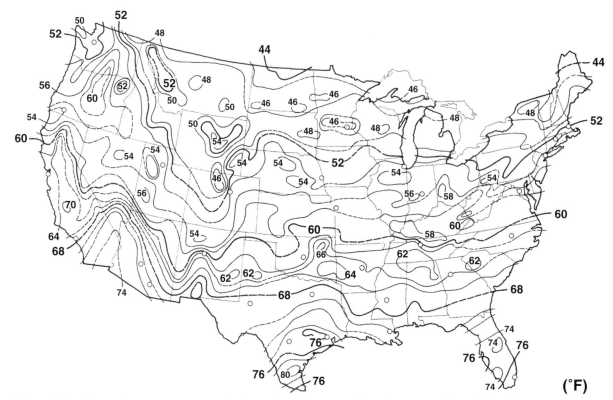

Figure 4.11 *Groundwater temperatures* (indicated in °F) remain relatively constant throughout the year, helping to moderate variations in stream water temperatures.

Data source: National Ground Water Association.

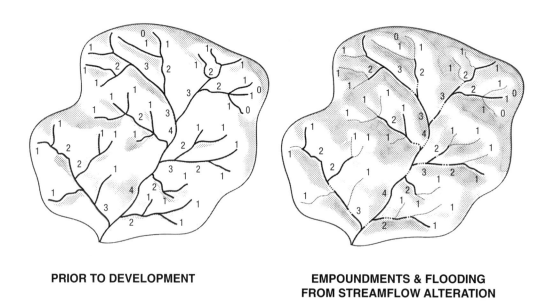

PRIOR TO DEVELOPMENT   **EMPOUNDMENTS & FLOODING FROM STREAMFLOW ALTERATION**

Figure 4.12 *Streams classified by reach:* Small headwater streams (zero-, first-, and second-order) represent at least 80% of the stream network in the United States.

Figure 4.13   *Zero-order stream in a Pennsylvania woodland:* Within several hundred feet, the stream channel becomes clearly defined with banks (first-order). Within less than a quarter mile, it joins a larger stream.

(PHOTO: James A. Schmid)

Figure 4.14   *Second-order stream in a Pennsylvania woodland:* Streambanks are clearly defined. The channel meanders, reducing erosive energy.

(PHOTO: Michele Adams)

support the mapping as a dashed blue line (intermittent) or solid blue line (perennial, or containing flow year-round). Rather, such decisions are often at the discretion of the mapmaker.[5] In detailed analysis, the Ohio Environmental Protection Agency found that small streams often are misclassified or unmapped. As a result of the lack of consistent mapping and the absence of regulatory requirements, there is little or limited protection for most headwater streams and virtually no protection for zero-order streams.

By current estimates, small headwater streams and flow paths make up at least 80% of the U.S. stream network. In terms of gross area, they provide more ecosystem services than any other water feature. Most biological and physical activity takes place in the area where the water makes contact with the saturated sediments in the channel (*hyporheic* zone) or where the water makes contact with the edges of the channel (*riparian* zone).

Headwater streams determine the capacity of a stream system to mitigate the flow of water downstream in extreme events. Small headwater streams can be thought of as a system of small reservoirs throughout the watershed, providing storage within the topography and surrounding soils as water levels rise. The topography of the channel provides storage capacity, especially in zero-and first-order streams, as the level of saturation in the soil rises during rainfall periods. When rainfall subsides, pools of water will remain along and in the channel, seeping into streambeds and banks, providing soil and groundwater recharge. The amount and rate of water discharged downstream is reduced.

Stream Channels

As first- and second-order streams combine to form larger streams, the width of the channel tends to increase. The shape of a stream channel is determined by both the amount of flow in the channel and the material that the channel moves through: bank material, underlying geology, and vegetation.

A stream channel is never static, and the location and shape of the channel will move over time. In an undeveloped watershed, these changes will happen slowly (on the order of eons). The channel shape itself is formed in response to the size and frequency of flows. *Bankfull flow* is the capacity of the channel flowing full, but not over, its banks. Stream channels are greatly affected by the frequency of bankfull flows. Statistically, bankfull flow has a recurrence interval of approximately 1.5 years, although in coastal areas bankfull flow may occur more frequently.[6]

Stream channels in undisturbed watersheds have meanders that tend to follow a sine-generated curve as the stream wanders back and forth. The meanders lengthen the overall flow path of the stream and hence reduce its slope and energy gradient. As the water travels through the bend, the flow is faster at the surface and tends to erode the outside bank. This material is deposited on the opposite side, creating a gradual slope that eventually forms a floodplain. As the channel moves, the floodplain is extended.

Stream channels also contain sequences of pools and riffles along the bottom of the channel, often formed as a result of the material generated by the bend in the channel. *Pools* are deeper areas of slower-moving water with very flat slopes. *Riffles* are shallow, steeper areas that often have more turbulent flow.

A stream forms a series of "steps" rather than a continuous slope. The repeated change from shallow to deeper waters increases the hydraulic resistance to flooding. The velocity of water moving in the channel is slowed when the channel includes pools and riffles and when the channel includes meanders and a longer flow path.

Floodplains

A *floodplain* is the flat area adjacent to a stream channel that is subject to inundation and flow in large events. The floodplain is shaped and formed by the same flow conditions of a watershed that shaped the channel. If those conditions change (more upstream volume of water), the floodplain may change in response. A floodplain is flat and may be on one or both sides of a channel.

Floodplains serve to reduce flooding by providing an increased area for the storage and slow movement of water. Floodplains tend to be flatter than the stream channel and also may have a rougher surface, both of which will slow the velocity of water. After floodwaters recede, water may remain in floodplains and slowly infiltrate, reducing the amount of water sent downstream.

Wetlands

Wetlands are areas where saturated surface conditions occur for all or part of the year (ephemeral wetlands), affecting the soils, vegetation, and fauna communities. Upland or terrestrial wetlands are almost always linked to stream networks and groundwater, whether these connections are visible at the surface or not. Nearly one in five upland wetlands has no visible surface connection to a stream system yet is connected to underlying groundwater. The inland wetland systems of Florida include many such areas, as do the prairie wetlands of Minnesota. These isolated wetlands may be protected under state or local laws but, based on a 2001 Supreme Court decision, are not protected by federal laws.

Wetlands, by definition, store water and, in doing so, reduce the volume and rate of water discharged downstream. The moist, but not saturated, conditions of the surface soils in wetlands improves their ability to absorb and infiltrate rainfall in the early portion of the storm.

Riparian Zones and Floodplains

Riparian zones provide significant ecosystem services by reducing the impacts of flooding.[7] Riparian zones have been found to be important areas of infiltration of overland flow, thereby reducing the flow in the stream system during a rainfall event. The soils and vegetation in riparian zones tend to be very effective at sediment reduction and nutrient sorption, specifically phosphorus, which tends to be bound to sediment and is responsible for excessive algal growth (*eutrophication*) in freshwater streams and water bodies. Riparian areas significantly reduce soluble nutrient levels, including nitrates that otherwise would contribute to coastal algal blooms.

Riparian habitats are often the richest and most diverse portion of a stream system. The microbial community in the riparian zone and shallow headwaters forms the foundation for the food web throughout the stream system. Most riparian areas remain unprotected unless specifically regulated under local wetland, floodplain, or stream setback requirements.

Summary of Stream Systems, Wetlands, Riparian Zones and Floodplains for Resilient Design

The watershed system of steams, wetlands, riparian zones, and floodplains combine to:

- Moderate downstream flooding by providing storage.
- Moderate downstream flooding by slowing the velocity of flow.
- Improve water quality by trapping sediments and nutrients.

- Improve water quality as a result of the biological activity that occurs within the sediment of bed bottoms and in the riparian zone.
- Promote infiltration, reducing runoff volumes. Slower-moving water is more likely to seep into bed and banks.
- Increase biodiversity and healthier ecosystems.

Notes

1. NOAA, Office of Hydrologic Development. Atlas 14, 2009. http://hdsc.nws.noaa.gov/hdsc/pdfs/.
2. K. R. Brye, J. M. Norman, L. G. Bundy, and S. T. Gower. "Water-Budget Evaluation of Prairie and Maize Ecosystems," Soil Science Society of America Journal 64 (2000): 715–724. Robert E. Horton, Erosional Development of Streams and Their Drainage Basins: Hydrophysical Approach to Quantitative Morphology (Boulder, CO: Geological Society of America, 1945).
3. Stephen S. O. Burgess, Mark A. Adams, Neil C. Turner, and Chin K. Ong, The Redistribution of Soil Water by Tree Root Systems (Dordrecht, the Netherlands: Springer, 1998).
4. Horton, Erosional Development of Streams and Their Drainage Basins.
5. Luna B. Leopold, A View of the River (Cambridge, MA: Harvard University Press, 1994); Judy L. Meyer et al., Where Rivers Are Born: The Scientific Imperative for Defending Small Streams and Wetlands (San Francisco: The Sierra Club Foundation and Turner Foundation and American Rivers, 2003).
6. Luna B. Leopold, M. Gordon Wolman, and John Miller, *Fluvial Processes in Geomorphology* (Mineola, NY: Dover Publications, 1995); Luna B. Leopold, *Water, Rivers and Creeks* (Sausalito, CA: University Science Books, 1997); and Christopher K. Metcalf, Shawn D. Wilkerson, and William A. Harman, "Bankfull Regional Curves for North and Northwest Florida Streams," *Journal of the American Water Resources Association* 45, no. 5 (October 2009): 1260–1272.
7. Meyer et al., *Where Rivers Are Born*; Metcalf et al., "Bankfull Regional Curves."

Figure 5.1   (A) *Before stream daylighting.* (B) *After stream daylighting.* Jordan Creek Daylighting and Greenway Project, Springfield MO.

(PHOTOS: Courtesy of City of Springfield and Terry Whalley, Ozark Greenways)

CHAPTER 5

THE ALTERED LANDSCAPE

The natural landscape—a system of vegetation, soils, stream networks, and natural features—has evolved over time in response to long-term rainfall patterns. Altering the natural landscape will alter water resources and increase flooding. Even within a small urban watershed, there can be thousands of homes, businesses, roads, and farm properties. Each site that disrupts the water balance will contribute to increased runoff volume and risk of flooding, in a sense, a "death by a thousand cuts."

Riverine flood conditions change due to three combined factors.

1. *Increased rainfall*, both in intensity and number of events. Global climate change is resulting in increased rainfall incidence, amount, and extremes.
2. *Loss of absorptive landscape.* The spread of urbanization and sprawl increases impervious surfaces that in turn increase the rates of stormwater flow.
3. *Siltation of waterways.* With increased stormwater discharge across altered landscapes, there is increased siltation of waterways. Constrictions to runoff that result from deposition of sand, sediment, and debris create ponding in previously dry areas.

Altering the landscape of natural vegetation can dramatically increase runoff and the volume of water discharged downstream. When building design and land development alter the landscape without consideration of watershed impacts, the local water balance is disrupted and water resource quality is diminished. As a result, the frequency and severity of flooding are made worse.

5.1 WHEN THE LANDSCAPE IS ALTERED

Vegetation
In land development, native vegetation often is replaced with nonnative species that lack the capacity to absorb rainfall effectively and may require supplemental irrigation. In terms of water resources and flooding, lawns are one of the most damaging types of vegetation replacement:

- The short, uniform, vertical nature of turf grass provides limited interception. Rainfall is conveyed directly down the stem and onto soils.

- Regular mowing required by turf grass compacts surface soils, compressing and eliminating the macro- and micropores that allow water movement into the soil.

- The root system of turf grass is shallow, usually not more than 2.5 inches (6 cm) deep. There is little opportunity for the roots to convey water into the soil. Rainfall rapidly becomes runoff.

- The monoculture of lawn changes the biological community of the soil with substantially less soil fauna and a decrease in soil porosity. The loss of biological community often is made worse by the use of pesticides and an imbalance in soil nutrients.

- The surface temperature of lawn is significantly greater than the surface temperature in forested or meadow conditions. This results in a rapid drying and hardening of the soil surface, with less absorptive capacity during precipitation. Increased surface temperatures also increase the temperature of runoff and alter the biological community.

Unlike forested systems, urban trees also often are limited in their ability to absorb water and reduce flooding. Because of very limited area, neglectful maintenance, as well as sand and salt from roadway deicing, urban trees have a limited life span, on average 32 years. Trees planted in parking lots average only 12 years. Urban trees rarely reach full maturity or succeed in developing an extensive canopy for rainfall interception. This is primarily due to lack of suitable soil conditions, compaction, or lack of soil volume for sufficient root growth or rainwater replenishment.

Removal of vegetation often is advocated to enhance groundwater recharge, especially in arid climates. While removal of nonnative vegetation may be worthwhile, native vegetation prevents damage to surface porosity of soils from heavy rainfall impact and increases the soil's ability to absorb water. Unless great care is taken, removing vegetation is likely to decrease rather than increase groundwater recharge.

Impervious Surfaces

Impervious surfaces—roads, driveways, sidewalks, building roofs, plazas, and patios—do not absorb water. They create runoff. Impervious areas created by development have a large impact on the water balance and flooding for several reasons:

- Virtually every rainfall event will generate runoff and will increase the overall volume of water occurring as runoff. Small storms that would not produce any runoff from a natural landscape will be translated almost entirely into runoff. During large precipitation events, the volume of runoff generated and discharged downstream will increase.

- Runoff begins almost immediately after rainfall begins. There is virtually no buffer time between the beginning of rainfall and the beginning of runoff.

Not all impervious surfaces are equal and do not have the same flooding impacts.

DIRECTLY CONNECTED IMPERVIOUS AREAS are areas where runoff is directed into a storm sewer, swale, or creek with no opportunity for the runoff to come into contact with absorptive soil or vegetation. These areas are the most damaging to stream health and flooding because all precipitation is translated immediately into runoff in the stream system. Examples include parking lot inlets that discharge directly to a storm sewer to the creek, roof downspouts that connect into a storm sewer, and roads that collect and discharge water directly into a stream.

DISCONNECTED IMPERVIOUS AREAS are impervious areas where the surface runoff is conveyed onto vegetation that has some ability to absorb water or slow the velocity of the flow. Examples include roof downspouts that are disconnected to discharge to the landscape or sidewalks that are sloped back toward the landscape instead of draining onto the street and into storm sewer inlets.

Although much of the runoff from disconnected impervious areas will eventually reach streams, the rate and intensity of the flow can be reduced. In urban areas, "disconnecting" impervious areas—ideally with naturalized features that hold and absorb run-off—can provide significant reduction in flood surges.

When precipitation falls on impervious surfaces such as pavements and roofs, some small amount of water will be captured in small crevices or spaces, or absorbed by sediment and debris. This is referred to as the *initial abstraction*. On small impervious surfaces, such as narrow roads and driveways, water that seeps through cracks is able to move laterally through the subbase material, reducing runoff.[1] In large pavement areas, such as parking lots, very little water is able to move through the subbase of the pavement, so that runoff begins almost immediately. The initial abstraction of impervious areas is generally 0.1 inches (0.3 cm) or less, so that with more than 0.1 inches of rainfall, runoff will be generated.

The U.S. Environmental Protection Agency estimates that watershed health begins to show measurable signs of decline at about 10% impervious cover. Highly urban environments, such as cities, urban centers, and campuses, often are 60% or higher in impervious cover, with values of 75% or more for ultra-urban areas. In the urban environment, streets and sidewalks together generally comprise slightly more than half of the impervious area. (Figure 5.2.)

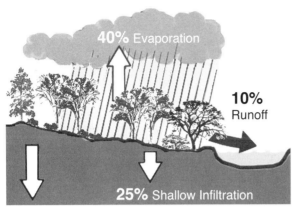

NATURAL LANDSCAPE
• native landscaping supported by rainfall
• soil replenished by tree succession
• natural areas support diverse wildlife

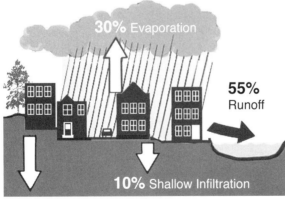

DENSE RESIDENTIAL
35% to 50% Impervious
• 24-hour water retention reduced by 20%
• aquifer recharge reduced by 40%
• evaporative cooling reduced by 12.5%

URBAN
75% to 100% Impervious
• runoff increased more than five fold
• 24-hour water retention reduced by 40%
• aquifer recharge reduced five fold
• evaporative cooling reduced by 25%

Figure 5.2   *Water balance and watershed resilience to flooding* can be correlated to the percent of porous versus impervious cover.

Source: U.S. Department of Agriculture, Soil Conservation Service. *Urban Hydrology for Small Watersheds*, Technical Release No. 55, 2nd ed. (Washington, DC: Author, 1986).

Compaction and Alteration of Soils

Healthy soil serves as Earth's filter, restoring and maintaining healthy water resources. By absorbing and slowing the movement of water toward streams and man-made conveyance systems, soils reduce both the volume and rate of stormwater runoff.

Soils in natural areas are able to absorb water *at the point of impact*. Due to human disturbance, removal of vegetation, and compaction, soils lose that capacity. The volume and rate of stormwater runoff both increase and, correspondingly, so does flooding.

Construction and maintenance practices result in the disturbance and compaction of soils. Topsoils are removed from any area of construction, including areas to be reestablished as lawn. As new landscape is regraded to the designed slopes, soils are redistributed and compacted, unless special precautions are taken and specifications are enforced. Landscaped areas are most often overly compacted, through grading equipment or unintentionally through normal construction operations.

Current practices and most regulations allow site disturbance as long as topsoil is stockpiled and erosion and sediment control measures—such as siltation fences—are in place to control the release of sediment from the site. Disturbance of soils eliminates macropores and soil capacity to absorb water. Topsoil often is replaced at a much thinner depth than existed before disturbance. The potential for emergence of a soil fungal community is eliminated.

Architects and engineers consider the structural abilities and constraints of soils for building and infrastructure purposes but are not trained to consider the hydrologic impacts of soil changes. The long-term impacts of changes in the soil and resulting impacts on flooding and water resources are not addressed in the typical regulatory process or site management practices.

Typical stormwater calculations do not account for changes in the soil response to precipitation, even where soils are removed, disturbed, compacted, replaced, or replanted as lawn. Lawn often is perceived as green space or a natural condition. Engineering calculations of runoff rarely make any significant distinction between lawn and other types of vegetation and often apply the same engineering coefficient values for lawn as would be applied for meadow or pasture. Heavily managed lawns and playfields are nearly as dense and as impervious as concrete. (Table 5.1.)

TABLE 5.1 PERMEABILITY MEASUREMENTS OF SAMPLED LAYERS WITHIN 20 INCHES OF SOIL SURFACE

Site	Bulk Density (g/cm³)	Permeability (in/hr)
Woods	1.42	15
Pasture	1.47	9.9
Single house	1.67	7.1
Subdivision lawn 1	1.79	0.14
Garage lawn	1.82	0.04
Cleared woods	1.83	0.13
Athletic field	1.95	0.01
Subdivision lawn 2	2.03	0.03
Concrete	2.2	0.0

Source: Ocean County Soil Conservation District, *Impact of Soil Disturbance during Construction on Bulk Density and Infiltration in Ocean County, New Jersey* (Washington, DC: U.S. Department of Agriculture, Natural Resources Conservation Service, 2001).

Loss of Groundwater Recharge

Loss of shallow interflow has a dramatic effect on vegetation. Impacts on the landscape may take years to become evident and thus are rarely associated with land use changes. Very typically, groundwater levels drop due to more water being removed first by well extraction and second by reduction or elimination of recharge flows. Protecting streams and wetlands by regulated setbacks alone will not ensure their long-term viability if the source of their groundwater discharge is disconnected. In coastal areas, reduction of seaward base flow of freshwater often will increase the saltwater intrusion, altering the gradient that sustains marshlands and shoreline buffers.

A decrease in stream base flow results in a corresponding increase in flood flows. This finding has been clearly established by research involving the monitoring of rainfall, streamflow, and land use over a significant time frame and in a number of locations, including Long Island, New York, and the Piedmont and coastal areas of North Carolina.[2]

Small changes in average stream temperature can alter the microbial community of a stream. The microbial community forms the basis of the food chain for the entire system.

A small change in average temperature can alter this community from a fungi-based system to a bacteria-based system, with impacts observed throughout the entire food chain.

5.2 ALTERED STREAM SYSTEMS AND INCREASED FLOOD DAMAGE

In a natural landscape, vegetation offers a "tortuous" path for stormwater to follow at both the small scale (natural swales and depressions) and the large scale (stream meanders and floodplains), storing and slowing water along the way. Downstream flood effects of extreme events are reduced in a complex system that begins with headwater streams.

Lost Headwater Streams and Upland Wetlands

Headwater streams, stream storage areas, and buffers tend to be forgotten in the development process. Small headwater streams comprise up to 80% of the stream channel miles. As more rainfall occurs, water levels may rise, but flow is generally slower than in a man-made system. As rainfall occurs, low depressions and swales absorb and hold rainfall through topography and depressions that feed small streams. This allows for a slower release downstream and a significant reduction in flooding. The topography of the headwater streams is critical to downstream flood protection.

Small headwater streams and depressions are not protected by regulatory requirements at the state or local level. At the local level, when headwater streams are filled and forgotten, they often become areas of localized "nuisance flooding," resulting in wet basements, lawns that are too soggy to mow, or areas of water ponding and structure damage. The flood-mitigating capacity of these areas generally is disregarded.

Incised Channels and Disconnected Floodplains

Beyond first- and second-order streams, stream systems tend to form floodplains, which are overflow ("overbank") areas that may experience flooding once every one to two years. Floodplains are low, flat areas along the stream channel. As water flow volumes increase and the water level rises, water moves easily and with little erosive damage beyond the channel banks and into the floodplain area. As rainfall diminishes, water in the floodplain gradually recedes. It returns to the stream channel, either directly through overland flow or through the gradual infiltration of water along the floodplain as the groundwater levels recede after the storm.

The capacity of floodplains to receive floodwaters is lost by changes in land uses upstream. As natural landscapes are converted to impervious and disturbed surfaces, the total *volume* of rainfall occurring as runoff increases and the *frequency* of runoff events increases, exceeding the capacity of the stream channel. The increase in total volume of runoff, as well as the increased frequency in runoff events, exceeds the capacity of the stream channel to convey this water during both large and small rainfalls. During the frequent smaller rainfalls, the volume of increased runoff will result in higher water levels in the stream channel for longer periods of time, more often than before. These flows are not high enough to reach the floodplain. In response, the stream will begin to erode and "cut down" its banks to accommodate the increased flow rate and frequency of flow.

The hydraulic forces that shape the geometry of the channel are most significant when filled to their banks (bankfull or near-bankfull) conditions, where the water level has risen but has not yet reached or overlapped into the floodplain. In a watershed with natural land use conditions, bankfull conditions occur at a frequency of about 1.5 years in upland areas and slightly more frequently in coastal areas.

In addition to erosion and steam siltation and pollution, the stream channel will "cut down" during bankfull conditions, which further disconnects the channel from the floodplain. When a larger rainfall occurs—one that normally would have discharged harmlessly to the floodplain—the flow can no longer reach the floodplain without detrimental impacts of flooding, erosion, siltation and pollution. As a result, even more water is discharged downstream, and the channel continues to cut down and erode, sometimes until it reaches bedrock. (Figure 5.3.)

After storm levels have passed and water levels recede, the channel is deeper than previously, with greater flow capacity. Because stream channels tend to form at the

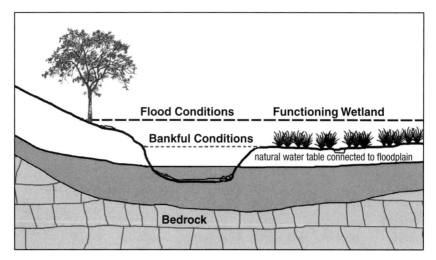

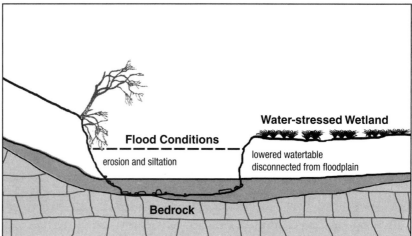

Figure 5.3 *Bankfull flow:* healthy stream (above) compared to eroded condition (below).

intersection of groundwater with the surface topography, interflow and shallow groundwater then discharge more rapidly into the channel. As a result, local groundwater levels and soil moisture conditions will drop, and streamside vegetation and riparian area will be lost.

During development, installation of pipes or outfalls often cause substantial draining of surface moisture, discharging onto the landscape and potentially creating erosion and sediment gullies, with further draining of area soil moisture. (Figure 5.4.)

The stream channel itself will lose its flood-mitigating capacity as the stream becomes more incised. In a natural channel, the velocity of water changes as it moves from deeper, slower-moving pools through shallow and

faster-moving riffles. This unevenness of stream topography provides the capacity for storage and buffering of water velocity as water levels rise during a storm event. As the channel cuts down and loses pools and riffles, the channel becomes "flashier," that is, rising and falling more rapidly. This may be more efficient at conveying water downstream but is far less effective at providing water storage along the way. Important stream habitat areas are lost.

The loss of freshwater floodplains in coastal areas is especially damaging. Coastal floodplains tend to be broader and "flatter" than upstream areas, with less slope and hence less energy. Coastal streams are shallow and experience out-of-bank flows into the floodplain more

(A)

(B)

Figure 5.4   (A) *Increased runoff* from adjacent development has caused this headwater stream bottom to be "cut down" below the organic soil layer. (B) *Close-up indicating groundwater discharge to lowered stream.* As a result, the soils of the woodland dry out more rapidly.

(PHOTO: Veridian Landscape Studio, LLC)

frequently than upstream areas. Floodplain flow occurs more frequently, with a recurrence interval of 0.9 to 1.0 times per year. Evapotranspiration is also significant in coastal freshwater wetlands. During the growing season, shallow coastal streams may not have any surface flow due to the high rates of evapotranspiration that lower the shallow groundwater table.

The capacity of coastal floodplains and vegetation to absorb the impacts of flood events is compromised by past damage from upstream areas as well as increased volume and frequency of floodwaters from those areas. Coastal communities thus can be impacted in the same storm event by both ocean coastal flooding and upstream inland flooding.

5.3 WHY DETENTION DOES NOT SOLVE FLOODING

Stormwater regulations have focused on controlling the rate of flow for *large or extreme storm events*, such as the 100-year, 10-year, or 2-year storms, defined respectively as storms that have the 1-in-100, 1-in-10, or 1-in-2-year statistical probability of occurring in any given year. Regulations traditionally have focused on the *rate* of flow but not the *volume* of flow. In other words, the total *volume* of water leaving a site may increase dramatically as long as the water not leave a site at a higher *flow rate* than it did before development during *large storm events* (2-year recurrence frequency or higher). Small storm events—comprising 90% or more the rainfall events in most locations—are generally not regulated, and both flow rate and volume may increase. Regulations vary significantly depending on local jurisdictions.

The use of detention basins—structures that hold and temporarily detain runoff for a few hours—has evolved from this approach to flood control. Detention measures have been widely implemented from site to regional scale with varied results, but most significantly, flooding generally has continued to occur and worsen, even with the use of detention basins. (Figure 5.5.)

There are two limitations to the detention basin approach, from both a flooding and a water resource perspective.

First, if a site is allowed to increase the total amount of water that is discharged from the site and is required only to control the rate of flow of that discharge, obviously there will be an *increase in the total amount or volume of water sent downstream*. As development occurs and more sites are altered, more and more water in the form of stormwater runoff is sent downstream. By controlling the rate of flow—also discharging a much greater volume of runoff than occurred before development—detention extends the time period that water is discharged from a site. More water at the same rate means that water is released over a longer time period.

Figure 5.5 *Valley Creek:* The last remaining stream with a wild brown trout population in the Philadelphia region has experienced rapid urbanization. Although several hundred stormwater detention basins were constructed, erosion of streambanks and loss of base flow continue due to increased runoff volume and the loss of recharge area.

(PHOTO: Michele Adams)

Increased volume of runoff water and extended duration of the flow increase downstream flow rates and flooding. Even if the rate of stormwater flow is controlled at the site, the combined volume from many sites leads to increased flow rates and water levels at the *watershed* level. From a watershed perspective, the primary goal of detention systems—flood control—is not achieved.

Second, flow-rate control traditionally has focused on large (and infrequent) storm events. For smaller, more frequent rainfall events, both rate and volume are unmanaged and usually are increased. As a result, stream systems are altered and existing floodplains are disconnected from the stream channel.

In some areas with significant flooding from urbanization, this problem has been recognized. Regulations now define maximum allowable flow rates of stormwater runoff from new development. The use of "extended detention basins" that discharge water over an even longer time period is required. Some local regulations require that the rate of flow from a project site be reduced to that which would occur from a smaller storm, such as controlling a 10-year rainfall down to flow rates that would occur during a 1-year or 2-year rainfall. This approach has evolved from recognition that a natural channel can safely convey the flow rate of a 1-year or 2-year rainfall without leaving its streambanks or causing erosion.

The flow rate or detention approach to flooding also disregards the value of the rainfall as a resource. Allowing small, frequent rainfall events to discharge rapidly downstream via a conveyance system disregards the need to replenish soil moisture and provide groundwater recharge. Healthy vegetation can no longer sustain itself. Stormwater management that focuses on controlling flow rates while increasing the volume of runoff sent downstream continues to foster the belief that stormwater is a nuisance to be managed and disposed of rather than recognizing the benefits of the rainfall.

5.4 SUMMARY: THE NATURAL LANDSCAPE AS A MODEL FOR RESILIENT DESIGN

A natural system employs many measures—of varying type and size in response to the amount of rainfall—to reduce the volume and rate of flow and to retain the water resource.

Most rainfall events are small, frequent precipitation events of 1.5 inches (3.8 cm) or less. Natural systems have evolved such that there is generally little or no stormwater runoff during these events. Rainfall is absorbed by vegetation and soils and stored in small local depressions in the landscape. During less frequent, larger rainfalls of 1.5.inches or more, soils and vegetation become saturated. If rainfall continues, water levels begin to rise in small soil depressions and larger landscape depressions. Surface saturation also will initiate more rapid water movement into soil through macropores. Water remains close to where it falls.

The greatest difference in runoff between a natural and an altered site occurs during small rainfall events and during the early portion of rainfall from a large storm event. Most of the increase in runoff volume occurs because the altered soils and groundcover cannot absorb the first portion of the rainfall and natural and varied depressions have been removed.

In an extreme event, such as a hurricane, healthy woodlands and urbanized areas both will generate runoff. But the woodland will not generate runoff in the early portion of the storm—the response is not as rapid because the woodland captures the first portion of the rainfall. A meandering pattern of water flow extends opportunities for retention and connection with groundwater recharge while also increasing diversity of aquatic and riverine habitat. Channelization has opposite results. While conveying stormwater elsewhere, channelization eliminates any effective flood mitigation that could be provided by slower-moving streams and functioning buffers.

Stormwater runoff from developed areas conveys an enormous pollutant load washed from the land surface. Area flooding is only one of the impacts, which also may include beach closings, seasonal water supply shortages and localized impoundment, soil saturation, and basement flooding.

Capturing runoff from the early part of an extreme rainfall is more effective than controlling the rate of flow at the height of the storm. Designing systems that mimic the natural system response is far more effective at reducing the flooding impacts of extreme weather than conventional approaches of detention and conveyance. (Table 5.2.)

Different design measures should be used to cover the range of type and size of all rainfall events and thus anticipate them. Many small and varied measures provide greater security and redundancy than any single approach, such as conveyance or detention alone. The range of Best Management Practices of watershed design for resilience to flooding is described in Chapter 6.

TABLE 5.2   COMPARISON OF THE RAINFALL RESPONSE OF NATURAL AND ALTERED LANDSCAPES SUMMARIZES THE ADVANTAGES OF MIMICKING NATURAL SYSTEMS IN LANDSCAPE DESIGN

Very Small Rainfalls (less than 1/2")

In most areas, more than 65% of all rain events are less than 1/2" precipitation.

vs.

NATURAL LANDSCAPE
Interception by vegetation
Infiltration into soils

ECOSYSTEM RESPONSE
No runoff
Water returned to atmosphere or groundwater

ALTERED LANDSCAPE
Impervious surfaces
Increased volume and frequency of runoff

Nearly all rainfall on impervious becomes runoff

Small Rainfalls (less than 1-1/2")

95% of all rain events are less than 1-1/2" in nearly every locale.

vs.

NATURAL LANDSCAPE
Depression storage
Groundwater levels rise
Headwater streams rise
Infiltration into soils

Little or no runoff

ALTERED LANDSCAPE
Loss of forest, meadow, and prairie
Increase in lawn, compaction of soils

Rainfall on landscape becomes runoff

Moderate Rainfalls (greater than 1-1/2")

Varies by location, generally between 1-1/2" and 4".

vs.

NATURAL LANDSCAPE
Streams flow full
Floodplains may flow

Runoff begins

ALTERED LANDSCAPE
Stream channel "cuts down" from too much runoff too often. Floodplain is disconnected from channel

Increased runoff volume is greater than capacity of streams and floodplains

---

Extreme Events

Storms that occur with a two year frequency or greater.

vs.

NATURAL LANDSCAPE
Local and watershed flooding

Floodplains slow flow and limit damage

ALTERED LANDSCAPE
Downstream flooding increases in frequency and level

Water is conveyed downstream faster and in greater amounts

Notes

1. Robert Pitt, *The Integration of Water Quality and Drainage Design Objectives*, 2003. www.rpitt.eng. ua.edu.

2. F. D. Shields Jr., S. S. Knight, and C. M. Cooper, *Effects of Channel Incision on Base Flow Stream Habitats and Fishes* (New York: Springer, 1994); and Dale L. Simmons and Richard J. Reynolds, "Effects of Urbanization on Base Flow of Selected South-Shore Streams, Long Island, New York," *Journal of the American Water Resources Council* 18, no. 5 (1983): 797–805.

Figure 6.1 (A) *Rainwater collection and native planting.* (B) *Drainage swale and interpretive trail.* Bird Johnson Wildflower Center, Austin, Texas. Overland Partners Architects.

(PHOTOS: Donald Watson)

CHAPTER **6**

DESIGN FOR INLAND FLOODING

There is a great opportunity to restore the capacity of building sites, communities, and regions to mitigate flooding.

Each building site is part of a watershed problem or a part of a watershed solution. Best Practice Measures (BMPs) undertaken as part of landscaping, infrastructure, building and remodeling can improve any project site and its role in the larger watershed: water collection, storage, and distribution; where and how to build; how to manage the runoff and to use and reuse the water resource that is available seasonally and annually.

The goals of an integrated approach to watershed protection and management that can be part of every construction project are to reduce flooding during extreme events, provide healthy water for human and natural needs, and restore impaired waters. These goals are achievable through many small measures, informed by how the water balance and natural systems support resilient design.

6.1 RESILIENT DESIGN FOR INLAND FLOODING

Protect Natural Features that Provide Ecosystem Services

The first step in resilient design for inland flooding is to identify and map areas of any existing natural features that resources that provide ecosystem services in absorbing rainfall. Develop a plan that protects or restores these features. These include:

- **Swales, depressions, and flow pathways**. Understand the movement of water through the area. Aerial photos can help to identify wet areas and flow pathways that are not obvious at eye level.

- **Wetlands, headwater streams, and stream systems**. Identify locations where surface water leaves a site and where it goes. Know the name of the watershed, the location within the watershed, and where water ultimately goes.

- **Vegetation**. Identify any remaining remnants of native vegetation and design to protect and maintain these areas if possible. Identify the type of vegetation that would thrive if human influences were not present.

- **Geology, soils, and slopes**. Identify and understand the underlying conditions. Geotechnical information for building construction, such as soil borings, can provide insight into site conditions.

- **Connectivity**. Provide corridors for native plant propagation and wildlife movement to adequate habitat.

In urban or previously disturbed environments, identify past conditions and alterations that have occurred:

- Buried streams may be reflected in the location of the storm sewers first utilizing topography, absorptive buffers, and wetlands.

- Native vegetation and soil conditions might provide information on what species and wetlands can be reintroduced.
- Current or past contamination or disturbance may be evident or may require scientific testing.

Reduce Impervious Land Cover

Identify opportunities to reduce the amount of proposed impervious surface or to reduce existing impervious surfaces:

- Reduced footprint: narrower streets or shorter driveways and reduced parking.
- Porous pavements to reduce impervious land cover.

POROUS PAVEMENT WITH INFILTRATION BED Also called *pervious paving*, porous pavement with an infiltration bed generally refers to any paving approach that allows water to infiltrate through it. The term, in a more limited definition, refers to a system of surface treatment and subsurface water storage. This typically is provided by porous (permeable) surface of asphalt, concrete, or pavers overlain on a subsurface, open-graded stone storage/infiltration bed. Porous pavement often looks the same as traditional asphalt or concrete but is manufactured without "fine" materials. It incorporates void spaces that allow for infiltration and is ideal for low-traffic parking areas and walkways. In extremely dense urban areas, porous pavement has been used in redevelopment projects, where it treats and stores stormwater without consuming extra land.

Porous pavements reduce stormwater runoff by allowing rainfall to drain directly through pavement instead of running off. In porous pavements, the underlying stone bed has many void spaces (approximately 40%). Rainfall is temporarily held in the voids of the stone bed and then slowly drained into the underlying, uncompacted soil below. Porous pavements must be designed with an emergency overflow so that the water level will not rise to the pavement level. A layer of geotextile filter fabric separates the stone aggregate from the underlying soil, preventing the migration of soil into the bed. Porous pavement beds should not be placed on compacted fill material, as infiltration will not occur.

Although porous pavement and the underlying stone infiltration bed are slightly more expensive than conventional materials, increased costs generally are offset by cost savings in reduced inlets, pipes, and excavation as well as in the reduction or elimination of separate detention facilities.

Porous asphalt and concrete surfaces provide better traction for walking paths in rain or snow conditions and are suitable to replace most roads, parking areas, walks, and other paved surfaces. (Figure 6.2.)

REINFORCED TURF SYSTEMS consist of cells of plastic, concrete, or other material that provide structural support for vehicles and prevent soil compaction while allowing vegetation or turf to grow within the

Figure 6.2a *Comparison* of standard asphalt (left on photo) and porous asphalt paving (right) during rainfall at the University of North Carolina Chapel Hill.

(PHOTO: Cahill Associates, Environmental Consultants)

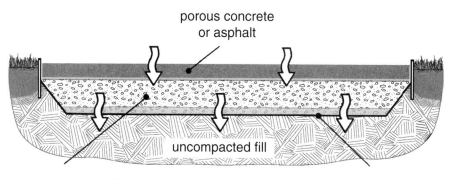

porous concrete
or asphalt

uncompacted fill

clean, washed
uniformly graded
aggregate

geotextile fabric lining
bottom and sides of bed

Figure 6.2b *Porous paving schematic.*

cells. Reinforced turf can be used in areas of temporary or overflow parking, to provide emergency vehicle access, or to provide structural stability along pedestrian paths for occasional vehicle movement. Reinforced turf soil mixes should include sufficient organic material to maintain porosity and the healthy growth of vegetation.

Design for Very Small Rainfalls

Most of the runoff in very small rainfall events (0.5 inch or less) will be generated by impervious surfaces, and so design for the first 0.5-inch of rainfall focuses on impervious areas. Avoid connecting and piping impervious areas to conveyance systems. Instead, first direct water flows onto vegetated areas. Identify all areas of impervious cover, and direct water toward vegetated areas. Do not collect and convey water to one location. Instead, allow rainfall to be managed close to where it falls. Use many small areas to disperse water in small rainfall events.

ROOF DOWNSPOUT DISCONNECTION AND PLANTER BOXES
Rather than piping water from building roofs to storm sewers, roof downspouts can be "disconnected" to discharge to vegetated areas, including lawns, rain gardens, and planter boxes. Grading must be designed so that water moves away from structures and into the landscape. Landscapes can be designed to receive this runoff. Care should be taken to avoid building designs that combine roof drainage into one location. Instead, design buildings that use many downspouts and disperse water throughout the landscape.

A stormwater planter is a structure typically formed from concrete or brick that is filled with absorbent soils and plants in order to temporarily store, evaporate, and treat rainwater. Planters are placed adjacent to the external downspouts of a building to receive rooftop runoff. Planters can be designed with open bottoms to infiltrate water or to discharge to the storm sewer system after capturing the first 0.5-inch of rainfall. Planters should be installed with an overflow connection to an outfall or storm drainage system. (See Figure 6.3.)

IMPERVIOUS AREA DISCONNECTION
Impervious surfaces, such as parking lots, streets, and sidewalks, can be graded toward vegetated areas rather than concentrating water and conveying it immediately to inlets and pipes. In low-traffic areas, eliminating curbs will allow water to disperse onto vegetated areas. (Figure 6.4.)

GREEN ROOFS
are engineered, vegetated systems installed on roofs to absorb rainfall. Installations may include additional layers, such as a root barrier and drainage and irrigation systems. Green roofs will absorb the initial rainfall of small events and slow the rate of flow during larger storms. Green roofs can be established on both existing and new roofs. The strength of the supporting structure as well as the size, slope, height, and directional orientation of the roof are critical factors that must be assessed before installation of a green roof.

Green roofs are described in various ways: single-layer systems with free drainage through the soil; systems with

Figure 6.3   *In-ground planter* at Waterview Recreation Center, Philadelphia, intercepts roof runoff from an existing 100-year old building in an urban setting.

(PHOTO: Michele Adams)

Figure 6.4   *Curb cut* accesses vegetated natural areas downslope of road and parking lot.

(PHOTO: A. P. Davis)

additional drainage layers; or systems with combined drainage and storage layer. *Extensive green roofs* consist of thin layers from .8 to 6 inches (2 to 15 cm) of growing media and lightweight plantings suited to thin media, such as sedums, grasses, and other small plants and are unirrigated. *Intensive green roofs* have deeper layers of soil (> 6 inches) that can support larger plants, including trees and shrubs, and often are irrigated.

Plant size and selection depends on the depth of the roof overburden (growing medium) and local climate, but the plants are almost always drought tolerant. Low-growing plants, such as grasses, sedums, and other cactuslike plants, are used where growing media depth is only a few inches. Where the media depth is several feet, shrubs and small trees can be used.

Green roofs extend the life span of a roof by mitigating temperature extremes on it. Green roofs control stormwater runoff, trap and break down airborne pollutants, and create habitat. Green roofs also mitigate urban heat island effects, recycle carbon, and conserve energy by stabilizing the indoor temperature and humidity of buildings. (Figures 6.5 and 6.6.)

CISTERNS TO CAPTURE AND REUSE WATER

Rooftops are cleaner than other impervious areas, such as pavements. Roof runoff has the potential to be detained and reused. A number of storage options are available for capturing rooftop runoff for reuse. Cisterns, rain barrels, and other vertical storage structures are large containers that store water draining via the external roof downspouts of buildings. Stored runoff can be used for passive irrigation, fire protection, or graywater reuse, including flushing toilets. In turn, the demand for potable sources of water for secondary uses is reduced. (Figure 6.7.)

To size water storage properly, it is necessary to consider the volume of water coming off a drainage area and the reuse demand for stored water. A further consideration is that the stored water must be used or discharged before the next rainfall. An overflow or bypass of large storm events

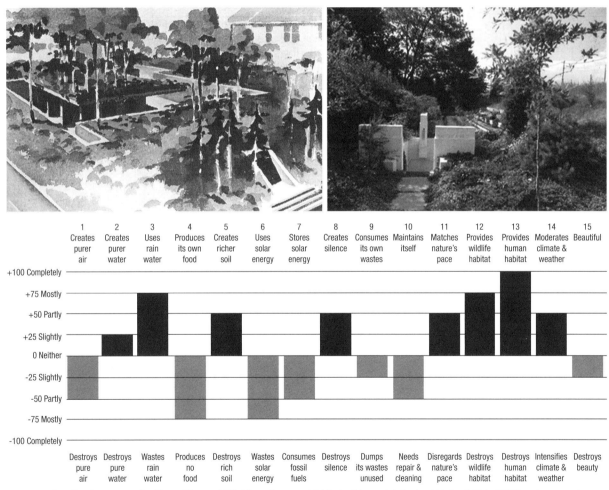

| | 1 Creates purer air | 2 Creates purer water | 3 Uses rain water | 4 Produces its own food | 5 Creates richer soil | 6 Uses solar energy | 7 Stores solar energy | 8 Creates silence | 9 Consumes its own wastes | 10 Maintains itself | 11 Matches nature's pace | 12 Provides wildlife habitat | 13 Provides human habitat | 14 Moderates climate & weather | 15 Beautiful |

Scale: +100 Completely, +75 Mostly, +50 Partly, +25 Slightly, 0 Neither, -25 Slightly, -50 Partly, -75 Mostly, -100 Completely

| | Destroys pure air | Destroys pure water | Wastes rain water | Produces no food | Destroys rich soil | Wastes solar energy | Consumes fossil fuels | Destroys silence | Dumps its wastes unused | Needs repair & cleaning | Disregards nature's pace | Destroys wildlife habitat | Destroys human habitat | Intensifies climate & weather | Destroys beauty |

Figure 6.5 *Earth-covered office, Cherry Hill, New Jersey, 1968.* Architect Malcolm Wells (1926–2009) advocated an environmental ethic and "gentle architecture" decades before green roofs and environmental rating systems were widely adopted.

Figure 6.6a   *Peco Energy Building, Philadelphia:* 45,000-square-foot green roof established with a low-maintenance sedum prevegetated mat installed over ultra-lightweight growing media. Located on the eighth-floor roof, it is accessible to building occupants and pedestrians.

(PHOTO: Courtesy of Roofscapes, Inc.)

must be provided on the storage device. Screens, covers, or other measures (e.g., constant agitation of the surface) should be implemented to prevent breeding of mosquitoes and other insects. Rain barrels and cisterns should be placed upgradient of reuse areas to reduce or eliminate pumping needs.

RAINWATER HARVESTING   As an extension of cisterns, additional measures may include designs to recover and reuse all water that falls on-site through integrated rainwater harvesting. The water may be stored in rainwater tanks or cisterns or directed into distribution systems that recharge groundwater. Stormwater runoff is not suitable for reuse as potable water unless water treatment is provided. Rainwater harvesting can provide lifeline water for human consumption, reduce water bills, and limit the need to build large reservoirs. Rainwater harvesting in urban areas provides supplemental water for landscape watering requirements and increases soil moisture, increases the ground water table through recharge, mitigates urban flooding, and improves the quality of groundwater. At a household

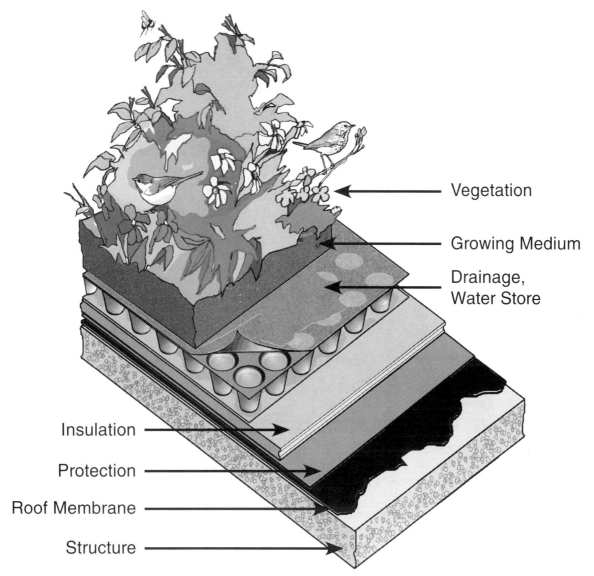

Figure 6.6b *Green roof* with combined drainage and storage layers.

(American Wick Drain Corporation)

level, harvested rainwater can be used for flushing toilets and washing laundry.

GRAYWATER SYSTEMS Freshwater is a precious resource, and its first use should be restricted to potable water. Increasingly, design innovations are demonstrating ways to extend water reuse. Rainwater harvesting often is combined with recovery of water used within building sinks or washer systems.

Any water that has been used once, except water from toilets, is called *graywater*. It can be reused for many other purposes, especially landscape irrigation. Plants thrive on used water containing small bits of compost. Dish, shower, sink, and laundry water make up 50% to 80% of residential "waste" water. The benefits of graywater recycling include:

• Lower freshwater use and related costs of supply

• Less strain on septic tank or treatment plant capacity

Figure 6.7 *Rainwater cistern:* Woodlawn Library, Wilmington, Delaware. Hillier Architects, Peggy Kehrer, Design Principal, and Rodney Robinson, Landscape Architects.

(PHOTO: Michele Adams)

- Highly effective topsoil treatment
- Less energy and chemical use
- Reclamation of otherwise wasted nutrients, helping to improve land fertility

WATER-SAVING FIXTURES Using water-saving fixtures can reduce water use and cost significantly. About 70% of the total water used in the home and offices is for toilet flushing, laundry, and baths. Water-saving fixtures are stand-ard options on such appliances, indicated by Environmental Protection Agency (EPA) ENERGY STAR ratings. Water use can be cut as much as 90% in some cases.

Design for Moderate Rainfalls

In moderate rainfall events between 0.5 and 1.5 inches (1.3 to 3.8 cm), altered landscapes such as lawns will begin to generate runoff, and runoff will continue to be generated from impervious surfaces. A natural landscape will absorb most of the rainfall in this category. Resilient design focuses on re-creating landscapes that can improve water capture or on designing structural measures that can capture water for infiltration, evapotranspiration, or very slow release.

Individual stormwater interventions should be designed with a safe "overflow" during larger rainfalls, with overflows connected to convey water safely. In small rainfall events, the designed interventions will capture and hold water. As rainfall continues in larger events, the components are connected as a system that safely and slowly conveys water toward the stream system or, in urban environments, toward a storm sewer.

URBAN FORESTRY AND REDUCTION OF LAWNSCAPE *Lawn areas* can be nearly as impervi-ous as pavement. If allowed to return to more naturalized state appropriate to the region, such as wildflower meadow or xeriscape, lawns can help reduce and retain runoff. Lawn areas provide outdoor activity space, so they serve a necessary function for recreation. Grading to direct the runoff from lawns toward natural planting areas will help to reduce lawn runoff. Existing soils can be amended to improve porosity, organic matter, and nutrients by decompaction and addition of organic matter rototilled into existing soils.

Where appropriate, replacing lawn and turf grass with tall grasses and other meadow vegetation greatly reduces the volume and velocity of stormwater runoff, especially on slopes. Meadow areas can be established to reduce mowing needs to twice per year (spring and fall) to avoid soil compaction. Lawns often attract geese, adding to pollution and runoff. Wildflower meadows substantially reduce watering and mowing maintenance. (Figure 6.8.)

Reestablishment of forest with understory, such as native shrubs and trees, restores natural hydrologic functions. Reforestation along streams and swales will provide additional benefit by creating a riparian buffer and reducing the runoff from developed areas, improving water quality, and providing shade for headwater streams.

Trees are indicators of a community's ecological health. When trees are large and healthy, the ecological systems that support them—soil, air, and water—are also healthy. The greater the tree cover and the less the impervious surface, the more ecosystem services are produced: reducing stormwater runoff, increasing air and water quality, storing and sequestering atmospheric carbon, and reducing energy consumption due to direct shading of residential buildings.[1]

NATIVE PLANTING   Once established, native planting requires little or no maintenance and is a cost-effective measure by which to reduce municipal costs and improve environmental benefits by replacing traditional lawn planting and care. Native plants grow well together—they evolved growing alongside one another—and to predictable sizes. In most prevailing conditions, native planting does not need watering (except during initial planting), nor do they require chemical fertilizers or any commercial biocides—herbicides, insecticides, and fungicides. They are adapted to local conditions and resistant to local insects. In contrast, manicured lawns and bark-mulch

Figure 6.8   *Lawn versus wildflower meadow:* Twin Brooks Park Trumbull, Connecticut.
(PHOTO: Donald Watson)

beds typical of commercial landscapes rely on synthetic chemicals, pesticides, and fertilizers. Additional negative impacts of traditional landscape include noise and air pollution from lawn cutting, which emits exhaust fumes and airborne chemicals.

Part of watershed management is to reduce pollutants from stormwater surges, especially those that flood lawn and agricultural areas that carry fertilizers, chemical pesticides, and other toxins into adjacent water bodies. Reducing and eliminating the source pollutants increases the effectiveness of native planting, riparian buffers, and access to water for recreation.

ALTERNATIVES FOR DEICING The common practice of deicing roadways, parking lots, and sidewalks has environmental impacts, adding to pollution of runoff and eventually stream and ground water systems. Of the commonly used deicing chemicals, *sodium chloride* (rock salt) is most harmful to watercourses and

most corrosive to building materials (often tracked into entryways and lobbies). *Calcium chloride* may result in similar but less severe detrimental impacts. Many management approaches combine deicing chemicals with other performance-improving agents to reduce corrosion or to increase traction. Other chemicals have been developed but may not be as effective at low temperatures. *Calcium magnesium acetate* (CMA) is least damaging but must be applied before snowfall and often continuously during snow removal. (Table 6.1.)

Sanding is an alternative and/or supplementary measure. Sand typically accumulates along edges of roads and walkways over a winter season and eventually may find its way into watercourses, adding to stream siltation and pollution.

Because of issues of safety and the severe risks of ice storms and snow blizzards, concerns about the environmental and water quality impacts are typically subsumed in snow and ice management necessary to ensure life safety

TABLE 6.1 COMMON DEICING CHEMICALS

Product	Lowest effective temperature	Method	Performance	Longevity	Corrosiveness	Concrete freeze/thaw resistance damage
Sodium Chloride (Rock Salt)	12°F	Melting	Very Good	Low	Very High	High
Calcium Chloride	–20°F	Melting	Excellent	Moderate	Moderate to High	Moderate to High
Magnesium Chloride	5°F	Melting	Good	Low	Low	Low
Potassium Chloride	12°F	Melting	Good	Low	Low	Low
Calcium Magnesium Acetate (CMA)	20°F	Loosening	Good (dependent on snow removal frequency)	High	None	None
Urea	15°F	Melting	Used only in special circumstances (e.g., runways)	Low	None	None

Source: Lawrence E. Keenan, AIA, PE, Hoffmann Architects.

for motor vehicle occupants and pedestrians. There are no perfect solutions. Nonetheless, the impacts of both salt and sand deicing measures should be addressed in a due diligence approach to watershed design.

To reduce risks associated with ice conditions, architectural and landscape measures should be considered to increase safety for drivers and pedestrians at site parking, drop-offs, and building entryways. Measures include abrasive surfaces (as might be provided by porous paving and gravel road and walkways), handrails along paths and exterior stairs, and ground lighting at transition points and covered drop-off areas. There may also be opportunity to use waste heat or solar thermal heat for snow melting at building entrances.

RAIN GARDENS AND SMALL BIORE-TENTION AREAS

A rain garden, also called a *bioretention area*, is a shallow depression intended to capture and soak up runoff from roofs or other impervious areas around buildings, driveways, walkways, and even compacted lawn areas. Rain gardens help to manage small storm events. They can be constructed with a subsurface sand or gravel bed for additional water storage capacity and an overflow to relieve larger rainfall events.

A rain garden typically is filled with several feet of amended soils and planted with native vegetation. The vegetation should be tolerant of salt and temperature changes (if exposed to road and parking runoff) and wet and dry conditions. Rain gardens become very wet when it rains but dry out between storms. Within these guidelines, rain garden can be richly planted with native trees, shrubs, flowers, and grasses. Rain gardens can be placed in lawn areas, in islands of paved areas, along roadways, and in other small open spaces adjacent to impervious surfaces. (Figure 6.9.)

SUBSURFACE INFILTRATION BEDS AND DRYWELLS

Subsurface infiltration beds are used for the temporary storage and infiltration of stormwater runoff and consist of a vegetated pervious soil layer or porous pavement layer placed above a uniformly open-graded aggregate bed. The aggregate has 40% void space and provides for the storage and slow infiltration of water. Subsurface infiltration beds are especially suited for expansive flat areas, such as athletic fields, and beneath parking lots, reducing site disturbance and managing the water within the built environment. Subsurface infiltration beds can be used on a slope if the beds are terraced or stepped. The base of the bed must be installed and remain level to distribute and infiltrate the water uniformly. (Figure 6.10.)

A drywell is a small, subsurface infiltration pit or chamber that is used to collect roof runoff from the downspouts of individual buildings. A drywell can consist of an excavated pit filled with clean-washed aggregate

Figure 6.9a *Rain gardens* at Penn State University Visitors Center retain roof runoff.

(PHOTO: Michele Adams)

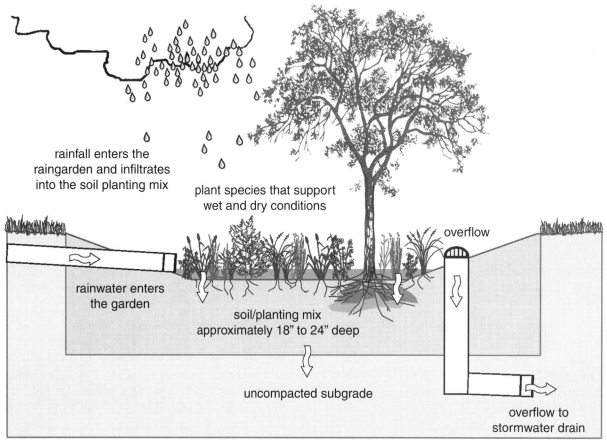

rainfall enters the
raingarden and infiltrates
into the soil planting mix

plant species that support
wet and dry conditions

overflow

rainwater enters
the garden

soil/planting mix
approximately 18" to 24" deep

uncompacted subgrade

overflow to
stormwater drain

Figure 6.9b   *Bioretention swale* schematic.

wrapped in nonwoven geotextile filter fabric, or it may be constructed from prefabricated storage chambers. Drywells may be located under planting areas, paths, or other uses and can be incorporated into the footprint of project disturbance. Drywells can be used at any site where there is a structure with roof leaders, soils with a sufficient infiltration rate, and adequate space to place them away from structure foundations.

INFILTRATION TRENCH   An infiltration trench is a linear infiltration bed that is used to capture, store, and infiltrate stormwater runoff in small storms but to convey water in larger storms via a perforated pipe. Infiltration trenches are best installed along a contour with a level or mild slope, and can be installed below a vegetated swale system to enhance its volume capacity. Impervious areas can be directed to an infiltration trench to distribute stormwater runoff.

TREE TRENCHES AND STRUCTURAL SOIL CELLS   A *tree trench* is a linear water management feature consisting of trees planted in amended planting soils designed to capture runoff from adjacent impervious areas. Tree trenches are suitable in linear areas with limited space to manage stormwater, such as along streets. In addition to managing stormwater, tree trenches enhance aesthetics by providing greening, improving air quality, and reducing the urban heat island effect. Tree trenches are cost effective as a stormwater and landscape improvement in highly developed areas and along roads. By providing soil and water availability to tree root bulbs, tree trenches facilitate healthier and longer-lasting urban treescapes. (Figure 6.11.)

Structural soil cells—types of grates or containers placed directly under a tree bulb—protect the hydric zone of the tree root soil against compression and help to ensure

Figure 6.10 *Infiltration bed* beneath playfield during and after construction at the Sadie Tanner Mosell Alexander School in Philadelphia.

(PHOTOS: Michele Adams)

long-term porosity.[2] As in tree trenching, tree roots are watered more directly, reducing requirements for the size of the soil bulb, while allowing paving (preferably porous) closer to the trees. With breathing and wetting room, soils do not break, expand, and push paving above grade, a typical result of urban sidewalk tree planters without such installations. As with tree trenches, soil cells make possible a full tree landscaping as part of stormwater measures within urban streets and parking areas (Figure 6.12.)

STREET BUMP-OUTS   Also knows as *curb exten-sions*, street bump-outs involve the widening of a typical

curb to create a small landscaped space to temporarily store, filter, and possibly infiltrate runoff from streets. Street bump-outs can be implemented in any street of adequate width but often are most effective at intersections to collect as much runoff as possible while improving pedestrian conditions. In addition to enhancing street aesthetics and providing stormwater management, street bump-outs provide traffic calming, which improves pedestrian safety.

Street bump-outs are constructed of formed concrete curb adjacent to the standard curb line in a long narrow strip with rounded ends. The center area of the

Figure 6.11a   Tree trench installation provides runoff water through porous concrete sidewalk at the Waterview Recreation Center, Philadelphia.

(PHOTO: Michele Adams)

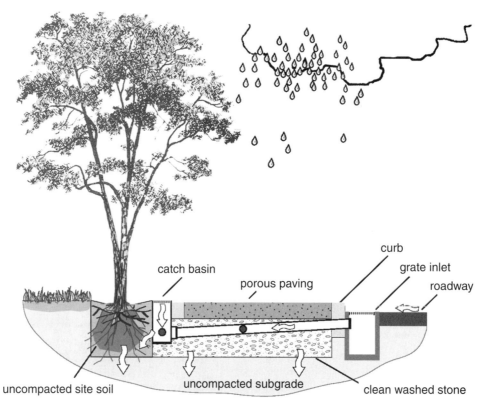

Figure 6.11b   Tree trench system schematic.

Figure 6.12a *Structural soil cells* and permeable paving installed under trees in an urban streetscape.
(PHOTO: Casey Trees)

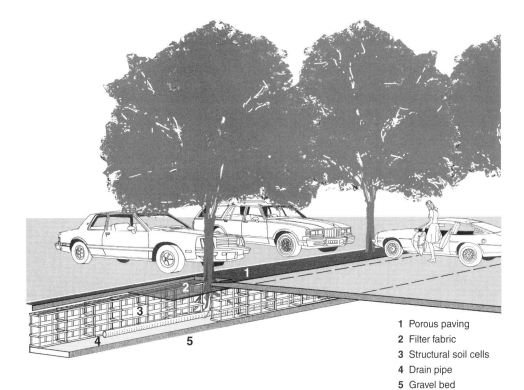

1 Porous paving
2 Filter fabric
3 Structural soil cells
4 Drain pipe
5 Gravel bed

Figure 6.12b *Greening of the city:* Structural soil cells create stormwater retention and tree root protection and watering for heavily trafficked areas.

(DeepRoot Urban Landscape Products Silva Cell Technical Bulletin)

bump-out should be excavated and filled with modified soils. The bottom of the planting area can be lined with an underdrain if infiltration is not feasible at the site. The soil mix should be high in nutrients, organic matter, and absorptive properties. Plants, which may be grasses, shrubs, and/or trees, selected for a vegetated swale should be native and salt tolerant and have a high potential for pollutant removal. Bump-outs are most cost effective along streets with minimal grade change (4% or less). Runoff can be directed into a street-bump via sheet flow through curb cuts, trench drain, or pipe. An overflow outlet is required for large storm events. (Figure 6.13.)

Design for Large Rainfalls

In large rainfall events from 1.5 to 3 inches (3.8 to 7.6 cm), a natural system of forest or prairie will begin to generate runoff. However, this runoff is slowed and stored in topographic depressions and small swales, along headwater streams, and in local wetland areas. The rate at which water moves through the landscape before reaching a stream is slowed and moderated.

RETENTIVE GRADING   refers to techniques that replicate the slowing of water in its movement toward the stream or storm sewer. Localized conveyance can be

Figure 6.13   *Street bump-out* accommodates stormwater retention in Portland, Oregon.

(PHOTO: Maria Cahill, Green Girl LDS)

achieved through secondary systems such as graded swales and depressions that replicate how a natural system conveys large events. Concentrated flow and overloaded inlets and pipes can be avoided or reduced. At the small scale, grading can create small depressions "fill" to fill with runoff and then continue in a network of swails to convey runoff from larger events. For example, grading in a manner that allows short periods of ponding in swales and drainage components, placed to avoid erosion or other damage, creates a slower, safer movement of runoff. Areas between buildings can be graded to allow temporary ponding or surface flow of water if done in a manner to protect structures and site features.

At the larger scale, remote areas of parking lots that are used infrequently are ideal areas for retentive grading. Grading can be done such that in extreme storm events, these areas provide several inches of water storage for a few hours, as necessary. The temporary inconvenience of local ponding in infrequently used areas can significantly reduce downstream flooding and impacts. Similarly, athletic playfields and public gathering spaces can be designed to detain water during storm events temporarily when they are unlikely to be used. Combining vegetation with retentive grading reduces runoff volumes, slows the flow, and removes pollutants.

VEGETATED SWALE   Also called a *bioswale*, a vegetated swale is an uncompacted, vegetated, unlined runoff channel that is shallow and planted with native grasses, shrubs, and/or trees that are drought and salt tolerant and have a high potential for water and pollutant uptake. A vegetated swale is a larger extension of the rain garden or bioretention area described earlier.

Vegetated swales convey water at a slower velocity and provide water storage on a temporary basis. Check dams constructed from wood, concrete, or stone in a vegetated swale can further slow the rate of flow, preventing erosion and providing temporary detention. The flow path, winding within the wide and shallow ditch, is designed to maximize the time water spends in the swale, which aids in filtering pollutants and silt.

As in a rain garden, plants act as biofilters, removing phosphorous, soil sediments, and other pollutants. Several classes of water pollutants may be arrested with bioswales, including silt, inorganic contaminants, organic chemicals, and pathogens. Water seeping from a bioswale typically is cleaner than when it came in. Vegetated swales are appropriate in areas with linear open space adjacent to impervious surfaces, such as around buildings, roadways, sidewalks, and parking lots. (Figure 6.14.)

Design for Extreme Events

During larger rainfalls and extreme events greater than 3 inches (7.6 cm), the capacity of any system, natural or man-made, to hold water eventually will be exceeded, and water will move downstream. In a natural system, the rate at which this runoff water moves downstream is buffered by wetlands, riparian buffers, and floodplains. These features serve to capture some volume of water and to slow the rate at which water moves to downstream locations.

If the *volume* of water from the smaller rainfall events is managed successfully at the site level, the need to control the rate of water is substantially reduced. Wetlands and floodplains serve to reduce flood damage on both site and watershed scale.

GREEN INFRASTRUCTURE   is a term that refers to the combination of stormwater, rain garden, tree planting, and other flood measures with public circulation networks, including parking, sidewalks, and utility rights-of-way. Combining elements of natural landscape—wildlife corridors, trees, bioswales, buffer zones, and parks—with pedestrian-safe and bike trails creates opportunities for stormwater management and amenities of community-wide greenways.[3]

RIPARIAN BUFFERS   are areas established by setbacks from streams, rivers, and wetlands. A *riparian buffer* preserves the stream's natural characteristics. It filters sediments, nutrients, and chemicals from surface runoff and shallow groundwater. Riparian buffers create opportunities for *wildlife corridors* for animals and plants. Birds and other animals find protective cover, water, food, and nesting sites and pathways between other open space areas. Native plants require fertile areas to propagate and extend their reseeding.

The width of setback for a riparian buffer often is determined by state and local wetland regulations, very typically established as 100 feet wide from a water course or wetland edge, so that a stream might have a total of 200 feet of riparian corridor. (Figure 6.15.)

The setback line established by local zoning or wetland regulations is defined as a "regulated area," requiring approval for development within the setback by local authorities. The "science" that establishes 100 feet as a

Figure 6.14a *Vegetated swale and rain garden* constructed within a preexisting foundation defines the entry courtyard at Rogers International School, Stamford, Connecticut. Tai Soo Kim Partners Architects.

(PHOTO: Donald Watson)

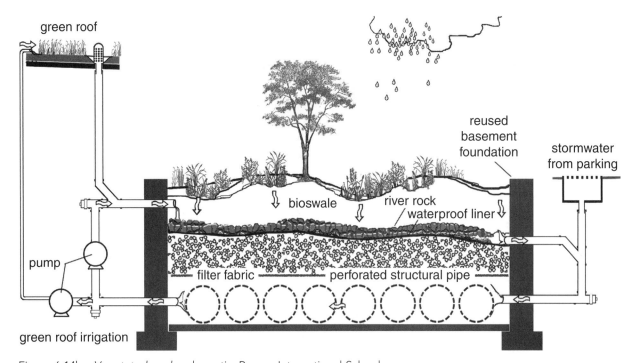

Figure 6.14b *Vegetated swale* schematic. Rogers International School.

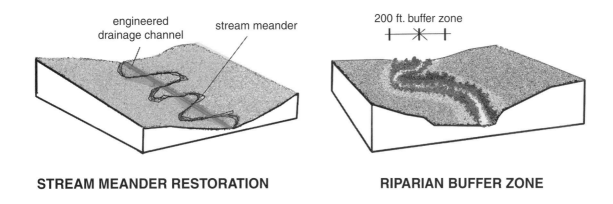

STREAM MEANDER RESTORATION   **RIPARIAN BUFFER ZONE**

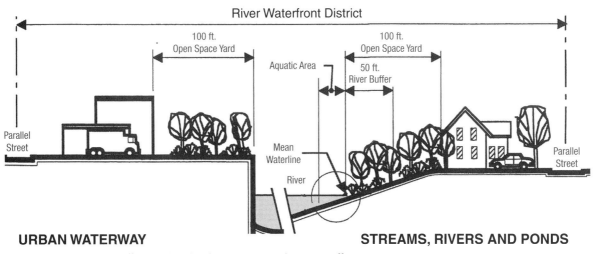

URBAN WATERWAY   **STREAMS, RIVERS AND PONDS**

Figure 6.15 *Riparian buffers and setbacks* are among the most effective Best Management Practices in protecting and improving flood control and water resources.

Source: Donald Watson, ed., *Time-Saver Standards for Urban Design* (New York: McGraw-Hill, 2003).

minimum required for the ecological vitality of a buffer is subject to interpretation. The determination of setback may also be based on local assessment of the specific site conditions, often leading to reduced setbacks in areas that do not otherwise threaten the health of the wetland or riparian zone. In many instances, it should be a larger setback and protected area. Local review boards are often lenient in allowing development within regulated setback areas. The goal of water resource protection and enhancement normally should impose restrictions on any alteration that limits the capacity of the wetland and its surround to control flooding and preserve water quality and habitat.

Riparian buffers can be connected within a community to provide "corridors" for wildlife and for native plant propagation. Greenway and trail projects can be ideal ways to restore and link riparian buffers.

WETLAND PROTECTION AND RESTORATION
A wetland is an exquisitely complex biological system that cleans water and air and provides a natural sponge for varying water flows and an ideal habitat for wildlife (amphibians and birds) that supply natural means of insect and pest control.

Where some detention is required for large storm events, newly created wetland areas will improve water quality and create habitat while providing detention. It is important that any created wetland be designed to be shallow with littoral shelves to encourage the healthy establishment of aquatic vegetation, with a steady source of water flow to prevent stagnant conditions.

Appropriate drainage is needed in order to optimize hydraulic behavior, water quality improvement, and biodiversity increase. Moderate vegetation density does not hinder the flow but rather increases dispersion. A proper design has to avoid hydraulic short-circuiting and provide a good distribution of the flow in vegetated zones. Reconstructed wetlands can be part of a nature park, available to schools for science-based educational programs and to the entire community for passive recreation. (Figure 6.16.)

PERMACULTURE/COMMUNITY-BASED AGRICULTURE

Urban farming benefits the interests of sound use of water resources and local food availability, that is, water security and food security. Food-producing plots in urban areas offer conservation advantages in monitored water irrigation and hydroponics, efficient use of compost along with other economic, and community benefits. Organic growers, community farm markets, and permaculture promote ecological approaches to urban farming advocates, wherein the entire food chain is managed in ecological terms.

Figure 6.16 *Constructed wetland* within former gravel pit.
(PHOTO: Donald Watson)

ECOLOGICAL WASTEWATER TREATMENT SYSTEMS Ecological wastewater treatment is a multi-stage process to remediate wastewater with biological processes before it reenters a body of water, applied to the land, or reused. Ecological treatment systems recover nutrients and reduce the environmental impact of wastewater (often referred to as "black water"). Building and community-scale systems include dry composting, biofiltration tanks, reed beds, and constructed wetlands. (Figure 6.17.)

Rainwater harvesting, stormwater treatment, and bioremediation of the campus including farm area runoff are combined in the design of the John T. Lyle Center for Regenerative Studies, California State University-Pomona.[4] (Dougherty + Dougherty Architects, LLP.)

COMBINED SEWER OVERFLOWS Combined sewer systems are site or district installations designed to collect rainwater runoff, domestic sewage, and industrial wastewater in the same pipe. Most of the time, combined sewer systems transport all of their wastewater to a sewage treatment plant, where it is treated and then discharged to a water body. During periods of heavy rainfall or snowmelt, the wastewater volume in a combined sewer system can exceed the capacity of the sewer system or treatment plant. For this reason, combined sewer systems are designed to overflow occasionally and discharge excess wastewater directly to nearby streams, rivers, or other water bodies. These overflows, called *combined sewer overflows*, contain stormwater but also untreated human and industrial waste, toxic materials, and debris. They are a major water pollution concern for more than 770 cities in the United States that have combined sewer systems. Watershed remediation requires change to EPA compliance requirements in order to credit distributed low-impact wastewater solutions and to encourage distributed storage approaches.

Figure 6.17a   Planter boxes, trellises, and rain gardens.

Figure 6.17b   Settling pond for first-stage
bioremediation.

Figure 6.17c   Constructed wetland.
(PHOTOS: Donald Watson)

EDUCATIONAL AND INTERPRETIVE FEATURES Watershed education is essential in promoting public understanding of water as a resource and the values of watershed design and management. Water is one of the basic raw materials for learning mathematics and science, developing language, and fostering social skills. A watershed design is best conveyed by the visible design measures supplemented by engaging interpretive settings (Figure 6.18) and watershed model displays (Figure 6.19).

6.2 TOOLS FOR WATERSHED PROTECTION

The BMPs and measures for watershed protection described in this chapter can be implemented by design of projects from smallest to largest scales. Just as flooding is created or increased by small changes in the land—"death by a thousand cuts"–remediation can be undertaken by individual actions at any scale.

Currently, most ecosystem and wildlife protection is achieved by legal tools that were devised before water and flooding became predominant concerns. They were not designed specifically to accomplish water quality and flood protection goals. For example, development that impinges wetlands and wetland-dependent species is regulated through laws and review processes established to permit activities within wetland setbacks or regulated areas. Uplands, including headwater streams and vernal pools, are not governed by wetland regulations. Approvals occur on a site-by-site basis. While every opportunity for watershed protection is important, these gain the greatest support as part the larger issues of community ecosystem health, habitat scale, and need for connectivity.

Figure 6.18 *Wayfinding and interpretive design.* Oregon Coastal Aquarium, Newport, Oregon: A stream parallels the pathway from parking to building entry and is represented as the way-finding "blue thread" through the exhibits. Fulton Gale Architects/SRG Architects.

(PHOTO: Donald Watson)

Figure 6.19 *Watershed exhibit.* Aquarium of the Pacific, Long Beach, California, allows visitors to trigger a "rainfall" within a large-dimensional model of the watersheds of greater Los Angeles. Main Street Exhibit Design.

(PHOTO: Aquarium of The Pacific)

In making the case for protection of wetlands and water-sheds, evidence that is presented as expert testimony in public hearings and reviews must be science-based, demonstrating the environmental impacts of development proposals. Claims for and against specific design and development proposals are part of this testimony. The several reports cited below provide valuable reference for such presentations.

A broad range of studies describing the assessment of values that communities and residents assign to open spaces—including wetlands, greenways, and farmland—are reviewed in "The Value of Open Space," a 2005 Report published by Resources for the Future. The report discusses advantages and disadvantages of methods used to represent how open space is valued in both qualitative and economic terms, along with a state-of-the-art review of present research on the values of conservation areas. Perceived benefits of open space while generally positive vary depending upon their type and location within a community. Wetlands in urban and suburban locations and those showing more open water are considered valuable, more than those in rural locations. Bird and fish habitat and protection of water quality rank as important attributes.[5]

New legislative models respond to the needs and opportunities of conservation area protection and community planning. The Conservation Overlay District developed by the New York Metropolitan Conservation Alliance provides a model ordinance to support adoption of watershed and ecosystem measures.[6] It is intended to supplement rather than replace existing regulations. Such approaches combine recreation and community values with measures that reduce habitat fragmentation, maintain biodiversity, and protect significant natural features.

The range of applications of Conservation Overlay District model is represented in the City of Boston's Groundwater Conservation Overlay District (GCOD), enacted in 2006 as Boston Zoning Code Article 32. The legislation provides for monitoring of groundwater levels and appropriate regulation in areas of Boston where receding groundwater threatens the extensive wood pilings that underpin many of the city's structures, susceptible to rot as a result of changes in groundwater levels.[7]

The following box provides a summary of the discussion in this and prior chapters on the role of the natural and altered landscape to mitigate flooding.

FINDINGS OF FACT: WATERSHED ECOSYSTEM SERVICES THAT DIRECTLY INFLUENCE HEALTH, SAFETY, AND WELFARE

Wetlands, Water Bodies, Watercourses

1. Wetlands and watercourses serve multiple functions, including:

   a. Provide surface water, recharge groundwater and aquifers, serve as chemical and biological oxidation basins, and function as settling basins for naturally occurring sedimentation.

   b. Control flooding and stormwater runoff by regulating natural flows, storing water, and desynchronizing flows.

   c. Provide critical nesting, migratory stopover, and over-wintering habitats for a diversity of wildlife.

   d. Support unique vegetative associations of various types.

   e. Provide areas of unusually high plant productivity, which support significant wildlife diversity and abundance.

   f. Provide breeding and spawning grounds, nursery habitat, and food for various species of fish and amphibians.

   g. Serve as nutrient traps for nitrogen and phosphorous and act as filters for surface water pollutants.

   h. Help to maintain biospheric stability by supporting particularly efficient photosynthesizers capable of producing significant amounts of oxygen and supporting bacteria that process excess nitrates and nitrogenous pollutants and return them to the atmosphere as inert nitrogen gas.

   i. Provide open space and visual relief from intense land development.

   j. Serve as outdoor laboratories for the study of natural history, ecology, and biology.

Floodplains

1. Floodplains temporarily store water and decrease storm velocity. These functions are enhanced by vegetation that enables water to spread horizontally and move more slowly.

2. Floodplains help control runoff, decrease the potential for catastrophic flooding, and allow for the infiltration of water into the groundwater table.

3. Floodplains capture and sequester sediment and nutrients, thereby enhancing the quality of water.

4. Floodplain trees and plants stabilize riverbanks, thereby reducing erosion.

5. Floodplains provide critical habitat for wildlife and aquatic species, including resting, feeding, and nesting areas. These areas provide a transition zone between watercourses and uplands.

6. Damage from flooding and erosion can be extensive, including destruction or loss of housing, public facilities, and injury to and loss of human life.

Aquifers

1. Aquifers store water for varying periods of time, acting as underground reservoirs.

2. Springs and spring-fed habitats are important for various species.

3. Aquifers contribute significantly to surface water and are important to sustaining vegetation.

4. Activities that prevent infiltration into aquifers cause increased runoff.

5. The groundwater underlying the conservation area district is a major source of existing and potential future groundwater supply, including drinking water and, as such, should be protected from contamination.

6. Unregulated development in areas with sensitive hydrogeologic formations of stratified drift aquifers and their primary recharge areas may threaten the quality of such groundwater supplies and related water resources in the conservation area's district, posing potential public health and safety hazards.

7. Preventive measures are needed to control the development of land and to control the discharge and storage of hazardous materials within the hydrologic formations to limit their adverse impacts.

Steep Slopes

1. Steep slopes are environmentally sensitive landforms and valuable natural resources that are of benefit to the entire community and the surrounding region. The environmental sensitivity of steep slopes often results from such features as shallow soils over bedrock, bedrock features, groundwater seeps, or watercourses and wetlands found on or adjacent to steep slopes.

2. Destruction of steep slopes by unregulated regrading, filling, excavation, building, clearing, and other such acts is inconsistent with the natural condition or acceptable uses of steep slopes. Steep slopes provide critical habitat for some wildlife species.

3. Effective protection of steep slopes requires preservation. Where steep slopes must be disturbed, careful regulation, including stringent mitigating measures of disturbance of soil and vegetation on steep slopes, is necessary.

4. Improper management of disturbances to steep slopes can aggravate erosion and sedimentation beyond rates experienced in natural geomorphological processes. Erosion and sedimentation often include the loss of topsoil, a valuable natural resource, and can result in the disturbance of habitats, alteration of drainage patterns, obstruction of drainage structures, damage to surface and subsurface hydrology, and intensification of flooding.

5. Inadequate control of disturbances to steep slopes can lead to the failure of slopes and mass movement of earth; damage to natural environment and man-made structures; risks to personal safety; and the loss of landscapes.

Woodlands, Forests, and Trees

1. Preservation and maintenance of trees are necessary to protect the health, safety, environment, and welfare.

2. Trees provide necessary shade and cooling, greenscape, and aesthetic appeal. They impede soil erosion, aid water absorption, and generally enhance the quality of life within a community.

3. Forests and stands of trees provide important habitat for wildlife. Forests and plants provide important ecosystem functions, such as carbon sequestration, filtering pollutants, moderating climate, and surface runoff.

4. The destruction and damage of trees and the indiscriminate and excessive cutting

of trees causes barren and unsightly conditions, creates surface drainage problems, increases municipal costs to control drainage, impairs stability of real property values, and adversely affects the character of the community.

Wildlife and Habitat

1. Areas that contain a diversity of wildlife species are a natural resource of local, state, national, and global significance.

2. Wildlife plays important roles in maintaining ecosystems through ecological interactions such as predation, pollination, and seed dispersal.

3. Wildlife provides valuable educational and recreational opportunities.

4. Wildlife populations can be sustained only if adequate measures are taken to maintain the habitats they require and the ecological connections between these habitats. Habitat protection enables wildlife to persist in a region as well as enabling the continuation of vital natural processes.

5. Poorly planned land development causes the fragmentation and reduces the functioning of habitat.

6. The effective protection of ecosystems is dependent on a basic understanding that few ecosystems are wholly contained within one municipality. Intergovernmental cooperation is necessary to ensure that ecologically sensitive landscapes are protected and maintained.

Source: Patricia Black, ed., *Conservation Area Overlay District: A Model Local Law*, Technical Paper Series No. 3 (Bronx, NY: Metropolitan Conservation Alliance, 2002). www.ecostudies.org/mca_technical_papers.html.

6.3 COMMUNITIES AND BUILDINGS IN FLOODPLAINS

Watershed design and management should strictly limit, if not prohibit, the location and construction of new structures in existing floodplains. To restore the functions of natural landscapes and water systems, it is essential to stop the harm and to avoid construction that would in any way reduce the floodwater storage and carrying capacity of floodplains. In urban areas, past development typically has already occurred within the floodplain. With increased development, the floodplain capacities are decreased and areas of flooding are increasing. Any development or upgrading of properties and structures within or near the floodplain should be required to protect or replace ecosystem services lost by altering the land. For urban areas, floodplain development must be designed carefully to protect structures and human health. Resilient design approaches require retrofit provisions for flood mitigation and control, including preparations for emergency evacuation.

Where streams have become disconnected from the floodplain, careful restoration of the stream channel and reconnection of the channel to the floodplain can return flood mitigation benefits. Successful restoration efforts tend to be substantial areas, involving at least several hundred feet of stream channel length. Floodplain restoration often is undertaken by larger municipal entities or government agencies.

Floodplain restoration can reduce flooding impacts in areas that are already urbanized. Open space, such as public lands along urban stream corridors, provides ideal locations for floodplain restoration as the stream corridor is under the control of a single entity. Restoration projects require a multidisciplinary design team including biologists, geomorphology experts, and hydrologists.

The EPA has issued guidelines that require federal project stormwater design to retain small events—95th percentile, or about 1.5 inches (3.8 cm)—within the site or otherwise to design for a "water balance" equal to its natural (pre-Columbian) state before any disturbance occurred.[8] Local regulations often mandate such design to comply with Federal Emergency Management Agency (FEMA) requirements. The regulatory and design requirements for flood control and flood-resistant design are presented in Part III of this book.

Notes

1. U.S. Department of Agriculture Forest Service, *Urban Watershed Forestry Manual* (September 2006), www.na.fs.fed.us/watershed/.../Urban%20Watershed%20Forestry%20Manual%20Part%203.pdf.

2. James Urban, Up by Roots: Healthy Soils and Trees in the Built Environment (Champaign, IL: International Society of Arboriculture, 2008).

3. U.S. Environmental Protection Agency, *Green Infrastructure Municipal Handbook*, Monograph Series, 2009, http://cfpub.epa.gov/npdes/greeninfrastructure/munichandbook.cfm.

4. For a user assessment of the J.T. Lyle Center, see S. R. Stine and W. B. Stine. "People, Place and Solar Possibilities," 2001, www.powerfromthesun.net/jtlyle-center.htm.

5. Virginia McConnell and Margaret Walls. "The Value of Open Space: Evidence from Studies of Nonmarket Benefits. Resources for the Future. January 2005. www.rff.org/Documents/RFF-REPORT-Open%20Spaces.pdf.

6. Patricia Black, ed., Conservation Area Overlay District: A Model Local Law, Technical Paper Series No. 3 (Bronx, NY: Metropolitan Conservation Alliance, 2002).

7. Boston Groundwater Conservation Overlay District. 2006. www.bostongroundwater.org/gcod.html.

8. U.S. EPA, Office of Water, "Technical Guidance on Implementing the Stormwater Runoff Requirements for Federal Projects under Section 438 of the Energy Independence and Security Act" (December 2009). www.epa.gov/owow/NPS/lid/section438/pdf/final_sec438_eisa.pdf.

PART III

FLOOD-RESISTANT DESIGN

Donald Watson, FAIA, and James Destefano, AIA, P.E., Structural Engineer

We can prepare for flooding, natural disasters, and climate change events by flood-resistant design of our floodplains and coastal communities and buildings.

The best thing one can do when it's raining is to let it rain.

—*Henry Wadsworth Longfellow, nineteenth century.*

CHAPTER 7   Flood Design Analysis

CHAPTER 8   The Coast

CHAPTER 9   Flood Design Practices for Buildings

IMPACT OF COASTAL FLOODING

Lessons of Katrina August 2007

Hurricane Katrina was one of the strongest storms to impact the coast of the United States during the past 100 years. Katrina reached Category 5 level over the Gulf of Mexico, weakened, and made landfall in Louisiana and Mississippi with strong Category 3 storm winds. The storm surge, however, did not diminish before landfall, and the record surge caused widespread devastation in the coastal areas of Alabama, Louisiana, and Mississippi. The storm surge caused failures of the levee system that protects the City of New Orleans from Lake Pontchartrain. Subsequently, 80% of the city flooded. (Figure C-15.)

Prior to Hurricane Katrina, Alabama, Louisiana, and Mississippi did not have statewide building codes for non-state-owned buildings. Many of the communities in areas that were heavily impacted by Hurricane Katrina either had not adopted up-to-date model building codes that incorporated flood and wind protection or had no building codes at all.

Storm surge and wave crest elevations from Hurricane Katrina exceeded the mapped base flood elevations (BFEs) in many coastal areas of the three states. The elevation of a building was the most critical factor in its success at withstanding the storm surge. In cases where Katrina's surge and waves rose above foundations and impacted floor beams and walls, most buildings were destroyed, regardless of foundation type.

The failure of levees and floodwalls that protect the City of New Orleans resulted in catastrophic flooding in the Greater New Orleans area, with flooding in many areas up to 8 feet above the lowest floor of the building. BFEs for the levee-protected area are determined based on the certification that the levee will provide protection from the base flood event. Many buildings constructed with the first-floor elevation above the BFE were severely damaged or destroyed when the floodwaters rose well above the first floor. The duration of the floodwaters in New Orleans contributed to further damages; some areas remained underwater for several weeks, which saturated some building materials beyond the point where they could be salvaged and contaminated them with chemical and biological substances in the floodwaters. The rampant growth of mold in flood-saturated buildings was another evident result of flooding.

Significance of Hurricane Katrina

Hurricane Katrina was the most severe hurricane to strike the Louisiana/Mississippi Gulf Coast since Hurricane Camille in 1969 and the most significant hurricane to strike the New Orleans area since Hurricane Betsy in 1965.

- Katrina exceeded the BFEs by as much as 15 feet (4.5 m) along parts of the Louisiana and Mississippi Gulf Coast. Flooding extended well beyond the inland limits of designated flood-prone areas and the highest storm surge in U.S. history was recorded on the Mississippi coast.

- The American Red Cross estimated that Katrina destroyed over 300,000 single-family homes throughout Louisiana and Mississippi.

- Coastal flood impacts covered a wide area, with severe flood damage extending along coastal Alabama and totally destroying over 100 houses on Dauphin Island.

- Levee failures led to severe flood damage throughout the City of New Orleans and surrounding areas of Plaquemines and St. Bernard parishes. Hundreds of thousands of people were displaced due to damage caused by the flooding.

- Katrina's wind speeds were less than the current code-specified speeds required for structural design for wind-resistance in most areas. Nonetheless, wind damage to both commercial and residential buildings was widespread throughout the southern portions of Louisiana and Mississippi.

- The operation of many critical and essential facilities was hampered or eliminated as a result of storm-induced damage or isolation due to coastal flooding.

- At least 1,836 people lost their lives in the hurricane and subsequent flooding. Damage estimates range upward of $100 billion. Four years later, thousands of displaced residents remain in temporary housing and trailers.

Source: Federal Emergency Management Agency, Summary Report on Building Performance Hurricane Katrina, 2005. FEMA 548 (April 2006).

Figure 7.1 *Atlantic coastal flooding at seasonal astronomical high tide.* Westhampton, Long Island, New York.

(PHOTO: © Robert Perron)

CHAPTER 7

FLOOD DESIGN ANALYSIS

Resilient design views flood-resistant design strategies at regional, community. and project site scale. One cannot be solved without the other. *Flood-resistant design* includes:

- **Prevention** by relocating buildings and community infrastructure out of harm's way and enhancing natural flood dissipation features of the land and coast.

- **Mitigation** by raising buildings above anticipated peak flood levels, engineering building structures and envelopes for severe wind and wave impacts, and using building materials that are waterproofed or otherwise impermeable to water damage.

7.1 DEFINITION OF TERMS

All regions of the United States experience flooding. *Riverine flooding* is the term of reference to describe inland flooding that results from precipitation overwhelming the base flow capacity of the watershed streams and rivers. *Coastal flooding* results from any combination of ocean storms, accompanying precipitation, tides, and storm surges. *Alluvial flooding* occurs in desert and mountain regions that may experience flash floods, in some cases with little recent or historic precedent. *Shallow flooding* can occur in any location.

- **Riverine flooding** is experienced in inland watersheds, including both slowly rising and accelerated force of river

flow in floodways close to the center of major streams and rivers. The history of Midwest and Mississippi floods covering river deltas across many states shows the extent of riverine flooding.

- **Coastal storm flooding** is experienced along coastline and shore areas subject to coastal storms, hurricanes, or tsunamis. Buildings in coastal areas generally have higher property values and thus higher risk exposure to storm damage and economic losses. In the United States, the rate of population growth has increased in coastal zones, imposing higher requirements for emergency preparedness and evacuation route capacities.

- **Alluvial fan and uncertain flow flooding** are experienced in desert and mountain regions where flash flood and mud flows occur and may follow uncertain, unmapped, and unpredicted paths. They occur in hilly or mountainous areas rich in sediments and where precipitation is not sufficient to carry the sediments downstream as rapidly as they accumulate. In the United States, these conditions exist primarily in the arid and semiarid regions west of the Great Plains, although there are alluvial fans in Alaska and Appalachia. *Flash floods* often emerge from canyon mouths and travel downstream at very high velocities, carrying water, sediment, and debris at great distances from the precipitation. They can also occur with spring snowmelt. The landward track of Hurricane Kathleen (shown in Figure 3.5) resulted in widespread alluvial fan and flash flood events in previously unmapped floodplains.[1]

- **Shallow flooding** is defined as flooding with an average depth of 1 to 3 feet (30 to 90 cm) in areas where a clearly defined channel does not exist. Shallow flooding can exist in any of these situations:

  - **Ponding**. In flat areas, water collects or "ponds" in depressions.
  - **Sheet flow**. In steeper areas where there are no defined channels or on flat plains, water will spread out over the land surface.
  - **Urban drainage**. Local drainage problems can be caused where runoff collects in yards or swales or when storm sewers back up.

Flooding events covered by the National Flood Insurance Program (NFIP) are defined as a "general and temporary condition during which the surface of normally dry land is partially or completely inundated. Two properties in the area or two or more acres must be affected." NFIP lists as causes of flooding:

- Overflow of inland or tidal waters
- Unusual and rapid accumulation or runoff of surface waters from any source, such as heavy rainfall
- Mudflow (i.e., a river of liquid and flowing mud on normally dry land areas)
- Collapse or subsidence of land along a lakeshore or other water body, resulting from erosion, waves, or water currents exceeding normal, cyclical levels[2]

A zone where repeated or hazardous flooding is likely to occur is designated as a Special Flood Hazard Area (SFHA). The SFHA designation imposes limits on developments through regulations defined by the NFIP. NFIP regulations establish the flood requirements that may apply to a building. Local governmental authorities are responsible for plan approvals and enforcement. (Figure 7.2.)

NFIP regulations[3] stipulate minimum requirements for building construction for:

- Height of lowest floor
- Installation of building utility systems
- Use of flood-resistant materials
- Use of the area below the lowest floor

Flood regulations adopted by local municipalities can be more restrictive than FEMA minimum requirements but not less restrictive. Flood regulations may vary from community to community even within the same coastal region. Requirements for flood resistant construction are also covered in local building codes by adoption of International Building Code International Residential Code codes of the International Code Council.

Limitations of NFIP Minimum Requirements

NFIP minimum requirements do not account for future changes in floodplains due to land development, coastal erosion, or sea level rise. And even if all NFIP requirements are met, large storm events or surge can impact a riverine or coastal site with flood levels well over the anticipated BFC. The limitations of minimum standards are recognized in the *No Adverse Impact Initiative* of the Association of State Floodplain Managers, which advocates "a new approach to dealing with the interaction of human beings and the environment that takes into account all aspects of both developed and natural systems."[4]

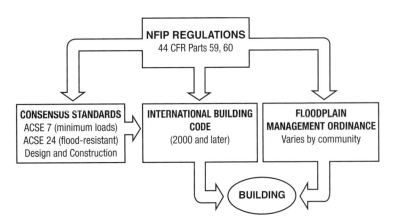

Figure 7.2   *NFIP Regulations* are incorporated into ordinances, codes, and standards.

Source: FEMA Mitigation Assessment Team Natural Disaster Reports, "Hurricane Ike in Texas and Louisiana: Building Performance Observations, Recommendations and Technical Guidance," FEMA P-757 (April 2009). www.fema.gov/library/viewRecord.do?id=3577.

DEFINITIONS OF THE FEDERAL EMERGENCY MANAGEMENT AGENCY (FEMA) PROGRAMS

National Flood Insurance Program (NFIP). A voluntary insurance program administered by FEMA to reduce loss of life and damage caused by flooding, to help flood recovery and promote equitable distribution of costs. Under the NFIP, substantially damaged and substantially improved buildings must meet flood-resistant construction requirements for new buildings. Damage to a building is considered "substantial" regardless of cause if the cost of restoring the building to its before-damage condition would equal or exceed 50% of the market value of the structure before the damage occurred.

Floodplain. Any land area susceptible to being inundated by water from any source.

Floodplain Management Regulations. The zoning ordinances, subdivision regulations, building codes, health regulations, special-purpose ordinances, emergency procedures, and other applications of enforcement used by a community to manage development in its floodplain areas.

Coastal Flood Hazard Area (CFHA). An area, usually along an open coast, bay, or inlet, subject to inundation by storm surge and, in some instances, wave action caused by storms or seismic forces.

Coastal Zone Management (CZM) Regulations, enacted 1972 and adopted by most coastal states, encourage adoption of coastal zone policies by U.S. coastal states in partnership with the federal government. Definition of each state's coastal zone boundary and interpretation of regulations varies and can be based on political jurisdictions or by natural features.

Special Flood Hazard Area (SFHA). Under NFIP, an SFHA is an area having special flood, mudslide and/or flood-related erosion hazards and shown on Flood Insurance Rate Maps as Zones A, AO, A1–A30, AE, A99, AH, V, V1–V30, VE, M, and E.

Coastal High Hazard Area (CHHA). These are areas of special flood hazard within an SFHA, defined from offshore to the inland limit of "a primary frontal dune along an open coast and any other area subject to high-velocity wave action from storms or seismic sources." On Flood Insurance Rate Maps, a Coastal High Hazard Area is designated Zone V, VE, or V1–V30. These zones designate areas subject to inundation by the base flood where wave heights or wave run-up depths are greater than or equal to 3 feet.

Coastal Barrier Resources Act (CBRA) of 1982. The CBRA protects vulnerable coastal barriers from development, to minimize loss of life, to reduce expenditures of federal revenues, and to protect fish, wildlife, and other natural resources. The CBRA does not prohibit privately financed development in coastal barrier areas. However, it prohibits most federal assistance, including NFIP coverage.

Source: FEMA. *Flood Hazard Assessments and Mapping Requirements* www.fema.gov/business/nfip/fhamr.shtm.

Not all areas prone to flooding are identified as SFHAs on flood maps. Shallow flooding can be a problem in developed areas where large storms overload drainage systems. Debris accumulation, ice jams, and extreme events can contribute to flooding beyond the mapped floodplain boundaries.

NFIP establishes the regulatory requirements that a designer and owner must meet. NFIP definitions and requirements are outlined in this chapter. In each region and project location, specific flood risk exposures must be carefully assessed to determine safety factors to design beyond minimum requirements.

Flood Maps and the Base Flood

NFIP flood data are established by FEMA for most locations of the United States, published as a Flood Insurance Rate Map (FIRM). (Figure 7.3.) The FIRM delineates zones for both 100-year and 500-year flood occurrence. The 100-year occurrence, defined as the *base flood*, has 1% annual probability of occurring in any given year. The base flood is used by the NFIP and federal agencies for purposes of flood insurance and regulating new development. Credits are given to communities and property owners who meet or exceed floodplain regulations. The Community Rating System is a FEMA program that decreases flood insurance rates for residents in communities that adopt effective hazard mitigation strategies.

Due the scale of flood zone mapping, it may be difficult to determine the exact flood zone, BFE, or flood boundary for a specific site. Additional information is included in Flood Insurance Studies (FIS). Site topography, landform, and nearby transect data from the local FEMA FIS provide additional data for evaluating a site and designing a building.

Beginning in 2009, FEMA has provided FIRMs in digital format, called Digital Flood Insurance Rate Maps (DFIRM), now available on the web for most communities.[5]

Base flood elevations are indicated on FIRM and FIS maps and become the reference elevation for design to meet regulatory requirements. *Regulatory floodways* may also be shown on the FIRM or on a separate Flood Boundary and Floodway Map (FBFM). More stringent development

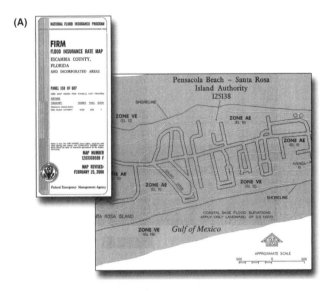

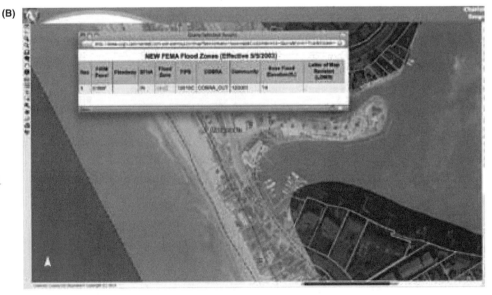

Figure 7.3   FIRMS
(A) *Print Format* (prior to 2010).
(B) *DFIRMs* (new format). DFIRM is a digital version of the FEMA Flood Insurance Rate Map design for use with digital mapping and analysis software.

FIGURES – COLOR INSERT SECTION

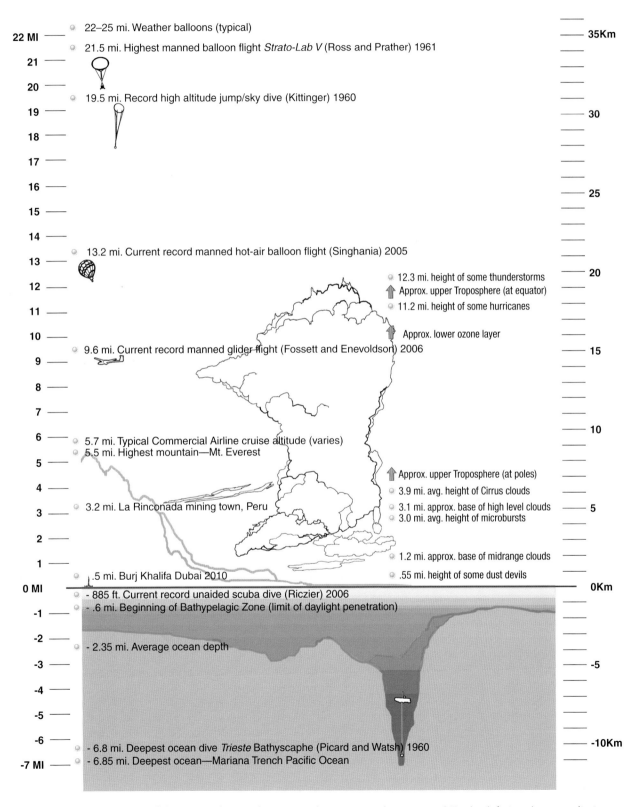

22 MI — 22–25 mi. Weather balloons (typical) — 35Km

21 — 21.5 mi. Highest manned balloon flight *Strato-Lab V* (Ross and Prather) 1961

20 —

19 — 19.5 mi. Record high altitude jump/sky dive (Kittinger) 1960 — 30

18 —

17 —

16 — — 25

15 —

14 —

13 — 13.2 mi. Current record manned hot-air balloon flight (Singhania) 2005

12 — 12.3 mi. height of some thunderstorms — 20

Approx. upper Troposphere (at equator)

11.2 mi. height of some hurricanes

11 —

10 — Approx. lower ozone layer

9 — 9.6 mi. Current record manned glider flight (Fossett and Enevoldson) 2006 — 15

8 —

7 —

6 — 5.7 mi. Typical Commercial Airline cruise altitude (varies) — 10

5 — 5.5 mi. Highest mountain—Mt. Everest

Approx. upper Troposphere (at poles)

3.9 mi. avg. height of Cirrus clouds

4 —

3 — 3.2 mi. La Rinconada mining town, Peru — 3.1 mi. approx. base of high level clouds — 5

3.0 mi. avg. height of microbursts

2 —

1 — 1.2 mi. approx. base of midrange clouds

.5 mi. Burj Khalifa Dubai 2010 — .55 mi. height of some dust devils

0 MI — 0Km

- 885 ft. Current record unaided scuba dive (Riczier) 2006

-1 — - .6 mi. Beginning of Bathypelagic Zone (limit of daylight penetration)

-2 —

- 2.35 mi. Average ocean depth

-3 — — -5

-4 —

-5 —

-6 — - 6.8 mi. Deepest ocean dive *Trieste* Bathyscaphe (Picard and Watsh) 1960 — -10Km

-7 MI — - 6.85 mi. Deepest ocean—Mariana Trench Pacific Ocean

Figure C.1 *Dimensions of the atmosphere:* Life exists within a narrow layer around Earth, defining the outer limits to challenges of unaided human reach.

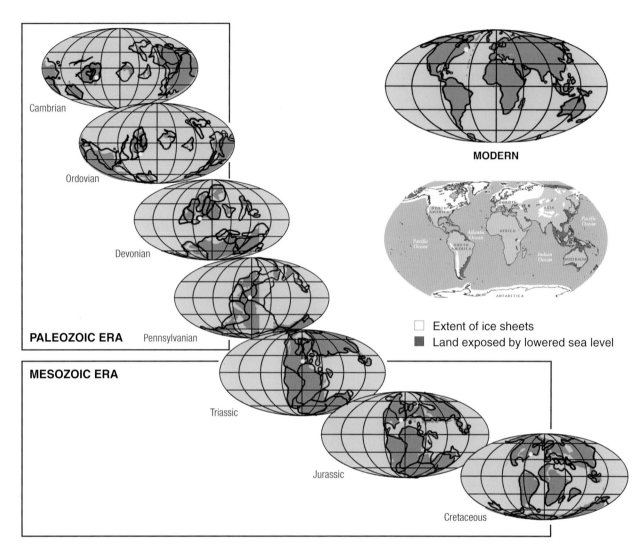

Figure C.2   *Geologic history:* The history of land and sea evolved out of billions of years of continental transformations and, in the modern era, millions of years of glacial and sea level advance and retreat.

MAJOR HURRICANE HISTORY
Data from 1949 in the Pacific, from 1851 in the Atlantic

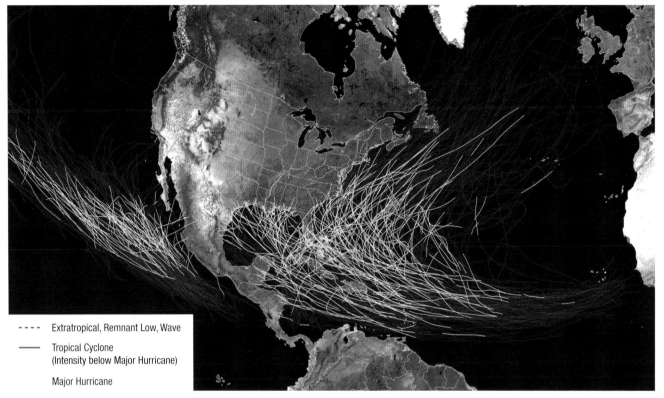

- - - - Extratropical, Remnant Low, Wave

——— Tropical Cyclone
(Intensity below Major Hurricane)

Major Hurricane

Figure C.3 *Major hurricane history:* Tracks of hurricanes Category 3 or greater in North Atlantic (1851–2008) and Eastern North Pacific (1949–2008).

Source: National Weather Service National Hurricane Coastal Services Center, Ethan J. Gibney, GISP, IMSG, NOAA.

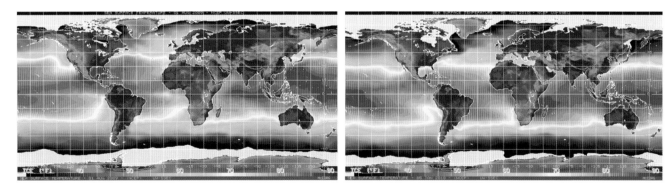

Figure C.4 *Sea surface temperatures* (LEFT: July 2009. RIGHT: January 2010). This six-month comparison is representative of winter and summer sea temperature and polar ice cover variations.

Source: Space Science and Engineering Center, University of Wisconsin-Madison. Images are produced for each day of the year and are accessible via the SSEC Web site.

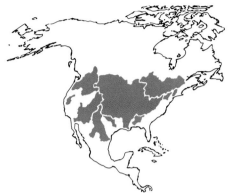

Land Cover and Use Variables

Percent Forest Cover:	73.0
Percent Grassland, Savanna, and Shrubland:	0.2
Percent Wetlands:	4.0
Percent Cropland:	9.1
Percent Irrigated Cropland:	0.0
Percent Dryland Area:	0.0
Percent Urban and Industrial Area:	17.4
Percent Loss of Original Forest Cover:	24.6

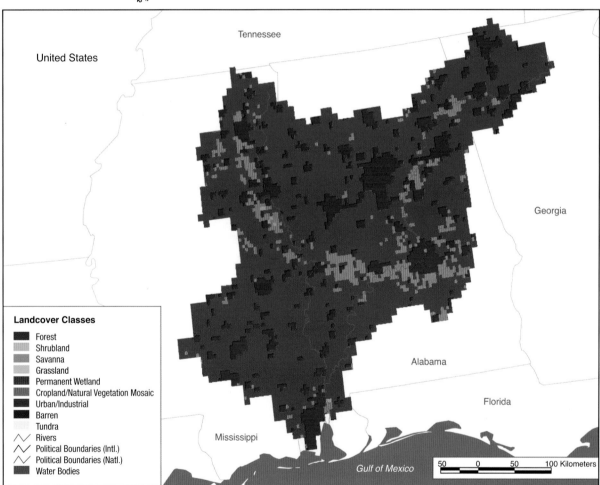

Figure C.5   Alabama & Tombigbee River Basins.

© World Resources eAtlas (by permission World Resources Institute)

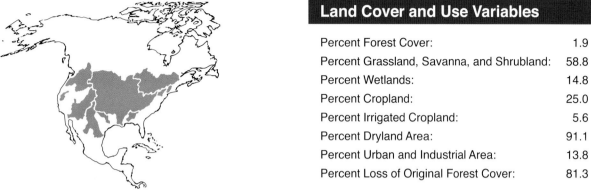

Land Cover and Use Variables

Percent Forest Cover:	1.9
Percent Grassland, Savanna, and Shrubland:	58.8
Percent Wetlands:	14.8
Percent Cropland:	25.0
Percent Irrigated Cropland:	5.6
Percent Dryland Area:	91.1
Percent Urban and Industrial Area:	13.8
Percent Loss of Original Forest Cover:	81.3

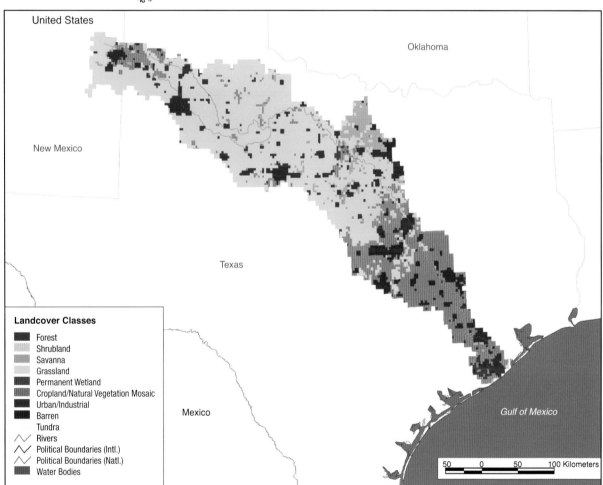

Landcover Classes

- Forest
- Shrubland
- Savanna
- Grassland
- Permanent Wetland
- Cropland/Natural Vegetation Mosaic
- Urban/Industrial
- Barren
- Tundra
- Rivers
- Political Boundaries (Intl.)
- Political Boundaries (Natl.)
- Water Bodies

Figure C.6   Brazos River Basins.

© World Resources eAtlas (by permission World Resources Institute)

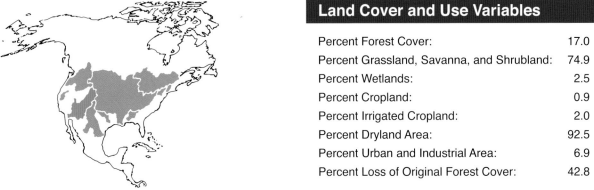

Land Cover and Use Variables

Percent Forest Cover:	17.0
Percent Grassland, Savanna, and Shrubland:	74.9
Percent Wetlands:	2.5
Percent Cropland:	0.9
Percent Irrigated Cropland:	2.0
Percent Dryland Area:	92.5
Percent Urban and Industrial Area:	6.9
Percent Loss of Original Forest Cover:	42.8

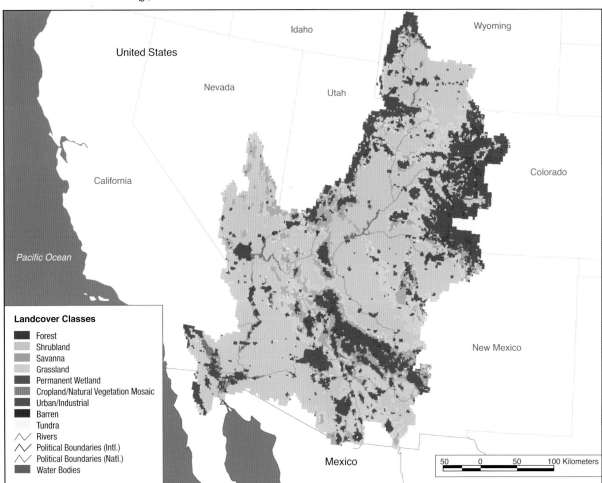

Landcover Classes
- Forest
- Shrubland
- Savanna
- Grassland
- Permanent Wetland
- Cropland/Natural Vegetation Mosaic
- Urban/Industrial
- Barren
- Tundra
- Rivers
- Political Boundaries (Intl.)
- Political Boundaries (Natl.)
- Water Bodies

Figure C.7   Colorado River Basins.

© World Resources eAtlas (by permission World Resources Institute)

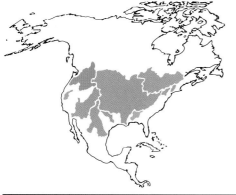

Land Cover and Use Variables

Percent Forest Cover:	50.0
Percent Grassland, Savanna, and Shrubland:	35.5
Percent Wetlands:	6.3
Percent Cropland:	6.4
Percent Irrigated Cropland:	3.6
Percent Dryland Area:	61.8
Percent Urban and Industrial Area:	7.3
Percent Loss of Original Forest Cover:	21.6

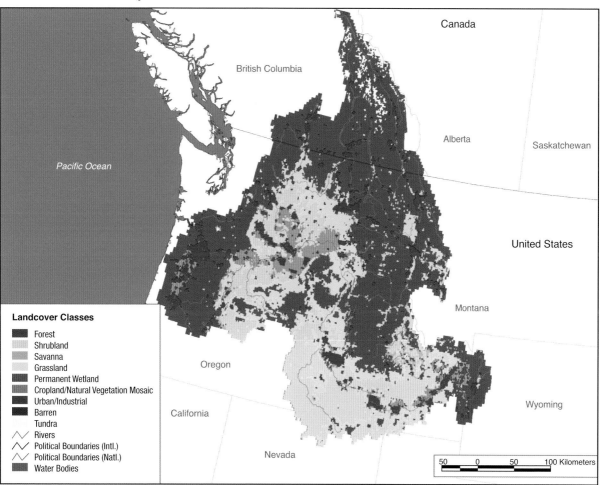

Figure C.8   Columbia Northwest River Basins.

© World Resources eAtlas (by permission World Resources Institute)

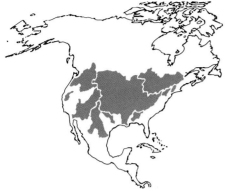

Land Cover and Use Variables

Percent Forest Cover:	76.3
Percent Grassland, Savanna, and Shrubland:	0.0
Percent Wetlands:	15.0
Percent Cropland:	0.3
Percent Irrigated Cropland:	0.0
Percent Dryland Area:	0.0
Percent Urban and Industrial Area:	22.8
Percent Loss of Original Forest Cover:	9.1

Figure C.9   Hudson River Basins.

© World Resources eAtlas (by permission World Resources Institute)

Land Cover and Use Variables

Percent Forest Cover:	22.2
Percent Grassland, Savanna, and Shrubland:	28.5
Percent Wetlands:	20.0
Percent Cropland:	35.8
Percent Irrigated Cropland:	3.1
Percent Dryland Area:	46.7
Percent Urban and Industrial Area:	12.6
Percent Loss of Original Forest Cover:	51.7

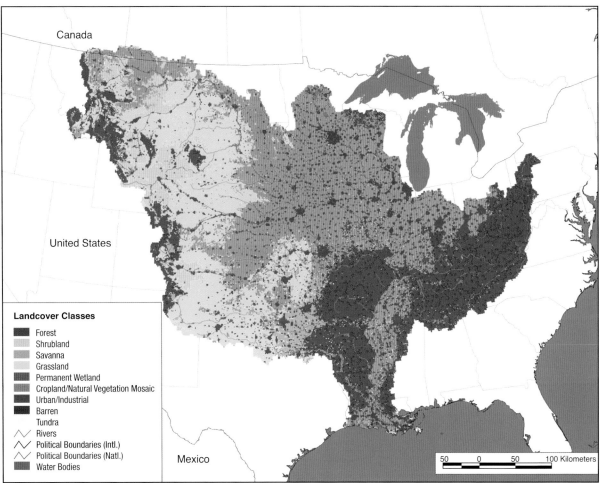

Landcover Classes

- Forest
- Shrubland
- Savanna
- Grassland
- Permanent Wetland
- Cropland/Natural Vegetation Mosaic
- Urban/Industrial
- Barren
- Tundra
- ⋀⋁ Rivers
- ⋀⋁ Political Boundaries (Intl.)
- ⋀⋁ Political Boundaries (Natl.)
- Water Bodies

Figure C.10   Mississippi River Basins.

© World Resources eAtlas (by permission World Resources Institute)

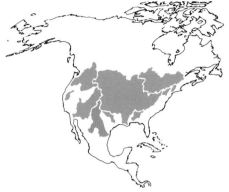

Land Cover and Use Variables

Percent Forest Cover:	7.5
Percent Grassland, Savanna, and Shrubland:	80.9
Percent Wetlands:	2.1
Percent Cropland:	5.2
Percent Irrigated Cropland:	2.6
Percent Dryland Area:	98.8
Percent Urban and Industrial Area:	6.0
Percent Loss of Original Forest Cover:	52.1

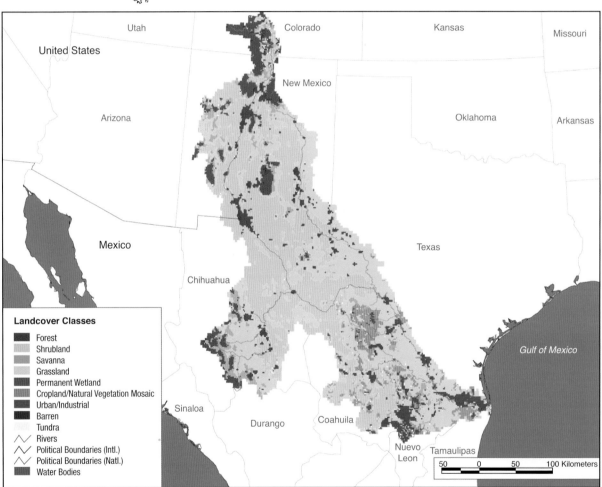

Landcover Classes

- Forest
- Shrubland
- Savanna
- Grassland
- Permanent Wetland
- Cropland/Natural Vegetation Mosaic
- Urban/Industrial
- Barren
- Tundra
- Rivers
- Political Boundaries (Intl.)
- Political Boundaries (Natl.)
- Water Bodies

Figure C.11   Rio Grande River Basins.

© World Resources eAtlas (by permission World Resources Institute)

Land Cover and Use Variables

Percent Forest Cover:	48.6
Percent Grassland, Savanna, and Shrubland:	33.3
Percent Wetlands:	3.0
Percent Cropland:	6.0
Percent Irrigated Cropland:	11.5
Percent Dryland Area:	29.3
Percent Urban and Industrial Area:	11.5
Percent Loss of Original Forest Cover:	26.0

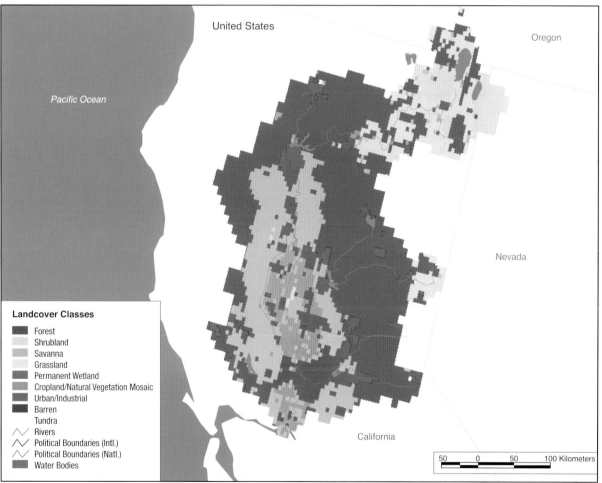

Landcover Classes

- Forest
- Shrubland
- Savanna
- Grassland
- Permanent Wetland
- Cropland/Natural Vegetation Mosaic
- Urban/Industrial
- Barren
- Tundra
- /\/\ Rivers
- /\/\ Political Boundaries (Intl.)
- /\/\ Political Boundaries (Natl.)
- Water Bodies

Figure C.12   Sacramento River Basins.

Land Cover and Use Variables

Percent Forest Cover:	43.5
Percent Grassland, Savanna, and Shrubland:	0.1
Percent Wetlands:	47.2
Percent Cropland:	16.4
Percent Irrigated Cropland:	0.2
Percent Dryland Area:	0.0
Percent Urban and Industrial Area:	14.5
Percent Loss of Original Forest Cover:	31.0

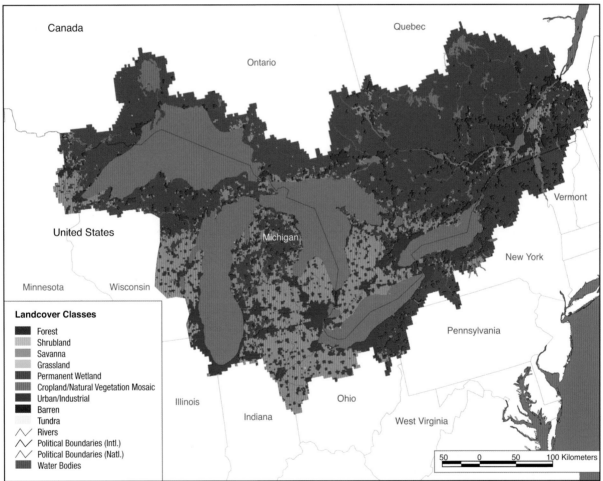

Figure C.13   St. Lawrence River Basins.

© World Resources eAtlas (by permission World Resources Institute)

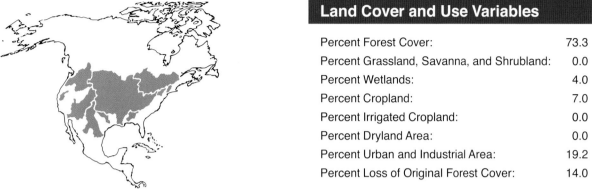

Land Cover and Use Variables

Percent Forest Cover:	73.3
Percent Grassland, Savanna, and Shrubland:	0.0
Percent Wetlands:	4.0
Percent Cropland:	7.0
Percent Irrigated Cropland:	0.0
Percent Dryland Area:	0.0
Percent Urban and Industrial Area:	19.2
Percent Loss of Original Forest Cover:	14.0

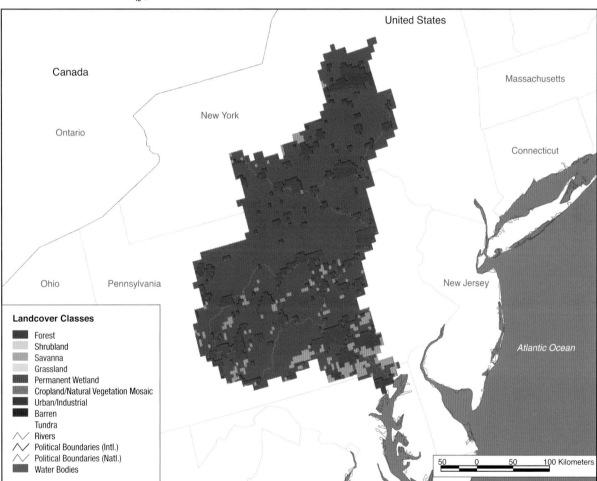

Landcover Classes

- Forest
- Shrubland
- Savanna
- Grassland
- Permanent Wetland
- Cropland/Natural Vegetation Mosaic
- Urban/Industrial
- Barren
- Tundra
- Rivers
- Political Boundaries (Intl.)
- Political Boundaries (Natl.)
- Water Bodies

Figure C.14   Susquehanna River Basins.

Figure C.15   Spring Glen, Wisconsin. Snow melts in areas already saturated from fall storms resulted in spring 2008 river levels that were higher than they had been for years.

(PHOTO: Walter Jennings FEMA Photo Library, July 11, 2008)

Figure C.16   New Orleans, St. Bernard's Parish after Hurricane Katrina. The storm surge caused failures of the levee system that protects the City of New Orleans from Lake Pontchartrain. Eighty percent of the city subsequently flooded.

(PHOTO: Michael Rieger FEMA Photo Library, September 8, 2005)

Figure C.17   Damage to utilities and municipal infrastructure is among the most vulnerable risks of flooding, also determining the schedule of recovery.

(PHOTO: Marvin Nauman FEMA Photo Library, September 30, 2005)

Figure C.18   Debris pile in a staging area in the Lakeview area of New Orleans. Approximately 58.8 million cubic yards of debris were collected in Louisiana in three years following Hurricane Katrina.

(PHOTO: Andrea Booker FEMA Photo Library, July 29 16, 2008).

Figure C.19   Environmental pollution: Thick oil leaking from storage tanks in Chalmette, New Orleans, after Hurricane Katrina.

(PHOTO: Marvin Nauman FEMA Photo Library, September 16, 2005).

Figure C.20 Stockpiled vehicles destroyed in the storm surge of Hurricane Katrina.

(PHOTO: Mark Wolf FEMA Photo Library, October 30, 2005)

Figure C.21 Blue roofs—temporary membrane covers—of homes in Ocean Springs, Mississippi, indicate the most widespread storm damage evident across the entire area impacted by Hurricane Katrina.

(PHOTO: Mark Wolf FEMA Photo Library, October 30, 2005)

Figure C.22 Best mitigation practices helped a Bay St. Louis, Mississippi, house to survive a 7-foot high surge and 125-mile winds of Hurricane Katrina: elevated construction, slab-on-grade, continuous path structural design, structural materials doubling as finishes, and a heavy green roof.

Allison and John Anderson, Unabridged Architects. (PHOTO: Mark Wolfe FEMA Photo Library, March 27, 2006)

NFIP FLOOD ZONES

Special Flood Hazard Areas (SFHA)	**Zone V and VE**	**V** The coastal area subject to a velocity hazard (wave action) where BFEs are not determined on the FIRM. **VE** The coastal area subject to a velocity hazard (wave action) where BFEs are provided on the FIRM.
	Zone A	The 100-year or base floodplain. There are seven types of A Zones: **A** The base floodplain mapped by approximate methods, i.e., BFEs are not determined. This is often called an unnumbered A Zone or an approximate A Zone. **A1–30** These are known as numbered A Zones (e.g., A7 or A14). This is the base floodplain where the FIRM shows a BFE (old format). **AE** The base floodplain where base flood elevations are provided. AE Zones are now used on new format FIRMs instead of A1–A30 Zones. **AO** The base floodplain with sheet flow, ponding, or shallow flooding. Base flood depths (feet above ground) are provided. **AH** Shallow flooding base floodplain. BFEs are provided. **A99** Area to be protected from base flood by levees or Federal Flood Protection Systems under construction. BFEs are not determined. **AR** The base floodplain that results from the decertification of a previously accredited flood protection system that is in the process of being restored to provide a 100-year or greater level of flood protection.
Outside SFHA or Undetermined Flood Hazard	**Zone B and Zone X (shaded)**	Area of moderate flood hazard, usually the area between the limits of the 100-year and 500-year floods. B Zones are also used to designate base floodplains of lesser hazards, such as areas protected by levees from the 100-year flood, or shallow flooding areas with average depths of less than 1 foot or drainage areas less than 1 square mile.
	Zone C and Zone X (unshaded)	Area of minimal flood hazard, usually depicted on FIRMs as above the 500-year flood level. Zone C may have ponding and local drainage problems that don't warrant a detailed study or designation as base floodplain. Zone X is the area determined to be outside the 500-year flood and protected by levee from 100-year flood.
	Zone D	Area of undetermined but possible flood hazards.

Source: FEMA, *Flood Hazard Assessments and Mapping Requirements* www.fema.gov/business/nfip/fhamr.shtm.

controls apply within the regulatory floodway to prevent or limit encroachment and restriction of floodwater flows.

The 500-year floodplain may be shown as a lightly shaded area labeled Zone B (older map) or Zone X (newer map). Although most communities do not impose special requirements in the 500-year floodplain, flood hazards in

these areas should be considered, such as location of critical facilities or storage of hazardous materials.

The FIRM represents flood hazards based on present-day shoreline and inland riverine floodplain configurations. It does not account for future development effects (e.g., increased runoff in riverine areas),

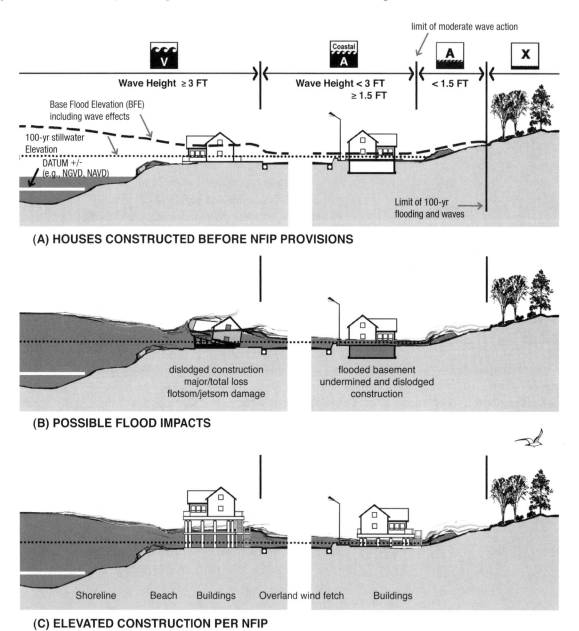

Figure 7.4 *Shoreline transect* illustrates FEMA zone classifications with the recommended Coastal A zone.

Source: FEMA, *Coastal Construction Manual: Principles and Practices of Planning, Siting, Designing, Constructing, and Maintaining Residential Buildings in Coastal Areas*, FEMA 55 (August 2005), www.fema.gov/rebuild/mat/fema55.shtm; also, FEMA, Local Officials Guide for Coastal Construction, FEMA P-762 (February 2009), http://www.fema.gov/library/viewRecord.do?id=3647.

long-term shoreline retreat, subsidence, or sea level rise that may occur in the future due to climate change. Thus, the FIRM represents minimum requirements under today's conditions only.

NFIP classifications of open coast floodplain are illustrated in Figure 7.4, as modified in a December 2008 FEMA Directorate. The Directorate defines the "Coastal A Zone" that may experience potential wave heights of the base flood between 1.5 and 3 feet and where VE zone design requirements should apply. The line between the Coastal A zone and the A zone is described on new DFIRMs as the LiMWA (Limit of Moderate Wave Action).[6]

"100-Year Flood"

The terms *100-year flood* and *500-year flood* are a source of confusion, often mistakenly interpreted to mean a flood event that occurs "only once in 100 years" and "once in 500 years." Flooding equal to a 100-year or 500-year event may follow one another in the same area within any one-year or decade.

When a "100-year flood" is adopted as the minimum elevation in regulations, it is referred to as the *base flood,* and its elevation is defined as the Base Flood Elevation, or BFE.

The designation of a "100-year flood" is properly defined as a "flood that has 1% probability of being equaled or exceeded in any one year." As the number of years increases, so does probability that a flood will occur

of the specified magnitude or greater. For example, during a 30-year period (representative of a standard mortgage and shaded in Table 7.1), the probability increases to 26%. During a 70-year period (representative of most buildings), the probability increases to 50%. The same principle applies to other natural hazard events with other recurrence intervals. The probabilities for recurrence intervals of 10, 25, 50, 100, and 500 years are indicated in Table 7.1.

Geodetic Data

Geodetic data are recorded as a set of constants specifying the coordinates of points on earth, including vertical datum of sea level elevation. The most recent FIRM maps reference the BFE to the North American Vertical Datum (NAVD) defined as the average sea level in 1988. Previous FIRM maps were based on the National Geodetic Vertical Datum (NGVD), the average sea level in 1929. Elevations indicated on a land survey may be based on a local datum that may not necessarily coincide with NAVD or NGVD.[7]

Floodways

The *floodway* is the central portion of a riverine floodplain that carries floodwater flow downstream. Floodways—overbanked streams and river sources—are subject to high velocities and risk to life safety and property damage during flooding.

TABLE 7.1 NATURAL HAZARD PROBABILITIES DURING PERIODS OF VARIOUS LENGTHS

Length of Period (years)	Frequency—Recurrence Interval				
	10-Year Event	25-Year Event	50-Year Event	100-Year Event	500-Year Event
1	10%	4%	2%	1%	0.2%
10	65%	34%	18%	10%	2%
20	88%	56%	33%	18%	5%
25	93%	64%	40%	22%	5%
30	96%	71%	45%	26%	6%
50	99+%	87%	64%	39%	10%
70	99.94+%	94%	76%	50%	13%
100	99.99+%	98%	87%	63%	18%

The percentages shown represent the probabilities of one or more occurrences of an event of a given magnitude or larger within the specified period. The formula for determining these probabilities is $P_n = 1 - (1 - P_a)^n$ where P_a = Annual probability and n = Length of the period.

The *Federal Register* defines *regulatory floodway* as:

The channel of a river or other watercourse and the adjacent land areas that must be reserved in order to discharge the base flood without cumulatively increasing the water surface elevation more than a designated height.[8]

FBFMs designate *regulated floodways* wherein any structure or fill that encroaches may obstruct or restrict the flow of floodwaters, thereby increasing flooding upstream.

Encroachment of any fill, landscape, or building obstruction is not allowed in a regulated floodway. If locating a structure, such as a bridge pier, road crossing, or culvert, within a floodway cannot be avoided, it is subject to local review and approval. Regulated floodway boundaries are delineated using computer modeling and often are not directly matched to the specific landform or construction features that are visible. A site-specific hydrological analysis of the watershed must demonstrate and certify that a proposed potential obstruction or encroachment will not significantly increase upstream flood elevations. (Figure 7.5.)

Wave and Water Forces on Structures

Analysis of flood-prone sites and structures must consider the full force of water and wave and related impacts. High-velocity flows can be created or exacerbated by the presence of man-made or natural obstructions along the shoreline and by "weak points" formed by roads and access paths that cross dunes, bridges or canals, channels, or drainage features. Design provisions for wave and water force include elevation of the building. Structural design measures to accommodate these forces are discussed in Chapter 9.

HYDROSTATIC FORCES are imparted by standing water or slowly moving water that can induce horizontal or lateral hydrostatic forces against a structure, especially when flood levels on different sides of a structure are unequal. Hydrostatic forces due to flooding can overcome the weight of a structure and cause vertical buoyancy and flotation.

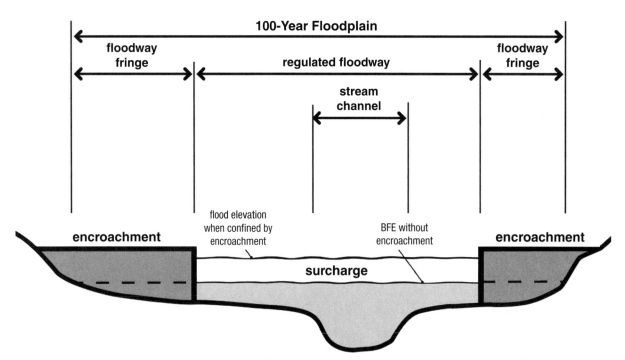

Figure 7.5   *Regulated floodway:* Any structures, fill, or other development existing or proposed in a floodway is subject to approval and cannot divert or confine floodwater flow or contribute to increased water depths and upstream impoundment during a flood.

HYDRODYNAMIC FORCES on buildings are created when floodwaters moving at high velocities impact the structure. They exert frontal impact forces while creating drag along the sides and suction on the downstream side. High-velocity flows are capable of destroying solid walls and dislodging buildings with inadequate foundations.

WAVE LOADS result from the force of impact, which can be 10 to 100 times higher than wind or other forces. Breaking wave loads can overwhelm nearly all wood-frame and unreinforced masonry walls below the wave crest elevation. Only engineered and massive structural elements are capable of withstanding breaking wave loads.

DEBRIS IMPACT LOAD are imposed on a structure or building element by flotsam material and objects carried by moving floodwaters. Debris may include dislodged tree trunks, fuel tanks, piers, building remnants, and, in severe cases, boats or barges.

EROSION AND LOCAL SCOUR that result from water and wave action can impact building performance. Erosion results from the force of water flow across unstable ground. Local scour results from turbulence of ground elements around foundation elements. Both erosion and scour can impact the lateral stability of a structure.

WAVE RUN-UP occurs as waves break and run up beaches, sloping surfaces, and vertical surfaces. Wave run-up can drive large volumes of water against or around coastal buildings, inducing fluid impact forces, current drag forces, and localized erosion and scour.

SHOALING WAVES beneath insufficiently elevated structures can lead to wave uplift forces. The most common example of wave uplift damage occurs are fishing piers and boat docks, when shoaling storm waves lift the deck from pilings and beams.

Levees
The United States has thousands of miles of levee systems, usually earthen embankments, designed and constructed to contain, control, or divert the flow of water and provide protection from temporary flooding.

Levee systems are designed to provide a specific level of protection and can be overtopped during larger flood events. Levee systems do not provide full protection from all flooding events. They can decay over time and require maintenance. When levee systems do fail, or are overtopped, the results can be catastrophic. Flood damage may be more significant than if the levee system had not been built.[9]

Assessing flood risk for levee-impacted areas is complex. FEMA does not examine levee systems to assess how they will perform during a flood. NFIP has criteria for crediting levee systems in insurance assessment calculations. Levee owners must provide data and documentation to show that the levee system meets these criteria.

None of the agricultural levee standards provides a level of flood protection considered minimally sufficient for cities and towns by FEMA's National Flood Insurance Program. Additionally, none of these standards accounts for the risks associated with earthquakes. All lands behind these levees, regardless of their certification, are considered to be at high risk of flooding.[10]

7.2 FLOOD ELEVATION: BASE FLOOD AND DESIGN FLOOD

Base Flood Elevation
FIRMs delineate a BFE for each flood zone. The BFE indicates the 100-year stillwater elevation predicted for riverine flooding and the wave crest elevation for coastal flooding. (Figure 7.6.) The BFE is the regulatory requirement for the elevation or flood-proofing of structures. The relationship between the BFE and a structure's elevation determines the flood insurance premium.

To determine BFE, FEMA computer modeling computes 100-year stillwater elevations, maximum wave heights and, in some areas, the maximum wave run-up, whichever is greater. Wave run-up is the maximum extent of wave uprush or overtopping above the wave height crest that results from the shoreline profile. Site-specific shore topography determines whether wave crest or wave run-up is greater. (Figure 7.7.)

Postdisaster damage inspection of selected floods, hurricanes, and tornadoes have helped to determine what has worked and what has not, using evaluation of actual storm

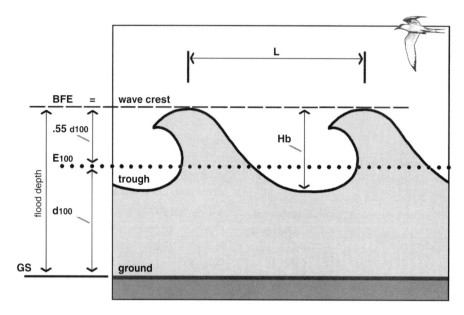

E100 = 100-year stillwater elevation in feet above datum

d100 = 100-year stillwater depth

GS = Ground surface elevation - Lowest eroded ground level

L = Wave length (crest to crest)

Hb = Wave height (wave trough to wave crest) = 0.78 d100

BFE = Base Flood Elevation = d100 + .55 d100

Figure 7.6 *Wave height* is the vertical distance between the trough and the crest. *Wave length* is the horizontal distance between wave crests. Maximum wave height is 78% of stillwater depth. Flood depth including waves can be as much as 55% greater than the stillwater depth.

Source: FEMA 55 and FEMA P-762.

DEFINITIONS FOR DESIGN CRITERIA FOR FLOOD ZONES

Base flood. Flood that has as 1% probability of being equaled or exceeded in any year.

100-year stillwater elevation. Projected elevation that floodwaters would assume, referenced to the NGVD or NAVD, or other datum, in the absence of waves resulting from wind or seismic effects. Stillwater elevation in a coastal area is determined by offshore ocean floor profile (bathymetry), astronomical tide, wind, and pressure setup.

Elevation (G). The elevation at the base of the structure, accounting for erosion during the flood. The *Coastal Construction Manual* defines this term as "GS," equal to ground level less the erosion. It does not account for localized scour.

Unit weight of water

62.4 pcf—unit weight of freshwater
64.0 pcf—unit weight of salt water

Wave height. Vertical distance between the wave crest and the wave trough.

Wave run-up. Rush of wave water up a slope or structure.

Sources: Bartlett Quimbey, P.E., "Beginner's Guide to ASCE 7.05 T," 2008, www.bgstructuralengineering.com; American Society of Civil Engineers, *Flood-Resistant Design and Construction*, SEI/ACSE 24-05, Reston, VA: Author, 2006.

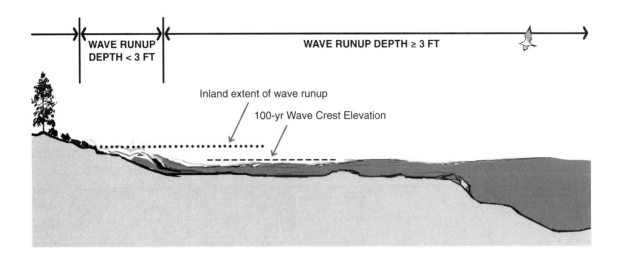

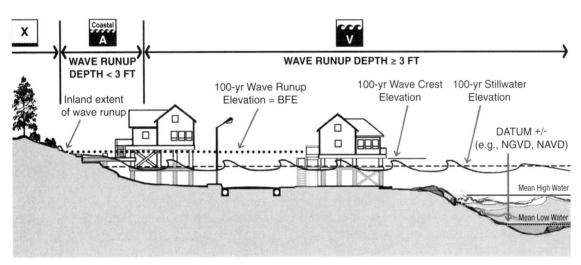

Figure 7.7   *Wave run-up*: The BFE is determined by the run-up elevation, where wave run-up along an embankment or shallow shoreline exceeds wave crest elevations.

Sources: FEMA 55 and FEMA P-762.

damage as a laboratory of research. The Reports of FEMA Mitigation Assessment Teams (MATs) provide a record of assessment and recommendations for building and infrastructure design and construction based on empirical evidence and real examples.[11] The MATs offer lessons learned that eventually may become part of FEMA handbooks and advisories.

Figures 7.8 and 7.9a illustrate NFIP requirements from FEMA 55 and FEMA P-762. Figure 7.9b represents best practice recommendations from recent FEMA Mitigation Assessment Team (MAT) reports.

With the possible exception of slab-on-grade and masonry construction, adhering only to minimum requirements for

BFE at the lowest floor elevation exposes the floor structure both below and immediately above the BFE to moisture, humidity, and mold damage.

Design Flood Elevation

The flood regulations for many communities require buildings to be designed for flood elevations 1 foot or more about the BFE. This requirement is called the *Design Flood Elevation* (DFE) and becomes the locally adopted reference elevation for design, typically referenced to the ASCE/SEI Standard 24-05, *Flood-Resistant Design and Construction*.[12] DFE as a term is not included in NFIP regulations, which

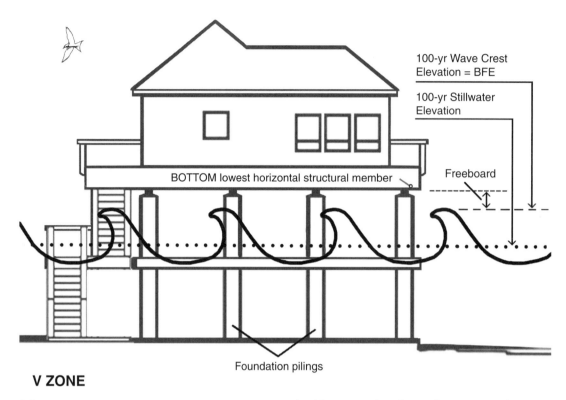

100-yr Wave Crest
Elevation = BFE

100-yr Stillwater
Elevation

BOTTOM lowest horizontal structural member

Freeboard

Foundation pilings

V ZONE

Figure 7.8 *Minimum NFIP V-zone requirements*: In V zones, buildings must be elevated on an open foundation (e.g., piling, piers) so that the bottom of the lowest horizontal member is at or above the BFE. Recommended best practice is to follow this requirement in Coastal A zones.

refer to BFE only as the minimum elevation to meet its requirements. The additional height above the BFE determined by local regulation is referred to as *freeboard*.

FREEBOARD is a safety factor to account for uncertainties in flood level and/or structural performance. Freeboard compensates for many unknown factors, such as local waves, debris, or increased hydrological effect of the watershed from inland flooding.

Increasing local regulations by adding freeboard above the BFE results in significantly lower flood insurance rates. Reduced flood insurance premiums pay for the cost of incorporating freeboard on average within fewer than six years.[13]

Additional Design Safety Factors

Potential for long-term impacts of flooding requires that design criteria go beyond current minimum standards and regulations. Flood mapping and model regulations are subject to updates. Flood and storm events are trending toward greater intensity. Meeting minimum regulatory requirements for the siting, design, and construction of a building does not guarantee that the building will be safe.

Adding freeboard above BFE or the locally mandated minimum DFE is one example of precautionary design, which adds to the margin of safety in design and construction.

Some states and communities require extra measures and margins of safety that exceed code minimum requirements.[14] The designer, in concert with the owner, is responsible for the assumptions that determine risk and resulting "margins of safety" for design. These assumptions should be based on analysis of risk over the predicted life of the building and site infrastructure.

Risk assessment must consider the possibility of multiple events, not just a single event. Any one area may experience several minor storms in a short period of time, causing more damage than a major storm. Assessment

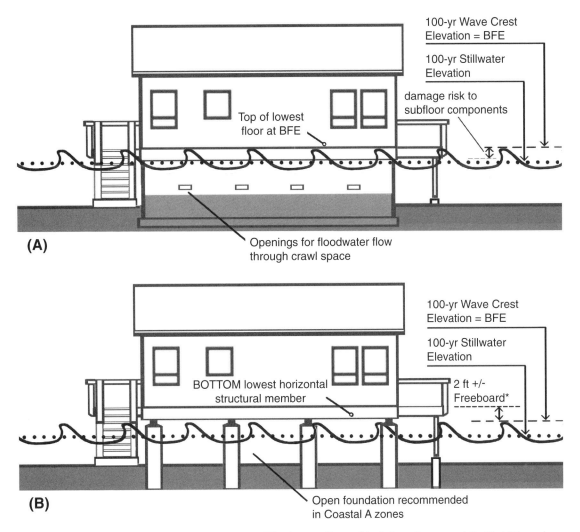

Figure 7.9 (A) *Minimum NFIP A-zone requirements*: The lowest floor of buildings in zones AE, A1-A30, and A must be at or above the BFE. (B) *Recommended best practice* for A zones is to exceed the minimum requirement by freeboard sufficient to avoid moisture damage to structure and materials exposed to floodwater splashing and wicking.

Source: FEMA Mitigation Assessment Team Natural Disaster Reports of Hurricane Ike. FEMA P-757/April 2009. www.fema.gov/rebuild/mat/mat_reprts.shtm.

should also consider the potential of bluff instability, shoreline fluctuations, and storm-induced erosion.

Christopher Jones, author of the *Flood Resistance of the Building Envelope* section of the *NIBS Whole Building Design Guide*, recommends additional steps in determining flood conditions.[15] (Figure 7.10.)

Following review of the FIRM and FIS, designers may wish to supplement those documents with updated calculations and flood hazard zone/flood level estimates. Although not usually required by communities, this step may be important for building planning and design in the case of old and out-of-date flood hazard maps. This step may also be important in the case of a rapidly urbanizing floodplain. Designers must consider designing to possible future conditions rather than historical flood hazards.

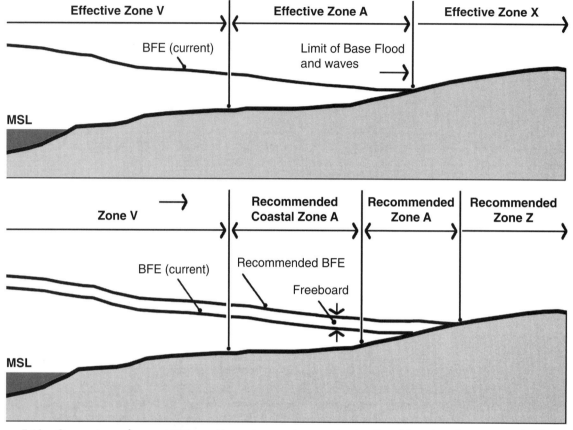

Figure 7.10 *Comparison* of current BFEs and hazard zones that may be in effect (above) and recommended freeboard and flood hazard zones (below).

Source: www.fema.gov/rebuild/mat/mat_reprts.shtm.

Notes

1. National Research Council, Commission of Geosciences, Environment and Resources, *Alluvial Fan Flooding*. Washington, DC: National Academies Press, 1996.

2. National Flood Insurance Program (NFIP), "Myths and Facts about the National Flood Insurance Program," Publication F-002, 2007, www.fema.gov/business/nfip.

3. Federal Emergency Management Agency (FEMA). Technical Bulletin "User's Guide to Technical Bulletins" and NFIP Technical Bulletins 1, 2, 5, and 9, 2009 www.fema.gov/pdf/fima/guide01.pdf.

4. Association of State Floodplain Managers, *No Adverse Impact Handbook*. Madison, WI. 2008, www.floods.org/NoAdverseImpact/CNAI_Handbook/CNAI_Handbook.pdf.

5. FEMA Digital Mapping Products http://www.fema.gov/plan/prevent/fhm/dfm_dfhm.shtm. FIRM maps can be viewed online at FEMA Map Service Center, http://msc.fema.gov. "Make a FIRMette" enables a printout of a selected portion of a map along with identifying information. See also How to Read a FIRM Online Tutorial www.fema.gov/media/fhm/firm/ot_firm.htm.

6. FEMA, "Memorandum for Regional Mitigation Division Directors," December 3, 2008. www.fema.gov/library/viewRecord.do?id=3481 The recommendation is representative of updating flood design measures based on continuing assessment of disaster events.

7. National Oceanic and Atmospheric Administration, National Geodetic Survey establishes maintains the current national geodetic vertical datum. www.ngs.noaa.gov/.

8. Congressional *Federal Register* (Title 44 CFR 59.1), www.access.gpo.gov/nara/cfr/waisidx_02/44cfrv1_02.html.

9. FEMA, "Levee System Information or Stakeholders" (2010), www.fema.gov/plan/prevent/fhm/lv_intro.shtm.

10. Robyn Suddeth, Jeffrey F. Mount, Jay R. Lund. "Levee Decisions and Sustainability for the Delta," Technical Appendix B (San Francisco: Public Policy Institute of California, August 2008). www.ppic.org/content/pubs/other/708EHR.

11. FEMA Mitigation Assessment Team (MAT) Natural Disaster Reports. Hurricane Ike in Texas and Louisiana: Building Performance Observations, Recommendations and Technical Guidance FEMA P-757/April 2009. The report summarizes damage to many different building types in coastal and urban locations impacted by Hurricane Ike, including highrise structures in downtown Houston, Texas. www.fema.gov/rebuild/mat/mat_reprts.shtm.

12. ASCE, *Flood-Resistant Design and Construction*, SEI/ACSE 24-05 (Reston, VA: Author, 2006).

13. American Institutes for Research, "Evaluation of the National Flood Insurance Program Building Standards," 2006. www.fema.gov/library/file?type…file=10_765_b.txt.

14. Ronald L. Geren, The Code Corner No. 12, "Flood-Resistant Design," (August 2009), www.specsandcodes.com/…/The%20Code%20Corner%20No.%2012%20-%20Flood-Resistant%20Design.pdf.

15. Christopher P. Jones. National Institute of Building Sciences. "Flood Resistance of the Building Envelope," 2009, Whole Building Design Guide, www.wbdg.org/resources/env_flood.php.

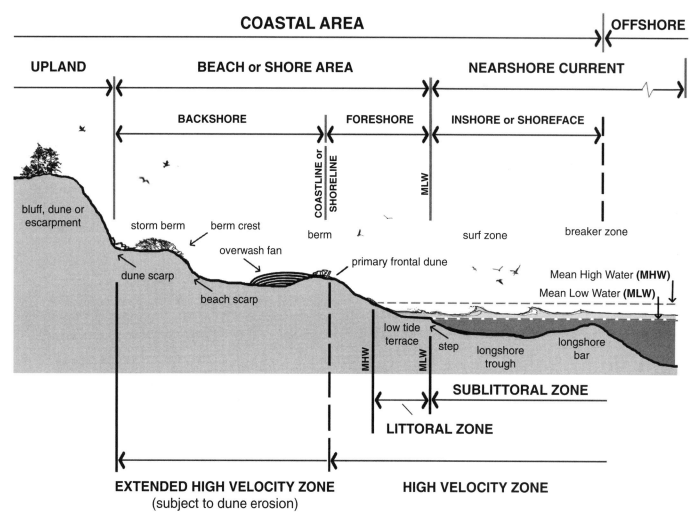

Figure 8.1 *Coastal area terminology.*

CHAPTER **8**

THE COAST

The edge between land and sea is in constant motion, changing with each wave and with each tide. Beaches are particularly dynamic landforms. On a calm day, the natural reshaping of the land proceeds at nearly imperceptible pace. During a storm, it can happen rapidly and violently. (Figure 8.2.)

8.1 COASTAL PROCESSES

Coastal processes combine daily and seasonal wind, wave, tides, and weather. Waves carry sand up and down the foreshore, to and from the sea. If waves approach at an oblique

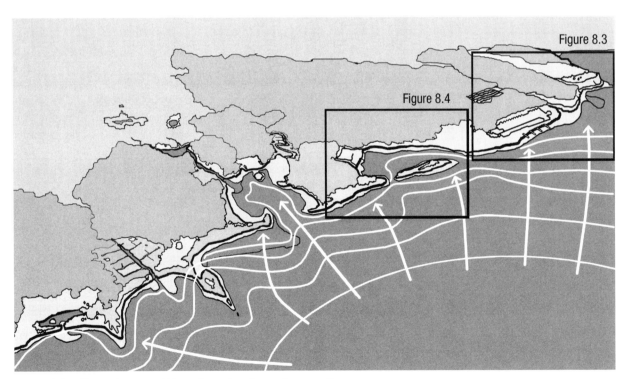

Figure 8.2   *Shore dynamics:* Wave dynamics shape the coastline.

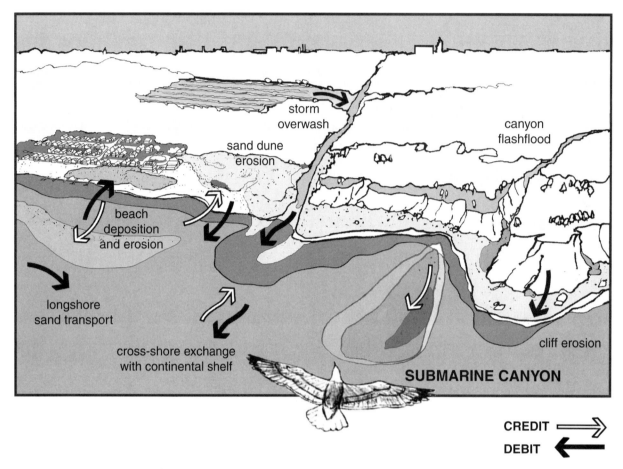

Figure 8.3 *Components of the sediment budget:* mainland shoreline backed by bluffs and dunes.

angle, the wave upwash (*swash*) moves sand along the face of the beach in a longshore movement referred to as *littoral drift.* This process causes barrier islands to migrate parallel to the shore. (Figures 8.3 and 8.4.)

- **Flood shoals** are sediment deposits formed by flood tidal currents just inside a tidal inlet.

- **Ebb shoals** are sediment deposits formed by ebb tidal currents just offshore of a tide inlet.

- **Longshore sand transport** is wave- and/or tide-generated movement of shallow-water coast sediments parallel to the shoreline.

- **Cross-shore sand transport** is wave- and/or tide-generated movement of shallow water coastal sediments toward or away from the shore.

Trends in the shoreline erosion and accretion can be analyzed by measuring differences in past and present shoreline delineation. LIDAR (Light Detection and Ranging) remote sensing cameras provide GIS-based data such as the mean high water line or specific elevation contours. Several NOAA Shoreline Web sites provide extensive data and tools for planners for analyzing shoreline elevations and trends.[1] (Figure 8.5.)

Waves

Waves are generated by forces that disturb a body of water. Most waves are created by wind moving across the surface of the water. Other influences include gravitational pull of the Sun and Moon, underwater earthquakes and landslides, and distant or nearby passing of ships. The size of wind-generated waves is established by wind speed, wind duration, and *fetch,* the distance of open water over which the wind blows without changing direction.

As a wave passes, water molecules move in circular orbits that diminish in diameter with water depth. Waves are a

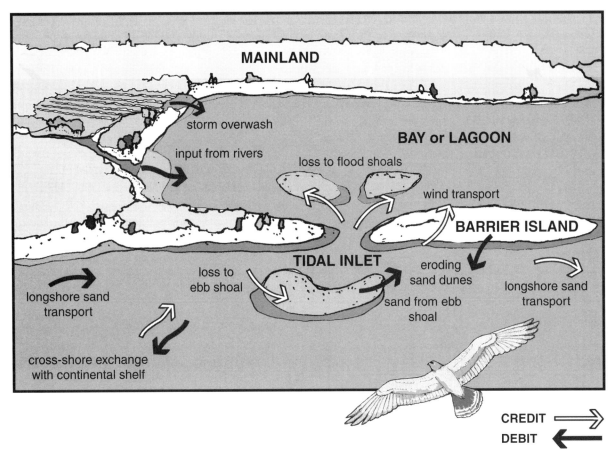

Figure 8.4 *Components of the sediment budget:* barrier island and spit.

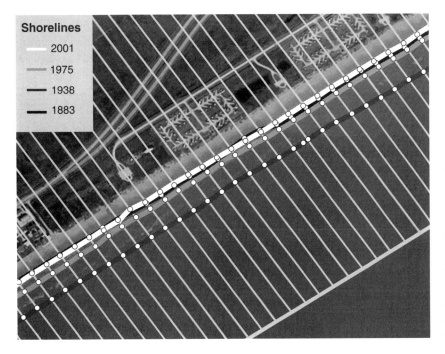

Figure 8.5 *Changes in the shoreline* are documented by LIDAR, providing comparative analysis of historic and present trends.

Source: NOAA Shoreline Web site, "A Guide to National Shoreline Data and Terms. Shoreline Change Analysis," <http://shoreline.noaa.gov/apps/index.html>.

disturbance of the water surface and do not carry water with them as the travel across the surface. Under sustained winds, wave height and steepness will increase until the waves break, forming whitecaps. When this occurs and the waves can no longer grow, the sea is said to be "fully developed."[2]

As waves approach the shore, the wave speed slows, wavelength shortens, and wave height increases as a wave passes over shallow depths along the inshore until breaking along the surf zone. (Figure 8.6.)

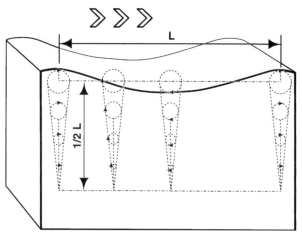

(A) DEEP WATER WAVE

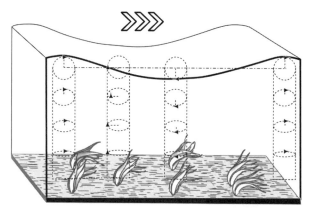

(B) SHALLOW WATER WAVE

Figure 8.6 *Mechanics of wave motion:* In deep water, water particles under force of wave motion follow an elliptical but near-circular path with a vertical momentum, decreasing in force as a function of depth. As the wave advances and is compressed in shallow water, the momentum of each particle is nearly flattened to horizontal and speeds the wave's shorebound trajectory.

As wave height increases, a wave begins to lose its generally rounded sinusoidal shape and its crest becomes peaked. When its height exceeds one-seventh of its wavelength, the wave becomes unstable and breaks. Different types of breaking waves, known intimately by surfers, are defined by the profile of the surf zone and nearshore slope. (Figures 8.7 and 8.8.)

Beaches, Bluffs, and Headlands

As waves approach a jagged shoreline, they refract and focus energy on projecting headlands. Over geologic time, waves pulverize rocky headlands and undercut bluffs, eroding the land until the hills and promontories are reduced to a low coastal plain. As the land erodes, fine-grain soils settle out in the deep ocean or in bays and marshes, leaving behind only coarse-grained sands and cobbles in the surf zone.

With time, the shoreline is transformed into a chain of thin barrier islands and sandy beaches facing the ocean, often separated from the mainland by a bay or lagoon. Barrier islands are a landform ideally suited to absorbing and dissipating the energy of ocean waves. With rising sea levels, barrier islands tend to migrate landward.

BAYS behind a barrier island and within transecting river deltas form *estuaries* where freshwater and saltwater mix and tidal marshes flourish. Sheltered from waves, and with a gradient of freshwater flow from the coastal upland mixing with the ocean water, these shallow brackish bays are a haven for wildlife, shellfish, and recreational boaters.

BEACHES are shaped and continuously reshaped by forces of waves and wind. (Figure 8.9.) Some shorelines may experience large seasonal fluctuations in beach width, profile, and elevation, a result of seasonal variations in wave conditions and water levels. (Figure 8.10.)

DUNES are low, parallel sandy ridges typical of natural beach backshore formation. Dunes provide a natural barrier that can prevent storm waves from moving inland. During a storm, wave erosion will cause beach berms and dunes to become steeper as sands are transported offshore, forming nearshore bars. Following a storm, calm weather

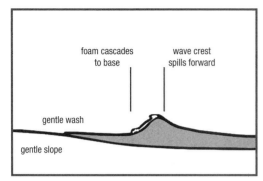

SPILLING BREAKER

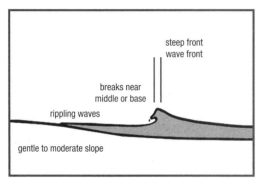

COLLAPSING BREAKER

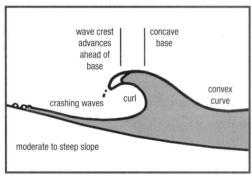

PLUNGING BREAKER

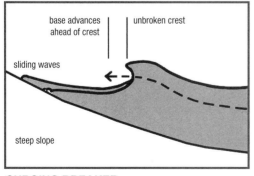

SURGING BREAKER

Figure 8.7 *Breaking waves* are defined by their shape as a function of nearshore beach profile.

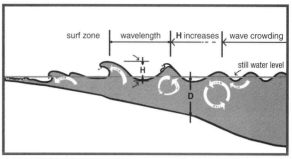

BREAKER FORMATION

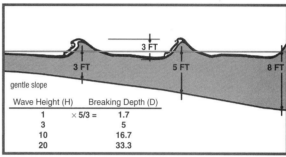

SPILLING BREAKERS

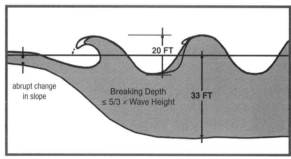

PLUNGING BREAKERS

Figure 8.8 *Breaker formation* can indicate the slope and depth of the nearshore beach profile.

waves eventually carry sand from the bars back to the shore, rebuilding the dunes and berms. Marine species of fish, shellfish, crabs, and birds find niches along the shore. The process of beach and dune formation is an enduring cycle, which, if left on its own, creates a self-sustaining ecosystem. (Figure 8.11.)

Beaches and barrier islands are resilient landforms that can absorb the energy of breaking waves by shifting and changing shape, rolling with the ocean's forces of tide and storms. The same dynamic makes some barrier islands or some significant portions of them unsuitable for building infrastructure and buildings.

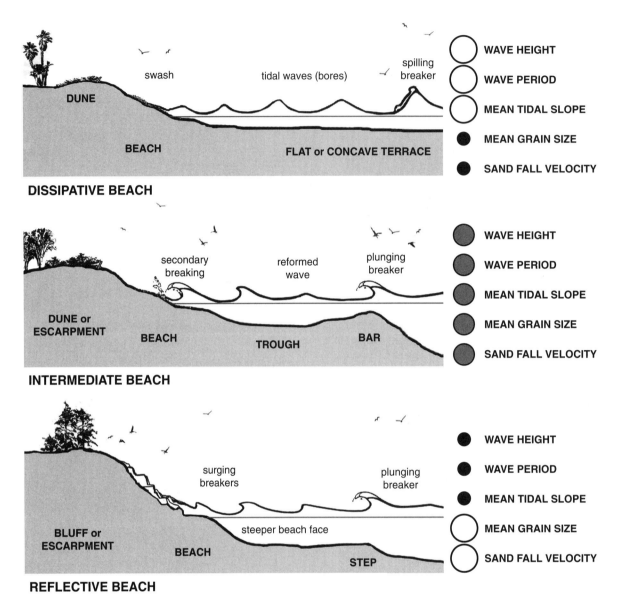

Figure 8.9 *Types of beaches* are defined by nearshore slope and profile and resulting character of waves and beach compositions.

Source: Graphic comparison after M. Herrman et al., "Testing the Habitat Harshness Hypothesis," *Journal of Molluscan Studies* *(2009)*, <mollus.oxfordjournals.org/cgi/reprint/eyp044v1.pdf>.

Protection of Coastal Wetlands and Marshes

Areas of shoreline that normally serve as buffers—inlets, estuaries, and wetlands—have been reduced or eliminated by erosion or development. Data from Hurricane Rita support a calculation that storm surge elevation could be reduced by approximately 1 foot in height for every 1.4 mile of inland reach of coastal wetlands.[3] Coastal marshes

and wetlands should be protected and expanded along with coastal vegetation and landscapes. (Figures 8.12 and 8.13.)

Protection of Rocky Coastlines

Rocky coastlines are generally resistant to dramatic erosion. Typical of the Pacific, Great Lakes, and New England, rocky coasts experience slow and incremental geologic processes including erosion, rockfall, and caving

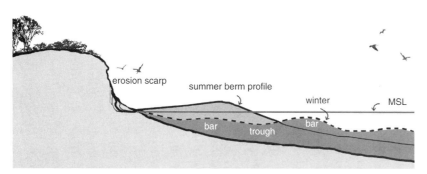

SUMMER AND WINTER BEACH EROSION

Figure 8.10 *Seasonal fluctuations* in beach width and elevation are part of the changing shoreline dynamic.

Figure 8.11 *Beach grasses and other vegetation* stabilize dunes, making them more resistant to storm erosion. Sandy Neck, Cape Cod, Massachusetts.

(PHOTO: Marja Watson)

Figure 8.12 *Wetlands and coastal marshes* absorb wind energy and blunt storm surges.

(PHOTO: James B. DeStefano)

Figure 8.13 *Vegetative buffer and dunes* along U.S. southeastern coastline.

(PHOTO: Donald Watson)

SUMMARY OF COASTAL FLOOD HAZARDS

- **High-velocity flows** can be created or exacerbated by man-made or natural obstructions along the shoreline and by points of least resistance opened by roads and access paths that cross dunes, bridges, or canals, channels, or drainage features.

- **Floodborne debris** may include decks, steps, ramps, breakaway wall panels, portions of or entire houses, heating oil and propane tanks, vehicles, boats, pilings, fences, and destroyed erosion control structures.

- **High winds** from tropical cyclones (hurricanes), coastal storms, and tornadoes generate the most significant coastal wind hazard. Wind speeds can increase on or near the crests of high coastal bluffs, cliffs, or dunes, or in gorges and canyons.

- **Windborne debris and rainfall penetration** can damage the building envelope. Even small failures in the building envelope will, at the least, lead to interior damage by rain penetration and winds. At worst, depressurization and complete collapse may result.

- **Erosion** can be an unexpected but significant impact of even mild flooding events, exposing landforms and structures to collateral damage during and after a storm event.

- **Localized scour** can occur when water flows at high velocities past an object embedded in or resting on erodible soil, undermining its structural stability.

- **Overwash and sediment burial**. Sediment eroded during a coastal storm travels to the offshore or laterally along the shore or inland. Overwash occurs when low-lying coastal lands are overtopped and eroded by storm surges and waves, carried landward along paths of least resistance by floodwaters, burying uplands, roads, and at-grade structures.

- **Salt spray and moisture effects** often lead to corrosion and decay of building materials in the coastal environment. Inspection of coastal buildings near salt water typically reveals deterioration of improperly selected or installed materials. These are a common source of construction failure.

- **Floating ice**. Some coastal areas are vulnerable to problems cause by floating ice. These include erosion, gouging of coastal shorelines, flooding due to ice jams, and

lateral and vertical ice loads on shore protection structures and coastal buildings.

- **Sea level rise and lake level rise**. Flood effects described earlier typically occur over a period of hours or days. With global warming, long-term rise in sea levels and temperatures is expected to increase the severity of coastal flood and storm events.

in response to elevated water levels, waves, and storms. Breakers erode the base of the cliff, forming caves in zones of weakness. Caves eventually may form arches, which then possibly collapse. Weathering causes rockfalls on the cliff face. Debris flows and avalanches on steep slopes are triggered by seismicity, heavy soil saturation, and loss of tree root strength. (Figure 8.14.)

Summary of Coastal Flood Hazards

Flood-resistant design rests on analysis of current and future coastal storm impacts, including high wind speeds, flooding, seismic activity, and erosion. Coastal flood hazards, introduced in earlier chapters, are summarized in the above box. Of these, storm surge is the most severe and dangerous impact. (Figure 8.15.)

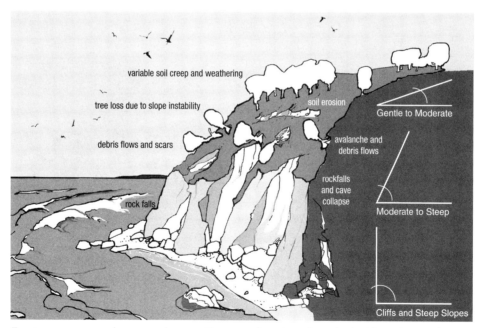

Figure 8.14 *Erosion processes along a rocky coastline* are a function of geological foundation, slope, vegetative cover, and wind and wave exposure.

Source: FEMA, *Coastal Construction Manual: Principles and Practices of Planning, Siting, Designing, Constructing, and Maintaining Residential Buildings in Coastal Areas* (FEMA 55) (August 2005), www.fema.gov/rebuild/mat/fema55.shtm.

Figure 8.15 *Storm surge* can be increased in height by inland flooding and peak astronomical tides.

8.2 SHORELINE PROTECTION

Structural Measures of Shoreline Protection

Coastal development typically requires measures to stabilize the shoreline and to prevent erosion. If there is inadequate supply of sand, "hard structures" cannot control erosion. In the absence of adequate sand, hard structures such as seawalls, bulkheads, and revetments can protect uplands but often at the expense of the beach. They reflect waves sharply, causing greater turbulence and increased erosion. Inappropriate "hard" measures can lead to more damage than would occur without them.

The U.S. Army Corps of Engineers regulates structures or work affecting navigable waters of the United States according to Rivers and Harbors Act (Title 33, United States Code, Section 403, 1899) and any activity that results in discharges of dredged or fill material into waters of the United States (which includes wetlands) according to Section 404 of the Clean Water Act.

SEAWALL AND BULKHEADS are intended as armoring the shoreline. While vertical seawalls are the most common of shore protection measures, they are possibly the most ineffective of measures because they do not prevent erosion of the beach. Waves striking the face of a vertical seawall reflect off the wall such that their energy is concentrated at its bottom or toe. This can cause rapid erosion in front of the wall, leading to loss of the beach there, and can eventually undermine the seawall foundations. In severe storms, vertical seawalls often are damaged or destroyed. If they withstand the storm, they often fail to prevent flood damage to lands and buildings behind. (Figure 8.16.)

REVETMENTS are armored slopes typically faced with large boulders, precast concrete, or riprap. Breaking waves will run up the sloped face of a revetment, dissipating their energy. (Figure 8.17.)

GEOTEXTILE CONTAINERS are available as single-cell (monotube) and connected multicell installations and are used primarily as dune protection. Although somewhat resilient, they are considered to be a form of structural revetment. When used for permanent installation, geotextile containers are filled with sand slurry. They help to protect and restore dunes in approved locations, wide beaches, proper slopes and installation details. In severe storm and hurricanes, some geotextile installations have been dislodged or resulted in additional erosion. In other installations, they have remained intact and in place. (Figure 8.18.)

GROINS are short structures built perpendicular to the shore, They are intended to intercept the littoral migration of beach sand. They usually are built of rubble stone mounds. Breakwaters and groins are effective in retaining sand and reducing erosion losses, thereby preserving the beach when there is an adequate supply of sand moving through the system but sometimes at the expense of unprotected downdrift beaches. Groins should

(A)

(B)

Figure 8.16 *Seawalls* provide only partial and limited protection. (A) Eroded beach along the Connecticut shore; (B) New Smyrna Beach, Florida, after Hurricane Wilma, 2005.

Source: Florida Department of Environmental Protection, *Critically Eroded Beaches Report*, 2005, http://www.dep.state.fl.us/beaches/publications/tech-rpt.htm#Critical_Erosion_Reports.

be no higher than the beach they are intended to build so that, when filled, they will pass sand to the downdrift coastline. Building groins or other structures that impede the natural littoral drift of a beach is no longer considered sound practice and is prohibited by some coastal programs.[4] (Figure 8.19.)

JETTIES are built in pairs on either side of a navigable channel, to create the channel. They are intended to confine the tidal flow of water to within the narrow channel to prevent shoaling within the channel. Jetties usually are built

Figure 8.18 *Subsurface dune restoration system (SDRS)*, September 7, 2004: Remained in place leaving accretion of sand at its base after Hurricanes Jeanne and Francis, Vero Beach Florida.

(PHOTO: Courtesy of Advanced Coastal Technologies)

Source: Florida Department of Environmental Protection, *Hurricane Frances and Hurricane Jeanne Post-storm Beach Conditions and Coastal Impact Report*, 2004, www.dep.state .fl.us/BEACHES/publications/tech-rpt.htm.

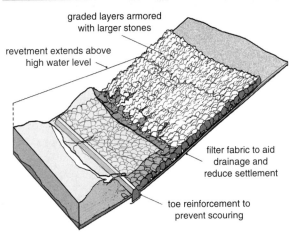

graded layers armored with larger stones

revetment extends above high water level

filter fabric to aid drainage and reduce settlement

toe reinforcement to prevent scouring

Figure 8.17 *Revetments* provide a measure of shore protection in locations where other measures are not feasible.

(PHOTOS: James B. DeStefano)

of rubble stone mounds that extend into deep water. Jetties block the natural littoral drift of sands along the shore and often result in the accretion of sand on the updrift side of the inlet and erosion on the downdrift side. (Figure 8.20.)

BREAKWATERS are built to create sheltered harbors for boats and ships. They absorb the energy of breaking waves and prevent waves from passing over them. Breakwaters usually have one end that terminates at the shore but sometimes are built offshore with no connection to the land. *Offshore breakwaters* can trap available littoral sediments and reduce the sediment supply to nearby beaches. This adverse effect must be mitigated by combining breakwater construction with beach nourishment. (Figure 8.21.)

Nonstructural Measures of Shoreline Protection

Nonstructural, or "soft," measures of shore protection are more effective and often less costly than structural approaches. They include dune restoration, vegetation, light protection such as fencing, and extension and nourishment of beaches. They typically have fewer potential adverse impacts.

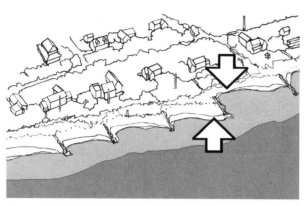

Figure 8.19 *Groins* can cause offset, uneven erosion and accretion, depicted in the illustration (above) and a Long Island Sound beach (below).

(PHOTO: James B. DeStefano)

Source: FEMA 55.

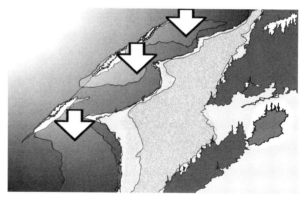

Figure 8.21 *Littoral sediments* are trapped behind offshore breakers. Presque Isle, Pennsylvania.

Source: FEMA 55.

Figure 8.20 *Construction of jetties* or similar structures at a tidal inlet of a bay, harbor, or river entrance often results in accretion on one side and erosion on the other, resulting in substantial shoreline offset. Ocean City inlet, Maryland—opened by a 1933 hurricane and stabilized by jetties in 1934–1935—now evidences extreme offset of accretion on one side and erosion on the other.

Source: FEMA 55.

VEGETATIVE SHORE PROTECTION

methods involve planting dune grasses or other native shoreline plant species along dunes adjacent to beaches. The plantings develop a dense root network that helps to stabilize the dunes. Dune vegetation should be protected from foot traffic by fencing and boardwalks. (Figure 8.22.)

Dune vegetation has to become established over years and decades. Dune systems are resilient, but severe storms exploit their weaknesses:

- A dune that is not covered by well-established vegetation in place for two or more growing seasons will be more vulnerable to wind and flood damage.

- A dune crossed by a road or pedestrian path will offer a weak point that storm waves and flooding will exploit.

BEACH NOURISHMENT is mechanical addition of sand from other locations to replenish or widen an eroded beach. Beach nourishment is a temporary measure

Figure 8.22 *Sea oat and sea grape vegetation* and dune over subsurface restoration system installed 1987, Palm Beach, Florida.

(PHOTO: Courtesy of Advanced Coastal Technologies)

that may last up to 10 to 15 years and is thus costly and often controversial. Sand can be trucked in from off-site or, more commonly, pumped onto the beach from offshore bars with hydraulic dredges. To prevent rapid erosion of the new sands, the profile of the nourished beach must be graded based on site-specific wave analysis.

8.3 FLOOD BARRIERS AND FLOODGATES

FLOOD BARRIERS—in various configurations called levees, dikes (or dykes), embankments, berms, floodbanks, or flood walls—are natural or artificial construction intended to contain water flow and flooding.

FLOODGATES   provide a means of access through a flood barrier. Floodgates and other measures that require

operators or active mechanical or electrical controls do not meet FEMA requirements in most V zones and Coastal SFHAs. In less impacted areas, flood barrier and floodgate approaches can provide a measure of property protection for building sites and communities. (Figures 8.23 and 8.24.)

Protection for severe flooding beyond an individual site scale involves large infrastructure investments. These measures are discussed in subsequent chapters as a response to sea level rise.

8.4 SUMMARY OF COASTAL PROTECTION MEASURES

The report of the Association of State Floodplain Managers (ASFPM) titled *No Adverse Impact in the Coastal Zone* advocates a comprehensive approach to coastal flood protection and mitigation.[6] The report sets as a goal the

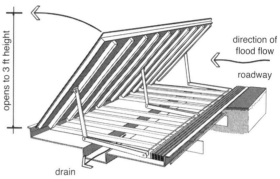

Figure 8.23 *Flood embankment and walls* installed after the Spring 1997 snowmelt flood of the Red River, Grand Forks, North Dakota.

(PHOTO: Michael Rieger FEMA Photo Library, March 27, 2007)

Figure 8.24 *Automatic roadway gate* Floodbreak™.

(PHOTO courtesy of Floodbreak Inc.)

avoidance or reduction of negative impacts of coastal development or flood-control action on adjacent properties, communities, and the coastal environment. Negative effects may be direct, such as erosion on the adjacent property, or indirect, such as impacting the economic value of a fishery or altering the filtration capacity of natural coastal zones, including marshes or estuaries. As a summary of this chapter, the next points recap ASFPM recommendations for coastal protection and enhancement.

Dissipate Flooding Impacts by Increasing Channels and Waterways

Flooding from storm surge or tsunami can be minimized by increasing the dissipation area available to floodwaters. Design and management should protect and increase adjacent wetlands and other low land along susceptible coastlines.

Minimize Use of Structural Protection Measures

Structural protection measures are increasingly considered a "last resort" for mitigation of erosion. Although bulkheads and other vertical walls may be needed in harbors and other waterways, they should be minimized as much as possible. Wave reflection can cause adverse impacts on other properties and on waterway activities. Revetments (and seawalls where required) should be located as far as feasible from the normal range of water's edge to minimize interactions between these structures and waves during more frequent storms and tidal ranges. Some measure of wave absorption should be required on new bulkheads if wave reflection could create a problem for others. An absence of grout between rocks or blocks in seawalls, revetments, and groins dissipates wave energy and allows vegetation to take hold. Revetments that deflect wave energy also can provide habitat for marine life where nooks and crannies are designed into the structure.

EROSION HAZARD CHECKLIST

General Information

- Property location and dimensions
- Land use at site and adjacent properties
- Historical flood and erosion damage descriptions at site and nearby

Coastal Flood Conditions—Observed and Predicted

- Flood elevations due to tides, storm surge, tsunami, or seiche
- Wave conditions at shoreline (height, period, direction)
- Erosion of beach, dune, and/or bluff
- Sediment overwash
- Breaching or inlet formation

Local Soils and Geology

- Soils, geology, and vegetation—site and region
- Site drainage—potential for erosion from surface water or groundwater
- Coastal morphology and coastal processes
- Wave climate
- Presence and influence of nearby inlets, harbors, coastal structures
- Littoral sediment supply and sediment budget
- Topography of near shore, beach, dune, bluff, uplands
- Relative sea level changes or lake level changes—land subsidence or uplift

Shoreline History

- Shoreline change maps and historical aerial photography
- Published erosion rates—long-term and short-term
- Spatial variability in erosion rates
- Temporal variability in erosion rates (seasonal, annual, long-term)
- Erosion/accretion cycles—magnitude and periodicity
- Most landward historical shoreline (most landward shoreline that has occurred over the past 50–70 years)
- Errors and uncertainties associated with erosion rates

Harbor/Inlet Navigation Projects; Erosion Control Projects

- Navigation projects (jetties, dredged channels) affecting site
- Shore protection structures, on property or nearby
- Dune/bluff stabilization projects, on property or nearby
- Beach/dune nourishment projects—completed on planned

Other Erosion/Sediment Considerations

- Erosion by wind
- Erosion by ice
- Burial by storm overwash or windborne sand
- Erosion due to channeling of flow between buildings or obstructions
- Local scour potential and presence of terminating strata

Source: FEMA. 2005. Coastal Construction Manual: Principles and Practices of Planning, Siting, Designing, Constructing, and Maintaining Residential Buildings in Coastal Areas (FEMA 55) August, 2005. www.fema.gov/rebuild/mat/fema55.shtm.

Use Nonstructural Protection Measures

Before resorting to structural measures, nonstructural options should be deployed, including:

- Adapt to natural coastal processes by substantial setback distances and removal of at-risk structures.

- Restore natural shorelines by retaining and nourishing beaches, revegetating the shore, conserving or constructing dunes and beach ridges, creating or restoring wetlands, modifying the ends of structures that must stay to minimize the end effects on other properties and natural resources.

- Reduce erosion by stabilizing coastal slopes, slowing wind erosion, improving existing protective structures, and tripping waves.

- Reduce shoreline erosion with hybrid stabilization techniques, such as a vegetation and geotextile measures. The hybrid approach provides more resistance to erosion than vegetation alone in moderate energy environments and increases diverse habitat compared to riprap or stone revetments.

Take Erosion Seriously

Erosion increases coastal flood hazards over time, due to loss of protective beaches, dunes and bluffs, and soil that support building foundations. Failure to account for long-term erosion is one of the common errors made in planning coastal buildings and communities.

Notes

1. NOAA Shoreline Web site, "A Guide to National Shoreline Data and Terms. Shoreline Change Analysis," http://shoreline.noaa.gov/apps/index.html; *also, Canvis-Digital Coast,* www.csc.noaa.gov/digitalcoast/tools/canvis/.

2. Scripps Institution of Oceanography Coastal Data Information Program, http://cdip.ucsd.edu/?nav=documents&sub=index&xitem=waves.

3. J. G. Wilkins et al., 2008. Louisiana Coastal Hazard Mitigation Guidebook. Louisiana Sea Grant College Program, cited in National Wildlife Federation, 2006 www.nwf.org/hurricanes/hurricanesand wetlands.cfm.

4. NOAA, "State, Territory and Commonwealth Beach Nourishment Programs: A National Overview," 2000, http://coastalmanagement.noaa.gov/resources/docs/finalbeach.pdf.

5. NOAA Coastal Services Center, "Beach Nourishment: A Guide for Local Government Officials," 2009. www.csc.noaa.gov/beachnourishment/html/geo/shorelin.htm.

6. Association of State Floodplain Managers, *No Adverse Impact Handbook* (Madison, WI. 2008, www.floods.org/NoAdverseImpact/CNAI_Handbook/CNAI_Handbook.pdf.

Figure 9.1 *Storm surge* exceeding the base flood elevation (BFE) by 2 to 5 feet (.6 to 1.5 m) swept across Gilchrist, Texas, upon landfall of Hurricane Ike. The few structures that survived had been elevated more than several feet above the BFE.

(PHOTO: Jocelyn Augustino, FEMA Photo Library, September 22, 2008)

CHAPTER 9

FLOOD DESIGN PRACTICES FOR BUILDINGS

Flood design must meet Federal Emergency Management Agency (FEMA) minimum requirements. In addition, designers should consider exceeding minimum requirements to design for risks from potential changes in floodplain and coastal conditions, including future development, erosion, and sea level rise.

Design for flooding is not limited to mapped floodplains. Flood regulations do not cover areas beyond the mapped floodplain and do not account for upland land use and development that can affect floodplain areas. The conditions of the entire watershed well beyond the regulated riverine or coastal hazard zones determine water budgets and flooding impacts. Along large river basins where flooding is regulated with varying standards of approvals and enforcement by different municipalities and communities, flooding conditions may be aggravated by development upstream of the regulated floodplain.

Professional Standard of Care

Recommended practices for flood design are regularly updated. New requirements and recommendations for flood resistant design follow from more accurate and extended postdisaster studies and risk assessments. New methods and materials of construction are being developed and help solve vexing issues.

In Special Flood Hazard Area (SFHA) V zones, construction plans for all new and substantially improved structures typically must be certified by a registered design professional (a licensed architect or engineer). Postdisaster mitigation assessment studies recommend that the same certification requirement be extended to Coastal A zones.[1]

Design professionals must exercise best judgment of where and how to go beyond minimum requirements to assure health, safety, and welfare of building occupants and communities. The flood design practices described in this chapter include those required for V zones, Coastal A zones, and other areas where flooding may occur.

9.1 OVERVIEW OF FLOOD DESIGN

Goals of Flood-Resistant Design

- **Reduce direct impacts** from flooding, high-velocity water flow, waves, scour and erosion, and debris impacts. Provisions for design in SFHAs provide minimum requirements. Poststorm assessments provide ample documentation that minimum requirements should be exceeded. Margin of safety factors should be determined by the designer and property owner, with consideration of insurance rating incentives, vulnerability of the site, and future climate and weather trends.

- **Reduce wind-induced and rain impacts.** Rain intrusion results when openings and building envelope are deficient or are damaged by hurricane wind and windborne debris, often concurrent with flooding events.

- **Reduce indirect impacts**, including degradation or contamination of building materials and mold.

- **Provide emergency refuge and escape**. Unlike earthquakes, and with the exception of flash floods, most flood threats can be anticipated so that evacuation from a building is possible. However, flooding and storm surge often exceed any prior or anticipated levels. Emergency egress of building occupants and access of first responders should be provided.

Flood-Resistant Design includes measures so that:

- Building foundation remains intact and functional.
- Building envelope (lowest floor, walls, openings and roof) remains structurally sound and capable of minimizing penetration wind, rain, and debris.
- Lowest floor is elevated sufficiently to prevent floodwaters from entering the building through the lowest floor and envelope during the design flood event.
- Utility connections (electricity, water, sewer, natural gas) remain intact with no threat to life safety, or are easily restored to service.

- Damage to breakaway enclosures and site elements below the design flood level do not cause further damage to foundation, utility connection, or the elevated portion of the building or to adjacent structures and properties.

The most effective measures to fully protect buildings and provide life safety from severe flood hazards are either to relocate or to elevate the building.

Relocation

Relocate the entire building away from the area subject to flooding. Relocation is the most reasonable of options to reduce or eliminate life safety and property risk. It is often necessary for those structures exposed to direct coastal surges or to cliff or riverine erosion. For many property owners, this option is economically feasible only if it is possible to relocate within their existing property, either to higher ground or with greater setback from a flood source. (Figure 9.2.)

Figure 9.2   *Building relocation*. FEMA assists in relocating highest-risk insured buildings that are repeatedly flooded. Skykomish River, Gold Bar, Washington.

(PHOTO: Marvin Nauman FEMA Photo Library, January 2007)

Elevation

When relocation is not feasible, elevation is the preferred and at times the only strategy of flood-resistant design. Elevation may be accomplished by raising and supporting a building structure on:

- Piles, posts, piers, or columns: required for V and recommended for Coastal A zones.

- Compacted fill: recommended only for A zones.

- Walls or a crawl space: allowable in A zones subject to openings, construction, and zone.

Elevation of an existing building to meet National Flood Insurance Program (NFIP) and community regulations involves raising the lowest floor (habitable space with permitted uses) to or above the Design Flood Elevation (DFE). A basement that is below grade on all sides is prohibited. The area under the elevated building may be used for storage, parking, or building access and stairs.

Lifting a building, such as a residence, above the ground presents both technical and aesthetic design challenges. In this section, the technical issues are reviewed. Aesthetic implications of raising the active building and living levels above the ground plain are discussed again at the end of this chapter. (Figure 9.3.)

ELEVATING A BUILDING IN V ZONES AND COASTAL A ZONES

Coastal waves and flooding can exert strong hydrodynamic forces on any exposed building element. NFIP requires that all new buildings, substantially damaged buildings, and substantially improved buildings in Coastal High Hazard Areas V zones be elevated to or above the base flood elevation

Figure 9.3a *Coastal community on Bolivar Peninsula, Texas*: Hurricane Ike exceeded the base flood elevation (BFE) by several feet, and 4,000 to 6,000 houses were destroyed in Bolivar. Those surviving were generally constructed well above the BFE.

(PHOTO: Jocelyn Augustino FEMA Photo Library, September 2008)

Figure 9.3b   *Elevated house, Baldwin County, Alabama: This house* survived Hurricanes Ivan and Dennis.

(PHOTO: Mark Wolfe FEMA Photo Library, July 2005)

Figure 9.3c   *Justine Plantation, Mandeville, Louisiana:* Photo shows one of few houses to survive the Hurricane Katrina storm surge that washed over seawalls at Lake Pontchartrain.

(PHOTO: Jeff Markham FEMA Photo Library, September 2005)

(BFE)—or DFE as determined by local regulations[2]—on open foundations consisting of piles, posts, piers, or columns. Similar design is recommended for Coastal A zones. The space below the elevated building must be "free of obstructions." The open foundations must allow high-velocity waves and water to flow beneath the building.

ELEVATING A BUILDING IN OTHER FLOOD-PRONE ZONES

For noncoastal flood zones or coastal floodplains subject to minimal wave action, NFIP regulations define the allowable BFE as the elevation of the top (walking surface) of the lowest floor while also requiring that materials below that level be flood-damage-resistant. With the possible exception of a concrete slab or floor plate, this minimum provision is insufficient to prevent water damage to building materials that typically are placed within a floor structure (insulation and finishes) or that rest just above the DFE. Conventional floor construction materials placed on or near the DFE are subject to water and moisture damage as a result of localized cresting, splashing, or capillary action. While they are permitted by regulation in A zones, due diligence design should assure that there is sufficient freeboard to raise the entire underfloor construction well above the DFE.

ELEVATION BASED ON FILL

In V zones, use of fill is prohibited. In Coastal A zones, elevating a building on open foundations of piers or piles is recommended. In some situations and subject to approval (noncoastal floodplains, coastal floodplains with minimal wave action), fill may be used to elevate the structure above the BFE and thus place it and the filled area above the floodplain. The foundation must be engineered so that any erosion of fill that is placed around or under the structure would not endanger the foundation itself. (Figure 9.4.)

In A zones and other lower-hazard zones, elevating the entire building construction on fill or partial fill may offer economic and aesthetic advantages. Fill can elevate a site above the DFE and thus relieve the building construction from certain NFIP requirements. Fill may be used to partially elevate the site to reduce the vertical distance between the ground and the elevated building. This may allow shorter foundations, such as posts or piers, to be used.

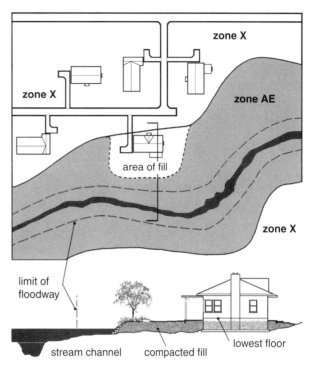

Figure 9.4a *Elevation based on fill.* A site and building could be elevated out of an AE zone by approved fill.

Source: FEMA, Technical Bulletin (TB) 10, "Ensuring that Structures Built on Fill in or Near Special Flood Hazard Are Reasonably Safe from Flooding," www.fema.gov/plan/prevent/floodplain/techbul.shtm.

Figure 9.4b *Mitigated house on fill,* Port Sulfur, Louisiana.

(PHOTO: Marvin Nauman FEMA Photo Library, April 2006)

Partial elevation also may improve building accessibility and keep interior living areas closer to outside areas.

Placing the entire structure at or above the level of the DFE will minimize flood risk and is the recommended approach to constructing on fill. Caution is still required: A structure with a basement adjacent to a floodplain may be impacted by subsurface water resulting from area flooding. Extensive regrading or filling could result in deflecting run-off and flooding impacts onto adjacent sites or structures.

Wet Floodproofing and Dry Floodproofing

The terms *wet floodproofing* and *dry floodproofing* are used in FEMA regulations and publications. They describe strategies that, where allowed, may be used in addition to or as a replacement for building elevation alone. (Figure 9.5.)

WET FLOODPROOFING is defined by FEMA as "permanent or contingent measures applied to a structure and its contents that prevent or provide resistance to damage that may result by allowing floodwaters to enter the structure."[3] Wet floodproofing is permitted only by variance or special exception. The basis of exception is proof of hardship where it is not possible or practical to elevate the structure above the DFE.

Wet floodproofing is appropriate for structures whose use is functionally dependent on close proximity to water, historic buildings, or accessory structures for used solely for parking or limited storage.

In addition to allowing flow of floodwater into portions of the building, wet floodproofing requirements include:

- Design entire structure for resistance to floodwater flow, collapse, and lateral movement.
- Use flood-resistant materials below the DFE.
- Locate all mechanical and utility equipment above the DFE, with any portions and connections below the DFE designed to be floodproofed.

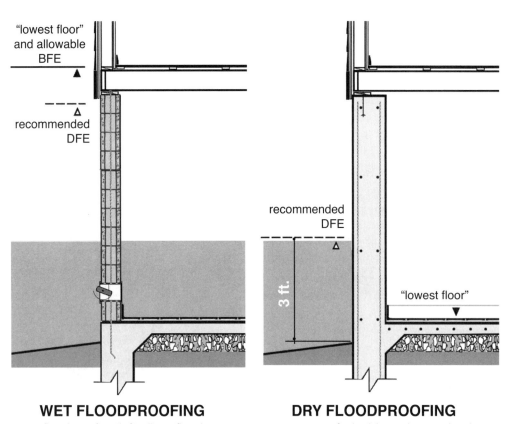

WET FLOODPROOFING **DRY FLOODPROOFING**

Figure 9.5 *Wet floodproofing* (left) allows floodwaters to enter portions of a building, along with other measures to protect the structure and contents, permitted only by variance or special exception. *Dry floodproofing* (right) excludes floodwaters and is permitted only for nonresidential structures.

NONRESIDENTIAL DRY FLOOD-PROOFING IN A ZONES

Dry floodproofing involves perimeter barriers to prevent floodwater intrusion into the interior and related measures that eliminate or reduce the potential for flood damage. Dry floodproofing is not allowed for any type of structure or building in V zones. It is not allowed for residential structures in A zones.

The NFIP allows a new or substantially improved nonresidential building in an A zone to be dry floodproofed, that is, to have some portion of the "lowest floor below the base flood elevation." It may be appropriate for existing nonresidential buildings in A zones or zones of lesser hazard subject to flood mitigation and renovation. In most cases, dry floodproofing is permitted only under very strict circumstances.

In addition to excluding floodwater from potions of the building, dry floodproofing requirements include:

- Anchor the building to resist flotation, collapse, and lateral movement.

- Install watertight closures for doors and windows.

- Reinforce walls to withstand floodwater pressures and impact forces generated by floating debris.

- Use membranes and other sealants to reduce seepage of floodwater through walls and wall penetrations.

- Install pumps and backup power generation to control interior water levels.

- Install backflow valves to prevent the entrance of floodwater or sewage.

- Install elevator(s) with all possible measures protecting the elevator equipment from flood damage.

Hydrostatic and hydrodynamic pressures exerted by rising floodwater can cause walls to buckle or collapse. Dry floodproofing construction is most appropriate with slab-on-grade structures and concrete or fully grouted and reinforced masonry walls. Concrete and masonry are more resistant to flood damage and stronger than other conventional construction materials. In such cases, detailing—mortaring and sealants, corrosion protection of embedded reinforcement and metal connectors—requires special care in specification and installation.

Dry floodproofing, where permitted, is acceptable within requirements just listed, where the DFE is not greater than 3 feet higher than the floor elevation as a practical limit of the structural capacity of enclosing walls. The maximum height may be further restricted and proscribed in local regulations. If doorways penetrate the enclosure, watertight doors or floodgates must be installed. Many commercial product choices are available for flood barriers for driveways, below-grade parking entrances, and building openings. (Figure 9.6.)

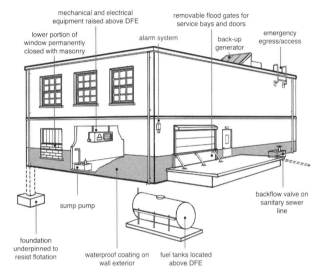

Figure 9.6a *Dry floodproofing measures* are applicable for flood mitigation of existing nonresidential buildings, subject to specific approvals and certifications.

Source: FEMA, TB 3, "Non-Residential Floodproofing—Requirements and Certification," www.fema.gov/plan/prevent/floodplain/techbul.shtm.

Figure 9.6b *Dry floodproofing measures* for approved nonresidential buildings include floodwalls, floodgates, and other removal panel systems.

(PHOTO: Courtesy of *FloodBarrier* Unlimited Applications Inc.)

Measures that require human intervention—often called "active techniques"—are appropriate only if there is adequate warning time (12 hours is a recommended minimum) and someone is reliably present to implement the required measures. Additional provisions include warning systems, safety and access, flood emergency planning, and inspection and maintenance protocols.

Repair and Remodeling of Existing Structures

Bringing an existing structure into compliance with flood regulations may require raising the elevation of the building, relocating mechanical and electrical equipment, or approved wet floodproofing spaces and materials. These measures are required for addition and alterations of existing buildings in regulated flood zones meeting the definitions of *substantial damages* or *substantial improvements*.[4]

Substantial damages are those of any origin sustained by a structure whereby the cost of restoring the structure to its before-damaged condition would equal or exceed 50% of the market value of the structure before the damage occurred. Improvement to structures determined to be substantially damaged are considered to be "substantial improvements," regardless of the extent of repair work performed.

Substantial improvements are defined as reconstruction, rehabilitation, addition, or other improvements of a structure, the cost of which equals or exceeds 50% of the market value of the structure (or a smaller percentage if established by the community) before the "start of construction" of the improvement. This term includes structures that have incurred "substantial damage" regardless of the actual repair work performed.

Certifications

Construction of buildings in SFHAs require a number of certifications defined by FEMA, depending on zone classification, and may include elevation, flood openings, floodproofing, V-zone design, and breakaway walls. In advance of construction, site-related issues such as floodway requirements may require hydrologic analysis and certification. As-built elements are certified by a licensed architect, engineer, or surveyor. Items that require certification may include utilities or equipment, anchoring, septic systems, gas well equipment, or flood-resistant materials.

Each of these items should be clearly indicated in construction documents with the required elevation data in order to establish a record for construction administration, commissioning, and certification.

9.2 FLOOD DESIGN AT THE BUILDING SCALE

Site

Site and landscape options are discussed in prior chapters, including Chapter 6 and Chapter 8.

A *coastal landscape* should be designed to stabilize the ground surface and to minimize erosion and debris during flooding. Alterations to the natural topography of a coastal site should be minimized. All exterior landscape elements—signs, lighting, fences, seating, outside patios—must be designed either to endure flooding and storm surge or to break away in order to minimize risks of obstruction, water-borne debris, and wind-borne projectile hazards. (Figure 9.7.)

An *inland riverine landscape* should be designed for water retention to minimize runoff. Measures such as avoiding impervious coverage, retaining or developing woody vegetation buffers, and using vegetated swales and rain gardens all help to minimize runoff impacts on the site and adjacent properties.

Foundations

FOUNDATION TYPES IN A ZONES   Subsoil conditions on waterfront sites are often unsuitable for supporting shallow foundations. Foundations need to be constructed at sufficient depth to prevent undermining by eroding soils and scour. Because of potential for undermining by erosion and scour, shallow-spread footing and slab foundations may be inappropriate for some Coastal A zones and for riverine and coast bluff areas outside of mapped floodplains.

In A zones and other zones, buildings can be elevated on fill and constructed with closed foundations, such as crawlspaces, stem wall foundation, or slab-on-grade foundations. *Closed foundations* typically consist of continuous

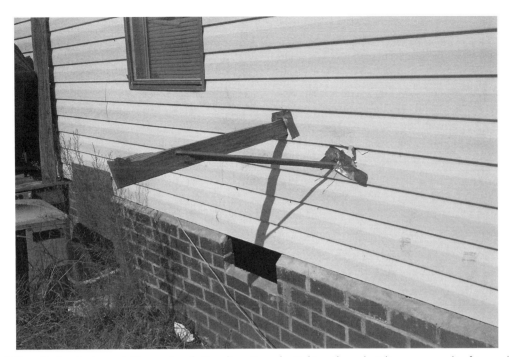

Figure 9.7a   *Projectile hazard*. Ithaca, South Carolina. Boards sticking though siding as a result of tornado spawned by Hurricane Frances.

(PHOTO: Marvin Nauman FEMA News Photo, October 2004)

Figure 9.7b   *Debris hazard*. Waveland, Mississippi. Hurricane Katrina's wind and tidal surge lodged a boat and stair on top of a house five miles inland.

(PHOTO: John Fleck FEMA Photo Library, September 2005)

perimeter foundation walls. A closed foundation can be a crawlspace, a stem wall (usually filled with compacted soil), or a slab-on-grade or monolithic foundation. *Crawlspaces* typically consist of perimeter masonry or concrete foundation walls and a system of interior beams and piers that support an elevated floor-framing system. In many instances, crawlspaces are used for mechanical equipment. *Stem wall foundations* consist of perimeter foundation walls, but the interior space is backfilled with soils that support a floor slab.

PILE DESIGN AND CONSTRUCTION IN V ZONES

Breaking waves exert enormous hydrodynamic forces. Structures in V zones need to be elevated on piers or pilings so that waves can pass freely under the structure. Any walls that enclose the space below the structure must be designed and constructed to break away under flood force. Loose sands or soft organic soils are commonly encountered near the water's edge, requiring deep foundations, such as driven piles. Inadequate depth of pilings, footings, and columns is a common cause of failure in elevated low-rise residential buildings. (Figure 9.8.)

FOUNDATIONS FOR WATERFRONT STRUCTURES

require substantial bracing to resist hydrodynamic wave and wind forces. Pile foundations typically need bracing bolted to the pilings. Poor structural connections (pile, pier, column to beam, joist to beam) have been a major cause of failure of residential structures, as documented in hurricane and other coastal storm assessments. Structures should be securely anchored to the pilings with corrosion resistance bolts.

GRADE BEAMS AND PIER COMBINATIONS

provide lateral stiffness, eliminating or reducing the need for diagonal cross-bracing or knee bracing. Pile foundations may be designed with grade beams, typically of concrete. Concrete pier foundations require steel reinforcing and often are tied together with underground concrete grade beams. Grade beams must be designed to be self-supporting elements and not rely on the soils beneath for vertical support. (Figure 9.9.)

DIAGONAL BRACING

provides lateral wind resistance and support to a pile or column foundation and is allowable. Bracing introduces the concern of potential obstruction to water and debris trapping. This concern may be partly addressed by placing bracing parallel to the primary direction of anticipated floodwater flow. Although not typically as effective as cross-bracing, knee bracing can be used to reduce the amount of bracing exposed to flow and debris forces. (Figure 9.10.)

Structure

WIND-RESISTANT DESIGN

Hurricane strength winds can destroy a structure that has not been designed to be wind resistant. Wind pressures act perpendicular to the surface of a wall or roof. The wind pressures are positive (pushing inward) on the windward or upwind side of a building and negative (suction) on the leeward or downwind side. Large negative pressures can develop adjacent to corners and at roof eaves, rakes, and ridge. Roof overhangs can be exposed to very large uplift forces. Wood-frame structures do not resist high wind forces as well as masonry or reinforced concrete structures.

The porosity of construction and openings—either left open or created during the storm—determine the extent of wind penetration to the interior and contribute additive (or subtract from) external pressure. (Figure 9.11.)

SHEAR WALLS

Waterfront homes often have open floor plans with large windows facing the water. Open plans and wide openings may not allow for sufficient length of shear walls for lateral bracing tied from roof to foundation. Without sufficient shear walls for lateral bracing, structural steel beams and columns may be required to resist lateral loads. Wood-frame shear walls typically require close nail spacing and hold-down anchors connected to the foundation.

CONTINUOUS LOAD PATH ANALYSIS

of forces as they are transferred within the structure is needed to establish the engineering design of structure and connections to resist loads that may result from high wind and water conditions. A building structure is only as strong as its weakest link. Continuous load path analysis starts at the point or surface where loads are applied (roof

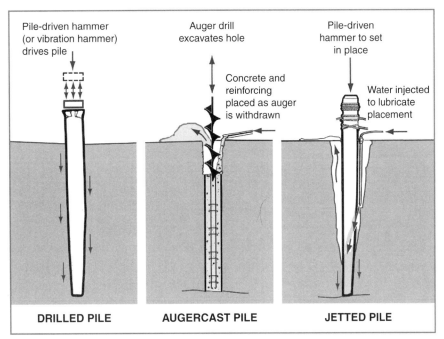

Figure 9.8 *Pile installation methods*: Pile design and installation establish the foundation for the life of the structure.

Source: FEMA, *Coastal Construction Manual: Principles and Practices of Planning, Siting, Designing, Constructing, and Maintaining Residential Buildings in Coastal Areas*, FEMA 55 (August 2005), www.fema.gov/rebuild/mat/fema55.shtm.

Pile Installation Method	Advantages	Special Considerations
Driven	Well suited for friction pile Common construction practice Pile capacity can be determined empirically	Difficult at times to reach terminating soil strata, which is not necessary for friction piles Difficult to maintain plumb during driving and thus maintain to column lines
Augered	Economical Minimal driving vibration to adjacent structures Well suited for end bearing Visual inspection of some soil stratum possible Convenient for low-headroom situations Easier to maintain column lines	Requires subsurface investigation Not suitable for highly compressible material Disturbs soil adjacent to pile, thus reducing earth pressure coefficients to 40% of that for driven piles Capacity must be determined by engineering judgment or load test
Jetted	Minimal driving vibration to adjacent structures Well suited for end bearing Easier to maintain column lines	Requires subsurface investigation Disturbs soil adjacent to pile, thus reducing earth pressure coefficients to 40% of that for driven piles Capacity must be determined by engineering judgment or load test

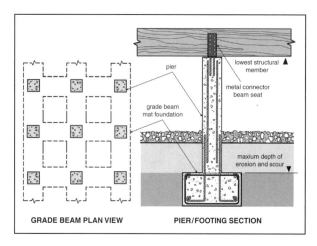

Figure 9.9 *Grade beam and concrete column system* is one of many grade beam configurations appropriate to specific conditions.

Source: FEMA, *Recommended Residential Construction for the Gulf Coast: Building on Strong and Safe Foundations* (FEMA 550) (April 2006), www.fema .gov/library/file?type=publishedFile&file=550_ch4.

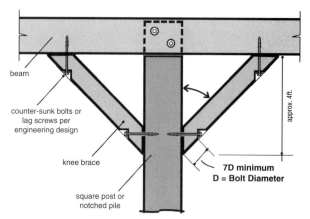

Figure 9.10 *Knee bracing* increases the stiffness of an elevated pile foundation and assists in reducing lateral forces.

Source: FEMA Technical Bulletin 5, "Free-of-Obstruction Requirements," www.fema.gov/plan/prevent/floodplain/ techbul.shtm.

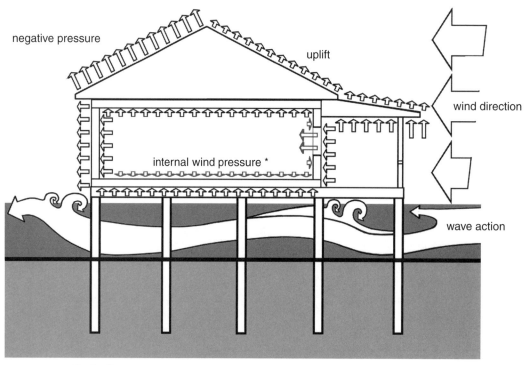

Figure 9.11 *Structural diagram* depicts hydrodynamic and wind-induced loads for elevated buildings.

Source: FEMA 55.

or other point of application), then moves through each link in the path, down to the ground. Both horizontal and vertical load paths must be analyzed. (Figure 9.12.)

CONNECTORS AND FASTENERS: INSTALLATION, MAINTENANCE, AND REPLACEMENT
In coastal environments exposed to salt air, corrosion-resistant structural connectors are required. Salt is very corrosive to metals, including concrete reinforcement that is exposed over time by cracking or spalling of the concrete. Dissimilar metals should not be allowed to come in contact with each other. Corrosion of light-gauge galvanized metals—connectors and nailing, straps and truss plates—is a

common cause of structural failure in buildings exposed to ocean salt air environments. Corrosion may be accelerated by chemical reaction with some preservative treatments. Stainless steel connectors should be considered for light-gauge fasteners and connectors in areas subject to salt spray.

A further precaution is to design for ease of replacement of critical structural elements as may be required over the life of a building. Access for inspection and component replacement should be provided.

Nailing sizes and patterns must be specified for engineered connections. Nail- and staple-gun installation can lead to incomplete attachment due to overdriving nails and staples or angled and splintered attachment. If used, nail guns must be adjusted and used correctly. Failure of roof

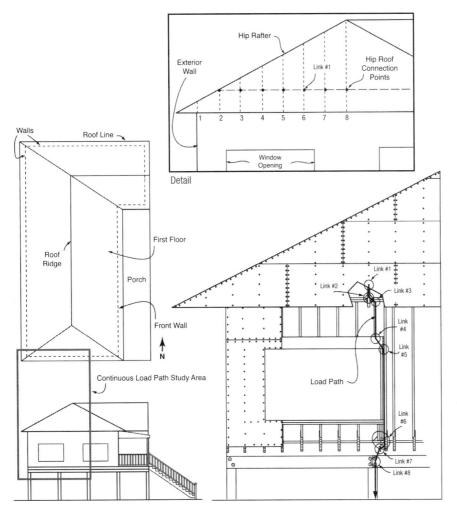

Figure 9.12 *Continuous load path example.* Load path of corner of representative hip-roof structure with more than eight critical links. Each link in the path must be strong enough to transfer loads without failure.

Source: FEMA 55.

sheathing fasteners can lead to loss of the entire roof and structure. All sheathing panel sides must be secured with full edge blocking. (Figure 9.13.)

BREAKAWAY AND "FREE-OF-OBSTRUCTION" REQUIREMENTS (V ZONES)

NFIP regulations require that the site and the building area below the lowest floor of elevated buildings in Coastal High Hazard V zones and recommended for Coastal A zones meet these conditions:

1. They must be free of obstructions.
2. If enclosures are used below the BFE, they should be constructed of nonsupporting breakaway walls, open latticework, or insect screening.

Breakaway walls, lattice, or screening is intended to collapse under wave loads without causing collapse, displacement, or other structural damage to the elevated building or foundation system. Most building codes require that breakaway walls be designed to withstand a lateral load greater than 10 pounds per square foot (psf), or the design wind load, or the design seismic load. If the breakaway wall design load is greater than 20 psi, the wall must be designed to collapse under flood loads during the base flood or lesser floods and must not cause damage to the foundation or elevated building when the wall breaks free. If the breakaway wall design load is greater than 20 psi, the design must be certified by a registered design professional to withstand the increased load conditions.

NFIP regulations specify that breakaway walls meet a "design safe loading" condition of not less than 10 psf and not more than 20 psf, or otherwise be certified by a registered design professional to meet approved design conditions.

A breakaway enclosure may also be considered for unfinished or flood-resistant enclosures that are used solely for parking of vehicles, building access, or storage. As defined by the NFIP, an "enclosure" is an area that is enclosed on all sides by walls. Other building elements covered by the breakaway provision include access stairs and ramps, decks, detached garages and accessory buildings, and fences. (Figure 9.14.)

Exterior Walls

FLOOD OPENINGS IN FOUNDATION WALLS

NFIP regulations require openings for flow of floodwaters in below-DFE foundation walls and enclosed crawlspaces in A zones. Flood openings allow free passage of floodwaters on both sides of enclosing walls in order to equalize hydrostatic forces that result from the unbalanced pressure of floodwaters. Bottoms of openings must be located no more than 1 foot above the exterior or interior grade (whichever is higher) on at least two different enclosing walls. In A zones, the requirement for flood openings applies to all enclosed areas below newly elevated buildings and below substantially improved buildings. A variety of options satisfy the requirements. The total net opening area to be provided depends on the size of the enclosed space and the method by which opening size is calculated. (Figure 9.15.)

FLOOD DAMAGE-RESISTANT MATERIALS

The International Building Code (IBC) defines flood damage–resistant materials as "capable of withstanding direct and prolonged contact with floodwaters without sustaining any significant damage that requires more than cosmetic repair." *Prolonged contact* is generally

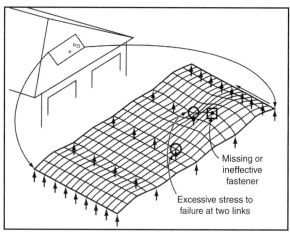

Figure 9.13 *The missing nail*: The FEMA *Coastal Construction Manual* details the multiplier effect that could result from one missing or defective fastener or unblocked edge of sheathing (highlighted in square). Other locations made critical by the missing nail are circled. With loss of sheathing, the entire interior is open to force of wind and rain and, possibly, total destruction.

Source: FEMA 55.

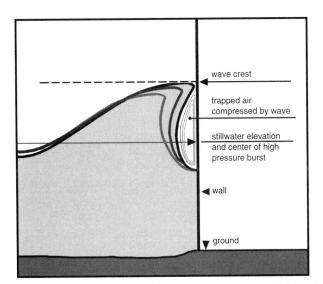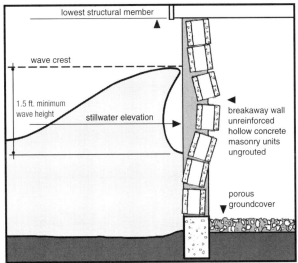

Figure 9.14 *Breakaway elements*: Masonry wall designed to break away provides a measure of privacy and security while it is heavy and small enough to minimize the risk of damaging debris upon collapse.

Source: FEMA Technical Bulletin 9.99, "Design and Construction Guidance for Breakaway Walls Below Elevated Coastal Buildings," www.fema.gov/plan/prevent/floodplain/techbul.shtm.

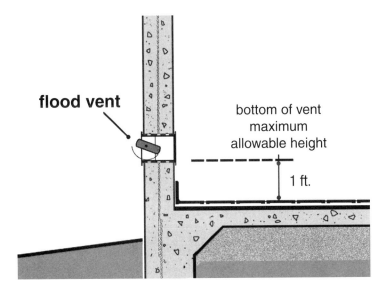

Figure 9.15 *Requirements of flood vent openings.*

Source: FEMA Technical Bulletin 1, "Openings in Foundation Walls and Walls of Enclosures," www.fema.gov/plan/prevent/floodplain/techbul.shtm.

Engineered Openings are Designed and Certified by a Registered Design Professional as Meeting Performance Requirements of the Regulation. Non-Engineered Openings Include Products and Designs that Meet the Following Requirements:

Designs for flood vent openings either must be certified by a licensed design professional or must meet or exceed these requirements for nonengineered openings:

- The openings shall have a total net area of not less than 1 square inch of net open area for each square foot of enclosed area subject to flooding.

- The openings' net area shall be at least 3 inches in diameter.

- Bottom of the openings must be no higher than 1 foot above the adjacent finished grade and should permit complete drainage from the interior lowest elevation.

- Openings may be equipped with screens, louvers, valves, or other coverings or devices, provided that they permit the automatic entry and exit of floodwaters. The area occupied by any obstructions must be subtracted when determining the "net area" of the opening. Insect screens do not affect the net open area but to prevent them from becoming clogged by debris, they should be installed so that they are removed under flush of water flow.

- As an alternative, proprietary flood vents are available that open automatically during a flood. Because the flow is not restricted by louvers, they permit smaller unobstructed openings or fewer openings.

- Crawl space vents are designed to facilitate the flow of air and generally do not meet the requirements for flood vents. However, additional ample openings above the DFE that facilitate ventilation will help dry the area following a flood.

- Windows, doors, and garage doors are not considered openings for flood venting purposes. However, openings that meet the flood vent standards can be installed in doors and windows.

- In areas where flow velocities can be expected to exceed 5 feet per second, flood vent openings may not be sufficient to protect solid perimeter foundation walls from hydrodynamic loads and debris impact and scour. In these areas, buildings should be elevated on fill or on open foundations, such as posts, columns, or pilings.

interpreted to equal at least 72 hours. *Significant damage* is any damage requiring more than cleaning or low-cost cosmetic repair, such as painting. (Table 9.1.)

Flood Damage-Resistant Materials Include:

- Glazed brick, concrete, concrete block, glass block or stone (with waterproof mortar or grout)
- Steel trusses, headers, beams, panels, or hardware.
- Naturally decay-resistant lumber, recycled plastic lumber, or marine-grade plywood
- Clay, concrete, rubber, or steel tiles (with chemical-set or waterproof adhesives)
- Cement board or cement fiberboard
- Metal doors, cabinets, and window frames provided with drainage weeps
- Mastic, silicone, or polyurethane formed-in-place flooring
- Sprayed polyurethane foam or closed-cell plastic foam insulation
- PVC trim, molding, rail, deck and sheets, impervious to moisture and insects

- Water-resistant glue
- Polyester epoxy paint (Mildew-resistant paint contains toxic ingredients and should not be used indoors.)
- Hot-dipped galvanized and stainless steel screws, nails

HUMIDITY AND MOISTURE MIGRATION

Humidity and moisture are a concern in any building structure. Structures exposed to water from flooding in enclosed areas, even if above the DFE, can be affected by excessive humidity and moisture migration.

Crawl spaces, lower-floor structural framing, and attached materials should be designed to prevent moisture entrainment that may result from capillary movement, evaporation, and condensation. Precautions to reduce moisture damage should extend to above the underside of buildings exposed to flooding. "Wicking" (capillary movement of moisture) may occur upward from materials that are partly wetted in a flood. Materials along the sides of outdoor wash zones and above enclosed spaces where floodwater may remain for any period of time should be

TABLE 9.1 CLASS DESCRIPTIONS OF FLOOD DAMAGE-RESISTANT MATERIALS

Highly resistant to floodwater. Damage, including damage caused by moving water. Floodwater is assumed to be "black" water that contains pollutants such as sewage, chemicals, heavy metals, or other toxic and hazardous substances. Moving water is defined as water moving at low velocities of 5 feet per second (fps) or less. At velocities greater than 5 fps, floodwaters may cause structural damage to building materials. These materials can survive wetting and drying and may be successfully cleaned after a flood to render them free of most harmful pollutants. Some materials can be successfully cleaned of most of the pollutants typically found in floodwater. However, some individual pollutants, such as heating oil, can be extremely difficult to remove from uncoated concrete. Materials in this class are permitted for partially enclosed or outside uses with essentially unmitigated flood exposure.

Resistant to floodwater. Damage from wetting and drying, but less durable when exposed to moving water. These materials can survive wetting and drying and may be successfully cleaned after a flood to render them free of most harmful pollutants. Materials in this class may be exposed to and/or submerged in floodwaters in interior spaces and do not require special waterproofing protection.

Resistant to clean-water damage but not floodwater damage. Materials in this class may be submerged in clean water during periods of flooding. Clean water includes potable water as well as "gray" water. Graywater is wastewater collected from normal uses, such as laundry, bathing, and food preparation. These materials can survive wetting and drying but may not be able to be successfully cleaned after floods to render them free of most harmful pollutants.

Not resistant to clean-water damage. Materials in this class are used in predominantly dry spaces that may be subject to occasional water vapor and/or slight seepage. These materials cannot survive the wetting and drying associated with floods.

Not resistant to clean water. Damage or moisture damage. Materials in this class are used in spaces with conditions of complete dryness. These materials cannot survive the wetting and drying associated with floods.

Sources: International Building Code (IBC), by reference to the International Residential Code (IRC), and ASCE 24, require the use of flood damage–resistant materials; also American Society of Civil Engineers, *Flood Resistant Design and Construction*, SEI/24-05 (Reston, VA: Author, 2006); also FEMA, Technical Bulletin 2, "Flood Damage–Resistant Materials Requirements," www.fema.gov/plan/prevent/floodplain/techbul.shtm.

able to withstand high humidity without damage or mold. Many modern construction materials are susceptible to deformation, deterioration, and mold if exposed to water or high humidity, either directly or through wicking. (Figure 9.16.) (following page)

SEALANTS, WEATHER STRIPS, AND TRIM

intended to protect weather tightness of the exterior enclosure are elements of construction most vulnerable to deterioration, decay, and damage. Coastal construction requires more vigilant preventive maintenance due to the critical role of all building elements.

Roofing

ROOF DESIGNS that incorporate gabled ends (especially unbraced ends) and wide overhangs are susceptible to failure. Wood roof truss construction has performed poorly under hurricane winds due to installation deficiencies, including inadequate or nonexistent bracing between the trusses. Effective cross-bracing is required to prevent a domino effect of trusses collapsing one on the other. Manufactured trusses can respond differently under uplift compared to gravity loads. Designers should consult with truss manufacturers to ensure that adequate resistance to uplift forces is included in truss engineering design. (Figure 9.17.)

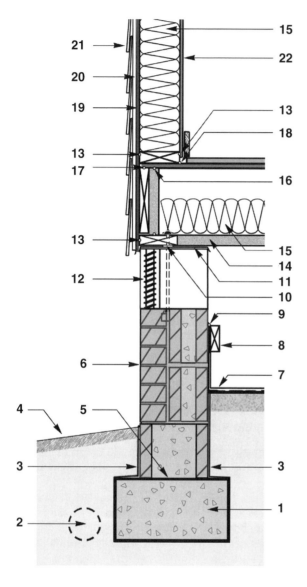

Figure 9.16 *Crawlspace moisture barriers* (Building Sciences Corporation).

1. Concrete footing below frost depth
2. Perimeter drain (not required where grade is lower than crawlspace grade)
3. Dampproofing
4. Slope away from foundation (.5%)
5. Capillary break over footing
6. Masonry foundation wall
7. Continuous polyethylene vapor diffusion retarder (joints overlapped)
8. Treated wood nailer
9. Waterproof sealant
10. Gasket
11. Capillary break top of foundation wall
12. Crawlspace vent
13. Sealant, adhesive or gasket
14. Rigid insulation (fire rated, sealed and taped joints)
15. Batt insulation
16. Sealant top and bottom
17. Adhesive
18. Sealant at corner of bottom plate and subfloor or gasket under bottom plate
19. Exterior sheathing
20. Vertical air space behind siding between vertical furring
21. Siding (all surfaces painted)
22. Gypsum board with vapor-permeable paint (latex)

Source: Joseph Lstiburek, P.E., "New Light in Crawlspaces," Building Sciences Corporation, 2009, www.buildingscience.com/documents/insights/bsi-009.new-light-in-crawlspaces/.

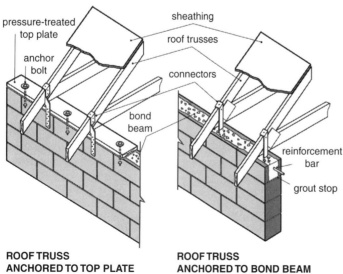

ROOF TRUSS ANCHORED TO TOP PLATE   **ROOF TRUSS ANCHORED TO BOND BEAM**

Figure 9.17 *Connections and anchors* ensure that trusses and overhangs resist vertical, lateral, and uplift loads.

Source: FEMA, *Home Builder's Guide to Coastal Construction Technical Fact Sheet Series*, FEMA 499, Fact Sheet No.16, "Masonry Details," www.fema.gov/rebuild/mat/mat_fema499.shtm.

Figure 9.18   *Hip roof construction*: Bolivar Peninsula, Texas. A home with hip roof and shuttered openings survived Hurricane Ike.

(PHOTO: Jocelyn Augustino FEMA Photo Library, September 2008)

Low-sloped roofs and flat roofs are susceptible to winds and rain damage, due to negative pressure uplift. Steeper slopes force wind pressure to compress and diffuse wind force downward in direction of continuous path construction. Of all roof configurations, hip roofs and similar multidirectional beam structures that distribute loads in several directions have performed well in extreme wind conditions. (Figure 9.18.)

ROOF OVERHANGS AND MULTI-STORIED DECKS

can induce significant structural damage, even during minor wind, flood, and erosion events. They should be supported by fully secure and embedded vertical members. Porch and deck roof overhangs should be designed to remain intact without vertical supports or their supports should be designed and installed to the same engineering standards as the main foundation. Roof decks should be designed to withstand all design loads, including uplift, and to prevent further damage in breakaway mode.

NAILING OF ROOF SHEATHING

is critical. During Hurricane Andrew in 1992, destruction of numerous homes was attributed to failure of oriented strand board roof sheathing that had been secured with staples rather than nails. If a panel of roof sheathing blows off the roof, wind can enter the building and lift the roof framing off its walls, resulting in a total collapse.

ROOF COVERING

Residential roofing materials are susceptible to damage from wind and wind-borne debris. Loss of roofing and protective rain cover is the most widespread damage in coastal storms, even those of minor magnitude. The quality of roofing that is specified and the care taken in installation, while very small in terms of total cost of the structure, determines the ultimate fate and value of the entire building and contents beneath.[5]

WINDOW AND DOOR PROTECTION

In high wind conditions, failures can be successive, beginning with failure of weak connections at openings, including all penetration of the structural envelope, windows, mechanical vents, doors, and garage doors. Rain entering the interior can result in near-total loss of building and contents. If windows are broken, internal wind pressures can precipitate a roof blow-off. For a building to be considered "enclosed," windows, glass doors and skylights must be fully protected.

STORM SHUTTERS AND LAMINATED (IMPACT-RESISTANT) GLASS help protect the building openings and minimize damage and life safety risk. (Figure 9.19.)

Services
MECHANICAL, PLUMBING, AND ELECTRICAL (MEP) SYSTEMS The NFIP requires that all new and substantially improved structures in flood-prone areas be designed and constructed by methods and practices that minimize or eliminate flood damage to electrical, heating, ventilation, air conditioning, plumbing, and other building utility systems. In V and A zones, and in residential and commercial properties that are not dry floodproofed, mechanical, plumbing, and electrical (MEP) equipment must be placed above the DFE and, wherever possible, located on upper floors or attics.[6]

The best way to protect MEP and service equipment is location in accessible locations above the DFE. MEP system components located below the DFE, such as water meters or underground fuel tanks, must be protected by watertight enclosures, protective utility shafts, and anchoring. Susceptible equipment should be protected against freezing.

If location or relocation to upper levels is not an available option—such as projects involving flood mitigation and upgrading of existing structures—MEP equipment may be suspended or placed above the DFE on pedestals or platforms. Similar precautions are appropriate for dry floodproofing installation in case the "active system" or other emergency provisions fail. Electrical and fuel ignition controls should be accessible in flood conditions for shut-off and recommissioning after a flood event. (Figure 9.20.)

ELECTRICAL EQUIPMENT—circuit breaker panels, transformers, motors, and wiring—must be located above the DFE except for wiring contained in watertight conduit. Utility risers and electric meters, and similar elements that must be located below the DFE must be installed to minimize flood damage.

To help to achieve this requirement:

- Equipment should not be attached to or penetrate through breakaway walls.
- Where possible, equipment should be located on the sides of piles and columns opposite from the anticipated direction of flood flow and wave approach.

Figure 9.19 *Hurricane shutters* protected this building on the coast of Melbourne, Florida, during Hurricane Jeanne.
(PHOTO: Michael Rieger FEMA Photo Library, September 2004)

Source: FEMA, *Home Builder's Guide to Coastal Construction Technical Fact Sheet Series*, FEMA 499, Fact Sheet No. 26, "Shutter Alternatives," www.fema.gov/rebuild/mat/mat_fema499.shtm.

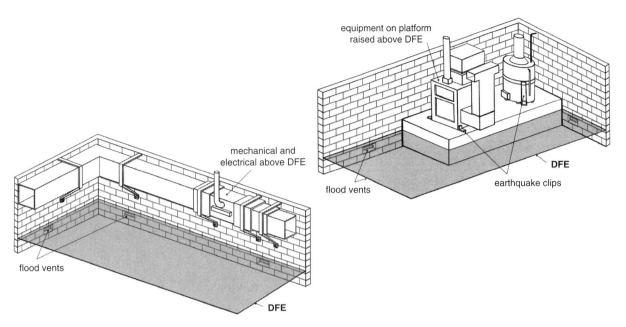

Figure 9.20 *Raising mechanical equipment* above DFE in wet floodproofed areas of mitigated existing structures may be an acceptable option where other alternatives are not possible.

EMERGENCY GENERATORS are required to protect vital equipment and processes during and after a flood event. These measures are recommended:

• Locate emergency generators as high as practical. At a minimum, the generator should be placed above the main electrical service equipment.

• Locate the emergency generator's transfer switches and electrical distribution equipment at least as high as the generator.

• Supply the generator with a reliable source of fuel that will not be interrupted during an event. If an emergency fuel tank is provided on-site, it must be anchored to prevent floatation.

• Ensure that access is provided to the generator for operation, refueling, and maintenance.

• Off-the-grid solar electric (photovoltaic) installations may provide emergency power. Grid-connected photovoltaic installations typically have a power interrupter that prevents this option in emergency situations.[7]

PLUMBING SYSTEMS must be protected by elevation of system components. Plumbing pipes that are enclosed may run through areas below the DFE, a practical necessity for connections to in-ground water and sewer services. Plumbing controls, tanks, shut-offs and vents must be located above the DFE, accessible for emergency access during flood, with backflow prevention installed on the wastewater connection to prevent contamination of the building water supply or interior.

The principal dangers that floodwaters present to water supply systems are:

• Damage to pipes and to the on-site wellhead (on sites that have water wells) resulting from the effects of velocity flow, wave action, and debris impact.

• Water supply contamination in the well, service feed pipe, and distribution system.

SUMP PUMPS Enclosed or partially enclosed areas that are below grade require sumps (depressions in the floor area) where water can be collected and removed by a sump pump. Emergency generator power must be available in case of power outage.

BACKFLOW AND AUTOMATIC SHUT-OFF VALVES Flooding can force sewage from sanitary sewer lines to back up into building drainage systems or interiors. Backflow valves are designed to temporarily block pipes and prevent flow into the building. They should be installed on any pipes that leave the building or are connected to equipment or sanitary systems located below the flood protection level. In addition to sanitary sewer and septic connections, this requirement may include water lines, washing machine drain lines, laundry sinks, downspouts, and sump pumps. Fuel supply lines must be equipped with float-operated automatic shut-off valves. (Figure 9.21.)

ANCHORING ACCESSORY STRUCTURES AND EQUIPMENT
If possible, fuel storage tanks should not be located below the DFE. This may prove impractical due to truck service access requirements of the fuel company. (Often the fuel supplier is the legal owner of the tanks that it maintains under a service contract.)

Where located below the DFE, tanks must be anchored to prevent floating or shifting during a flood. Even if located belowground, buoyancy forces on a partially filled oil tank or any gas tank during a flood can be substantial, requiring a counterbalance provided by concrete hold-down pad and

attachments. Tanks and other containers should have water-tight fill caps and vents that extend above the BFE. They should be visibly labeled so that if the tank breaks loose, emergency personnel know what it contains.[8]

SWIMMING POOLS AND SPAS
NFIP permits a swimming pool or spa placement beneath an elevated building only if the top of the pool/spa and accompanying deck or walkway are flush with the existing grade, and only if the space around the pool/spa remains unenclosed.[9] Some states and communities may prohibit or restrict pools and spas beneath elevated buildings.

Several conditions govern the placement of swimming pools and spas under or adjacent to buildings in V zones:

- The pool and/or spa configuration may be disallowed due to NFIP use limitations for enclosed areas under elevated buildings. Pools may be considered as "recreational" and therefore not allowed as one of the approved uses for building entry, parking, or storage.

- The pool or spa may lead to increased flood loads on buildings or exacerbate scour and erosion near buildings.

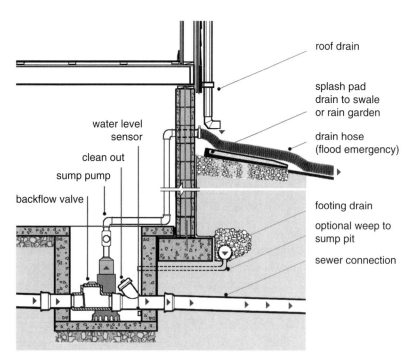

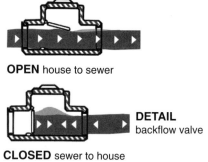

OPEN house to sewer

DETAIL backflow valve

CLOSED sewer to house

Figure 9.21 *Backflow valve and sump pump installation* provide back-up measures of flood control. Subject to elevations and local approvals, the sump can receive water from the footing drain to lower the water level around the foundation.

Source: Canada Mortgage and Housing Corporation, "Avoiding Basement Flooding," www.cmhc-schl.gc.ca/en/co/maho/gemare/gemare_002.cfm.

TABLE 9.2 SUMMARY: NFIP REGULATORY REQUIREMENTS AND RECOMMENDATIONS FOR EXCEEDING THE REQUIREMENTS

	V Zone Guidance	Coastal A Zone Guidance[a]	A Zone Guidance[a]
General Requirements			
Design	Requirement: Building and its foundation must be designed, constructed, and anchored to prevent flotation, collapse, and lateral movement due to simultaneous wind and water loads.	Requirement: Building must be designed, constructed, and anchored to prevent flotation, collapse, and lateral movement resulting from hydrodynamic and hydrostatic loads, including the effects of buoyancy. Recommendation: Same as a V zone.	Requirement: Building must be designed, constructed, and anchored to prevent flotation, collapse, and lateral movement resulting from hydrodynamic and hydrostatic loads, including the effects of buoyancy.
Materials	Requirement: Structural and nonstructural building materials at or below the BFE must be flood-resistant.	Requirement: Structural and nonstructural building materials at or below the BFE must be flood-resistant.	Requirement: Structural and nonstructural building materials at or below the BFE must be flood-resistant.
Construction	Requirement: Building must be constructed with methods and practices that minimize flood damage.	Requirement: Building must be constructed with methods and practices that minimize flood damage.	Requirement: Building must be constructed with methods and practices that minimize flood damage.
Siting	Requirement: All new construction shall be landward of mean high tide; alteration of sand dunes and mangrove stands that increases potential flood damage is prohibited. Recommendation: Site new construction landward of the long-term erosion setback and landward of the area subject to erosion during the 100-year coastal flood event.	Requirement: Encroachments into the SFHA are permitted as long as they do not increase the BFE by more than 1 foot[c]; encroachments into the floodway are prohibited. Recommendation: Same as V zone.	Requirement: Encroachments into the SFHA are permitted as long as they do not increase the BFE by more than 1 foot[c]; encroachments into the floodway are prohibited.

(continued)

TABLE 9.2 (CONTINUED)

	V Zone Guidance	Coastal A Zone Guidance[a]	A Zone Guidance[a]
Foundation			
Structural Fill	Prohibited.	Allowed but not recommended; compaction required where used; protect against scour and erosion.[d]	Allowed; compaction required where used; protect against scour and erosion.[d]
Solid Foundation	Prohibited.	Allowed but not recommended.[d]	Allowed.[d]
Open Foundation	Required.	Not required but recommended.[d]	Allowed.[d]
Lowest Floor Elevation	Not applicable.[e]	Requirement: Top of floor must at or above BFE.[f] Recommendation: Elevate bottom of lowest horizontal structural member to or above BFE[f] (see next category below); orient member perpendicular to wave crest.	Requirement: Top of floor must at or above BFE.[f]
Bottom of Lowest Horizontal Structural Member	Requirement: Bottom must at or above BFE.[f]	Allowed above BFE[f] but not recommended. Recommendation: Same as V zone.	Allowed above BFE[f] but not recommended. Recommendation: Same as V zone.
Orientation of Lowest Horizontal Structural Member	No requirement. Recommendation: Orient perpendicular to wave crest.	No requirement. Recommendation: Same as V zone.	No requirement.
Freeboard	Not required[f] but recommended.	Not required[f] but recommended.	Not required[f] but recommended.

Enclosures below the BFE (Also see Certification below.)	Prohibited except for breakaway walls, open lattice, and screening.[9] Recommendation: If constructed, use open lattice or screening instead of breakaway walls.	Allowed but not recommended; if an area is fully enclosed, the enclosure walls must be equipped with openings to equalize hydrostatic pressure; size, location, and covering of openings governed by regulatory requirement. Recommendation: If enclosure is constructed, use breakaway walls, open lattice, or screening (as required in V zone)[g,h]	Allowed; if an area is fully enclosed, the enclosure walls must be equipped with openings to equalize hydrostatic pressure; size, location, and covering of openings governed by regulatory requirements.[g,h]
Nonstructural Fill	Allowed for minor landscaping and site drainage as long as the fill does not interfere with the free passage of floodwaters and debris beneath the building or cause changes in flow direction during coastal storms that could result in damage to buildings.	Allowed.[f] Recommendation: Same as V zone.	Allowed.
Use of Space below BFE[i]	Allowed only for parking, building access, and storage.	Allowed only for parking, building access, and storage.	Allowed only for parking, building access, and storage.
Utilities[i]	Requirement: Must be designed, located, and elevated to prevent floodwaters from entering and accumulating in components during flooding.	Requirement: Must be designed, located, and elevated to prevent floodwaters from entering and accumulating in components during flooding.	Requirement: Must be designed, located, and elevated to prevent floodwaters from entering and accumulating in components during flooding.
Certification — Structure	Required: Registered engineer or architect must certify that the design and methods of construction are in accordance with accepted standards of practice for meeting the design requirements described under GENERAL REQUIREMENTS.	Recommendation: Same as V zone.	Recommendation: Same as V zone.

(continued)

TABLE 9.2 (CONTINUED)

	V Zone Guidance	Coastal A Zone Guidance[a]	A Zone Guidance[a]
Breakaway Walls (Also see Enclosures below the BFE.)	Required: Either of the following: (1) Walls must be designed to provide a safe loading resistance of between 10 lb/ft^2 and 20 lb/ft^2 OR (2) a registered engineer or architect must certify that the walls will collapse under a water load associated with the base flood and that the elevated portion of building and its foundation will not be subject to collapse, displacement, or lateral movement under simultaneous wind and water loads.[g,h]	Not required but recommended.[g,h]	Not required.[g,h]
Openings in Below-BFE Walls (Also see Enclosures below the BFE.)	Not applicable.[k]	Required: Unless number and size of openings meets regulatory requirements, registered engineer or architect must certify that openings are designed to automatically equalize hydrostatic forces on walls by allowing the automatic entry and exit of floodwaters.	Required: Unless number and size of openings meets regulatory requirements, registered engineer or architect must certify that openings are designed to automatically equalize hydrostatic forces on walls by allowing the automatic entry and exit of floodwaters.

[a] "Prohibited" and "Allowed" refer to the minimum NFIP regulatory requirements; individual states and communities may enforce more stringent requirements that supersede those summarized here. Exceeding minimum NFIP requirements will provide increased flood protection and may result in lower flood insurance premiums.

[b] In this column, "TB" means NFIP Technical Bulletin (e.g., TB 1 = Technical Bulletin 1), and "CFR" means the U.S. Code of Federal Regulations.

[c] Some communities may allow encroachments to cause a 1-foot rise in the flood elevation, while others may allow no rise.

[d] Some coastal communities require open foundations in A zones.

[e] Bottom of lowest horizontal structural member must be at or above the BFE.

[f] State or community may regulate to a higher elevation (DFE).

[g] Some coastal communities prohibit breakaway walls and allow only open lattice or screening.

[h] If an area below the BFE in an A-zone building is fully enclosed by breakaway walls, the walls must meet the requirement for openings that allow equalization of hydrostatic pressure.

[i] Placement of nonstructural fill adjacent to buildings in coastal AO zones is not recommended.

[j] There are some differences between what is permitted under floodplain management regulations and what is covered by NFIP flood insurance. Building designers should be guided by floodplain management requirements, not by flood insurance policy provisions.

[k] Walls below BFE must be designed and constructed as breakaway walls that meet the minimum requirements of the NFIP regulations.

Source: FEMA 55.

Notes

1. FEMA Mitigation Directorate, *Hurricane Opal in Florida: A Building Performance Assessment*, FEMA-281 (August 1996), www.fema.gov/library.

2. Note: As introduced in prior chapters, *base flood elevation* (BFE) is the term of reference used in the NFIP as the minimum base elevation for flood regulations. Local communities may or may not add "freeboard" in designating the design flood elevation (DFE). Except where specifically quoting FEMA references, the term *DFE* is used here to indicate the elevation of the flood elevation requirement to which designers must adhere.

3. FEMA, Technical Bulletin 7, "Wet Floodproofing Requirements," www.fema.gov/plan/prevent/floodplain/techbul.shtm.

4. FEMA, "Substantial Improvement/Substantial Damage for Flood Administrators Mitigation Fact Sheet," www.floodplain.ar.gov/Substantial%20Damage%20Toolkit.pdf.

5. FEMA, *Home Builder's Guide to Coastal Construction Technical Fact Sheet Series*, FEMA 499, Fact Sheets Nos. 18–21 on various roofing methods and materials, www.fema.gov/rebuild/mat/mat_fema499.shtm.

6. FEMA, *Protecting Building Utility from Flood Damage: Principles & Practices for the Design & Construction of Flood Resistant Building Utility Systems*, FEMA Publication 348 (November 1999), www.fema.gov/library/viewRecord.do?id=1750.

7. FEMA, "Design Considerations for Improving Critical Facility Functionality during Flood Events: Midwest Floods Recovery Advisory Report" (October 2009), www.fema.gov/library/viewRecord.do?id=3824.

8. FEMA Publication 348.

9. FEMA, *Technical Bulletin* 5, "Free of Obstruction Requirements," www.fema.gov/plan/prevent/floodplain/techbul.shtm.

PART IV

DESIGN FOR RESILIENCE

Resilient design for flooding is a proactive and precautionary approach to increase water resource sustainability while reducing climate change risks.

Anything is right which tends to preserve the integrity, stability and beauty of the biotic community. It is wrong when it tends otherwise.

—Aldo Leopold, 1949

CHAPTER 10 Flood-Resistant Design for Sites and Communities

CHAPTER 11 Sea Level Rise

CHAPTER 12 Design for Resilience

Figure 10.1 *Community visioning workshop:* "Collecting the Voices" Workshop. Jefferson Parish, New Orleans. Louisiana Recovery Authority.

(PHOTO: Marvin Nauman FEMA Photo Library, January 21, 2006)

CHAPTER **10**

FLOOD-RESISTANT DESIGN FOR SITES AND COMMUNITIES

10.1 COASTAL COMMUNITIES

Many of the older coastal area communities in the United States have a tradition of informal construction, principally a result of their first use as seasonal vacation destinations and part-year occupancy. In some instances, shore communities subsisted on uneven spurts of tourism for much of the twentieth century. Only later in the century did many coastal communities realize increased property values, population growth, and now predominantly year-round use. Other coastal towns historically were founded on maritime commerce, dating from late nineteenth-century whaling, ocean fishing, and trading, and since that time have followed the fortunes of commerce and tourism.

For a mix of these reasons, many older coastal communities in the United States are without formal planning or with plans compromised by preexisting conditions. Coastal properties and infrastructure have been developed in areas either historically or only now susceptible to coastal storm and flood risk. Coastal planners have the task of working around these properties and conditions. Communities most at risk are those built in prior decades with informal and now-stressed infrastructure, many with street and lot layouts that increase flooding risk and would no longer be approved under modern flood regulations.

The most risk-exposed of lot plan arrangements are homes and other buildings situated directly on an exposed

beach or barrier strand, with backlot homes close behind. Storm surge and floodwaters follow the path of least resistance as may be created by beach access roads, carrying water, sand, and debris along interior roads, blocking or destroying infrastructure and access routes.[1] Any unmoored structure joins the debris path, capable of damaging neighboring homes even if these conform to all flood regulations. Coastal construction is exposed to more severe flooding impacts due to growth and infill of shoreline communities as well as exposure to extreme storm surge and possibility of sea level rise. (Figures 10.2 and Figure 10.3.)

Criteria for Resilient Design of Coastal Sites and Communities

Options of shoreline protection are variously described as structural versus. nonstructural, or engineered versus natural, or hard versus soft. In any situation, any one strategy may prove inadequate. A mix of strategies should always be considered, subject to site and community conditions and approvals. (Figure 10.4.)

Strategies of resilient design of coastal communities meet all best practice standards of flood-resistant design and represent the next criteria. The first four criteria represent a first line of defense and typically are required of property owners undertaking new or substantially improved construction projects.

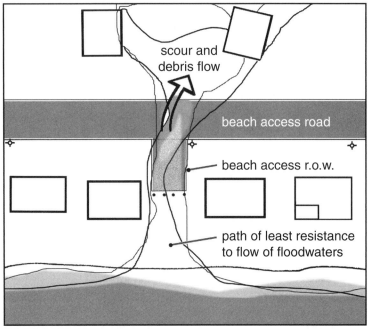

Figure 10.2 *Flood flow* follows the path of least resistance, such as beach access roads and utilities. Bolivar Peninsula, Texas.

(PHOTO: Jocelyn Augustino FEMA Photo Library, September 20, 2008)

1. Provide shoreline stabilization and protection through structural and nonstructural measures capable of reflecting, reducing, or diffusing storm surge by elevation, construction, and run-up profile.
2. Avoid or prevent increased erosion or other flood impacts to adjacent properties and, in the case of wave reflection, to adjacent waterways and water-edge structures.
3. Restore or create natural features that provide ecosystem services to absorb, filter, and diffuse severe storm and rising sea level impacts.
4. Construct and maintain floodplain landscape features that meet the designated zone regulations for breakaway

and free-of-obstruction requirements and are replaceable and maintainable in poststorm recovery.

A second set of criteria goes beyond typical regulatory requirements and may be undertaken by project developers, community associations, and community agencies to include:

5. Provide areas for diffusion and absorption of flooding that diverts and reduces threat of life safety and of infrastructure and property damage.
6. Secure routes for emergency egress and for access for first responders and postevent return.

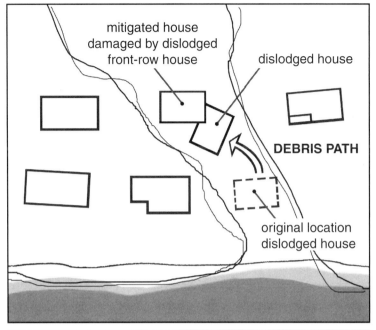

Figure 10.3 *Dislodged houses* present risk of damage to adjacent structures that may meet all mitigation requirements. Dauphin Island, Alabama.

(PHOTO: Marvin Nauman FEMA Photo Library, September 9, 2005)

7. Secure utility, water, and sewerage connections for prestorm or automatic disconnect and postevent recommissioning.

8. Establish a community emergency communication system and management procedures for storm preparation, evacuation, and emergency response.

Of the options illustrated in Figure 10.4, the extremes of both soft and hardened construction may provide protection of a particular site or structure but, deployed, alone each is insufficient. Some, such as area flood barriers (Photo A1), may have adverse impacts elsewhere, a result of confining and accelerating floodwater flow and erosion of adjacent areas. Armored building structures

may survive, but they may become isolated in communities whose infrastructure, access, and economy has been destroyed (C2).

Hardened construction engineered to high design standards is a means to provide buildings of sufficient scale and strength to be safe, secured by structural measures to withstand a severe storm (C1). Buildings that are "soft," even if properly mitigated with elevated wood-frame structures and breakaway stairs, can remain exposed to unsupportable risk, depending on location and the viability of other safety measures (A3).

The middle range of examples in Figure 10.4 represents hybrids, that is, a mix of soft and hard strategies. Shown in Photo A2, beach revetments of geotextile monotubes were exposed and beach sand transported inland when Hurricane Ike crossed Bolivar Peninsula, Texas, with a storm surge exceeding the base flood elevation (BFE). Houses that survived were those that exceeded the BFE by more than that height. The coastal access road is well removed and out of the high-velocity zone.

Photo B3 depicts Myrtle Grove Marina Estates, Empire, Louisiana. It escaped severe damage during Hurricane Katrina due to elevation and prior mitigation. The ground landscape level is given an active use and community life with outdoor patios, decks, and boat docks.

A mixed-use marine complex shown in Photo B1 is within a protected inlet in the intercoastal community of Jupiter, Florida. A coastal public park nearby (B2) preserves large natural buffer areas, with selected mid-rise structures interspersed and connected by walkways hardened to withstand coastal flooding.

hardened coastline

hybrid coastline

soft coastline

soft construction

Figure 10.4 *Summary of coastline and construction strategies:* Hybrid solutions may be most appropriate to the specific circumstances of each region and locality.

Sources: (A1) PHOTO: Jacinta Quesada FEMA (A2) PHOTO: Jocelyn Augustino FEMA (A3) PHOTO: Dave Gatley FEMA (B1) PHOTO: Donald Watson (B2) PHOTO: Donald Watson (B3) PHOTO: Marvin Nauman FEMA (C1) PHOTO: George Armstrong FEMA (C2) PHOTO: John Fleck FEMA (C3) PHOTO: Leif Skoogfors FEMA.

The Reconfigured Coastline

The elevation and profile of the coastline determine risk and severity of storm surge exposure, the most critical impact of flood events. Existing communities with buildings that are not mitigated to current FEMA standards are at risk in every respect. (Figure 10.5.)

Low-lying coastal communities can be mitigated, one building at a time, with elevation the single measure most available for any individual property. Even after mitigation, such homes remain at risk of damage from other nonconforming structures as well as from damage or loss of infrastructure and access (shown as Alternative B in Figure 10.5).

Figure 10.4   (Continued)

hybrid construction   **hardened construction**

Relocation of structures back from the foreshore allows dune enhancement and erosion controls, providing space for storm and wave diffusion and reducing risk of wave heights associated with the coastal high-velocity zone. Figure 10.5C illustrates a planning strategy that meets the resilient design criteria for coastal communities.

Many subdivision plans place shoreline and interior homes at risk of storm surge, flood debris flow, and erosion, as illustrated in Figures 10.2 and 10.3. Local communities may prohibit such layouts, based on evidence of poststorm assessment. Lot arrangements known as "flag lots" or "key lots" are often used instead, avoiding interior roads, but still placing building structures at risk, along both the shore and the interior. A more suitable arrangement that achieves the same density but creates sufficient setback to create a buffer zone is

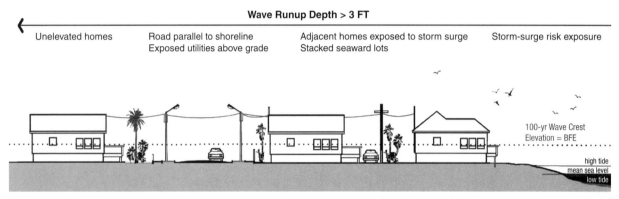

(A) Existing development fully exposed to coastal storm and flood hazard

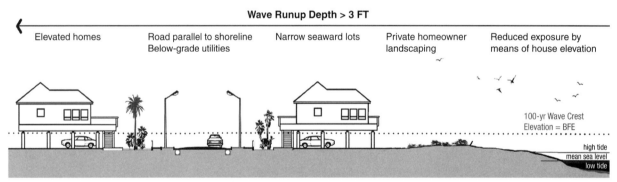

(B) Shorefront homes removed and rear lot homes elevated to NFIP requirements

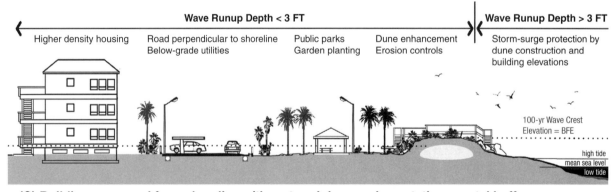

(C) Buildings removed from shoreline with restored dune and vegetative coastal buffer zone

Figure 10.5   *Alternatives to mitigation and transformation of the coastal communities* illustrate a phased plan of shoreline community retreat and reconstruction.

zero-lot-line layout. The deep lot with conservation zone in Figure 10.6C illustrates a strategy that meets the resilient design criteria for coastal communities.

For larger area developments, sufficient setback from the shore should be provided to protect the shore with a naturalized dune and vegetated buffer. This can be achieved with site layouts that have the same or better real estate values as conventional subdivisions, increasing the number of housing units with direct view and access to the shore. The plan configuration shown in Figure 10.7C is adaptable to

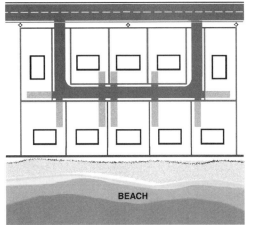

Interior lots exposed to damage from front lot building debris

Interior roads increase debris and scour paths

Beachfront lots exposed to high velocity storm surge

No beach erosion controls

(A) NOT RECOMMENDED Conventional lot subdivision

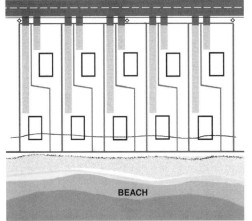

Interior lots exposed to damage from front lot building debris

Beachfront lots exposed to high velocity storm surge

No beach erosion controls

(B) NOT RECOMMENDED "Flag Lot" or "Key Lot" subdivision

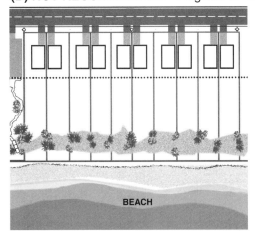

Compact infrastructure; deep, narrow lots

No infrastructure or building within high velocity zone

Dune protection and maintenance

(C) RECOMMENDED Deep lots with conservation zone regulation

Figure 10.6   *Three approaches to coastal low- to mid-rise development. Deep lots with conservation setbacks have reduced flooding risk and greatest resilience. Sufficient space is provided to comply with setback requirements and avoid dune damage.*

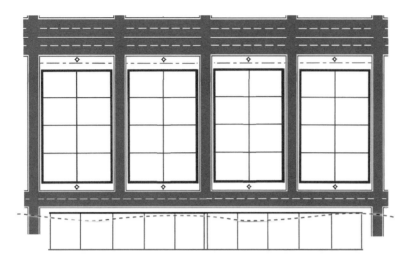

No vegetative buffers to absorb
stormwater and storm impacts

Interior lots and utilities
exposed to scour and debris
damage

Shore roads exposed to flood
erosion and debris

Beachfront lots in high velocity
flood hazard zone

No provision for beach erosion
control

(A) NOT RECOMMENDED Conventional coastal lot subdivision

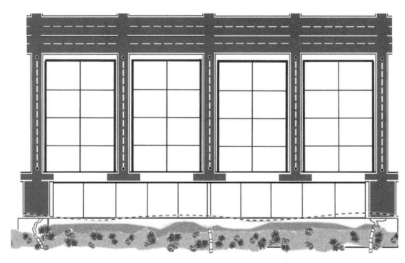

Below-grade utilities with
shut-off valves on water and
sewer lines

Limited-access driveways for
service and emergency with
redundant exitways

Beachfront lots set back behind
dunes and high hazard zone

Defined dune/vegetative buffer
for erosion control

(B) IMPROVED Coastal community subdivision

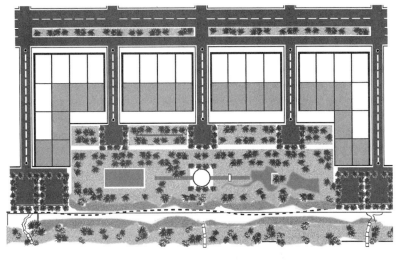

Reduce road with traffic calming with parking, combined with water retention planting

Smaller lots with near equal seaward views and access

More than 50% of site is landscape, including natural area planting

Additional buffer zone as long-term precaution for shoreline recession

Entire shore exposed to high hazard flooding managed as protected dune and landscape

Equal access to beach and shore

(C) RECOMMENDED Planned development with conservation zone regulation

Figure 10.7   *Three approaches to coastal development.* (A) Beach lots, shore roads, and utilities are vulnerable to storm effects and erosion. (B) An improved alternative is to create lots and infrastructure without the shore-parallel road and install shutoff valves on water and sewer lines. (C) The best approach is to create a conservation preserve along the beach and shoreline, increasing direct views, access, and value of previously interior lots while also protecting community infrastructure and emergency access.

low-rise, mid-rise, or high-rise development. It can meet the resilient design criteria for coastal communities. It provides a model by which existing coastal communities at risk of flooding and sea level rise can effectively "retreat" while reestablishing and enhancing the natural features of coastal protection.

10.2 COMPREHENSIVE PLANNING FOR RESILIENT COMMUNITIES

Comprehensive planning by definition defines all interacting elements of a community, typically represented in a plan of conservation and development. For coastal and riverine communities, floodplain and coastal area provisions may be regulated by setbacks, defining regulated areas where construction is subject to local approval. Elements of a comprehensive plan may include:

• Floodplain management plans

• Stormwater management,

• Hazard mitigation plans

• Provisions for emergency management

The rigor of local interpretation and rulings that permit development within regulated areas varies. Some communities prohibit any encroachment of building in regulated areas with strict adherence to requirements of wetlands and their need for buffering, typically represented by setbacks of from 50 to 100 feet (15 to 30 m). In many instances, developers interpret "regulated setback" as that area where site engineering can compensate for natural system alteration and thus justify full build-out within setbacks. Local officials and commissions provide site plan review and approval of such proposals. Their rulings may be governed by guidelines promoted by state environmental agencies. A body of law supported by rulings within each state's judicial system provides the legal precedents. Such rulings may vary by jurisdiction. The actual practices of watershed design and planning ultimately are resolved by review and approval procedures in each local community. The need for assessing wetland and ecosystem services is often lost in the process. (Figure 10.8.)

Wetlands may support rare and endangered species, such as turtles, that may require up to four times the area defined as regulated setback. Loss of critical habitat becomes inevitable in many cases where land development subdivides and separates natural areas. The Conservation Overlay District ordinance described in Chapter 6 provides a policy and legislative tool to protect and connect riverine corridors within community plans.

ASFMP *No Adverse Impact* Vision for Coastal Zone and Floodplains

The *No Adverse Impact Handbook* of the Association of State Floodplain Managers (also cited in Chapter 8)

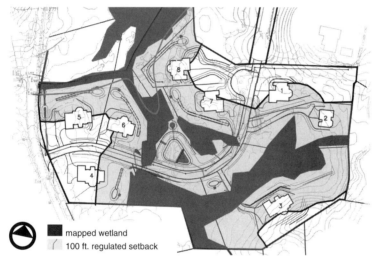

(A) DEVELOPER PROPOSAL: > 80% footprint within regulated wetland setback

mapped wetland
100 ft. regulated setback

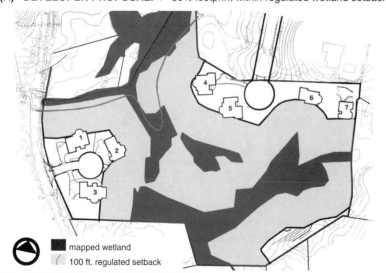

(B) INTERVENOR COUNTER PROPOSAL: < 5% footprint within regulated

mapped wetland
100 ft. regulated setback

Figure 10.8 *Alternative development proposals within regulated wetland setback.* Based on an actual case, a developer proposes to construct roads, bridge, revetments, stormwater retainage, and rain gardens within a 100-foot regulated wetland setback area. The proposal was represented as meeting all local codes and floodplain measures. The infrastructure of the development separates elements of the larger wetland system. An intervenor counterproposal submitted in a public hearing proposes an alternative plan, eliminating one building lot (#8) but otherwise matching all elements of the developer proposal while also preserving the entire wetland as a contiguous and functioning wetland, edging only slightly within the regulated setback.

envisions the desirable outcome of comprehensive planning that accounts for flood risk, with this vision:

The community's high-risk coastal floodplains provide open space, parks, recreation opportunities, habitat for wildlife and fish, and hiking and biking trails and add to the quality of life the residents and tourists enjoy. Owners of waterside property do not encroach onto the beach or into near shore waters, so public access for recreation, fishing, and other uses are protected. The direct and indirect consequences of increased growth are mitigated so they do not affect others. Development is done in a manner that does not pass the cost of living near the sea along to other properties, other communities, or future generations.[2]

NOAA Smart Growth Principles for Coastal and Waterfront Communities

NOAA advocates smart growth principles and provides short case studies that exemplify each of its 10 principles as models:[3]

1. Mix land uses, including water-dependent uses.
2. Take advantage of compact community design that enhances, preserves, and provides access to waterfront resources.
3. Provide a range of housing opportunities and choices to meet the needs of both seasonal and permanent residents.
4. Create walkable communities with physical and visual access to and along the waterfront for public use.
5. Foster distinctive, attractive communities with a strong sense of place that capitalizes on the waterfront's heritage.
6. Preserve open space, farmland, natural beauty, and the critical environmental areas that characterize and support coastal and waterfront communities.
7. Strengthen and direct development toward existing communities and encourage waterfront revitalization.
8. Provide a variety of land- and water-based transportation options.
9. Make development decisions predictable, fair, and cost-effective through consistent policies and coordinated permitting processes.
10. Encourage community and stakeholder collaboration in development decisions, ensuring that public interests in and rights of access to the waterfront and coastal waters are upheld.

USGBC New Orleans Principles

A coherent and inspirational statement forms the basis of *The New Orleans Principles*, published by the U.S. Green Building Council (USGBC) in a summary of a post-Katrina community design charrette.

The USGBC New Orleans charrette facilitators and contributors to the statement, including Robert Berkebile

---

THE NEW ORLEANS PRINCIPLES

1. Respect the rights of all citizens of New Orleans.

   Displaced citizens who wish to return to New Orleans should be afforded the opportunity to return to healthy, livable, safe, and secure neighborhoods of choice.

2. Restore natural protections of the greater New Orleans region.

   Sustain and restore the coastal and floodplain ecosystems and urban forests that support and protect the environment,

   economy, communities, and culture of southern Louisiana, and that contribute to the economy and wellbeing of the nation.

3. Implement an inclusive planning process.

   Build a community-centered planning process that uses local talent and makes sure that the voices of all New Orleanians are heard. This process should be an agent of change and renewal for New Orleans.

4. Value diversity in New Orleans.

   Build on the traditional strength of New Orleans neighborhoods, encourage mixed uses and diverse housing options, and foster communities of varied incomes, mixed age groups, and racial diversity. Celebrate the unique culture of New Orleans, including its food, music, and art.

5. Protect the city of New Orleans.

   Expand or build a flood protection infrastructure that serves multiple uses. Value, restore, and expand the urban forests, wetlands, and natural systems of the New Orleans region that protect the city from wind and storms.

6. Embrace smart redevelopment.

   Maintain and strengthen the New Orleans tradition of compact, connected, mixed-use communities. Provide residents and visitors with multiple transportation options. Look to schools for jump-starting neighborhood redevelopment and for rebuilding strong communities in the city.

7. Honor the past; build for the future.

   In the rebuilding of New Orleans, honor the history of the city while creating twenty-first-century buildings that are durable, affordable, inexpensive to operate, and healthy to live in. Through codes

and other measures, ensure that all new buildings are built to high standards of energy, structural, environmental, and human health performance.

8. Provide for passive survivability.

   Homes, schools, public buildings, and neighborhoods should be designed and built or rebuilt to serve as livable refuges in the event of crisis or breakdown of energy, water, and sewer systems.

9. Foster locally owned, sustainable businesses.

   Support existing and new local businesses built on a platform of sustainability that will contribute to a stronger and more diverse local economy.

10. Focus on the long term.

    All measures related to rebuilding and ecological restoration, even short-term efforts, must be undertaken with explicit attention to the long-term solutions.

Source: U.S. Green Building Council, *The New Orleans Principles: Celebrating the Rich History of New Orleans through Commitment to a Sustainable Future.* Report of the November 2005 New Orleans Planning Charrette, ed. Alex Wilson, www.usgbc.org/ShowFile.aspx?DocumentID=4395.

and Bill Browning, have decades of experience with environmental design charrettes, so that the principles represent an invaluable summary of professional experience. A lesson represented in these charrettes is to find consensus around a set of goals that makes the outcome real and thus realizable, focusing discussion on removing barriers and establishing steps to create what Architect David Lewis has aptly called "the memory of the future."[4]

In the New Orleans report, editor Alex Wilson compiled a set of detailed policy and action recommendations. The "Selected Practices" in the boxed section above give a summary of principles that have direct application to community planning for resilience.

10.3 LOCAL ACTIONS TO BUILD COMMUNITY RESILIENCE

Community measures for resilient design and flood mitigation require collaborative efforts. Often these efforts are difficult as a function of scale: The larger the community, the longer and more complex the collaborative process. Several measures, however, can be undertaken by individual or small groups of property owners, or community associations.

SELECTED PRACTICES TO IMPLEMENT RECOMMENDATIONS OF THE NEW ORLEANS PRINCIPLES

Infrastructure

1. *Rebuild Levee System.* Upgrade the existing levee system to withstand a Category 5 storm with redundant systems throughout. Internal levees should be incorporated to isolate flooding in case of a breech in the primary levees.

2. *Urban Linear Parks.* Use a redesigned, reinforced, and buttressed levee system and embankments as recreational areas, as segments of a system of linear parks with biking, walking, and jogging trails. These linear parks can also be a component of a coordinated evacuation strategy.

3. *Emergency Evacuation Routes.* Look for creative opportunities to share the costs of creating a better levee system by focusing on recreational opportunities—for example, a new national park could be funded by the National Park Service, and an emergency evacuation system could be funded by the Department of Homeland Security.

4. *Critical-Needs Facilities on Higher Ground.* Locate higher-density housing and critical-needs buildings such as hospitals, schools, and emergency response services along the redesigned waterway system, building on higher, more protected ground.

5. *Use Demolition Waste Creatively.* Use suitable demolition waste (such as crushed concrete, aggregate, and bricks) to raise ground levels in especially low-lying regions of the city and along expanded levee banks.

6. *Water-Resistant Construction.* Require new construction in low-lying areas to be built to withstand expected future flooding though careful material selection, elevated floor levels, and careful placement of utilities. Design structures to resist water intrusion and mold growth.

7. *Reliable Pumping System.* Redesign pumping stations so that they can function and be operated safely during even the most severe storm events.

8. *Reduce Stormwater Loading with On-Site Strategies.* Reduce the city's stormwater loads through the design of its new buildings and infrastructure. By reducing the stormwater loading, the rate at which stormwater reaches pumps is reduced, lessening flooding and allowing use of smaller pumps operating at substantially lower cost. Open, green areas that accept stormwater and have controlled discharge structures act as temporary storage and further reduce flooding risk.

   Require:

   • Use porous pavement wherever feasible to reduce stormwater loading. Despite the city's high water table, porous pavement is helpful in reducing flooding that results from small and moderate storms.

   • Install green roofs for most large structures, both to reduce stormwater loading and to reduce the urban heat island effect, thereby cooling the city as a whole and reducing energy consumption.

   • Use rainwater harvesting systems, including on-site cisterns, both to lessen the stormwater loading and to provide water for other uses (landscape irrigation, toilet flushing, cooling/heating systems, and maintenance).

9. *Survivable Wireless Systems.* Develop a reliable and survivable cell phone system and citywide high-speed wireless access to the Internet.

Passive Survivability

1. *Passive Survivability.* Make it the policy of the City of New Orleans that all homes, schools, churches, and civic buildings that could be used as emergency shelters be designed and built to provide life-support shelter in times of crisis—a criteria referred to here as *passive survivability.* These buildings should be designed to maintain survivable thermal conditions without air conditioning or supplemental heat through the use of cooling-load avoidance strategies, natural ventilation, highly efficient building envelopes, and passive solar design. Schools and other public buildings should be designed and built with natural daylighting so that they can be used without power during the daytime. Co-locate healthcare facilities with schools as part of the community anchor and to strengthen survivability.

2. *Water Systems.* Provide incentives to homeowners and other building owners for installing emergency water systems, including rooftop rainwater harvesting, in their buildings. Configure rainwater harvesting systems to provide landscape irrigation during normal times (reducing potable water consumption), but with an option so that during power outages or in the event of water supply interruptions, stored water can be used for drinking (with filtration), toilet flushing, bathing, and other uses in the building.

3. *Backup Power for Municipal Sewage.* Provide backup generator power at sewage treatment plants and pumping stations so that minimal sewage line operation can be maintained during extended power outages. Part of the problem is that sewer systems are not sealed. Rain or floodwater enters the system either by infiltration or through vents and manholes. If floodwater overwhelms the system, it backs up into buildings and untreated waste is released from the treatment plant. One-way valves mitigate this problem, but increase maintenance costs.

4. *Distributed Infrastructure.* Implement a distributed infrastructure (including power supply, water supply, and communications) to provide these critical services and to ensure emergency response capability during times of crisis. Include renewable energy strategies in achieving this requirement.

5. *Solar Electric Systems.* Seek federal funding through the Solar Roofs Program to provide rooftop photovoltaic (PV) systems on new homes and other buildings in the city. Configure these grid-connected systems so that they can provide emergency power within the building when the electricity grid is down (this will necessitate some battery backup as well as equipment to safely disconnect the PV system from the grid during blackouts). In normal times, these systems will reduce the owner's need to purchase electrical power, reduce peak demand, and lower regional pollution levels.

6. *Solar Water Heating.* Provide incentives for homeowners, schools, and businesses to install solar water heating systems on buildings.

7. *Bury/Protect Infrastructure.* Make it the policy of the City of New Orleans to install new electric, communications, and gas lines below ground and protected

from stormwater and floodwater loadings.

8. *Areas of Refuge.* Ensure that each neighborhood or community in New Orleans has a designated building (typically a school, but alternately a public library, church, or other civic building) that can serve the community during times of emergency or extended power outage. Construct or rebuild schools as neighborhood centers and potential refuges. Fund an outreach program to educate residents about this emergency shelter system.

9. *Highway System.* Upgrade the existing highway system to withstand future Category 5 storms, both to provide safe egress from the city and to save the expense of having to rebuild them after a future storm.

10. *Emergency Access.* At schools and hospitals and in recreation areas, include spaces that, during an emergency, can be used as assembly areas, helicopter landing areas, and distribution points.

Focus on the Long Term

1. *Visionary Master Plan.* Use the opportunity to remaster a city and regional plan that corrects past mistakes. Make decisions that will serve New Orleans well for the next several hundred years.

2. *Temporary Basic Services.* Provide temporary solutions for basic services (including water, sewage treatment, electricity, and security) that will allow system-wide improvements to be made in the context of integrated needs assessment and planning.

3. *Temporary Structures.* Phased solutions, such as temporary housing and classrooms, can be implemented in a manner that allows longer-term solutions to be fully planned and implemented.

4. *Establish Priorities.* Prioritize the implementation of long-term, environmentally responsible, and economically responsive improvements to the city.

Source: U.S. Green Building Council, *The New Orleans Principles*, www.usgbc.org/ShowFile .aspx? DocumentID=4395.

Compensation for Ecosystem Services

Ecosystem services—also referred to as ecological goods and services—are benefits derived by people, plants, and animals from the ecological functions of healthy ecosystems.

Rural and suburban communities often have open spaces that serve as reservoirs of biodiverse natural communities. Landscape and parcels developed and converted from their natural state most often lose part or all of their ecological functions. A market may be created wherein ecological goods and services are demanded by society and supplied by public and private landowners. Giving economic value to the ecological services provided by natural landscapes can help establish support for conservation and protection of natural resources as well as a basis of just and fair compensation for portions that are protected from development.

An example is compensation to farmers to set aside portions of land that would otherwise be in production or be sold to development, representing a shift in thinking from "polluter pays" to the "beneficiary pays." Many innovative legal and financial instruments

THE UNITED NATIONS 2004 MILLENNIUM ECOSYSTEM ASSESSMENT REPORT

The UN assessment report places ecosystem services into four broad categories.

Provisioning Services

• Food (crops, wild foods, and spices)

• Water

• Pharmaceutical, biochemical, and industrial products

• Energy (hydropower, biomass fuels)

Regulating Services

• Carbon sequestration and climate regulation

• Waste decomposition and detoxification

• Purification of air and water

• Crop pollination

• Pest and disease control

Supporting Services

• Nutrient dispersal and cycling

• Seed dispersal

• Primary production

Cultural Services

• Cultural, intellectual, and spiritual inspiration

• Recreation including ecotourism

• Scientific discovery

Source: Millennium Ecosystem Assessment, *Ecosystems and Human Well-Being: Synthesis* (Washington, DC: Island Press, 2005). www.wri .org/. . ./millennium-ecosystem-assessment-ecosystems-and-human-well-being-synthesis

provide means to protect the ecological services of land and marine resources, including municipal ordinances, zoning regulation, conservation easements and private land trusts, as well as market incentives and tax rebates. (Figure 10.9.)

Geologic Hazard Abatement Districts

Geologic hazard abatement districts (GHADs) were established in California in 1979 as a means to abate an immediate, existing geologic hazard, such as landslides and mudslides that could at any time impact private properties

as well as community infrastructure and vital services. Its first applications were to encourage preventative measures and rapid mitigation of "geologic hazards" defined as "an actual or threatened landslide, land subsidence, soil erosion, earthquake, or any other natural or unnatural movement of land or earth."[5] GHADs have evolved in California as independent state-level public entities authorized to oversee geological hazard prevention, mitigation, abatement, and control. It has authority similar to other public agencies including taxing, bonding, and legal immunity.

GHADs are an administrative and legal instrument to finance and implement measures required to mitigate

Figure 10.9   *Preserving ecosystem services:* New Jersey Farmland Preservation Program.

(PHOTO: Donald Watson)

Source: State of New Jersey Department of Agriculture. 2009. State Agriculture Development Committee.
www.nj.gov/agriculture/sadc/farmpreserve/.

flooding. GHADs offer the advantages of local financing, direction, and control. They are able to undertake preventive maintenance and mitigation quickly and appropriately to local situations, without reliance on any larger, more burdensome approvals. Once established, a GHAD may issue bonds, purchase and dispose of property, acquire property by eminent domain, levy and collect assessments, sue and be sued, and construct and maintain improvements. This scope of GHAD applications could be extended to other weather and storm hazards, flood prevention, mitigation of wave damage, wetland protection, repair of damaged shorelines, and monitoring and maintenance of stormwater infrastructure.[6] (Figure 10.10.)

Figure 10.10 *Capacity for local action:* GHADs provide a means for local control of flood prevention and mitigation programs.

(PHOTO: John Shea FEMA Photo Library, January 1, 2005)

Notes

1. FEMA, *Coastal Construction Manual: Principles and Practices of Planning, Siting, Designing, Constructing, and Maintaining Residential Buildings in Coastal Areas,* FEMA 55 (August 2005), www.fema.gov/rebuild/mat/fema55.shtm.

2. Association of State Floodplain Managers, *No Adverse Impact Handbook.* Madison, WI. 2008, www.floods.org/NoAdverseImpact/CNAI_Handbook/CNAI_Handbook.pdf.

3. NOAA, "Coastal & Waterfront Smart Growth" (December 2009), http://coastalsmartgrowth.noaa.gov/casestudies.html.

4. Donald Watson, *Environmental Design Charrette Workbook.* Washington, DC: AIA Press, 1996 [out of print]; also Donald Watson and Chad Floyd, "Community Design Charrettes" in *Time-Saver Standards for Urban Design* (New York: McGraw-Hill, 2003).

5. Robert B. Olshansky, "Geologic Hazard Abatement Districts," California Geology 39, no. 7 (1986): 158–159.

6. Robert B. Olshansky and Jack D. Kartez, "Managing Land Use to Build Resilience," in R. J. Burby (ed.), *Confronting Natural Hazards: Land-Use Planning for Sustainable Communities* (Washington, DC: National Academy/Joseph Henry Press, 1998); also personal communication with R.B. Olshansky, November 9, 2009.

Figure 11.1   *Bring Your Boots: Opportunities of Failure:* Rising Tides Competition, 2009.

(PHOTO: © Royston Hanamoto Alley and Abey)

CHAPTER **11**

SEA LEVEL RISE

The poetic notion of "the ever-constant sea"—however expressive of the enduring state of the oceans—has to be reworded to account for global climate changes. The condition and continuing health of the sea is not so predictably enduring.

U.S. communities are experiencing flood events with greater frequency and severity. Precipitation patterns are changing. Hurricanes, if less frequent, are more damaging, including more powerful storm surges. The prospect of sea level rise is acknowledged to be a result of global

---

CLIMATE CHANGE AND SEA LEVEL RISE

The consensus in the climate science community is that the global climate is changing. The effects of climate change are highly variable across regions and difficult to predict. Two effects of atmospheric warming on coasts are sea-level rise and an increase in major cyclone intensity.

Instrument observations over the past 15 years show that global mean sea level has been highly variable at regional scales around the world. On average, the rate of rise appears to have accelerated over twentieth-century rates, possibly due to atmospheric warming causing expansion of ocean water and ice-sheet melting.

In some regions, such as the Mid-Atlantic and much of the Gulf of Mexico, sea level rise is significantly greater than the observed global sea level rise due to localized sinking of the land surface, attributed to ongoing adjustment of Earth's crust due to the melting of former ice sheets, sediment compaction and

consolidation, and withdrawal of hydrocarbons from underground.

Global sea level elevations at the peak of the last interglacial warm cycle were 13 to 20 feet (4 to 6 m) above present levels and could again be realized within the next several hundred years if warming and glacier and ice-sheet melting continue. Results of climate model studies suggest sea level rise in the twenty-first century will significantly exceed rates over the twentieth century. Rates and the magnitude of rise could be much greater if warming affects dynamic processes that determine ice flow and losses in Greenland and Antarctica.

Source: Williams, S. Jeffress et al., *Sea-Level Rise and Its Effects on the Coast*, chap. 1, "Coastal Sensitivity to Sea-Level Rise: A Focus on the Mid-Atlantic Region," Final Report. U.S. Global Change Research Program (USGCRP), 2004, www.climatescience .gov/…1/final-report/sap4-1-final-report-all.pdf.

warming. These combine in what are called the unpredictable impacts of climate change.

The challenge and charge of resilient design is to address global warming and climate change through three realizable steps:

1. Reduction of risk by mitigation and adaptation measures
2. Restoration of ecosystem services
3. Revitalization and reinvestment toward community and regional sustainability

11.1 SEA LEVEL RISE: THE ISSUES

Even small increases in sea level rise will create risks for natural systems. A rise of several inches will drive ocean salinity inland, spilling into freshwater aquifers. Existing built infrastructure will be similarly impacted by slight elevation of sea level. Every shipping port facility has equipment and docks precisely calibrated for functional transfer between water to land. Urban stormwater and sewer outfalls typically function by gravity to elevations determined by current sea elevations.

More disruptive and unpredictable property and life-safety risks result from severe weather events associated with tropical cyclones and mid-latitude storms. Lower temperatures increase the moisture in the air, leading to larger snow and rainfall events. Low atmospheric pressure and high winds produce large storm surges, which are especially serious if they coincide with high tide.

Sea Level Measurement

Sea level is measured by tide gauges and by satellites. Tide gauges measure the height of water with respect to a fixed, nearby point on land. Satellite altimeters have made precise measurements of sea level continuously since the early 1990s. By combining data from these sources, sea surface topography can be determined to within less than an inch. Oceanographers analyze sea level changes as one of many indices of climate change.

Sea level measurement is an average, based on the evident assumptions that the oceans are ultimately intercon-

nected and that water tends to find its own level. Earth's ocean surface geometry approximates a flattened sphere (ellipsoid). To estimate the mean, tides and seasonal variations are averaged out over a long period, typically 19 years, to account for the effect of the 228-month Metonic cycle of phases of the Moon and the 223-month eclipse cycle on the tides.

Mean sea level (MSL) is the average height of the ocean surface midway between mean high and low tide, measured over a period of time. Measurements may vary regionally and locally. Designated as *local mean sea level* (LMSL), the data are defined with reference to a local land benchmark and used in designating surveyed land elevation.

The term *eustatic* refers to global changes in sea level due to water mass added to or removed from the oceans. Increase of sea level due to melting of glaciers is an example of eustatic sea level rise. The term *steric* refers to global changes in sea level due to variations in thermal expansion and salinity.

Sea level rise calculation must also account for vertical movements of the land, referred to in geology as *postglacial rebound*, which can be of the same order of magnitude as sea level changes. Postglacial rebound (also called *continental rebound*) is the rise of landmasses depressed by the weight of ice sheets during the last glacial period. In land formations, Earth's crust was depressed under weight of ice while a rise (*forebudge*) pushed the crust up and ahead of the advancing glaciers. When the glaciers retreated, Earth's surface rebounded upward where the glaciers had been and subsided along the glacial front where a forebudge was formed. This rise and fall continues today at reduced rate. In some regions, such as Great Lakes region of Canada and United States, both rebound and subsidence are evident.[1]

Range of Measurements and Estimates of Sea Level Rise

The surface of the oceans forms an amorphous continual shape, constantly in motion and neither perfectly spherical nor uniform. The height variations of ocean surface topography can be more than 6 feet (2 m) and are influenced by ocean circulation, ocean temperature, and salinity. Topographical features and weather patterns cause parts of the Atlantic Ocean to be 16 inches (40 cm) lower than parts of the Pacific Ocean. The Panama Canal spans a sea level difference of 8 inches (20 cm). Ocean currents are recorded by studying the hills and valleys in charts of the height of the sea surface relative to the geoid. Earth's *geoid* is a calculated surface of equal gravitational potential energy and represents the shape the sea surface would be if the ocean were not in motion.

Sea level has risen and fallen with the recent 100,000-year glacial-interglacial cycle. During glacial periods, sea level has been as much as 400 feet (120 m) lower than current levels, whereas during the warmer interglacial periods, sea level has been as much as about 20 feet (6 m) higher than the present. The northern hemisphere has experienced variations in temperature considered as climatic anomalies, reflected in changes in sea level as well as cultural history.

During the twentieth century until the 1990s, sea level rise occurred at a mean rate of 0.75 inches (19 mm) per decade, a small range compared to historic and current perspectives. The emerging concern of sea level rise is driven by a near doubling in the annual rate of sea level rise in the past two decades. (Figure 11.2.)

Increasing global temperatures result in sea level rise by thermal expansion of water and by the addition of water to the oceans from the melting of continental ice sheets. As a point of reference—no one is suggesting the possibility—if the entire mass of glaciers and ice sheets were to melt, global sea level would rise by approximately 250 feet (80 m).[2]

Estimates reported in scientific literature for predicted sea level rise over the course of the next century vary from 3.5 to 35 inches (90 to 880 mm), a tenfold disagreement. Ongoing research and authoritative reports tend to the higher estimates, leading to concerns that have now been raised to national and international policy levels.[3]

A 2010 Report of the U.S. National Academy of Sciences supports the principal findings of the Intergovernmental Panel on Climate Change, a United Nations study released in 2007 and later criticized for containing errors. The National Academy Report incorporates findings of newer research and concludes that earlier IPCC projections were conservative and underestimated the potential rate of sea level rise. While framing its conclusions with emphasis upon uncertainty, the report supports the soundness of scientific-consensus studies that indicate sea levels could rise as much as 6.25 feet (1.9 m) by 2100 if greenhouse gas (GHG) reduction efforts are not effective. The report states that the higher projections, along with increased uncertainty, derive from incomplete

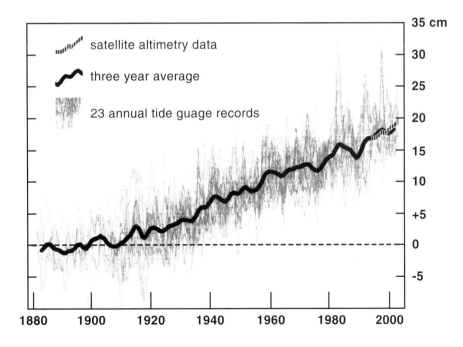

Figure 11.2   *Recent sea level rise, 1880–2010.*

Source: After Wikipedia contributors, "Current Sea Level Rise," *Wikipedia, The Free Encyclopedia*, http://en.wikipedia.org/wiki/Current_sea_level_rise.

understanding of ice sheet melting and collapse, as well as the potential for rapid and sudden changes. In effect, the Report supports continuing concern for the high risk of sea level rise, while avoiding prediction of "how much" and "how soon."[4]

The term *relative sea level rise* refers to the change in sea level compared with land elevation at a particular location. The regional differences have considerable importance in defining the extent and timing of regional and local options for protection and mitigation strategies.

Climate change–induced sea level rise is a function of greenhouse gas (GHG) emissions and global warming. Steps to reduce GHG are necessary to reduce sea level rise impacts. IPCC's *Synthesis Report* includes among its "robust findings" that:

- The rise in sea level during the twenty-first century will continue for further centuries.

- The sooner the better: Early GHG reduction will have the greatest impact on reducing projected global warming and sea level rise.

- Anticipatory actions of adaption and mitigation are needed in advance of evident or severe impacts because

of the inertia in the interacting climate, ecological, and socioeconomic systems.

- Adaptation cannot prevent all damages, but can reduce adverse effects of climate change and can produce immediate ancillary benefits.[5]

This last finding, that sea level rise will continue even if GHGs are reduced, underscores the importance of resilient design protection, mitigation, and adaption strategies. Even if carbon dioxide (CO_2) emissions are reduced and atmospheric concentrations are stabilized, surface air temperatures will continue to rise slowly for a century or more, due to inertia in ecological systems. Thermal expansion of the oceans and melting of ice sheets would thus continue sea level rise for many centuries. (Figure 11.3.)

For architects, planners, officials, and managers of properties at risk of sea level rise, the uncertainty about the amount and rate of sea level rise presents a problem whose solution is not evident, because risks and level of responses cannot be determined easily. Any responsible design and construction program is dependent on agreement on the extent and rate of sea level rise.

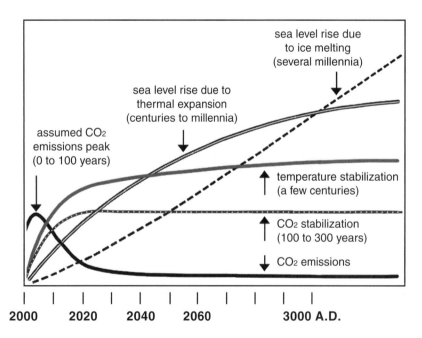

Figure 11.3 *Sea levels will rise even if all climate mitigation strategies succeed:* This graph is a general depiction of stabilization of global climate indices assuming CO_2 at any level between 450 parts per million (ppm) and 1,000 ppm. Therefore, it has no units on the response axis. Impacts become progressively larger at higher concentrations of CO_2.

Source: Intergovernmental Panel on Climate Change (IPCC). *Climate Change 2001: Synthesis Report. Summary for Policy Makers: An Assessment of the Intergovernmental Panel on Climate Change,* eds. Robert T. Watson et al. (New York: Cambridge University Press, 2001).

Building investments and impacts endure for many centuries in many U.S. coastal harbors and ports cities that were established more than 300 years ago and for millennia on other continents. To aspire to the goals of sustainability, one designs for the ages. No matter how one addresses ongoing debate over predictions, sea level rise will be evident within the present century. There appears to be no precautionary design choice other than to plan for sea level rise—to plan for the centuries and the risks and possibilities of climate change, known and unknown. Proposals that respond to the challenge and opportunities of sea level rise are presented in the next section.

11.2 SEA LEVEL RISE: DESIGN RESPONSES

The IPCC Coastal Zone Management Subgroup[5] recommends that coastal regions, authorities, and planners begin the process of adapting to sea level rise "not because there is an impending catastrophe, but because there are opportunities to avoid adverse impacts by acting now, opportunities that may be lost if the process is delayed." This is consistent with precautionary design to include coastal zone planning and best management practices, whether climate-driven sea level rise occurs or not.

Precautionary Actions to Increase Protection of Properties at Risk

- **Stop the harm.** Stop removing wetland, river, and estuarine buffers, coastal landscapes of forest, marsh, and mangroves that buffer storms.
- **Start doing the right thing.** At any scale, begin projects that mitigate harm and protect coastal resources, increasing water and food resources.

- **Plan for the longer term.** Planning is the least costly strategy and requirement for due diligence, to assess risk and determine solutions, ready to be implemented as opportunities and needs appear.

The 1990 IPCC Coastal Zone Management Subgroup defines three strategic responses required to protect human life and property from impacts of sea level rise: retreat, accommodation and protection. Quoting from the report:

- *Retreat involves no effort to protect the land from the sea. The coastal zone is abandoned and ecosystems shift landward. This choice can be motivated by excessive economic or environmental impacts of protection. In the extreme case, an entire area may be abandoned.*

- *Accommodation implies that people continue to use the land at risk but do not attempt to prevent the land from being flooded. This option includes erecting emergency flood shelters, elevating buildings on piles, converting agriculture to fish farming, or growing flood- or salt-tolerant crops.*

- *Protection involves hard structures such as sea walls and dikes, as well as soft solutions such as dunes and vegetation, to protect the land from the sea so that existing land uses can continue.*[6]

The "Pioneering Proposals" examples on the pages that follow present an overview of responses to sea level rise. Some are visionary and require very large and long-term programs of enterprise and investment. Others proposals are specific to sites and projects and thus more immediately realizable. A range of strategies borrow equally from design inspired by nature and technological innovation. All indicate ways of turning risk of flooding and the threat of sea level rise into opportunity to design for resiliency in buildings, communities, and regions.

PIONEERING PROPOSALS

THE SOUTH DADE WATERSHED PROJECT

- South Florida Water Management District 1992
- AIA Urban and Regional Design Honor Award 1999
- Daniel E. Williams, FAIA, APA, Research Associate Professor, Center for Urban and Community Design, University of Miami School of Architecture, 1992–1994

Hurricane Andrew destroyed communities within the 160-square-mile (414-square-km) South Dade area. A regional charrette produced a vision plan that redirects development toward higher ground and establishes a "carrying capacity" based on water supply and flooding mitigation. The plan helped to inform the South Dade Land Use Plan 2020.

- Transportation corridors connect people to work and civic amenities.
- Greenway/blueways connect water to use, storage, and flood mitigation.
- Sewage compost is returned to horticultural and agricultural uses.
- Water is recharged to aquifers after cleanup.
- Development is redirected to higher areas away from hurricane surge and sea level rise.
- Open space is designed to be available as floodable "hydric parks."

Source: Daniel E. Williams, *The South Dade Watershed Project* (West Palm Beach, FL: South Florida Water Management District, 1992), www.dwa-design.com/data/documents/Audubon_Dade_WIN.pdf.

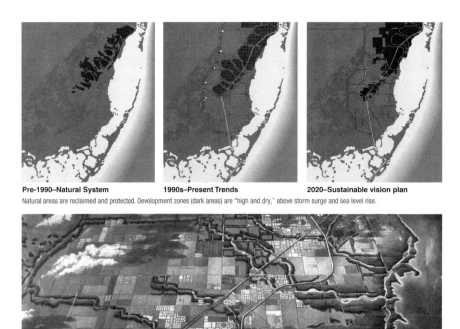

Pre-1990–Natural System   1990s–Present Trends   2020–Sustainable vision plan
Natural areas are reclaimed and protected. Development zones (dark areas) are "high and dry," above storm surge and sea level rise.

Figure 11.4 *South Dade Watershed Project* is an early 1990s example of flood mitigation and conservation planning.

EASTWARD HO: SOUTHEAST FLORIDA COASTAL SMART-GROWTH STUDY 1998

- South Florida Regional Planning Council
- AIA Urban Research Design Honor Award 2000
- Daniel E. Williams, FAIA, APA, Director, Education and Research Center, University of Florida, 1997–1999

The Eastward Ho! study developed a vision plan for a 2,400-square-mile (6,216-square-km) area of Southeast Florida. The study proposes a comprehensive regional framework for smart growth and sustainability, including storm mitigation and prospect of sea level rise.

Source: Daniel E. Williams, *Sustainable Design: Ecology, Architecture, and Planning* (New York: John Wiley & Sons, 2007); also Daniel E. Williams, *Eastward Ho: Vision for Southeast Florida* (Tallahassee: Florida Department of Community Affairs, 1998).

HYDRIC ZONES

A Everglades—Agricultural Zone

In this floodplain zone, existing geology and soils act as the region's water storage and aquifer recharge area. The area corresponds to land susceptible to sea level rise of 6 ft (2 m).

B Coastal Ridge and Transverse Glade Zone

This zone (darker tone) is the historic urban development area. This location receives the most rainfall but has the most amount of impervious surface. Glades reestablish natural water flow and recharge the groundwater aquifers.

C Hydric Parks and Blueway Zone

"Hydric parks" combine recreational and aesthetic benefits of greenways and blueways with the water resource objectives of flood protection and aquifer recharge.

D Florida Southeast Sea Level Rise Zone

Located to the right of the vertical line are the land uses most impacted by hurricanes and sea level rise. This zone historically provided a natural buffer from hurricane storm surge and an ecological and economic transition zone from impacts of sea level change as well as the nursery ground for the aquatic food chain.

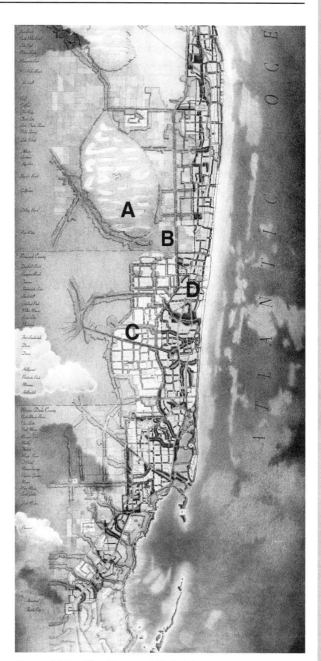

Figure 11.5   *The Eastward Ho! vision* encompasses 120 miles of coastline, 70 municipalities and population of 4.5 million people.

CLIMATE'S LONG-TERM IMPACTS ON METRO BOSTON

■ Paul H. Kirshen, William P. Anderson, Matthias Ruth

"Climate's Long-term Impacts on Metro Boston" (CLIMB) was the first of a recent series of studies on potential impacts of climate change on infrastructure systems in metropolitan Boston. It reviews and recommends strategies to prevent, reduce, or manage the risk of potential sea level rise (SLR), higher summer peak temperatures, and more variable and intense precipitation. The study considered impacts on regional water supply and quality, wastewater treatment, flood management, transportation and communication, health, building, and energy demand. It estimated the expected annual residual damages and costs of climate change impacts and adaptation strategies.

Four scenarios were compared to determine the cost and effectiveness of different adaptation

responses to increased coastal flooding from rising sea levels. For study purposes, it was assumed that SLR could reach either 24 inches (0.62 m) or 39 inches (1 m) over the next 100 years and that the area of study could be exposed to storm damage by a maximum of one storm per year. The analysis compared the implications of each scenario in terms of initial and continuing costs of emergency response, adaptation, and residual damage over 100 years (2000 to 2100).

Ride-it-Out Scenario

In this scenario, Boston would continue development in floodplains over the next 100 years as it does now. Existing flood insurance provisions would repair storm damage by returning buildings to their original condition. Using an assumed economic model

Figure 11.6 *Adaptation measures illustrate options for protection for sea level rise and coastal storms (subject to local planning regulations).*

Source: P. Kirshen, M. Ruth, and W. Anderson, "Climate's Long-term Impacts on Urban Infrastructures and Services: The Case of Metro Boston," chapter 7 of M. Ruth, K. Donaghy, and P.H. Kirshen (eds.), *Climate Change and Variability: Local Impacts and Responses* (Cheltenham, UK: Edward Elgar, 2006); also P. H. Kirshen, K. Knee, and M. Ruth. "Adaptation to Sea Level Rise in Metro Boston," *Climatic Change* 90, no.4 (2008): 453–473.

Figure 11.7 *East Boston waterfront* adjacent to Condor Street Urban Wild, as it exists today and after illustrative dune/beach protection measures. The CLIMB study has been followed by studies focused on local adaptation strategies, including impacts of increased coastal flooding on a generally low-income coastal neighborhood. Adaptation options include protection with hard and soft structures adjustable as the sea level rises while increasing economic and recreation opportunities for the neighborhood.

Source: Personal communications, Ellen Douglas of the University Massachusetts-Boston; Paul Kirshen of Battelle; Matt Shultz of The Woods Hole Group. November 29, 2009.

of development along the waterfront and expected flood damage over the next century with a SLR of 24 inches (0.62 m), the size of the area flooded will more than triple compared to no SLR. This would impose $20 billion in total costs over the next 100 years. If the sea level rises to 39 inches (1 m), the total property damage adaptation and emergency costs could reach $36 billion.

Build-Your-Way-Out Scenario

This approach would also allow current development to continue without floodproofing buildings but assumes that, after a second storm at the level of a 100-year storm, the region would construct seawalls and bulkheads to protect coastal development. Because flooding losses will be mitigated, damages from this scenario with 24 inches (0.62 m) of SLR would be $5.9 billion over 100 years instead of $20 billion in the Ride-It-Out scenario. Construction could cost up to $3.5 billion. Maintenance costs would be high. Seawalls would have a negative impact on the environment, separating beachfronts from dunes and increasing vulnerability to erosion.

Green or Planned Adaptation Scenario

In this scenario, new development in 100-year and 500-year floodplains would be flood-proofed, including existing residences and commercial and industrial buildings, before being sold. Retrofitting homes would each cost between $3,500 and $17,000, depending on location. This scenario would require $1.8 billion in expenditure for flood proofing but would result in reducing the total damages to 2100 to $4 billion, a reduction to one-quarter of the Ride-It-Out scenario, all other factors remaining equal.

Retreat Scenario

This scenario assumes that no more residential, commercial, or industrial development is allowed in floodplains and that no rebuilding after a

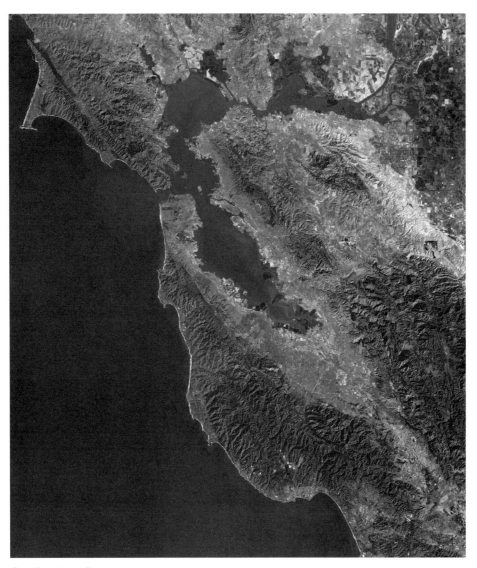

Figure 11.8   *San Francisco Bay.*

(PHOTO: USGS)

Source: San Francisco Bay Conservation and Development Commission Rising Tides Competition, 2008, www.risingtides competition.com/risingtides; also *Sea Level Rise Strategy for the San Francisco Bay Region*, www.bcdc.ca.gov/planning/ climate_change/climate_strategy.pdf.

structure is damaged by flood is permitted; that is, there would be no damage threshold below which an owner can repair instead of abandon. The total costs are very high, $17.1 billion, due to the high value of abandoned land and buildings in the coastal region. This scenario has least environmental impacts of other scenarios. As land is abandoned, it may revert back to such natural systems as wetlands and beaches, increasing regional ecosystem services.

A common finding of the CLIMB studies on various infrastructure systems is that failure to take any adaptation action is the least effective and the most costly policy and that Planned Adaptation is most effective and least costly long-term policy.

San Francisco Bay Rising Tides Competition

SAN FRANCISCO BAY CONSERVATION AND DEVELOPMENT COMMISSION (BCDC)

Historic records show that sea level in San Francisco Bay has risen nearly 8 inches (20 cm) in the past century. The California Governor's Climate Action Team (CAT) has projected that sea level will rise "between 20 to 55 inches" (50 to 140 cm) by the year 2100.[a]

The San Francisco Bay Conservation and Development Commission (BCDC) has developed a strategy for addressing climate change in the Bay region. The Commission has prepared studies using GIS data and maps showing that a 55-inch rise in the level of the Bay could flood over 332 square miles of land and development around the Bay. From this estimate, the Pacific Institute reported that over $62 billion worth of public and private shoreline development could be at risk in the Bay Area.

BCDC has identified changes and initiatives in state law so that to implement such a Statewide comprehensive strategy. It include new State regulations requiring each local government to be required to develop a sea level rise protection program along with relocation and resource enhancements program.

Announced as an "International Competition for Ideas Responding to Sea Level Rise in San Francisco Bay and Beyond," BCDC organized the Rising Tides competition in 2009, sponsored by the National Oceanic and Atmospheric Administration (NOAA), with a goal to define "a bold, new plan for the Bay...a vision for resilient communities and adaptable natural areas around a dynamic and changing Bay that will have different sea level elevations, salinity levels, species and chemistry than the Bay has today. A new pattern of development will be needed to respond to these changing conditions."

The competition program challenged planners and designer to:

• Rethink how to build new communities in areas susceptible to future inundation.

• Retrofit valuable public shoreline infrastructure.

• Protect existing communities from flooding.

• Protect wetlands.

• Anticipate changing shoreline configurations.

Images and texts on the pages that follow selected from entries represent a range of program responses. They include protective measures of dykes and weirs, but in almost all cases address "soft shoreline" approaches to restore and extend the ecological services of lagoons, marshes, and watersheds. They reinforce that the entire range of watershed, coastal, and green infrastructure concepts best address the challenge of severe weather and sea level rise.

---

[a] California Climate Action Team, Executive Summary (March 2006), p. 15, www.climatechange.ca.gov/climate_action_team/index.html.

[b] Personal communication, Brad McCrae, December 11, 2009; also see www.risingtidescompetition.com. The kind assistance of Brad McCrae, Bay Design Analyst, and Alice Chung, Intern, of San Francisco Bay Conservation and Development Commission is gratefully acknowledged.

TOPOGRAPHICAL SHIFTS AT THE URBAN WATERFRONT

- Rising Tides Competition winner 2009:
- Wright Huaiche Yang and J. Lee Stickles, San Francisco, California

The proposed green infrastructure shifts and alters with time, extending ecological, cultural, and civic infrastructure.

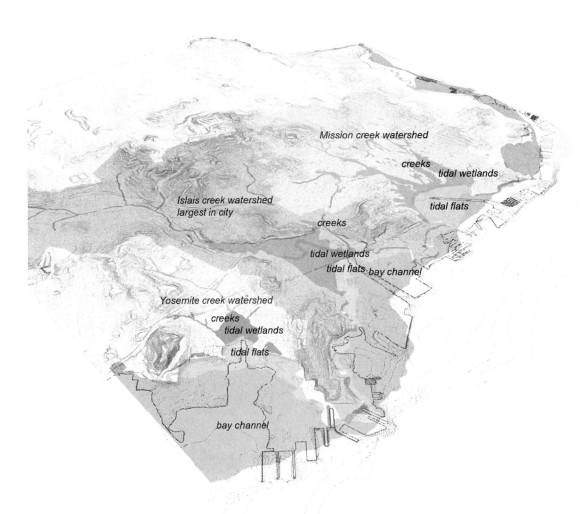

(A) ORIGINAL WATERSHED AND SHORELINE EDGE

Figure 11.9   Topographical shifts at the urban waterfront.

(Map: Courtesy San Francisco Planning Department.)

(B) EXISTING INDUSTRIAL LAND Transport and urban barrier

Figure 11.9   Topographical shifts at the urban waterfront.

(Source: EPA.)

(C) TOXIC SITES TO BE REMEDIATED BEFORE SEA LEVEL RISE

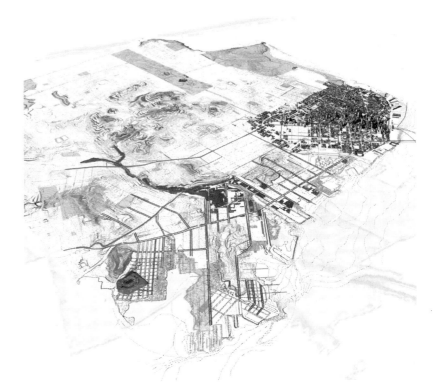

(D) PROPOSED ECOLOGICAL NETWORK, PARKS AND CITY FABRIC

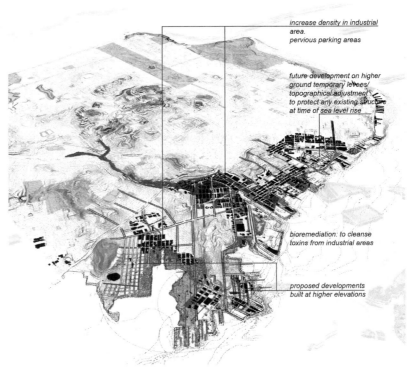

increase density in industrial area.
pervious parking areas

future development on higher ground temporary levees/ topographical adjustment to protect any existing structure at time of sea level rise

bioremediation: to cleanse toxins from industrial areas

proposed developments built at higher elevations

Figure 11.9   Topographical shifts at the urban waterfront.

(E) DIVERSIFY THE EDGE - Economy, culture, and ecology

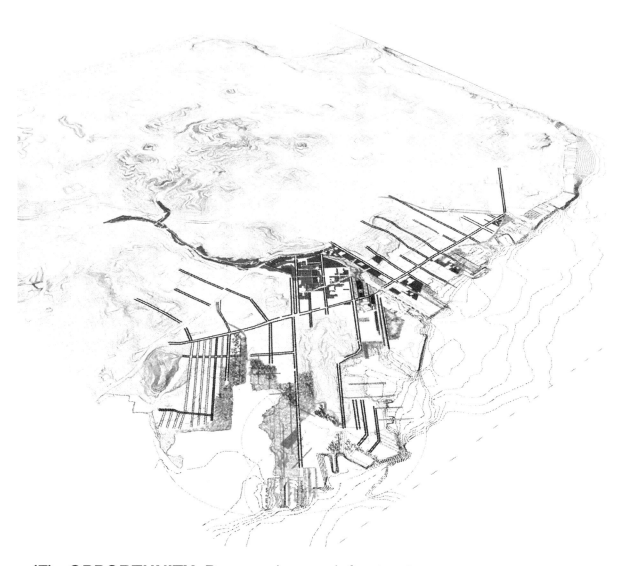

(F) OPPORTUNITY: Proposed green infrastructure

Figure 11.9   Topographical shifts at the urban waterfront.

ESTUARINE CITY

■ Rising Tides Competition honorable mention 2009

Mithun Architecture, San Francisco, California
Bionic Landscape Architecture and Planning
Regenesis Regenerative Planning
NSI Wetlands Planning

Emergent response. Learn and adapt through time. Privilege self-organizing biological processes over industrial ones.

Pattern transferability. This is one watershed, one bay of many. Principles and patterns are transferable. Techniques and structures may not be.

Place relating. Encourage differentiation: local responses to local conditions with access to natural and cultural legacy and economic opportunity.

Elegant holism. Orient to whole systems potential rather than dismantled parts, problems, and solutions. Find leverage points: Economize through elegance.

Life-concentrating zones. Layer, concentrate, enrich, and intensify uses. Establish harmonious equilibrium among human density and wildness.

Restored freshwater systems, wetlands, and soils purify storm and wastewater, recharging the aquifer. Daylighted stream and salmon runs, parks, green streetscape, and open spaces provide filtration.

Canal neighborhoods extend the urban estuary interface. Spoil for canal cutting creates buildable platforms and aquaculture gardens in otherwise inundated areas.

Abandoned districts become tidal ecosystems with oyster beds, eelgrass, and juvenile fish, serving as surge protectors, habitat, and sources of economic activity.

1 Oyster reefs
2 Wetlands
3 Canal neighborhoods
4 Aquaculture
5 Biofuels
6 Transit neighborhoods
7 Salmon streams
8 Coastal redwoods

Figure 11.10   *Estuarine City.*

(© Mithun)

EVOLUTIONARY RECOVERY

- Rising Tides Competition winner 2009
- Yuni Lee + Leon Tae Kim, LANDplus Design, San Francisco, California with EPRI Giyoung Park, Architect

This proposal for the bay's Evolutionary Recovery defines collaborative actions and recovery zones: protection, operation, and adaption.

PROTECTION
SFO

Protect Shoreline Infrastructure.

- Protect the shoreline infrastructure: Airports, Ports, Highways, and Utilities.
- Create physical barriers and wetlands as double shoreline protection.
- Maintain and manage low grounds and landfill developments.

OPERATION
Foster City

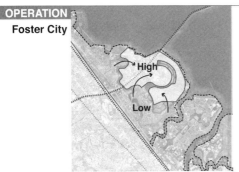

Operate Low-Grounds / Landfill Development.

- Retreat: Existing development susceptible to future inundation.
- Relocate: Creating new high-ground for relocation.
- Revitalize: New high-density development.

ADAPTATION
South Bay

Adapt Existing Wetlands / Salt Ponds.

- Tidal wetlands function as natural buffers against flood events.
- Salt ponds will be released as dredge materials and sediment washes into newly opened salt ponds.

Figure 11.11   Evolutionary recovery.

(Courtesy Lee + Kim, LANDplus Design.)

Bring Your Boots: Opportunities of Failure

- Rising Tides Competition honorable mention 2009

- Royston Hanamoto Alley and Abey, San Francisco, California

- Team members: Aditya Advani, Seth Babb, Masahiro Inoue, Sarah Kassler, Nathan Lozier, John Martin, Simon Schmid, and Jordan Zlotoff

"Bring Your Boots" is a system of selective elevation and flooding that changes the fundamental relationship to the water and accepts the unpredictability of time and environment.

+1-Foot (.3 M) Preparation

In areas at risk of inundation, existing shoreline protection is maintained as a temporary measure. Incentives are given to encourage the relocation of buildings and land uses that are not compatible with periodic flooding and inundation. Vacated lowlands serve as parks, farms, and habitat areas. Higher areas within this zone are built up, recycling clean wastes as fill to create "cell mounds." Uses atop these land-forms relate to the management and experience of the bay and lowlands.

+3-Foot (1 M) Adaption and Advancing Waters

As waters rise, older levees are retired, allowed to fail, and wetlands and open water encroach on the lowlands, creating a diverse and vibrant habitat zone. Cell mound land uses leverage their proximity to the bay. Here are oyster and algae farms, fishing and hunting lodges, parks for camping and exploration by kayak. The wetlands and landforms provide a buffer, protecting inland areas from storm surges.

+5-Foot (1.5 M) Co-Evolution with the Bay

As sea level rises and shorelines shift, get ready, the future is as unexpected as a gorilla in pink boots.

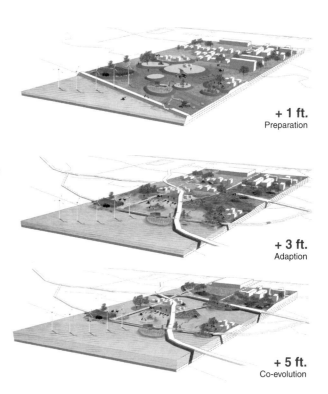

+ 1 ft.
Preparation

+ 3 ft.
Adaption

+ 5 ft.
Co-evolution

Figure 11.12   *Co-evolving adaptation.*

(Courtesy: Royston Hanamoto Alley and Abey.)

IT'S THE DELTA, STUPID

- Rising Tides Competition honorable mention 2009

- Drew Adams and Fadi Masoud, John H. Daniels Faculty of Architecture, Landscape and Design, University of Toronto

Susceptibility: Compared to the delta, very little urbanized land in the Bay Area of California will be impacted by a 3-foot (1 m) sea level rise. Much of what would be affected is already at risk of earthquake-induced soil liquefaction. Future development must avoid such areas entirely.

Subsidence and fragility: Currently, over 1,100 miles (1,770 km) of levees protect the delta, one of the most productive agricultural areas in the United States and world. The land protected has subsided as much as 25 feet (7.6 m) below sea level, due to aridity and extraction of groundwater. Breaches of these fragile levees are not infrequent. In event of a significant breach, salt water would rush rapidly into the delta. Soil productivity and water supplies would be contaminated and disrupted for years.

Living Levee System. For the Bay Area, California, and beyond, the delta is a unique agricultural resource. A Living Levee System is expandable in multiples line of defense to prevent a catastrophic intrusion of salt water into the delta. It enables normal flows at the bay–delta interface. A system of basins would provide a permeable barrier—responsive to salinity levels, ecosystem requirements, and rising sea levels over time. The water pressure of a new freshwater reservoir at Sherman Lake is a buttress against sea rise while increasing both storage capacity and habitat area. This aligns with regional objectives to increase water security along with ecosystem restoration and improved levee system integrity.

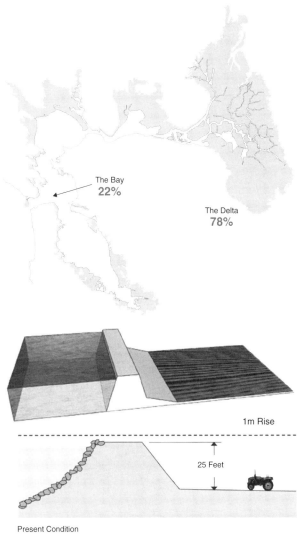

SUBSIDENCE AND FRAGILITY

Figure 11.13 *Comparison of Bay and Delta ecosystems* illustrates the regional (and national) impact of sea level rise beyond the immediate Bay Area.

(Courtesy Drew Adams and Fadi Masoud.)

NEW YORK CITY PROPOSALS

Lower Manhattan, from On the Water: Palisades Bay

- Winner AIA College of Fellows 2007–2009 Latrobe Prize 2007

- Architecture Research Office (ARO), Guy Nordenson & Associates, and Catherine Seavitt Studio, New York, New York

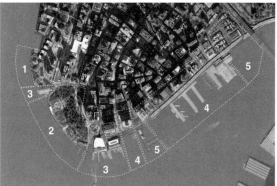

1   Narrow parkscape waterfront with small buildings
2   Wide parkscape waterfront
3   Ferry terminal structures to remain with caisson breakwater structures
4   Elevated highway with adjacent high-rises to remain
5   Elevated highway with low-rises beyond to be redeveloped into parkscape
▨ Pier structures
— Hard-edge seawalls/revetments
---- Soft-edge organic barriers

Figure 11.14   *Proposed waterfront mitigation plans* illustrate shorelines measures in Lower Manhattan.

(Courtesy: ARO.)

"On the Water—Palisade Bay" is a proposal for the adaptive transformation of the New York/New Jersey Upper Bay in light of climate change, sea level rise, and storm surge flooding from hurricanes and northeasters. The objectives are to:

- Consider alternatives to hard-engineering solutions for flood control while minimizing the impacts of flooding.

- Envision a new and versatile system of coastal planning, enriching ecology and the health of urban estuaries.

- Reconceptualize the relationship between adaptive infrastructure and ecology in the twenty-first-century waterfront city.

Plans focus on revitalized and ecologically restored waterfronts on Manhattan and adjacent communities of Staten Island, Brooklyn, and New Jersey, with flexible ecological measures as alternatives to concrete dams and storm barriers. Piers, parks, wetlands, oyster beds, and artificial islands define a new waterfront to mitigate rising sea levels and blunt the force of violent storm surges.

Figure 11.15   *Water table study* of surge buffers.

(Courtesy: ARO.)

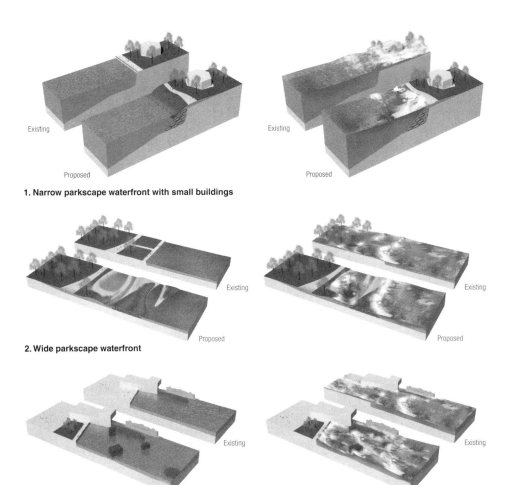

1. Narrow parkscape waterfront with small buildings

2. Wide parkscape waterfront

3. Ferry terminal structures to remain with caisson breakwater structures

Figure 11.16   *Shoreline measures* are based on shore transect and edge conditions.

(Courtesy: ARO.)

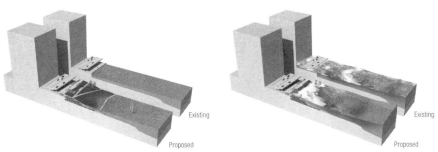

4. Elevated highway with adjacent high-rise buildings to remain

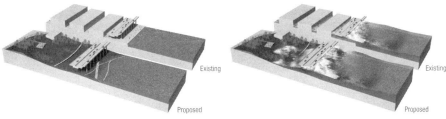

5. Elevated highway with low-rise buildings to be redeveloped into parkscape

Figure 11.17   Selection of shoreline measures are based on shore transect and edge conditions.

(Courtesy: ARO.)

Figure 11.18   *Caisson breakwater structures/marine habitat.*

(Courtesy: ARO.)

Regional Plan Association H209 Forum and Charrette

In September 2009, the Regional Plan Association (RPA) organized a half-day charrette in partnership with the Netherlands Water Partnership and Martin Zogran of the Harvard-Netherlands Project on Climate Change, Water, Land Development and Adaptation.

The charrette created a set of case studies that address flooding and sea level rise challenges on several waterfront sites in New York City. Teams combined professional architects and planners from the Netherlands and the United States. The resulting approaches were characterized in a report of the charrette:

The Dutch, in their centuries of adapting to the sea, have generally taken a "living with water" approach, a "Water-in" approach. Meanwhile, Americans have more generally fought to tame the shoreline with bulkheads and other harsher restrictive action, a "Water-out" approach. An example of this would be that instead of keeping water out via a higher bulkhead (the American approach), water could be brought into the city via a canal (the Dutch approach).

A Dutch expert at the public review epitomized this point with the comment, "You treat water like a drowning person. We treat it like a long distance swimmer."

Source: Sarah Neilson, "Water In, Water Out: Learning from the Dutch," *Newsletter of the Regional Plan Association* 8, no. 17 (2009), www.rpa.org/publications.html. The kind assistance of Robert Freudenberg, Senior Planner, and Robert Pirani, Director of Environmental Programs of the Regional Plan Association, is gratefully acknowledged.

BLUE AND GREENPOINT

- RPA H209 Charrette

- Design Team: Rob Lane, Eric van de Kooij, Joke Klumper, Tricia Martin, Colin Cathcart, Howard Slatkin, Milton Puryear, Ad Hereijgers, Frans van der Ven, Robert Freudenberg, Sarah Neilson

The Greenpoint Williamsburg proposal envisions links between the rivers, the bay, and upland water resources, using stormwater as a nutrient resource. The design incorporates Newtown Creek and a new swath of soft, wet landscape extending to the new Bushwick Inlet Park, to act as major sinks for large stormwater or flooding events. The neighborhood-level design responds to opportunities of its location: a new esplanade design and floodable streets.

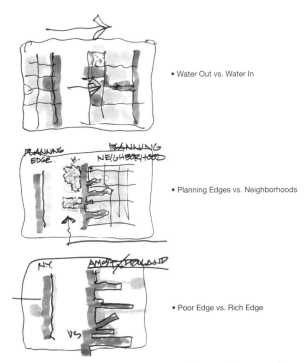

• Water Out vs. Water In

• Planning Edges vs. Neighborhoods

• Poor Edge vs. Rich Edge

Figure 11.20   Contrasting approaches to design with water.

(Courtesy: RPA.)

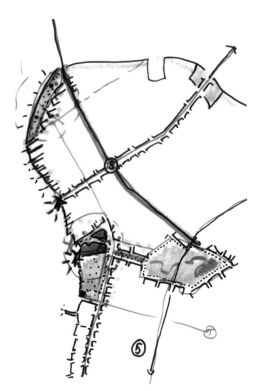

Figure 11.19   *Greenpoint Plan* indicates strategic retreat from flood-prone areas and revitalization along adaptively mitigated edges.

(Courtesy: RPA.)

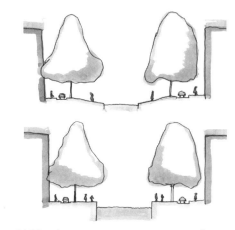

Figure 11.21   *Access to water*—two contrasting approaches. Small design adjustments make waterways a feature of community, not a barrier.

(Courtesy: RPA.)

SUNSET PARK: A BLUE-GREEN SEAPORT

- RPA H209 Charrette
- Design Team: Bonnie Harken, Han Meyer, Manju Chandrasekhar, Jan Elsinga, Michiel de Jong, Margie Ruddick, Christopher Steinon, Camiel Van Drimmelen, Wilbur Woods, Andrew Genn, Lou Venech

Blue + Green Identity
- Reenvision seaport with global economy
- Connect waterfront & neighborhood
- Use energy from tides, sun & wind

Hard and Soft Edges
- Preserve deep waterport option
- Use softer edges for recreation

Industrial Synergies
- Hold large industrial anchors
- Leverage with smaller businesses

Multipurpose Infrastructure
- Combine Expressway renovation with
- Flood protection, open space access

Living with Water
- Bring water inland
- Create urban wetlands
- Flood-proof waterfront buildings

Regional Visibility and Access
- Create network of water transport
- Promote as metro-regional attraction

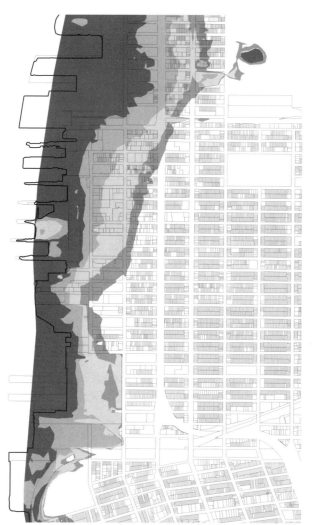

Figure 11.22 *The context plan* indicates the existing vulnerability to area flooding.

(Courtesy: RPA.)

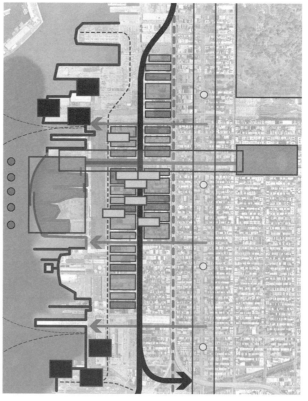

Figure 11.23 *Sunset Park Plan* proposes six themes to enhance economic, social, and ecological resources with flood protections measures.

(Courtesy: RPA.)

STATEN ISLAND AND "CENTRAL PARK HARBOR"

- RPA H209 Charrette:
- Design Team: Martin Zogran, Yttje Feddes, Robert Balder, Elizabeth Case, Marga Donehoo, Susannah Drake, Bob Englert, Len Garcia-Duran, Tom Jost, Kate Van Tassell, Luc Vronlijks

The St. George Staten Island team proposed a "Central Harbor Park" with St. George Ferry Terminal as an iconic, intermodal transport hub within the harbor —creating high-value properties at the water's edge. This concept changes the waterway from "backyard" to a central focus of economic and recreational activity and environmental rehabilitation. Blue-green corridors provide pedestrian and public transit access to the ferry network, transforming outmoded industrial uses near the water's edge and connecting uplands to the harbor.

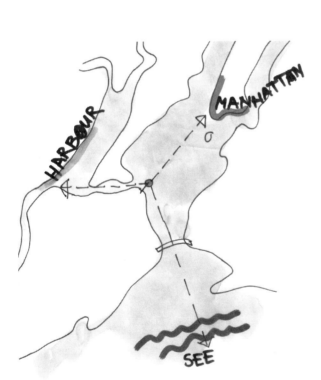

Figure 11.24 *Concept of "Central Park Harbor"* offers a bold revisioning that views the risk of sea level rise as the opportunity for urban revitalization.

(Courtesy: RPA.)

Figure 11.25 *Sketch plan* details how water transport can connect and intensify harborside development.

(Courtesy: RPA.)

FLOATING STRUCTURES

FLOAT House, Ninth Ward, New Orleans, Louisiana

- Make It Right Foundation Demonstration House 2009

- Morphosis Architects, Santa Monica, California

The FLOAT House prototype is constructed in New Orleans Ninth Ward for the Make It Right Foundation. It is proposed to fulfill three goals:

1. Sustain its own water and power needs.

2. Survive the floodwaters generated by a storm the size of Hurricane Katrina.

3. Be able to be manufactured as low-income housing.

Like the New Orleans shotgun house, the FLOAT House sits on a 4-foot (1.2 m) base. The FLOAT House can rise vertically on two guideposts placed within the interior construction,

able to float up to 12 feet as water levels rise. In the event of a flood, the house's chassis acts as a raft. The guideposts act as masts, anchored to the ground by two concrete pile caps supported in turn by six 45-foot deep piles.

Rather than permanently raising the house on high stilts, the house rises only in case of severe flooding from levee failure or overtopping, as occurred in Katrina. This also preserves the community's vital porch culture and facilitates accessibility for elderly and disabled residents.

While not designed for occupants to remain in the home during a hurricane, the FLOAT House buoyancy minimizes catastrophic damage and preserves the homeowner's investment in the property. It allows for the early return of occupants in the aftermath of a hurricane or flood.

Figure 11.26   *FLOAT House.*

(© Morphosis Architects)

FLOATING HOUSE, LAKE HURON, ONTARIO CANADA 2005

- MOS LCC Architects, New York, New York

A vacation cabin sits on a platform of steel pontoons to ride the fluctuations of Lake Huron. The concept was developed as a means to fabricate the structure off-site at a construction shop. It was transported 50 miles (80 km) on skids to its remote island location when the Lake was frozen. MOS Architects.

(A)

(B)

Figure 11.27

(A) *Floating House.*

(PHOTO: © Florian Holzherr)

(B) Cross-section of model.

(Courtesy: MOS Architects.)

Buoyant Foundation Project
Amphibious House

■ Dr. Elizabeth English, University of Waterloo

■ School of Architecture Cambridge, Ontario

The Buoyant Foundation Project is a nonprofit research initiative founded in 2006 at Louisiana State University Hurricane Center with the goal of designing and implementing retrofitable buoyant foundations for New Orleans' "shotgun" houses. The project was inspired by amphibious houses at Maasbommel in the Netherlands. The technology is based on designs used for over 30 years at Raccourdci Old River in Pointe Coupee Parish, Louisiana, where polystyrene foam blocks are used as a retrofit measure to accommodate rising and falling levels of the bayous.

Buoyant Foundation Project Web site (www .buoyantfoundation.org/) lists among the advantages:

• Can be retrofitted for existing houses.

• Can be accessed by wheelchair-bound persons and others without mechanical lifts.

• Structures remain low to ground except during a flood.

• Elevates house to above flood level, regardless of depth of flooding (i.e., above base flood elevation).

• Preserves the traditional character of street, porch, and houses.

The Buoyant Foundation Project designs are undergoing research and development testing of various construction process and material options. In current configurations, a structural steel frame attaches flotation blocks to the underside of the house. Four vertical guidance poles are located close to the corners of the house, proposed as telescoping tubes of new structural composites of recycled materials that do not corrode. These are exterior to the house for "retrofit" applications. The tops of the poles are attached to the steel frame. The poles telescope out of the ground, allowing the house to move up and down to any depth as a function of the length of telescoping

guideposts. Utility lines have either self-sealing breakaway connections (gas and sewer lines) or long, coiled umbilical lines (water and electrical). When flooding occurs, the flotation blocks lift the house, carried on the steel frame platform and restrained in place by the poles.

Source: Personal communication, Dr. Elizabeth English, February 20, 2010.

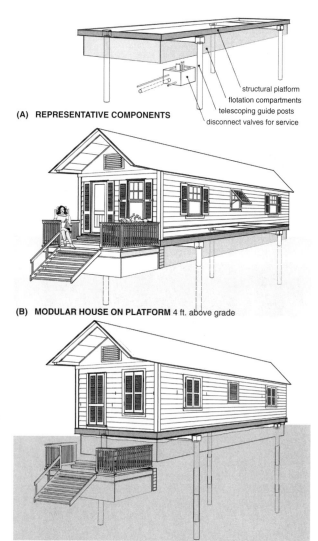

(A) **REPRESENTATIVE COMPONENTS**

structural platform
flotation compartments
telescoping guide posts
disconnect valves for service

(B) **MODULAR HOUSE ON PLATFORM** 4 ft. above grade

(C) **HOUSE FLOATING ABOVE RISING FLOODWATERS**

Figure 11.28 *Buoyant Foundation Project* is developing options for each of the components of amphibious construction.

CELLULAR GROWTH

- Rising Tides Competition submission 2009
- Dimitris Gourdoukis, Object-e architecture, Thessalonica, Greece

Cellular Growth is a system for self-organizing and indeterminate construction that can adapt to the level of rising water. Modular components with detachable connections and mechanized construction allow the community infrastructure and building to adapt to conditions they encounter and adjust to them. All necessary infrastructure, including rain collectors, water tanks and treatment, are generated and replaceable each time a new level is added. Solar, wind, and water turbines are proposed to generate electricity.

Figure 11.29 *Infrastructure Protocol*: Cellular Growth.

(Courtesy: Dimitris Gourdoukis/Object-e architecture, 2009.)

LILYPAD FLOATING CITY, OCEANS, THE WORLD

- A Floating Ecopolis for Climate Refugees 2008
- Vincent Callebaut, Architect, La Louvière, Belgium

Lilypad Floating City is designed as a structure for 50,000 inhabitants, to serve as amphibious and self-sustaining communities capable of floating ocean currents. The structure is inspired by the nutrient-processing capacities of the giant Amazon water lily, *Victoria Amazonica.*

Figure 11.30   *Lilypad Floating City.*

(© Vincent Callebaut)

LEVEES

Levees, dikes, and large-scale flood barriers have a long history in maritime construction as well as in control of flooding in agricultural lands within deltas and flood basins. U.S. federal and state agencies have adopted a variety of standards for levees applicable to public and privately owned levees. Due to susceptibility of failure and overtopping and the need for long-term maintenance, levees alone do not eliminate severe flood hazard. (Figures 11.31 and 11.32.)

In many instances, existing levee systems were built to conditions that no longer prevail (e.g., wetlands that previously reduced storm impacts have been lost, along with increased storm events).[7] The risk of sea level rise makes levee design, construction and maintenance a continuing subject of evaluation and improvement. They should be considered as one measure of a series in a redundant system of protection, mitigation and adoption measures.

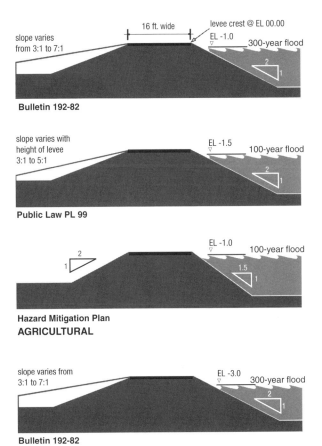

Figure 11.31 *Representative range of levee standards.* These standards are now subject to review and greatly improved provisions for increased storm severity and climate change impacts.

Source: California Department of Water Resources. "Actions and Priorities: Delta Flood Protection Act," Division of Planning Document D-031175 (March 1990), www.water.

ca.gov/floodmgmt.

(A)

(B)

Figure 11.32 *Large-scale levee and floodgate infrastructure.*

(A) Levee construction in New Orleans following Hurricane Katrina.

(PHOTO: Marvin Nauman FEMA Photo Library, March 3, 2006);

(B) new floodgates at London Street Canal, New Orleans.

(PHOTO: Ed Edahl, FEMA Photo Library)

GOLDEN GATE PERMEABLE FLOOD BARRIER

- Rising Tides Competition submission 2009

- Kim von Blohn and Steven Reel

The proposal is to install a permeable barrier with ship gates just east of the Golden Gate Bridge in water generally less than 100 feet (30 m) deep. The barrier is approximately 2.6 miles (4 km) long and constructed of reinforced concrete modules that are built on land, towed into place and sunk to the Bay floor. The typical module includes large-diameter butterfly valves that are controlled by hydraulic actuators. Normally open, the valves are sized to minimize impact on typical tidal flow. A pair of rotational gates located at the existing shipping channel locations handles ship traffic. During moderate high-tide events, the butterfly valves are closed, forcing tidal action to flow through the gates, which function as a weir to slow tidal inflow and limit the tide peak. At extreme tide and storm events, the butterfly valves and gates are fully closed to effectively seal off the Bay for the duration of the event. (Figure 11.33.)

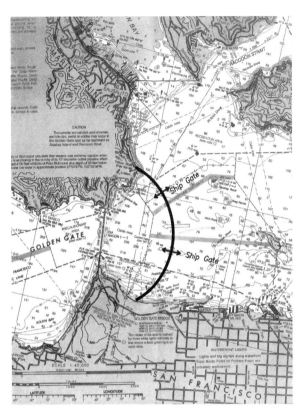

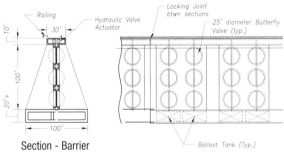

Section - Barrier

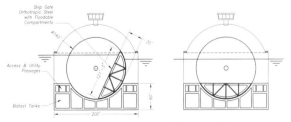

Section - Ship gate closed   Section - Ship gate open

Figure 11.33   *Golden Gate Permeable Flood Barrier* plan and cross section.

(Courtesy: Kim Von Blohn.)

PERPETUAL PROTECTION PLAN (P³) AGAINST SEA LEVEL RISE

- Rising Tides Competition submission 2009

- Warren R. Uhte, CA, CE

P³ is a proposal is to install a system of protection facilities—dikes, levees, and flood control structures—strategically located throughout the San Francisco Bay. The components include swing tide gates and a swing drawbridge to allow boat access and pumping facilities to keep upstream area free of water damage during storm or high tide conditions.

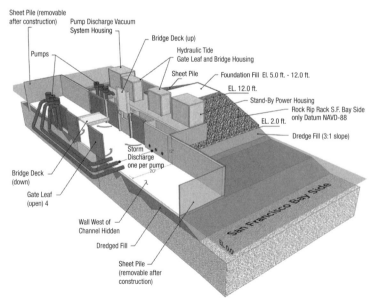

Model 2 Protection Facility

Figure 11.34 *Perpetual Protection Plan (P³).*

(Courtesy: Warren R. Uhte.)

SUPER LEVEES OF JAPAN

In response to devastating flooding from rapid-flowing rivers as well as coastal storms, Japan has developed a range of flood control measures, including levees, flood-activated floodgates, and multipurpose flood detention basins to control riverine flooding. As part of this flood management program, "super levees" (higher standard embankments) are constructed, utilizing the landside areas for new development. These areas gain higher value due to views and access to river and river-edge public parks.

The detention basins increase the area available as floodplains and provide a series of pocket catchments along the course of rivers to reduce the total volume of downstream flooding in extreme events. Buildings and functions suited to a scheduled and controlled use, such as sports stadiums and event venue parking, are located within the detention basins, where structures are raised on piers and meet other flood-resistant construction standards.

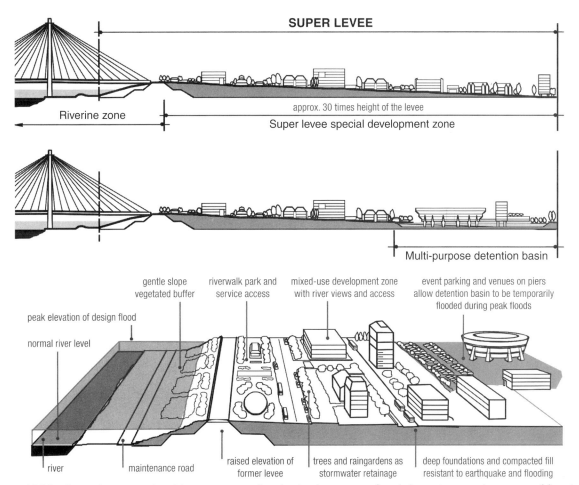

Figure 11.35 *Super levees and multipurpose retarding basins (temporary flood detention areas) are part of flood control, river enhancement, and urban reinvestment zone initiatives.*

Source: Hitomi Godou, Japan Ministry of Land, Infrastructure, Transport and Tourism. "River Basin Management in Japan: Flood Control Measures, Water Resources Management," www.mlit.go.jp/river/basic_info/english/pdf/conf_10.pdf.

Notes

1. J. William Kamphius, *Introduction to Coastal Engineering and Management* (River Edge, NJ: World Scientific Publishing, 2010).

2. K. O. Emery and D. G. Aubrey, *Sea-Levels, Land Levels and Tide Gauges* (New York: Springer-Verlag, 1991).

3. James G. Titus and Vijay K. Narayanan, *Probability of Sea Level Rise* (Darby, PA: Diane Publishing, 1998); National Assessment Synthesis Team, Global Change Research Program, Climate Change Impacts on the United States, ed. Donald F. Boesch, John C. Field, and Donald Scavia, "The Potential Consequences of Climate Variability and Change Overview: Coastal Areas and Marine Resources," Report 21, NOAA Coastal Ocean Program Decision Analysis Services, 2000.

4. U.S. National Academy of Science National Research Council America's Climate Choices: Advancing The Science of Climate Change. May 2010. "Projections of Future Sea Level Rise" page 191 www.nap.edu/catalog.php?record_id=12783.

5. Intergovernmental Panel on Climate Change (IPCC). *Climate Change 2001: Synthesis Report. Summary for Policy Makers: An Assessment of the Intergovernmental Panel on Climate Change*, eds. Robert T. Watson et al. (New York: Cambridge University Press, 2001).

6. IPCC, *Strategies for Adaption to Sea Level Rise*. IPCC Response Strategies Working Group (Geneva: United Nations Environment Programme and World Meteorological Organization, 1990). p. iv. U.S. Green Building Council, *The New Orleans Principles: Celebrating the Rich History of New Orleans through Commitment to a Sustainable Future*, Report of the November 2005 New Orleans Planning Charrette, ed. Alex Wilson, www.usgbc.org/ShowFile.aspx?DocumentID=4395.

Figure 12.1a *Waterfront revitalization.* Providence, Rhode Island. Downtown Providence is connected with public spaces created by "daylighting" the Providence River, now the focal point of the Capital Center area.

(PHOTO: Donald Watson)

Source: NOAA, *Coastal and Waterfront Smart Growth*, "Element 7: Providence, Rhode Island's Downcity Providence and Waterplace Park," 2009, http://coastalsmartgrowth.noaa.gov/casestudies.html#7.

Figure 12.1b *Shoreline Restoration* of coastal "softscape" vegetation and earth-bermed and green-roof building on a prior landfill and paved drive-in theater. Save The Bay Center, Providence, Rhode Island. Architect: Croxton Collaborative Architects.

(PHOTO: Donald Watson)

CHAPTER 12

DESIGN FOR RESILIENCE

12.1 THE WAVE OF THE FUTURE

Design for resilience is an emerging paradigm for the design professions. Its agenda is to create buildings, communities, and regions that restore and improve the ecological services of our natural resources and that mitigate threats of extreme weather and climate change. Resilient design can be the "wave of the future," to catalyze a program of revitalization of floodplains and coastal zones. Resilient design can counter the threat of that other "wave" of increased flooding, storm surge, and sea level rise that climate change may bring.

Resiliency describes the capacity to respond to stress and change of climatic conditions. Resiliency is evident in natural systems in strategies to adjust to variable and extreme conditions. Characteristics of resilient systems include buffering, storage, redundancy, self-reliance, decentralization, diversity, energy conservation, rapid adaptability, and replacement. (Figure 12.2.)

Resilient design defines a **precautionary design ethic** for buildings, communities, and regions to anticipate and prepare for extreme weather and flooding by protecting and enhancing the resilient capacities of the natural and built environment.

Resilient design builds on and incorporates the lessons of **sustainability and green building design** that provide exemplars of buildings and communities that are energy efficient, low impact and "regenerative," for example, recycling water and waste, returning waste nutrients to landscape and farming.

Resilient design adopts lessons from nature to protect, restore, and enhance the **ecosystem services** of the natural environment in mitigating the impacts of flooding, extreme weather and climate change.

The agenda of resilient design can be expressed by three key conclusions:

1. Multiple scales of impact
2. Collaborative design
3. Innovation in design, technology, and policy

MULTIPLE SCALES OF IMPACT Resilient design principles and practices are applicable in any region and at any scale, with greatest economic and practical advantage when implemented together. If a community development or building project is not designed for resilience, it is part of the problem. Design for resilience is part of the solution.

COLLABORATIVE DESIGN Resilient design goes beyond conventional practice to build on the combined knowledge and skills of regional and community planning and floodplain management, landscape design and architecture, civil and water engineering and construction, as well as science-based and ongoing findings of biologists and climate scientists. This creates the need and opportunity for collaborative and comprehensive planning of our watershed regions, communities, and developments.

INNOVATION IN DESIGN, TECHNOLOGY, AND POLICY Resilient design is based on measures that are available and economical. The challenges of climate change, severe weather, and sea level rise require the

Figure 12.2 *Lessons from nature.* Leaves exemplify the resilience of trees and forests. Leaves are nourished by sunlight and moisture, carry nutrients to and from their roots, adapt to their microclimate with sizes and shapes determined by their place in the sun, are able to heal and continue life functions when damaged by storms or attacked by animals and insects, carry time-release nutrients to nourish the soil, and, in some tree species, signal chemical messages when threatened by disease to initiate new roots and offshoots or slowly build immunity through regeneration.

(PHOTO: Donald Watson)

LESSONS OF NATURE APPLICABLE TO DESIGN AND CONSTRUCTION

Absorption. Watershed planning and design (reservoirs, retention ponds, green roofs).

Buffering. Breaks, riparian buffers, rain gardens, shuttering.

Core protection. Zoning, decentralization, self-reliant subsystems.

Diffusion. Meanders, wetland and coastal zone landscape, open foundations.

Rapid response. Smart grid, early warning, emergency responsive systems.

Redundant circuits. Green infrastructure, wildlife corridors, and multiple service routes.

Storage capacity. Aquifers, wetlands, reservoirs, cisterns.

Waste/nutrient recovery. Sustainable stormwater design and waste systems.

rebuilding of our coastal and riverine floodplain infrastructure and buildings. The rebuilding process can foster innovations at all steps of policy and projects, including planning criteria, design features and building technologies that increase community preparedness to natural hazards.

Multiple Scales of Impact

Design improvements in flood control, landscape and natural area restoration, water quality and quantity are achievable through measures of resilient design at all scales of regional, urban, community and building projects.

The greatest impact is achieved when all points of the scale, from region to site, are addressed as a watershed, riverine, and/or coastal system. (Table 12.1.)

Collaborative Design

Resilient design concepts are best implemented by creative design collaboration and integration of landscape architecture, architecture, and site/building engineering.

There are many opportunities to advance resilient design principles and practices through professional development and collaborative efforts of professional design associations. (Table 12.2.)

Innovation in Design, Technology, and Policy

Measures outlined in this book for flood-resistant design and watershed restoration and enhancement are market ready. There remain great opportunities for innovation in design, technology, and policy formation.

Many resilient design concepts reduce the cost of conventional approaches, such as native landscaping, which, once established, can reduce landscape management costs. Many concepts can be applied immediately in professional practice and simply need to be better known, such as tree trenching and structural soil cells. Promising design concepts are being developed but may require more research and demonstration, such as gray water and ecological wastewater systems where health standards demand utmost reliability, or amphibious foundations, which have been used in very few locations.

Many promising innovations—in some cases concepts that are technically proven and potentially cost effective if adopted widely—require policy and institutional innovations to smooth their adoption. Strategic relocation and

enhancement of coastal zones requires new ways to reconfigure property alignments and agreement of many property owners and community authorities. These options offer a rich mix of design, technology, and institutional measures to create an agenda for resilient design. (Table 12.3.)

12.2 MODELS FOR NATIONAL AND INTERNATIONAL ACTION

For the past several decades, catalyzed by the Rio Earth Summit,[1] responses to environmental degradation and natural hazards, and now climate change, have commanded attention at national and international scale. A number of signal declarations and programs have emerged that address flooding and water resources; they have been cited throughout the chapters of this book. By way of summary, several of these agendas are worth referencing again, even at risk of repetition. They offer valuable direction and consensus in framing any agenda for resilient design where collaborative action is required at regional, national, and/or international scales.

The lessons of flood mitigation and water resource protection apply throughout the world. Responding to climate challenge is an international agenda. Lessons learned in one place will be needed in another. In the process, as always, design professionals with international practices can play a leading role.

FEMA Floodplain Management Strategy

The FEMA Management Strategy published in 2009 defines four "strategies" for flood mitigation measures detailed in FEMA publications and summarized in Part III of this book. Quoting from the strategy statement:[2]

Strategy 1: Modify human susceptibility to flood damage. Reduce disruption by avoiding hazardous, uneconomic or unwise use of floodplains.

- *Regulate floodplain use by using zoning codes to steer development away from hazardous areas or natural areas deserving preservation, establishing rules for developing subdivisions, and rigorously following building, health, and sanitary codes.*

TABLE 12.1 ENVIRONMENTAL AND NATURAL HAZARD THREAT AND PROFESSIONAL DESIGN RESPONSE	1 Regional	2 Infrastructure	3 Landscape	4 Building
Normal Climate & Weather Events				
Stormwater & inland riverine flooding	●	●	●	○
Snow/ice storm		●	○	○
Coastal flooding	●	●	●	○
Drought/salinization	●	●	●	○
Extreme Weather/Natural Disasters				
Cyclone/hurricane/tsunami	●	●	●	○
Storm surge	●	●	●	○
Cyclone/tornado/earthquake	●	●		●
Snow avalanche/landslide/mudslide	●	●	●	○
Development/Land Use				
Soil erosion/sinkholes	●		●	○
Groundwater depletion/pollution	●	●	●	●
Wildfire (drought/desertification)	●	○	●	○
Eutrophication/shellfish bed loss	●	●	●	
Industry/Agriculture Uses				
Industry water consumptions	●	●		○
Wastewater disposal	●	●		○
Pollution (air and water)	●	●	○	○
Acid rain deposition	●	●	○	
Climate Change				
Sea level rise/increased storm surge	●	●	●	○
Land subsidence/loss	●	●	●	○
Saline water intrusion	●	●	●	
Ocean acidification		○	○	

● Design responsibility for mitigation

○ Indirect design influence

1 Regional planning policy and watershed/floodplain management

2 Infrastructure scale, civil engineering/stormwater design and water engineering

3 Landscape architecture and design

4 Building project scale, architecture, and construction

- *Establish development and redevelopment policies on the design and location of public services, utilities, and critical facilities.*
- *Acquire land in a floodplain in order to preserve open space and permanently relocate buildings.*
- *Elevate or floodproof new buildings and retrofitting existing ones.*
- *Prepare people and property for flooding through forecasting, warning systems, and emergency plans.*

	1 Regional	2 Infrastructure	3 Landscape	4 Building
TABLE 12.2 BEST PRACTICE MEASURES AND PROFESSIONAL DESIGN RESPONSE				
Regional and Urban Scale				
Watershed planning	●	●	●	
Riperian buffer/wildlife corridor	●	○	○	
Native planting/ecosystem restoration	●		●	○
Remediated Combined Sewer Overflow (CSO)		●		
Community & Public Landscape Scale				
Green infrastructure	●	●	●	●
Permaculture/urban farming/mariculture	○		●	○
Stormwater retention/porous paving	○	●	○	
Rain garden/bioswales/aquifer renewal	○	○	●	○
Building/Project Site Scale				
Energy conservation	○	●	○	●
Green roof/living wall			●	●
Water conservation/graywater systems	○	○	○	●
Ecological wastewater treatment	○	●	●	○
Flood Hazard Zones				
Levee/floodwater diversion	●	●		
Shoreline reconstruction/enhancement	●	●	●	●
Structural retreat/relocation	○	●	○	
Elevation and flood-resistant design	○	●		●

● Design responsibility for mitigation
○ Indirect design influence
1 Regional planning policy and watershed/floodplain management
2 Infrastructure scale, civil engineering/stormwater design, and water engineering
3 Landscape architecture and design
4 Building project scale, architecture, and construction
Source: An earlier version of this table was prepared for Daniel E. Williams and Donald Watson (eds.), "Water + Design Conference Report" (September 2006), AIA and EPA Watershed Grants Program, unpublished monograph, www.dwa-design .com/documents/menu/water+design.

- *Restore and preserve the natural resources and functions of floodplains.*

Strategy 2: Modify the impact of flooding. Assist individuals and communities to prepare for, respond to and recover from a flood.

- *Provide information and education to assist self-help and protection measures.*

- *Follow flood emergency measures during a flood to protect people and property.*
- *Reduce the financial impact of flooding through disaster assistance, flood insurance, and tax adjustments.*
- *Prepare post-flood recovery plans and programs to help people rebuild and implement mitigation measures to protect against future floods.*

TABLE 12.3 INNOVATION CYCLE: MARKET READINESS, R&D OPPORTUNITIES AND INSTITUTIONAL BARRIERS

	1 Market Ready	2 Added cost	3 R&D required	4 Institutional barriers
Regional and Urban Scale				
Watershed planning	●	◐ [1]		◐
Riparian buffer/wildlife corridor	●	◐	◐	
Native planting/ecosystem restoration	●	◐ [1]		◐
Remediated Combined Sewer Overflows (CSO)	●	●		
Community & Public Landscape Scale				
Green infrastructure	●	◐ [1]	●	●
Permaculture/urban farming/mariculture	●			●
Stormwater retention/porous paving	●	● [1]	●	
Rain garden/bioswales/aquifer renewal	●			
Building/Project Site Scale				
Energy conservation	●	● [1]	●	
Green roof/living wall	●	●	●	
Water conservation/graywater systems	●	●	●	● [2]
Ecological wastewater treatment		●	●	● [2]
Flood Hazard Zones				
Levee/floodwater diversion	●	●	●	
Shoreline reconstruction/enhancement	●	●	●	◐ [2]
Retreat/relocation	●	●	●	◐
Elevation/flood-resistant design	●	●	●	[2]

● Strong and direct influence

◐ Partial or indirect influence

1 Market ready: code compliant, commercially available

2 Adds cost to conventional capital project construction budgeting

3 Opportunity for research and design (R&D) to develop innovative design/technologies

4 Currently facing institutional, legal, or regulatory barriers

[1] Appropriate measures can reduce project costs

[2] Some innovative systems require special approvals

Source: An earlier version of this table was prepared for Daniel E. Williams and Donald Watson (eds.), "Water + Design Conference Report."

Strategy 3: Modify flooding itself. Develop projects that control floodwater.

- *Build dams and reservoirs to store excess water upstream from developed areas.*

- *Build dikes, levees, and floodwalls to keep water away from developed areas.*

- *Alter channels to make them more efficient, so overbank flooding will be less frequent.*

- *Divert high flows around developed areas.*

- *Treat land to hold as much rain as possible where it falls, so it can infiltrate the soil instead of running off.*

- *Store excess runoff with on-site detention measures.*

- *Protect inland development with shoreline protection measures that account for the natural movement of shoreline features.*

- *Control runoff from areas under development outside the floodplain.*

Strategy 4: Preserve and restore natural resources. Renew the vitality and purpose of floodplains by reestablishing and maintaining floodplain environments in their natural state.

- *Use floodplain, wetlands, and coastal barrier resources or land use regulations, such as zoning, to steer development away from sensitive or natural areas.*

- *Develop policies on the design and location of public services, utilities, and critical facilities.*

- *Acquire land for open space preservation, permanent relocation of buildings, restoration of floodplains and wetlands, and preservation of natural functions and habitats.*

- *Inform and educate people to become aware of natural floodplain resources and functions and how to protect them.*

- *Use tax adjustments to provide a financial initiative for preserving lands or restoring lands to their natural state.*

- *Maintain natural flood protection features by beach nourishment and dune building to protect inland development.*

NSTC Great Challenges Report

The National Science and Technology Council Committee on Environment and National Resources is an advisory group that contributes to the While House Office of Science and Technology Policy. Its 2005 report, "Grand Challenges for Disaster Reduction," promotes the concept of resilience in infrastructure and facilities, and the technology innovation opportunities for disaster mitigation. Quoting from the NSTC report:[3]

Create resilient structures and infrastructure systems using advanced building technologies.
Develop more advanced construction materials and technologies that create resourceful, intelligent, and self-healing structures. Structural systems must continue to be designed with disaster resilience in mind, and new materials and technologies must be available to create

facilities that remain robust in the face of all potential hazards. "Smart" building technologies, which allow for self-diagnosis of damage and structural stability, should be employed.

Support structural advances with effective non-structural mitigation.
All advances in building technology must be supported by appropriate nonstructural mitigation measures including land use and zoning regulations based on climatological and geological data. Community planning decisions should be designed to minimize damage and aid recovery.

Quantify the monetary benefits of disaster mitigation using economic modeling.
Economic modeling is necessary to support investment decisions and demonstrate that substantial savings can be achieved by instituting disaster mitigation policies on a local and national level prior to investment in mitigation projects.

Develop science and technology to prevent cascading failures in public infrastructure systems.
Develop tools and models to provide a more robust understanding of infrastructure interdependencies in order to protect the public infrastructure, to allow continuity of services, and to prevent cascading failures. Robust infrastructure systems should guard against damage from natural and technological hazards and feature redundant, rapidly resolving systems that allow any failures to be isolated and repaired with no disruption to other components. Additionally, infrastructures must be designed to protect people from secondary or cascading hazards.

Enhance the ability to protect public health before and after a hazard event.
Increased understanding of hazard events and their impact on public health can help protect the public before and after a hazard event. Communities should be designed to maintain sanitary conditions and prevent contamination to water supplies during and after hazard events. Scientific knowledge of potential threats to public health should be used in the creation of emergency response plans.

Assess the resilience of the natural and human environment.
Comprehensive assessments must include examination of the impact of natural and technological hazards on both the constructed and natural environment. Further,

community planning must include steps based on scientific research to prevent loss of natural resources during a hazard event.

Learn from each hazard event.
All hazard events should be analyzed and the results made public to support ongoing hazard research and future mitigation plans. Pre-disaster planning should be put into effect immediately following any hazard and should be the driving force behind all response and recovery actions for future events.

Raise public awareness of local hazards.
Reliable and integrated all-hazard data must be available to citizens and local decision makers to drive appropriate planning, mitigation, response, and recovery decisions.

Warn people with consistent, accessible, and actionable messages and a national all-hazards emergency communication system.
Comprehensive emergency communication systems are needed to warn people and to specify actions to be taken in the event of a hazard. Emergency communications systems should utilize all available media outlets including mobile phones, cable television, and the Internet. The seriousness of the threat must be conveyed and real-time information provided as hazard scenarios evolve.

NOAA Mainstreaming Adaptation to Climate Change

The NOAA report "Mainstreaming Adaptation to Climate Change" (MACC) describes environmental risk to coastal zones of the Caribbean Island nations. The report addresses the significant impacts of climate change, increased storm severity, and sea level rise:

- Submergence of low-lying wetland and dry land areas
- Erosion of soft shores by increasing offshore loss of sediment
- Increased salinity of estuaries and aquifers
- Rising coastal waters
- Increasing severity of coastal flooding and storm damage

The MACC report recommendations apply widely and, with appropriate local adaptation, are suitable for any coastal nation in the world. Quoting and summarizing from the report's summary:[4]

4.1 Regulatory Recommendations

4.1a Introduce building codes that account for climate variability and change . . . .

    1. *Modify engineering designs to include climate change projections, particularly for sea level rise, in addition to historical data typically used,*
    2. *Limit the siting of new structures in hazardous areas, restricting siting of any new public buildings in such areas,*
    3. *Add additional specifications to ensure that new buildings are built to better withstand wind and flooding . . . .*

4.1b Introduce regulations to phase out development in high hazard areas . . . .

    1. *Prohibiting the construction of protective structures in sensitive high hazard areas,*
    2. *Prohibiting the reconstruction of storm-damaged property in high hazard areas,*
    3. *Conditioning land ownership in high hazard areas to expire when property ownership expires or when sea levels reach a particular point along a map.*

4.1c Strengthen regulations to protect ecological buffers . . . .

4.2 Land-use planning & land protection

4.2a Develop comprehensive land-use plans . . . .

4.2b Develop and implement integrated coastal management plans . . . .

4.2c Develop coordinating mechanisms to ensure that watershed management plans are implemented at both the ministerial and private sector levels . . . .

4.2d Employ a "retreat approach" to planning and development in high hazard areas along the coastline . . . .

4.2e Integrate regional disaster mitigation strategies with national/physical planning . . . .

4.2f Employ land protection tools (easements, purchased and transferred development rights and acquisition) to maintain, preserve and restore ecological buffers and encourage retreat from high hazard areas . . . .

4.2g Enhanced Coastal Protection where Retreat and Accommodation strategies are not possible . . . . (Table 12.4.)

4.3 Economic and Market-Based Incentives Recommendations . . . .

4.3a Market-based incentives to promote a sustainable tourism industry . . . .

4.3b Link property insurance with construction quality . . . .

4.3c Eliminate subsidies or incentives that continue to promote development in high hazard areas . . . .

4.3d Establish a revolving loan fund for home improvement . . . .

4.4 Public Awareness and Education

4.4a Improve public awareness and education concerning vulnerability . . . .

4.4b Involve impacted communities in formulation of policies, programs and projects.

4.5 Research, Monitoring & Hazard Mapping

4.5a Continue to build and expand long-term beach monitoring programs . . . .

4.5b Promote increased use of GIS [geographic information systems] and remote-sensing/spatial planning applications . . . .

TABLE 12.4 LAND PROTECTION TOOLS

Land Protection Tools	Pro	Con
Demonstrated conservation easement	Permanent protection from development; Landowners receive tax benefits. Little to no cost to the local unit of government. Land remains in private ownership and on the tax rolls	Tax incentives may not provide sufficient compensation. Limited governmental control over which areas are protected
Purchase of development rights	Permanent protection from development. Property owner paid to protect land. Estate and property tax benefits. Local units of government can target locations. Property remains in private ownership and stays part of tax base	Costly
Transfer of development rights	Permanent protection. Landowner paid to protect land. Estate and property tax benefits to landowner. Local units of government can target locations. Low cost to local units of government. Utilizes "free market" approach. Land ownership remains in private hands and on tax roll.	Complex to manage. Receiving area must be willing/able to accept higher densities
Land acquisition	Permanent protection from development and full public control for preservation and restoration. Land can be managed for natural ecosystems services including buffering capacity	Costly

4.5c Establish a computer network linking sea level rise and climate change monitoring institutions . . . .

4.5d Expand hazard mapping of coastal zones, based on climate change . . . .

Experiences of Other Nations

The topics of water resources, climate change, and flooding will engage all nations. Flood disaster preparedness programs and practices are widely published and shared in professional colloquia. The Netherlands historic experiences with dikes and below-sea-level land management provide lessons for coastal mitigation and preparation for sea level rise. In 2000, the Dutch government began a 50- to 100-year program of coastal protection and

riverine retreat. In response to rapid river rise and urban flooding, Japan has a well-advanced program of riverine protection and enhancement, including innovative measures to increase flood detention in high-density urban districts.

THE NETHERLANDS: "MAKING ROOM FOR WATER" Water and flood management in the Netherlands has for centuries been a matter of public law. The water authorities are the oldest public bodies in the Netherlands. The dike infrastructure is extensive. Many cities and large areas of the Netherlands, with the highest density in Europe, lie below mean sea level. Predicted threat of severe weather and sea level rise due

TABLE 12.5 SUMMARY: VULNERABILITY VERSUS ADAPTATION MEASURES. ADAPTATION RECOMMENDATIONS ADDRESS THE INCREASING VULNERABILITY OF COASTAL INFRASTRUCTURE AND LAND USES DUE TO CLIMATE VARIABILITY AND CHANGE

Issues To Address	Regulatory Measures	Land-Use Planning & Land Protection Tools	Economic & Market-Based Incentives	Public Awareness & Education	Research, Monitoring & Hazard Mapping
Growth of tourism and water-based Industry		Develop a comprehensive land use plan	Market-based incentives to promote sustainable tourism and businesses	Public awareness and education	
Intensive & uncontrolled coastal development		Develop a comprehensive land use plan Integrate regional disaster mitigation strategies with national/physical planning	Eliminate subsidies that promote development in high hazard areas		Establish a computer network linking major sea level rise and climate change monitoring institutions
Location of coastal infrastructure in hazardous areas	Introduce regulations to phase out development in high hazard areas	Utilize a retreat approach to development in high hazard areas Utilize land protection tools to preserve/restore ecological buffers	Eliminate subsidies that promote development in high hazard areas	Public awareness & education	Expand hazard mapping of coastal zones, based on climate change Continue to build and expand long-term beach monitoring programs

Inadequate waste disposal systems	Strengthened regulations to protect ecological buffers		Market-based incentives to promote sustainable tourism	
Quality of building construction & insurance incentives	Strengthened building codes		Link property insurance with construction quality Establish a revolving fund for home improvement loans	Public awareness & education
Destruction of ecological buffers	Strengthened regulations to protect ecological buffers	Utilize land protection tools to preserve/restore ecological buffers Develop & implement integrated coastal management plans		Public awareness & education	Use of GIS mapping
Continued reliance on top-down approaches to land-use planning		Develop & implement integrated coastal management plans Implement watershed management		
Destructive agriculture & forestry practices		Develop a comprehensive land use plan Implement watershed management		Public awareness & education

to climate change is a national concern and agenda in the Netherlands.[5]

Dutch programs and policies, having experienced more severe storms and larger floods, address land subsidence and climate change–induced sea level rise. The Dutch national plan uses as a first line of defense the strategy of protection to improve its levee infrastructure. Flood defense standards have been raised to take account of changes in the frequency with which the dikes are over-topped, which has increased due to greater runoff from increased precipitation and climate change as well as the altered land use due to higher population density. Protective measures of improved levees are proposed as primary and secondary defenses along with additional pumping stations, estimated in 2000 costs at $19 billion to $25 billion, through phased investments over 50 to 100 years.[6]

The Dutch plan also includes a retreat strategy to surrender substantial portions of floodplain that have been sectioned by dikes along the Rhine and Meuse rivers. The strategy gives the rivers more room for flooding. By 2050, 222,000 acres (90,000 ha) will be opened to increase the size of the river floodplain, allowed to return to natural forests and marshland. Another 62,000 acres (25,000 ha) of pasture will be designated as temporary retention areas for floodwaters. Land use practices are defined for an additional 185,000 acres (75,000 ha) of farmland, with agricultural uses adapted to tolerate soggy conditions in winter and spring.

The Dutch plan is called "Making Room for Water," yielding to natural river flow the areas that are particularly subject to serious flooding events when a levee was breached. The retreat strategy was determined by the prospect of greater precipitation and storm severity as a result of global climate change. Larger levees were built and subsequently breached by a larger-than-predicted flood or a winter ice jam, resulting in greater damage than would have occurred without dikes.

This does not necessarily result in loss of land productivity or value. As a result of this long-term conversion of land to water, innovative proposals are being put forth in the Netherlands for amphibious structures and communities, including floating houses, farms, commercial parks, and towns that could be stationed in the flood-retainage areas.

JAPAN'S PROGRAM FLOOD MANAGEMENT MEASURES

Japan is an island nation exposed to the sea storms and surges, compounded by earthquakes. Due to mountainous geology with rivers that are short, steep, and rapidly flowing, Japan experiences river flooding, most typically with spring snowmelt but also occurring with increased storms and precipitation events, along with loss of natural floodplain. Fifty percent of Japan's population and 75% of property are concentrated on floodplains that have been severely impacted by urbanization of the river basins.

Japan's river laws have evolved to meet the changing circumstances, now including flood control, water utilization, and river environmental protection as three equal guiding principles for regulation. Current projects include very substantial civil engineering flood control measures required

as part of urban and regional water infrastructure. In high-density urban districts, runoff and river flood controls include underground viaducts to divert flooding away from underground public spaces to large-capacity in-ground storage tanks that provide temporary floodwater retention. In urban areas along rivers, super levees are combined with large flood multiuse retainage areas, or detention ponds, within which appropriate flood resistant facilities and parking are located (illustrated in Chapter 11, Figure 11.32). In the urban edge and agricultural zones, natural and nonstructural measures are deployed to provide naturalize river buffering through revegetation and meander restoration. These measures are combined to meet the flood requirements of the urban watershed, while retaining or increasing land values through development of river-edge parks and communities.[7]

12.3 DESIGN RESOLUTION

The threats created by flooding, severe storms, and climate change are manifest. It impacts individuals, communities, regions, and nations. Through innovative design and construction, there is opportunity to combine resilient design principles and practices to mitigate flooding while providing community investment and renewal.

Within the creative mix of the design and building professions, contributions of research, design and construction go hand in hand. Innovative concepts in architecture, building, and infrastructure have always emerged from a broad range of catalysts: experimental building groups, university-based academic research units, government laboratories, building product fabricators, and architectural and engineering practitioners. In many cases architectural projects and community and urban developments become both proof-of-concept prototype and paradigm that creates models for practices throughout the world.

The "curve of innovation" depicts how innovative ideas begin small and undergo a series of steps before becoming commercially viable. The wave is impelled by a series of steps that include test bedding, demonstration, performance monitoring, then often have to rely on significant sponsorship and advocacy. Innovative ideas are then advanced and promoted through professional colloquia and peer consultation, and then often showcased in premier buildings and community projects. The progress of an innovation can be "pushed" into the market by research support and test bedding of new concepts in prototype and demonstration projects. This is appropriate for ideas in early phases. An innovative concept can be "pulled" into the market by programs that increase widespread acceptance, such as tax incentives to initiate sufficient demand to benefit from economies of scale and commercialization.

The design professions and building industry share a part in the problem of global warming. Buildings consume energy and impact the environment. The decisions that a building designer makes can either increase or decrease the energy use and environmental footprint of the resulting building. Land development practices have removed natural buffers and placed buildings and communities in locations in floodplains and coastal areas that are at increasing risk.

By that same capacity, the design and building professions can use the best of the many ways to advance innovative designs for buildings and communities, to be part of the solution. (Figure 12.3.)

Rather than reactive measures undertaken as disaster recovery, resilient design offers a positive and proactive response to climate change. It calls forth the best of the art and science of architecture and engineering, the inspiration of landscape architecture and environmental design, the creative collaboration of the construction disciplines, and innovative capacity of the U.S. building industry and the many financial, policy, and program managers who make projects possible.

Innovation does not come about simply by evolution or by revolution. Creative and innovative design come about by *resolution*, that is, by the human resolve to bring creativity and insight to improve on the standard ways of doing things.

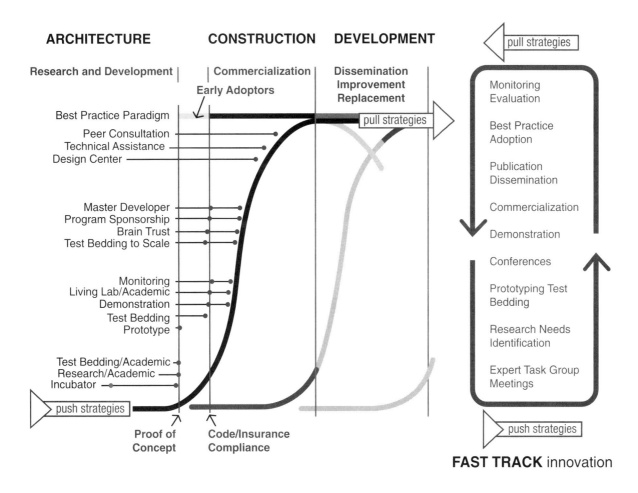

Figure 12.3 *The innovation curve:* the wave of resilient design by which innovative design and construction can contribute significantly to climate mitigation and flood management objectives.

Our design resolution should then be to address the challenge of climate change with the resolve to imagine and build a sustainable future through resilient design.

Notes

1. NOAA, "Coastal & Waterfront Smart Growth" (December 2009), http://coastalsmartgrowth.noaa.gov/casestudies.html "Element 7: Providence, Rhode Island's Downcity Providence and Waterplace Park."

2. FEMA, "Floodplain Management Strategies: Managing Floodplain Development through the NFIP," 2009, www.fema.gov/library/viewRecord.do?id=2108.

3. NSTC Committee on Environment and National Resources, Subcommittee on Disaster Reduction, "Grand Challenges for Disaster Reduction." National Science and Technology Council (June 2005), www.sdr.gov/SDRGrandChallengesforDisasterReduction.pdf.

4. NOAA National Ocean Service, "Mainstreaming Adaptation to Climate Change (MACC). Climate Change Impacts on Land Use Planning and Coastal Infrastructure," by Clement Lewsey, Gonzalo Cid, Edward Kruse, and John Virdin, www.oas.org/macc/Docs/LUPInfrastIssues.doc.

5. Van der Vlies, Arie, Kees Stoutjesdijk and Hans Waals, "Effects of Climate Change on Water Management in the Netherlands," *Proceedings of the Water Environment Federation* (2006): 7712–7232.

6. Colin Woodward, "Netherlands Battens Its Ramparts Against Warming Climate," *Christian Science Monitor*, September 4, 2001, http://news.nationalgeographic.com/news/2001/08/0829_wiredutch_2.html.

7. Kazuhiko Fukami, Kenji Kanoa, and Katsuhisa Shioji. "Japanese Experience: Structural Measures for Flood Management." Tokyo: PWRI Public Works Research Institute of Japan, 2009, www.mrcmekong.org/.../4-200504_Fukami_PWRI_Japan_d.pdf.

EPILOGUE

Before flooding is threatened, the prevailing attitude may be, "It won't happen here, not once in a hundred years." When rivers begin to rise and overflow their banks, hasty provisions are made, lifting belongings to upper stories and sandbagging where one can. Every inch in floodwater rise becomes critically important. When flooding increases to unprecedented levels and extent, the effect is devastating upon victims, who react with the entire range of emotions of disbelief and disorientation, anger and grief. Once-familiar ground is covered with polluted waters. Buildings that were once sanctuaries are invaded by a muddy ooze. Flooding may last for days, weeks, or longer. It may start slowly, sufficient to give some notice, or may strike without warning as a flashflood. With hurricanes, there are early warnings, although imprecise until the penultimate hours of landfall, by which time emergency routes may be jammed or impassable. Depending on the extent of a flooding, recovery can take months or years. Nothing about the experience of a flood disaster is fun.

First responders to emergencies provide a modicum of positive action to help individuals and communities in distress. Where flooding could have been predicted, but advanced preparations not put in place, emergency response teams are often too late. An earlier response is required: "advanced response teams." These are planners, designers, and municipal officials who are able to put in place precautionary design to prepare for flooding. Just as first responders are trained to work with a tunnel vision, focused upon the reality of facts at hand, advanced response teams must anticipate best and worst cases, to prepare for the reality of what may be.

For much of the second half of the last century, the floodplains and coastal areas that were historically prone to only very rare flooding and storm events have been intensively developed and altered. In some cases, built infrastructure and development has caused the loss of the entire vegetative cover, wetlands, and natural systems that had always provided water balance and resiliency to extreme weather. For much of that time, many of these floodplain communities may have flourished, beating the odds and probabilities represented by the 1% annual risk of a 100-year flood event. All this was good and "good riddance" to nightmares of past disasters that fade over time, such as now-distant memories of the 1938 Atlantic Hurricane that devastated East Coast communities.

Present-day projections of the impacts of climate change tell us to take remedial action and to set precautions in place now. Recent extreme flood events that reached "500-year" levels—in the Spring of 2010 in Rhode Island and Tennessee—give evidence that that due-diligence precaution is fully deserved.

Architects, engineers, builders, community planners, and officials can and should be part of that "advance response team." The message of this book is stated that simply.

In that charge, every community opportunity is critical to protect and extend the natural landscape along roadways, rivers, open space, and stormwater networks, to heal the wounds of "a thousand cuts" that have contributed to increased runoff, flashier streams and rivers, and loss of stormwater retention. In every building site in or near a flood-prone area, there are opportunities of tree planting, building location, and roof and gardenscapes to retain and reuse rainwater. In the architectural and structural design of buildings, every inch of elevation is important to protect from water and moisture damage. In coastal construction especially, attention to detail, structural connections, and attachments are critical, down to the minutia of nailing pattern for a secure and properly installed roof.

The disaster of flooding can be mitigated by design. Buildings and communities can be made resilient to flooding and extreme weather by design. Flooding can be anticipated and utilized as a way to sustain land and water needs in a balance of community and conservation values.

Poetic images of water—fresh falling rain replenishing the land or the rhythm of ocean waves lapping the shore—are part of the stories and metaphors of renewal and certitude inculcated in cultures throughout time. These images can continue to be restorative and inspirational dreams of a protective earth, rather than nightmares of potential disasters of a damaged earth, if we succeed in design for flooding and resilience of our buildings and communities.

GLOSSARY

Terms used in watershed and coastal flood design.

Adaptation (i) Genetically based capacity or behavior that allows an organism to be better suited to its environment; (ii) measures to reduce the vulnerability of natural and human systems to actual or expected *climate change* effects.

Aerobic With or requiring air, oxygen.

Albedo The fraction of solar radiation reflected by a surface or object, often expressed as a percentage. Snow-covered surfaces have a high albedo, the surface albedo of soils ranges from high to low, and vegetation-covered surfaces and oceans have a low albedo.

Algae Chlorophyll-containing nonvascular organisms, plant or plantlike.

Algal bloom A reproductive explosion of *algae* in a lake, river, or ocean.

Alluvial deposit Soil, mud and *detritus* transported by a river and deposited—usually temporarily—at points along the *floodplain* of a river. Commonly composed of sands and gravels.

Anerobic, anaerobic Without air, no oxygen. Also see *anoxia*.

Angle of repose Maximum slope (measured from the horizontal) at which soils and loose materials on the banks of canals, rivers, or *embankments* will remain stable.

Anoxia The absence of oxygen (e.g., in *water*). Also see *hypoxia*.

Anthropogenic Resulting from or produced by human beings.

Aquaculture The science and business of farming marine or freshwater food fish or shellfish under controlled conditions.

Aquifer A geologic formation that is water bearing and transmits water from one point in the formation to another.

Astronomical tides Daily tides controlled by the Moon, as distinct from wind-generated tides.

Atmosphere Envelope of air surrounding Earth to an approximate height of 621 miles (1,000 km), retained by the gravitational field, comprised of the *troposphere, stratosphere*, mesosphere, and ionosphere. (Figure G.1.)

Attenuation (i) Reduction in magnitude, such as lessening of wave height or lowering of peak *runoff* discharge rates; (ii) decrease of water-particle motion with increasing wave depth; (iii) reduction of contaminant concentrations, such as the action of biodegradation in *wetlands* or *bioretention*.

A zone Designation used in the *National Flood Insurance Program (NFIP)* to designate areas subject to inundation by the *100-year flood* where *wave* action does not occur or where waves are less than 3 feet high.

Barrier beaches Spits of sand that form parallel to the shore.

Barrier islands *Barrier beaches* with a cross-section profile that often includes *dunes*, shrub thickets, *maritime forests*, and *salt marshes*.

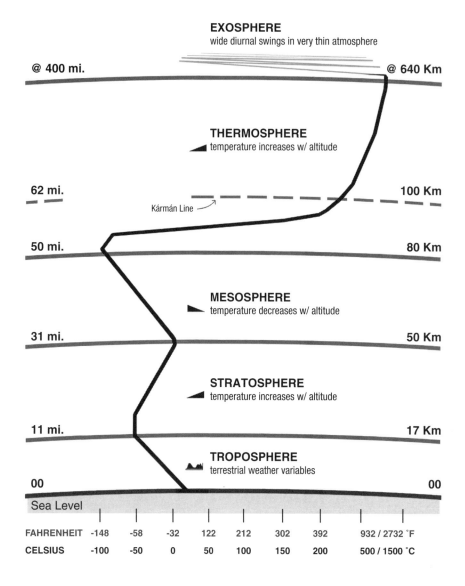

Figure G.1 *Layers of the atmosphere.*

Base flood In *National Flood Insurance Program (NFIP)*, defined as *flood* that has a 1% probability of being equaled or exceeded in any given year. Also known as the *100-year flood*.

Base Flood Elevation (BFE) Elevation of the *base flood* in relation to a specified datum, such as the National Geodetic Vertical Datum (NGVD) or the North American Vertical Datum (NAVD). The BFE is the basis of the insurance and *floodplain management regulations* of the *NFIP*.

Base flow The flow in a stream between storm events, supplied by *groundwater*.

Bathymetry The study of underwater depth of lake or ocean floors.

Beach Zone of unconsolidated material that extends landward from the low water line to where there is marked change in material or physiographic form, or to the line of permanent vegetation (usually the effective limit of storm waves). The seaward limit of a beach—unless otherwise specified—is the mean low water line.

Beach nourishment Replacement or augmentation of beach sand removed by ocean waters. It may occur naturally by longshore transport or be brought about artificially by the deposition of dredged materials or material from upland sites.

Beaufort scale Classification of the force of the winds according to a scale first described by Rear Admiral Sir

TABLE A. BEAUFORT WIND SCALE

Beaufort Number	Wind Speed (knots)	WMO Description
0	<1	Calm
1	1–3	Light air
2	4–6	Light breeze
3	7–10	Gentle breeze
4	11–16	Moderate breeze
5	17–21	Fresh breeze
6	22–27	Strong breeze
7	28–33	Near gale
8	34–40	Gale
9	41–47	Strong gale
10	48–55	Storm
11	56–63	Violent storm
12	>64	Hurricane

Francis Beaufort in which the range of intensity varies from 0 to 12. (Table A. Also see, page 19).

Bedrock The solid rock that underlies gravel, soil, and other superficial material. Bedrock may be exposed at the surface (an outcrop) or it may be buried under a few inches to thousands of feet of unconsolidated material.

Benthic Living on or in ocean, lake, or stream bottoms.

Biodiversity Diversity and number of *species* of plants and animals at various scales in a defined area, or *habitat*, measured by a variety of indices such as number of species and distribution of individuals among species.

Biome Major and distinct regional element of the *biosphere*, typically consisting of several *ecosystems* (e.g., forests, rivers, ponds, *swamps*) within a region of similar climate.

Bioretention A water quality practice that utilizes landscaping and soils to treat *runoff* by collecting it in shallow depressions and filtering it through a planting soil media.

Biosphere Part of the Earth system comprising all *ecosystems* and living organisms in the *atmosphere*, on land (terrestrial biosphere), or in the oceans (marine biosphere), including derived dead organic matter, such as litter, soil organic matter, and oceanic *detritus*.

Biota All living organisms of an area; the flora and fauna considered as a unit.

BMP (Best Management Practice) State-of-the-art method or measure for achieving a desired benefit, such as improved water quality.

Bore A very rapid rise of the tide in which the advancing water presents an abrupt front of considerable height. In shallow estuaries where the range of tide is large, the high water is propagated inward faster than the low water because of the greater depth at high water. If the high water overtakes the low water, an abrupt front is presented, with the high-water crest finally falling forward as the tide continues to advance.

Boreal forest Forests of pine, spruce, fir, and larch stretching from the east coast of Canada westward to Alaska, continuing from Siberia westward across Russia to the European Plain.

Buffer A vegetated strip immediately adjacent to a stream, river, or water body intended to protect the water from *sediment* and pollutant *runoff* and *siltation* from upstream areas. Other benefits may include rainfall *infiltration* and *habitat* enhancement.

Bulkhead Wall or other structure, often of wood, steel, stone, or concrete, designed to retain or prevent sliding or *erosion* of the land. Occasionally bulkheads are use to protect against *wave* action.

Carbon dioxide (CO_2) Naturally occurring gas, also a by-product of burning fossil fuels and biomass, or result of industrial processes or *land use changes*. It is the principal *anthropogenic greenhouse gas (GHG)* that affects the Earth's radiative balance.

Carbon sequestration Uptake of carbon-containing substances, in particular *carbon dioxide*.

Cation An ion or group of ions having a positive charge and characteristically moving toward the negative electrode in electrolysis.

Cation exchange capacity (CEC) In soil science, the capacity of a soil for ion exchange of cations between the soil and the soil solution. CEC is used as a measure of soil fertility, nutrient retention capacity, and the capacity to protect groundwater from contamination.

Central Pressure Index (CPI) The estimated minimum barometric pressure in the eye (approximate center) of a particular *hurricane*. The CPI is considered the most stable index to represent the intensity of hurricane wind velocities in the periphery of the storm; the highest wind speeds are associated with storms having the lowest CPI.

Channel (i) A natural or artificial waterway of perceptible extent that either periodically or continuously contains moving water, or that forms a connecting link between two bodies of water; (ii) the part of a body of water deep enough to be used for navigation through an area otherwise too shallow for navigation; (iii) a large strait, as the English Channel; (iv) the deepest part of a stream, bay, or strait through which the main volume or current of water flows.

Channel capacity The maximum flow that a channel is capable of transmitting without its banks being overtopped.

Channelization Creation of a channel or channels resulting in faster water flow.

Chenier A ridge formed by lateral transport and reworking of *deltaic deposits*, usually containing large amounts of shell deposits; named for the oak trees (*chene* is French for "oak") found growing on the ridges.

Climate The average weather typically represented by the statistical means and variables of temperature, *precipitation*, and wind over a period of time.

Climate change (i) Change in temperature and weather patterns; (ii) defined in the United Nations Framework Convention on Climate Change as "a change of climate attributed directly or indirectly to human activity that alters the composition of the global *atmosphere* in addition to natural climate variability observed over comparable time periods."

Coastal A zone Under the *NFIP*, the portion of the *special flood hazard area (SFHA)* landward of a *V zone* or landward of an open *coastline* without mapped V zones (e.g., shorelines of the Great Lakes), in which the principal sources of *flooding* are *astronomical tides*, *storm surge*, *seiches*, or *tsunamis* (not *riverine* sources). The flood forces in coastal A zones are highly correlated with coastal winds or coastal seismic activity. Coastal A zones may therefore be subject to *wave* effects, velocity flows, *erosion*, *scour*, or combinations of these forces. See *A zone* and *noncoastal A zone*. (NFIP regulations do not differentiate between coastal A zones and noncoastal A zones.)

Coastal barrier Depositional geologic feature such as a bay barrier, *tombolo*, spit, or *barrier island* that consists of unconsolidated sedimentary materials; is subject to wave, tidal, and wind energies; and protects landward aquatic habitats from direct *waves*.

Coastal currents (i) Currents that flow roughly parallel to the shore and constitute a relatively uniform drift in the deeper water adjacent to the surf zone. These currents may be tidal currents, transient, wind-driven currents, or currents associated with the distribution of mass in local waters; (ii) for navigational purposes, a current in *coastline* shipping lanes where the tidal current is frequently rotary. Also see *rip current*.

Coastal flood hazard area (CFHA) Under the *NFIP*, an area—usually along an open coast, bay, or inlet—that is subject to *flood* by *storm surge* and, in some instances, *wave* action caused by storms or seismic forces.

Coastal high hazard area (CHHA) Under the *NFIP*, an area of special flood hazard extending from offshore to the inland limit of a primary frontal dune along an open coast and any other area subject to high-velocity wave action from storms *tsunami*, or seismic sources. On a *Flood Insurance Rate Map (FIRM)*, the CHHA is designated as a *V zone*, indicating the area is subject to a *base flood* with wave heights or wave *run-up* depths greater than or equal to 3.0 feet.

Coastal zone management Integrated and general development of the coastal zone. Coastal zone management is not restricted to coastal defense works but includes development in economic, ecological, and social terms.

Coastline (i) Technically, the line that forms the boundary between the coast and the shore; (ii) commonly, the line that forms the boundary between the land and the water (e.g., the water of a sea or ocean).

Coliform bacteria Bacteria commonly found in intestinal colon and used as an indicator of water contamination.

Combined Sewer Overflow (CSO) Outflows or overflow of sewers designed to collect rainwater *runoff*, domestic sewage, and industrial wastewater in the same pipe.

Commensalism Form of symbiotic relationship in which one species gains from the interaction and the other is neither positively nor negatively affected.

Condensation The process in which water vapor changes into liquid water (such as dew, fog, or cloud droplets).

Contamination Undesirable element, impure or unclean, something that is not supposed to be there (such as oil, *pollution*, or insecticides in water).

Contour, contour line A line on a *topographic map* connecting points at the same elevation; also called an isobath to represent equal water depth.

Conservation Preservation and protection of ecological processes and *biodiversity* of the environment.

Coriolis effect (i) In physics, an apparent deflection of moving objects when viewed from a frame of reference that itself is rotating; (ii) in meteorology, the effect due to the centrifugal force to Earth's rotation combined with Earth's gravitation, causing air masses and weather events to be deflected to the right in the northern hemisphere and to the left in the southern hemisphere, also capable of generating currents.

Cryosphere Component of the *climate* system consisting of all snow, ice, and frozen ground (including *permafrost*) on and beneath the surface of Earth and ocean.

Cuspate bar Crescent-shape bar uniting with the shore at each end. It may be formed by a single spit growing from shore and then turning back to again meet the shore, or by two spits growing from the shore and uniting to form a crescent. It may eventually grow into a *tombolo* linking the feature to the mainland.

Decomposer An organism that feeds on and breaks down dead plant or animal matter, thus making organic nutrients available to the *ecosystem*.

Delta An area formed from the deposition of *sediment* or *alluvial deposit* at the mouth of a river or stream; normally built up only where there is no tidal or current action capable of removing the sediment at the same rate as it is deposited; hence the delta builds out from the coastline.

Deltaic deposits Mud and sand deposited at the mouth of a river.

Denitrification *Anaerobic* microbial conversion of nitrogen to nitrogen gas.

Density Ratio of the mass to the volume of any substance.

Desertification Land degradation, soil loss, and *desiccation* in arid, semiarid, and dry subhumid areas resulting from various factors, including climatic variations and human activities.

Desiccation Loss of water, drying.

Design storm Hypothetical extreme storm for which coastal protection structures will often be designed to withstand. The severity of the storm (i.e., return period) is chosen in view of the acceptable level of risk of damage or failure.

Design Flood Elevation (DFE) Elevation that is reference for design, specified by local regulatory authorities, which establishes the elevation of the lowest floor member or horizontal structural components. The DFE may be the same as BFE, or higher, as an additional safety factor at the discretion of local communities.

Detritus Newly dead or decaying organic matter in the process of bacterial decomposition.

Dike, also Dyke A constructed wall or *embankment* along a shore to prevent *flooding* of low-lying land. Also see *levee*.

Discharge A volume of fluid passing a point per unit of time, commonly expressed in cubic feet per second, millions of gallons per day, or gallons per minute.

Dissolved oxygen Oxygen dissolved in water available for respiration by aquatic organisms; a key indicator of the condition of a water body.

Disturbance Any event that opens up space for colonization, such as the falling of a tree in a forest or removal of marsh grass by storm *waves*.

Diversion Turning aside or alteration of the natural course or flow of water. In coastal *restoration*, this usually consists of action by *channelization*, or via pipe or conduit to introduce water and water-borne resources into a receiving area.

Dune A low hill or ridge of drifted sand in coastal areas that can be bare or covered with vegetation. The *primary dune*, also called *primary frontal dune*, is the critical first line of coastal defense exposed to harshest conditions of erosion, wind, waves, and salt air, requiring hardy vegetation for stabilization.

Easement A granting of one or more property rights, such as an accessible strip of land, by the property owner to and/or for the use by the public, or private person or entity.

Ebb The receding tide when the water moves out to the sea and the water level lowers.

Ecosystem A system of living organisms interacting with each other within its physical environment (*habitat*), including biological, geochemical, and geophysical systems. An ecosystem may range from very small spatial scales to, ultimately, the entire earth.

Ecosystem services A term of reference to identify and credit the economic, health and social benefits derived from functioning natural environments, land, vegetation, water, and living organisms.

Elevation The vertical distance from mean sea level or other established datum plane to a point on Earth's surface; height above sea level. Although sea floor elevation below *MSL* should be marked as a negative value, many charts show positive numerals for water depth.

El Niño, El Niño Southern Oscillation (ENSO) The warm equatorial ocean current that flows southward along the coast of Peru and Ecuador during February and March of certain years. It is caused by poleward motions of air and unusual water temperature patterns in the Pacific Ocean, leading to reversal in normal north-flowing cold coastal currents. During many El Niño years, storms, rainfall, and other meteorological events in the western hemisphere are measurably different from during non-El Niño years. The cold phase of ENSO is called *La Niña*.

Embankment An elevated human-made or natural deposit of soil, rock, or other materials placed with sloping sides and with a length greater than its height. Usually an embankment is wider than a *dike*.

Embayment *Shoreline* inlet or indentation resembling a bay.

Emergent plant A plant with stems and leaves that grows in periodically or permanently flooded areas. Parts of the plant extend through and above the water.

Encroachment Any physical object placed in a *floodplain* that hinders the passage of water or otherwise affects *flood* flows.

Endangered species Defined in Code of Federal Regulations as "a plant or animal in danger of extinction throughout all or a significant portion of its range." See also *threatened species*.

Endemic Restricted or peculiar to a locality or region. With reference to health, endemic can refer to a disease or agent present or usually prevalent in a population or geographical area.

Environmental impact statement (EIS) Documentation of the positive and negative environmental effects of a proposed action and possible alternatives.

Erodible soil Soil subject to wearing away and movement due to the effects of wind, water, or other geological processes of *erosion* during a flood or storm or over a period of years.

Erosion Process of the gradual wearing away of land or landmasses. In general, erosion involves the detachment and movement of soil and rock fragments, during a *flood* or storm or over a period of years, through the action of wind, water, or other geologic processes.

Escarpment A more or less continuous line of cliffs or steep slopes facing in one general direction that is caused by *erosion* or faulting.

Estuarine Of, or relating to, an *estuary*.

Estuary (i) A semi-enclosed body of water that has a free connection to the open sea or river that is affected by tides; (ii) region near a river mouth in which freshwater of the river mixes with the salt water of the sea and that receives both fluvial and littoral sediment influx.

Eustasy, also Eustatic sea level change A uniform worldwide change in sea level caused by the amount of water taken up or melted by continental and polar *ice caps*, or by a change in the capacity of ocean basins.

Eutrophication Process by which large additions of nutrients causes an overgrowth of *algae* and subsequent depletion of oxygen (*hypoxia*).

Evaporation The process by which any substance is converted from a liquid state into, and carried off in, vapor (e.g., evaporation of water).

Evapotranspiration The combined processes of *evaporation* from the water and soil surface and from *transpiration* of water by plants.

Exotic species Plant or animal species that has been intentionally or accidentally introduced and that does not naturally occur in a region.

Extended detention A function provided by *BMP* measures, which incorporate water quality storage. BMPs with extended detention intercept *runoff* and then release it over an extended period of time.

Extirpation Disappearance of a *species* from part of its range; local extinction.

Fathom Unit of measurement used for water body depth soundings equal to 6 feet (1.83 m).

Federal Emergency Management Agency (FEMA) Federal agency created in 1979 to provide a single point of accountability for all federal activities related to disaster *mitigation* and emergency preparedness, response and recovery. FEMA administers the *National Flood Insurance Program (NFIP)*.

Fetch Distance or area of a water body over which wind acts on the water surface to generate *waves*; sometimes used synonymously with "fetch length."

Filter strip Vegetated boundary installed with uniform mild slopes and absorptive materials. Filter strips may be provided downgrade of developed tracts to trap *sediment* and sediment-borne pollutants and to reduce imperviousness. Filter strips may be forested or vegetated turf. Filter strips located adjacent to water bodies are called *buffers*.

Fiord, also fjords Narrow, deep, steep-walled inlet of the sea, usually formed by entrance of the sea into a deep glacial trough.

500-year flood Flood that has as 0.2% probability of being equaled or exceeded in any given year. See *100-year flood*.

Flood, flooding A general or temporary condition of partial or complete inundation of normally dry land areas from overflow of inland or tidal waters; unusual and rapid accumulation or runoff of surface waters from any source; or mudslides (mudflows) caused by flooding.

Flood elevation Height of the water surface above an established elevation datum such as the NGVD, NAVD, or *mean sea level*.

Flood Insurance Rate Map (FIRM) Under the *NFIP*, an official map of a community, on which the Federal Emergency Management Agency has delineated both *special flood hazard areas (SFHA)* and the insurance risk premium zones applicable to the community.

Floodplain (i) Area that is flooded periodically by the lateral overflow of rivers; (ii) in *hydrology*, the entire area that is flooded at a recurrence interval of 100 years; (iii) under the *NFIP*, synonymous with 100-year *floodplain*, any land area susceptible to being inundated by water from any source, with a 1% probability of being equaled or exceeded in any given year.

Floodplain management regulations Under the *NFIP*, any and all zoning ordinances, subdivision regulations, building codes, health regulations, special-purpose ordinances, and other applications of police power, which provide standards for flood damage prevention and *mitigation*.

Floodway Part of the *floodplain*, centered on the stream that will convey most of the flow during overbank *flood* events.

Food chain (i) Plants and animals linked by their food relationships; (ii) a representation of the flow of energy among producers, consumers, and decomposers.

Foreshore The area between mean low water and mean high water.

Freeboard (i) Under the NFIP, a factor of safety above the *base flood elevation (BFE)*, usually expressed in feet. Freeboard is intended to plan for many unaccounted or unknown factors that could contribute to *flood* elevations greater than the BFE calculated for a selected condition; (ii) on a ship, the distance from the waterline to main deck or gunwale.

Freshwater marsh Grassy *wetlands* that occur along rivers and lakes, typically dominated by grasses, reeds, rushes, and sedges.

Frontal dune The *dune* closest to the water's edge.

Fujita scale Also called the Fujita-Pearson scale, used to rate tornado intensity based on ground or aerial surveys of storm damage. The scale was modified and updated by the National Weather Service in 2007. The Enhanced Fujita scale has ratings from EF1 (moderate damage) to EF5 (extreme damage).

Gabion Structure composed of masses of rocks, rubble, or masonry held tightly together usually by wire mesh so as to form blocks or walls. Sometimes used on heavy erosion areas to retard wave action or as a foundation for breakwater or *jetty*.

Geographical Information System (GIS) Database of information that is geographically referenced, usually with an associated visualization system.

Geologic cycle The dynamic transitions through *geologic time* among the three main rock types: *sedimentary*, metamorphic, and igneous.

Geologic time The total time involved since formation of Earth to the present time, spanning millions or billions of years.

Geomorphology (i) Branch of physical geography that deals with the form of Earth, the general configuration of its surface, and distribution of land and water; (ii) study of the history of geologic changes through the interpretation of topographic forms. (Figure G.2.)

Geotextile A fabric manufactured from synthetic fiber designed to achieve specific engineering objectives, including seepage control, media separation (e.g., between sand and soil), filtration, or the protection of other construction elements, such as geomembranes.

Glaciation Modification of the land surface by action of glaciers in middle and high latitudes and alpine environments, including distinct *erosion* and present-day *watershed* elements. (Figure G.2.)

Figure G.2   *Remnants of the last glacial period* evident in North American landforms, wetlands, and waterways.

GEOLOGIC TRACES IN NORTHERN LANDSCAPES

1. **Esker:** A long winding ridge of stratified sand and gravel, left by ice flows in glacial formations.

2. **Moraine:** An accumulation of boulders, stones, or other debris deposited by a glacier, often creating significant aquifers.

3. **Kettle lakes and ponds:** Water bodies originating from large ice blocks left in the wake of glacial retreat. Steep sided (like a "kettle"), over time they may become silted and filled in as bogs.

4. **Drumlin:** An elongated hill of glacial deposits, formed by glacial ice flow.

5. **Braided streams:** A network of small channels that result when a discharge of water, ice, or sediment increases in speed or is constrained in depth or width and cannot otherwise transport its load, typical of glacial melt and river deltas, resulting in a braided appearance.

6. **Glacial erratic:** A boulder deposited by glacial ice, often carried over great distances, remaining distinct in the landscape due to its size and type.

Global warming An increase of Earth's temperature by degrees, resulting in an increase in the volume of water that contributes to *sea level rise*.

Glycophytes Plants that cannot live in high-*salinity* environments; most plants.

Gradient (i) A measure of slope (soil or water surface, such as a stream or river) in terms of rise or fall per horizontal distance; (ii) a change of a value per unit of distance (e.g., the *gradient* of a *halocline* zone of freshwater and salt water mixing); (iii) with reference to winds or currents, the rate of increase or decrease in speed, usually in the vertical or the curve that represents this rate.

Greenhouse gas (GHG) Gaseous constituent of the *atmosphere*, both natural and *anthropogenic*, that absorbs and emits radiation at specific wavelengths within the spectrum of thermal infrared radiation emitted by Earth's surface, the atmosphere itself, and clouds. This process causes the greenhouse effect.

Greenway A strip or belt of vegetated land that typically includes both upland and *riparian zones*. Greenways are often used for recreation or to provide as a land use *buffer*, or to provide a corridor and *habitat* for wildlife.

Groin Narrow structure built perpendicular to the *coastline* to reduce longshore currents and/or to trap and retain littoral material. Most groins are of timber or rock and extend from a seawall, or the backshore, well onto the *foreshore* and rarely farther offshore.

Groundwater Water contained belowground in soil and rock. Also see *aquifer*.

Groundwater recharge Process by which external water is added to an *aquifer*, via percolating rainwater.

Habitat Environment occupied by individuals of a particular *species*, population, or *biome*. (Figure G.3.)

Halcocline Zone in which salinity changes rapidly.

Harmful algal bloom (HAB) An algal bloom that causes negative impacts to other organisms by producing natural toxins. The causes of HABs are not clearly established. Their appearance in some locations may be entirely natural, while in others a result of human impacts. Not all HABs are dense enough to cause water discoloration, and not all algae blooms are harmful. Examples of harmful effects of HABs include:

- Toxins that cause mass mortalities in fish, seabirds, and marine mammals.
- Risk of human illness or death via consumption of contaminated seafood.

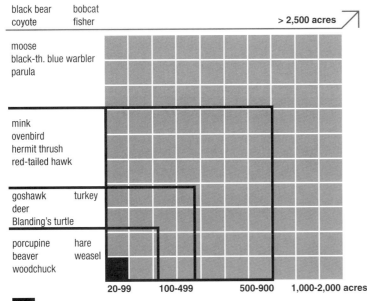

Figure G.3 *Habitat*: representative wildlife area requirements.

Sources: Maine Department of Inland Fisheries & Wildlife; Maine Audubon Society.

- Mechanical damage to marine organisms, gills of fish, resulting in asphyxiation.

- Oxygen depletion of the water (*hypoxia* or *anoxia*).

Herbaceous A plant with no persistent woody stem aboveground.

Highest astronomical tide (HAT) The highest level of water that can be predicted to occur under any combination of astronomical conditions. This level may not be reached every year.

High-velocity wave action Condition in which *wave* heights or *wave run-up* depths are greater than or equal to 3.0 feet.

High water (HW), also high water line Maximum height reached by each rising tide. The height may be solely due to the periodic tidal forces or it may have superimposed on it the effects of prevailing meteorological conditions; non-technically, also called high tide. The shoreline delineated on the nautical charts of the National Ocean Service is an approximation of the high water line.

100-year flood *Flood* that has as 1% probability of being equaled or exceeded in any given year. See *500-year flood*.

Hurricane Tropical cyclone, formed in the *atmosphere* over warm ocean areas, in which wind speeds equal or exceed 75 miles/hour (65 knots or 33.5 m/sec) or more and blow in a large spiral around a relatively calm center, or eye. Term is used in the Atlantic, Gulf of Mexico, and eastern Pacific. Hurricane circulation is counterclockwise in the northern hemisphere and clockwise in the southern hemisphere.

Hydric soil Soil that is saturated, flooded, or ponded long enough during the growing season to develop *anaerobic* conditions. Hydric soil in areas having indicators of hydrophytic vegetation and wetland *hydrology* is *wetland* soil.

Hydrological cycle The continuous movement of water on Earth between the *atmosphere*, land, and oceans in its various forms of liquid, vapor and ice. The amount of water, or *water balance*, with Earth's *atmosphere*, remains fairly constant over time. (Figure G.4.)

Hydrology Pattern of water movement on Earth's surface, in the soil and underlying rocks and *aquifers*, and the atmosphere.

Hypoxia (hypoxic) Very low oxygen levels; condition of low dissolved oxygen concentrations.

Ice cap A dome-shape ice mass, usually covering a highland area, which is considerably smaller in extent than an ice sheet.

Ice sheet A mass of land ice sufficiently deep to cover most of the underlying bedrock topography. Most ice is discharged through fast-flowing ice streams or outlet glaciers There are only three large ice sheets in the modern era, one on Greenland and two on Antarctica (the East and West Antarctic ice sheets).

Ice shelf An extensive floating sheet of ice of considerable thickness and usually of great breadth extending seaward from the continental *coastline*; common along polar coasts (Antarctica, Greenland).

Impervious surface Surface in the landscape that cannot infiltrate rainfall, such as rooftop, pavement, sidewalk, driveway, and compacted earth.

Infiltration Downward movement of water from the surface of the land to subsoil.

Intermediate marsh A marsh occurring where the salinity is about 3 parts per 1,000 (ppt); a transitional area between fresh and brackish marshes.

Intertidal Alternately flooded and exposed by tides.

Invasive species Nonnative *species* of plants or animals that outcompete native species in a specific *habitat*.

Invertebrate An animal that does not have a backbone, such as snails, worms, and insects.

Isostacy (i) General equilibrium of forces tending to elevate or depress Earth's crust; (ii) elastic response of Earth's lithosphere and mantle to changes in surface loads.

Jetty Wall built out into the water to restrain currents or protect a *coastline* or structure, to prevent shoaling of a *channel* by *littoral* materials, and/or to direct and confine the stream or tidal flow. Jetties may also be built at the mouths of rivers or tidal inlets to help deepen and stabilize a channel.

Karst (geology) An area of irregular limestone in which *erosion* has produced fissures.

Katabatic wind Wind caused by cold air flowing down slopes due to gravitational acceleration.

Kinetic energy (waves) In a progressive oscillatory wave, a summation of the energy of motion of the particles within the wave.

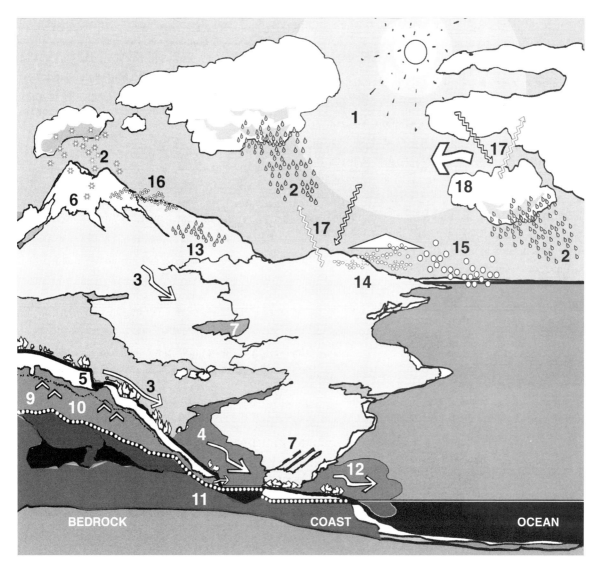

ATMOSPHERE TO SURFACE
1 Moisture in Atmosphere

2 Precipitation
3 Surface Runoff
4 Streamflow
5 Ground Infiltration

6 Storage in Ice and Snow
7 Freshwater Storage in Swamps and Lakes
8 Ground Water Storage/Aquifer
9 Water Table

10 Groundwater Percolation
11 Groundwater Seepage/Springs
12 River Discharge

SURFACE TO ATMOSPHERE
13 Condensation (air to liquid)
14 Transpiration (foliage to air)
15 Evaporation (liquid to air)
16 Sublimation (snow and ice solid to air)
17 Radiative Transfer (heating and cooling)
18 Cloud Formation/Transport

Figure G.4   *Hydrologic cycle.*

Knot The unit of speed used in navigation and in some weather data equal to 1 nautical mile (6,076.115 ft or 1,852 m) per hour.

Lacustrine flood hazard area Area subject to inundation by *flooding* from lakes.

Laminar flow Slow, smooth flow, with each drop of water traveling a smooth path parallel to its neighboring drops. Laminar flow is characteristic of low velocities and particles of *sediment* in low-flow zones.

Land use and land use change (i) The total of arrangements, activities, and inputs undertaken in a certain land cover type; (ii) in the sense of the social and economic purposes for which land is managed (e.g., grazing, timber extraction, and *conservation*). Land cover and land use change may have an impact on the surface *albedo*, *evapotranspiration*, sources and sinks of *greenhouse gases (GHG)*, or other properties of the climate system.

Larval Stage of some animal's life cycles (most *invertebrates*) between egg and adult.

Levee, levée (i) A long, low ridge or *embankment* built up by a stream on its *floodplain* along one or both banks of its *channel*, deposited by *flooding*; (ii) a linear mound of earth or stone, often having an access road along the top, constructed to prevent a river from overflowing. Also see *dike*.

Littoral Of or pertaining to the shore, especially of the sea; coastal. Often used as a general term for the *coastline* zone influenced by wave action or, more specifically, the shore zone between the high and low water marks.

Littoral drift Movement of sand by transport parallel (longshore drift) and sometimes also perpendicular (cross-shore transport) to the shore.

Lowest astronomical tide (LAT) The lowest tide level that can be predicted to occur under average meteorological conditions and any combination of astronomical conditions. This level may not be reached every year.

Low-flow channel An incised or paved *channel* from inlet to outlet in a dry basin, designed to carry low *runoff* directly to the outlet without retention.

Low water (LW), also low water line The minimum elevation reached by each falling tide. Nontechnically, also called low tide.

Liquefaction, soil Term to describe the behavior of soils from solid to liquefied state, having consistency of a heavy liquid, that may result due to earthquake loading or coastal storm wave action. Building foundations that bear directly on soils or sand that liquefies will experience a sudden loss of support, resulting in substantial settlement or failure.

Maritime forest Broadly defined as coastal forest community within range of salt spray or mist typically dominated by closed canopies of evergreen (northern areas), broadleaf (temperate areas), or tropical hammocks (subtropical and tropical zones), located on the mainland side of a barrier beach or *barrier island*.

Marsh *Wetland* periodically or continuously flooded to a shallow depth, where terrestrial and aquatic *habitats* overlap dominated by *herbaceous* or nonwoody grasses, cattails, and other low plants, often emerging in shallow ponds or depressions, river margins, tidal areas, and *estuaries*.

Meander A bend or curve in a river course; a single *channel* having a pattern of successive deviations in alignment that results in a more or less sinusoidal course. Often preserved or created to maximize *riverine* areas, *habitat*, and *bioretention*.

Mean sea level (MSL) Average height of the sea for all stages of the tide, usually determined from hourly height observations over a 19-year period on an open coast or in adjacent waters having free access to the sea; the average sea level that would exist in the absence of tides.

Mesohaline Intermediate levels of *salinity*, about 15 ppt.

Meteorological tides Tidal constituents having their origin in the daily or seasonal variation in weather conditions that may occur with some degree of periodicity.

Metonic cycle An approximate 19-year cycle of lunar orbit around Earth and Earth around the Sun, used in spacecraft trajectory calculations, prediction of eclipses, and the basis for the Hebrew calendar and significant dates of many religions.

Mitigation (i) An action taken to reduce or permanently eliminate the long-term risk to life and property from natural hazards; (ii) replacement of functional values lost when an ecosystem is altered. Mitigation can include replacement, *restoration*, and enhancement of functional values.

Mollusks Soft-bodied, shelled animals such as clams, oysters, nudibraches, and octopi (the latter two have either small remnant shell within their bodies or an embryonic shell).

Monsoon A tropical and subtropical seasonal reversal in both the surface winds and associated *precipitation*, caused by differential heating between a continental-scale landmass and the adjacent ocean. Monsoon rains occur mainly over land in summer.

Mudflat Shallow water *benthic* zone of *coastline* alternately covered or uncovered by the tide, comprised of extremely fine *sediment*, typically fine silt and clay.

Mudslide Slow-moving mudflow precipitated by rain and *flooding*.

Mutualism Form of symbiotic relationship in which both species involved gain from the interaction (e.g., lichen and fungi).

National Flood Insurance Program (NFIP) Federal program created by Congress in 1968 that makes flood insurance available in communities that enact and enforce satisfactory *floodplain management regulations*.

Native plant A plant that has evolved naturally in an area.

Nautical mile The length of a minute of arc, 1/21,600 of an average great circle of Earth. Generally 1 minute of latitude is considered equal to 1 nautical mile. The accepted U.S. value is 1,852 meters (6,076 feet), approximately 1.15 times as long as the U.S. statute mile of 5,280 feet.

Neap tides Average tides that occur between full and new moons.

Noncoastal A zone Portion of a *special flood hazard area (SFHA)* in which the principal source of *flooding* is *runoff* from rainfall or snowmelt. In noncoastal A zones, flood waters may move slowly or rapidly, but *waves* are usually not a significant threat to buildings. See *A zone* and *coastal A zone*. (*NFIP* regulations do not differentiate between noncoastal A zones and coastal A zones.)

Nonnative plant Also called introduced, vegetation that has been brought to an area by humans or migrated and otherwise becomes established. Some nonnative plants become *invasive species*.

Nonpoint source pollution Indirect or scattered sources of *pollution* that enter a water system, such as drainage or *runoff* from agricultural fields, airborne *pollution* from crop dusting, and runoff from urban areas and construction sites.

No-take zones Aquatic or coastal areas in which all extractive activities (such as fishing) are prohibited.

Organic matter Materials and debris that originated as living plants or animals.

Oxidation (of organic matter) Decomposition (rotting, breaking down) of plant material through exposure to oxygen.

Ozone (O_3) The triatomic form of oxygen, a gaseous atmospheric constituent. In the *troposphere*, ozone is created both naturally and by photochemical reactions involving gases resulting from human activities (smog). Tropospheric ozone acts as a greenhouse gas. In the *stratosphere*, ozone is created by the interaction between solar ultraviolet radiation and molecular oxygen (O_2). Stratospheric ozone plays a dominant role in the stratospheric radiative balance.

Peak rate (of runoff) The maximum instantaneous rate at which *runoff* is discharged from a site as the result of a precipitation event, usually measured in cubic feet per second.

Pelagic Of or in the ocean or open water; in the *water column*.

Percolation, also percolation rate Downward movement of water under the influence of gravity movement and under hydrostatic pressure through the interstices of the rock or *sediment*.

Perennial Persisting for more than one year. Perennial plant species persist as woody vegetation from year to year or resprout from their rootstock annually.

Permafrost Permanently frozen subsoil layer occurring in the polar regions, in some areas to depth of 5,000 feet (1,500 m).

Permeability The property of bulk material (sand, crushed rock, soft rock) that permits movement of water through its pores.

pH A dimensionless measure of the acidity of *water* (or any solution). Pure water has a pH = 7. Acid solutions have a pH smaller than 7 and basic solutions have a pH larger than 7. Measurement of pH is on a logarithmic scale. A pH decrease of 1 unit corresponds to a 10-fold increase in acidity. (Figure G.5.)

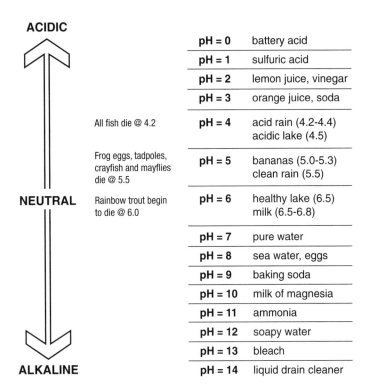

Figure G.5   Table of pH values.

Photic zone The area of a water body receiving sunlight, within which the light is sufficient to sustain photosynthesis. The depth of this layer varies with water clarity, time of year, and cloud cover but is about 330 feet (100 meters) in the open ocean.

Photosynthesis Process by which green plants, *algae*, and some bacteria take *carbon dioxide* from the air (or bicarbonate in water) to build carbohydrates.

Phytoplankton Floating plants or plantlike photosynthetic single-cell organisms.

Pier Structure, usually of open construction, extending out into the water from the shore, to serve as a landing place or facility rather than to afford coastal protection or affect the movement of water.

Piezometric surface The level at which the hydrostatic water pressure in an *aquifer* will stand if it is free to seek equilibrium with the *atmosphere*. For artesian wells, this is above the ground surface.

Pioneer species Plant species that first establishes itself in primary succession of unvegetated area.

Plankton Free-floating organisms drifting in water, unable to swim against currents.

Point source pollution Pollution from a clearly defined, localized source such as a sewage outfall, pipes, ditches, wells, vessels, and containers.

Pollution *Contamination* of natural environment.

Polyhaline High *salinity*, about 30 to 335 ppt.

Porosity A measure of the void spaces in a material, indicated as a fraction of the volume of voids over the total volume, between 0 to 1, or as a percentage between 0% to 100%; percentage of the total volume of a soil sample not occupied by solid particles but by air and water.

ppt Parts per thousand. Abbreviation used in representing small quantities in water (e.g., *salinity*).

Precipitation Rain, snow, sleet, freezing rain, mist.

Primary dune, also primary fontal dune See *dune*; also see *setback*.

Primary succession Plant colonization in a pristine *habitat*, such as bedrock areas left from devastating disturbances such as glaciers or wildfire. Secondary *succession* is a response to natural or human disturbance (e.g., fire, *flooding*, construction, or tree clearing).

Probability The chance that a prescribed event will occur, represented by a number (p) in the range 0 to 1. It can be estimated empirically from the relative frequency—that is, the number of times the particular event occurs—divided by the total count of all events considered in that class.

Recharge The addition of new water to an *aquifer* or to the zone of saturation.

Reef Chain or string of coral, oysters, rocks, or other hard substrate.

Relative sea level change The sum of the sinking of the land (*subsidence*) and eustatic sea level change; the change in average water level with respect to the surface. Also see *eustacy*.

Resilience The ability of a social or ecological system to absorb *disturbances* while retaining the same basic structure and ways of functioning, the capacity for self-organization, and the capacity to adapt to stress and change.

Respiration Process that, using oxygen, releases stored chemical energy to power an organism's life processes; opposite reaction of *photosynthesis*.

Restoration Make physical changes in a destroyed or impaired site to return it to the type of *habitat* that existed prior to alteration or disruptive impacts.

Revetment (i) A facing of stone or concrete to protect an *embankment* or shore structure against *erosion* by wave action or currents; (ii) a retaining wall, typically sloped.

Riffle A steep gradient section of streams recognizable by the rapid movement of water over a coarse substrate resulting in rough flow, turbulent surface, and high dissolved oxygen levels in the water. Riffle and deeper pool complexes associated with them provide valuable *habitat* for fish and wildlife.

Riparian (i) Pertaining to the banks and edges of a stream or river; (ii) plant communities occurring in association with any spring, lake, river, stream, or creek through which waters flow at least periodically.

Riparian zone Land and vegetation bordering flowing or standing water such as streams, rivers, lakes, and ponds. Riparian zones provide a variety of *ecosystem services* and help to improve or maintain local water quality.

Riprap Broken stone, cut stone blocks, or rubble layered on slopes as protection from *erosion* or scour caused by *flood* or *wave* action.

Rip tide/rip current Strong undertow of water flowing seaward from the shore through the surf line, normally in a low point or trench between two sandbars. (Figure G.6.)

Risk analysis Assessment of the total risk due to all possible environmental inputs and all possible mechanisms.

Riverine (i) Relating to or resembling a river; (ii) living or situated along a river.

Runoff Precipitation that drains into a water body from the surface of the surrounding land.

Run-up Rush of *wave* water up a slope or structure.

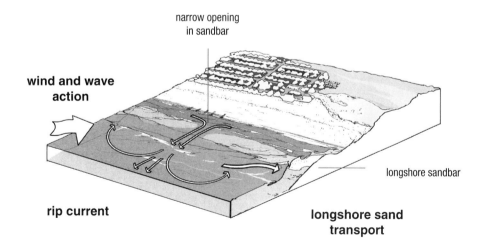

Figure G.6 *Rip currents can occur on any beach (ocean or large lake) with breaking waves.*

Salinity The concentration of dissolved salts in a body of water, commonly expressed as parts per 1,000 (ppt). Ocean water is about 3.5% salt, measured by salinity typically between 33 and 37 ppt. (Table B.)

Salinity gradient Change in salinity levels in a mixing zone where salt water meets freshwater flowing downstream from land.

Salt marsh Saltwater *wetlands* (15–18 ppt or greater) occurring along the coast, flooded regularly by tidal, *brackish* water, dominated by saltwater grasses such as *Spartina alterniflora* (oyster grass).

Saturated soil Soil in which the pore space is completely filled with water.

Saltwater intrusion Displacement of fresh surface water or *groundwater* by the advance of salt water due to its greater density. This usually occurs in coastal and estuarine areas due to reducing land-based influence (e.g., from reduced *runoff* and associated groundwater recharge, or from excessive water withdrawals from *aquifers*) or increasing marine influence (e.g., *relative sea level rise*).

Scarp An almost vertical slope along the beach caused by *erosion* by *wave* action. It may vary in height, depending on wave action and the nature and composition of the beach. See also *escarpment*.

Scour Removal of soil or fill material by waves and currents and/or the flow of floodwaters, especially at the base or toe of a shore structure.

Sea level rise (SSL) Sea level change, both globally and locally, due to changes in the shape of ocean basins, in the total mass of water, and in water density. Factors due to *global warming* include increase in the total amount and mass of *water* from the melting of land-based snow and ice, and decrease in water density due to thermal expansion from increase in ocean temperatures and salinity changes.

TABLE B WATER SALINITY BASED ON DISSOLVED SALTS IN PARTS PER THOUSAND (PPT)

Freshwater	<0.5 ppt
Brackish water	.5–30 ppt
Saline water	30–50 ppt
Brine	>50 ppt

Sea surface temperature The subsurface temperature in the top few meters of the ocean, measured by ships, buoys, and drifters. From ships, earlier measurements of water samples in buckets were mostly switched in the 1940s to samples from engine intake water. Satellite measurements of skin temperature (uppermost layer; a fraction of a millimeter thick) in the infrared or the top centimeter or so in the microwave spectrum are also used but must be adjusted to be compatible with the bulk temperature.

Sediment Particles deposited by air, wind, ice, and water. Other sediments are precipitated from the overlying water or form chemically, in place.

Sedimentary rock Rock formed by the consolidation of *sediment* particles or the remains of plants and animals.

Sediment plume Caused by *sediment*-rich rainwater *runoff* entering the ocean. The runoff creates a visible pattern of brown water that is rich in nutrients and suspended sediments that forms a kind of cloud in the water, spreading out from the coastline.

Sediment transport The means by which sedimentary materials are moved are gravity (gravity transport), running water (rivers and streams), ice (glaciers), wind, and the sea (currents and *littoral drift*). The mechanisms include rolling or traction, in which the sediment moves along the bed but is too heavy to be lifted from it; *saltation*; and suspension, in which particles remain permanently above the bed, sustained by the turbulent flow of the air or water.

Seiche Pronounced *saysh*. A standing wave oscillation of an enclosed water body that continues, pendulum fashion, after the cessation of the originating force, which may have been either seismic or atmospheric. Tides are considered to be seiches induced primarily by the periodic forces caused by the Sun and Moon. In the Great Lakes area, any sudden rise in the water of a harbor or a lake, whether it is oscillatory or not. (Although inaccurate in a strict sense, this usage is well established in the Great Lakes area.)

Setback In planning regulations, a limiting distance for location of construction, typically from the edge of a water body within which development is either prohibited or regulated and subject to specific plan approval or variance. Setbacks are established by local regulation for the purpose of maintaining open space next to wetlands, streams, lakes, *coastlines*, and other water bodies. The area within setbacks is frequently used for *flood* control, recreation, preservation of drinking water supply, and wildlife *habitat* enhancement. (Figure G.7.)

deep lot
building
setback

edge of
primary dune

mean high
water

Figure G.7 *Setback* limitations for coastal construction preserves *foreshore dune* and additional *buffer* that remove structures from the *Special Flood Hazard Area (SFHA)*.

Sequestration Carbon storage in terrestrial or marine reservoirs. Biological sequestration includes direct removal of carbon dioxide from the *atmosphere* through land use change, reforestation, carbon storage in landfills, and practices that enhance soil carbon in agriculture.

Sheet flow Water flow with a relatively thin and uniform depth; sheet flow may include *sediment* particles transported in the direction of flow.

Shoaling Decrease in water depth and shallowing of an open water area through deposition of *sediments*. The transformation of wave profiles as they propagate inshore.

Shore, shoreline The narrow strip of land in immediate contact with the sea, including the zone between high and low water lines. Also used in a general sense to mean the *coastline*. The line delineating the shoreline on NOAA nautical charts and surveys approximates the mean high water line.

Shoreline retreat Progressive movement of the shoreline in a landward direction caused by the composite effect of all storms considered over decades and centuries (expressed as an annual average *erosion* rate). Shoreline retreat considers the horizontal component of erosion and is relevant to longterm land use decisions and the siting of buildings.

Siltation Deposition of water-born silt and fine-particles of *sediment* in a body of water, a common result of *erosion*.

Special Flood Hazard Area (SFHA) Under the *NFIP*, an area having special *flood, mudslide*, and/or flood-related *erosion* hazards and shown on *Flood Insurance Rate Map*

(FIRM) as a *Zone A*, AO, A1–A30, AE, A99, AH, or *Zone V*, V1–V30, VE, M or E.

Species A classification of related organisms that can freely interbreed.

Spring tides Extreme high and low tides that occur about twice a month, with the full and new moons.

Stillwater elevation Projected elevation that floodwaters would assume, referenced to the established datum for that locale, in the absence of *waves* resulting from wind or seismic effects.

Stomata In botany, the pore structures found on the outer skin of leaves and plants that are used for gas exchange with the air.

Storm sewer system Pipes, conduits, *swales*, and other human-made improvements designed to carry *runoff*.

Storm surge A rise above normal water level on the open coast due to extreme meteorological conditions coincident to tides. In addition, wind-driven *waves* are superimposed on the wave height above the mean tidal elevation what would have occurred at that time and place. Storm surge resulting from a *hurricane* also includes that rise in level due to atmospheric pressure reduction as well as wind.

Stratosphere The highly stratified region of the atmosphere above the troposphere, extending from about 6 miles (10 km) ranging from 5 miles (9 km) in high latitudes to 10 miles (16 km) in the tropics on average to about 31 miles (50 km) altitude.

Streambank erosion Removal of soil particles from a bank slope primarily due to water action. Changes in *land* *use, climate,* ice, debris, and chemical reactions can also lead to streambank erosion.

Structure Defined for *floodplain management regulations* in the *NFIP* as "a walled and roofed building, including a gas or liquid storage tank that is principally above ground, as well as a manufactured home."

Sublittoral zone Portion of rocky shore always submerged.

Submerged Lands Act U.S. federal legislation first enacted in 1953 granting to coastal states federal rights to natural resources on or within 3 nautical miles of the *coastline* (up to 9 miles for Texas and the Gulf Coast of Florida). The federal government maintains the right to regulate offshore activities for national defense, international affairs, navigation, and commerce.

Subsidence A gradual sinking of land with respect to its previous level.

Substantial damage In the *NFIP*, damage of any origin sustained by a *structure* whereby the cost of restoring the structure to its before-damaged condition would equal or exceed 50% of the market value of the structure before the damage occurred.

Substrate In biology, substance or surface to which an organism attaches and grows.

Succession Progressive replacement of populations in a *habitat*; the temporal changes of plant and animal *species* in an area. Also see *primary succession.*

Succulent Plants that possess organs that store water in their roots, stems and leaves, facilitating survival during drought conditions (e.g., cacti).

Surface water Water in streams, brooks, rivers, ponds, and lakes.

Swale Constructed or natural depression or trough intended to hold and divert water *runoff.*

Swamp Lowland, generally saturated with water and covered with trees and aquatic vegetation; may be a deepwater swamp, such as the cypress tupelo, which has standing water all or part of the growing season or bottomland hardwood forests flooded periodically.

Swash zone Zone of wave action on the beach *foreshore,* which moves as waves and water levels vary, extending from the limit of run-down to the limit of *run-up.*

Symbiosis A close ecological relationship between two (or more) species. Symbiotic relationships may include one or the other species providing nutrition, shelter making, transportation, pollination, or predator and disease defense. Some scientific references consider mutual benefit to be the defining character of symbiosis. Others sources define variations, including:

Mutualism	Both species benefit by trading resources or services.
Commensalism	One species is benefited, the other is unaffected.
Parasitism	One species is benefited, the other is harmed.

Thermohaline circulation (THC) The global oceanic upwelling and circulation driven by density gradients between deep-water temperatures mixing with surface heat and freshwater as a function of heat (*thermo*) and salinity (*haline*)—as distinct from wind-driven currents and tides due to gravity of the Moon and Sun—also referred to as the ocean conveyor belt.

Threatened species Defined in the Code of Federal Regulations as a *species* "in danger of becoming an endangered species in the foreseeable future throughout all or a significant portion of its range." Also see *endangered species.*

Tide, and tidal current The periodic rising and falling of the water that results from gravitational attraction of the Moon and Sun and other astronomical bodies acting on the rotating Earth. Although the accompanying horizontal movement of the water resulting from the same cause is also sometimes called the tide, it is preferable to designate the latter as *tidal current,* reserving the name *tide* for the vertical movement.

Tidal wave (i) Wave motion of the tides; (ii) in popular usage, any unusually high and destructive water level along a shore, usually referring to *storm surge* or *tsunami,* which are not tidal phenomena at all.

Tombolo Sandbar that connects an island to mainland or other island, often resulting from longshore drift of sand and *sediment*; tombolos may also form on the leeward side of constructed offshore breakers.

Topographic map Line and symbol representation of natural and artificially created features in an area on which elevations are shown by *contour lines.* A topographic map may typically indicate locations or streams, roads, and buildings.

Tornado A violent, rotating column of air in contact with the surface of Earth and a thundercloud. The United States experiences more tornadoes than any country, due to the unique geography of the continent. (Figure G.8.)

Transition zone Area between habitats or *ecosystems*. Frequently, *transition zone* refers to the area between uplands and *wetlands*. In other cases, wetlands are referred to as transitional areas between uplands and aquatic ecosystems.

Transpiration Loss of water to the *atmosphere* by evaporation from plant leaves and stomata, facilitating flow of nutrients and water from roots to plant stems and leaves.

Tropical cyclone Storm characterized by large low-pressure center, released when moist air rises, originating near the equator, with some rotary circulation at the water surface. Called a *tropical depression* when characterized by moving thunderstorms and with slight or no rotary circulation at the water surface and a *tropical disturbance* when maximum sustained wind speeds are up to 39 miles per hour (32 knots); these may be early phases in the development of a *hurricane*.

Trophic level (trophic) Level of flow of nutrition in a *food chain* (e.g., producer, primary consumer, secondary consumer, tertiary consumer).

Troposphere The lowest part of the *atmosphere* from the surface to about 10 km in altitude in mid-latitudes (ranging from 9 km in high latitudes to 16 km in the tropics on average), where clouds and weather phenomena occur. In the troposphere, temperatures generally decrease with height.

Tsunami One or a series of ocean seismic waves caused by displacement of a large volume of water by subduction related to earthquakes, volcano, landslides, and other disturbances above and below ocean waters. On the open ocean, tsunamis have small amplitude (*wave height*) and long wave length (period) but grow in height as they approach a shoreline. Commonly miscalled tidal wave.

Turbidity Level of suspended *sediments* in water; opposite of clarity or clearness.

Typhoon The term applied to *tropical cyclones* in the western Pacific Ocean. See *hurricane*.

Upland General term for dry, nonwetland elevated land within a *watershed* above the *floodplain* and lower areas along streams of between hills. Often used as a general term to mean high land far from the *coastline*.

Vector In epidemiology and public health, an organism such as an insect that transmits a pathogen from one host to another.

Vertical stratification Gradient or layering of freshwater on top of salt water, also known as salt wedge effect; occurs when the fresh- and saltwater bodies join and are not vigorously mixed together by turbulence.

V zone See *coastal high hazard area (CHHA)*.

Water Molecule-composed compound of hydrogen and oxygen. Defined in the Code of Federal Regulations as "the part of the aquatic ecosystem in which organic and inorganic constituents are dissolved and suspended." Water forms part of a dynamic aquatic life-supporting system. Water clarity, nutrients and chemical content, physical and

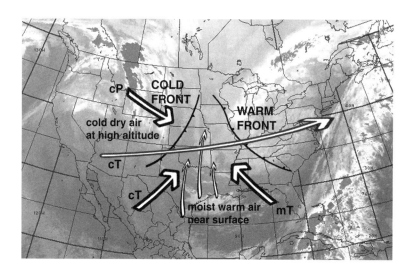

Figure G.8 *Tornado formation*

biological content, dissolved gas levels, pH, and temperature contribute to its life-sustaining capabilities.

Water balance In *hydrology*, the equation that describes the flow of water in an out of a system, at any scale, and including all forms of physical states and water storage.

Water column Volume of water from the bottom (pond, lake, or seafloor) to and including the water surface. The water column typically contains free-swimming, or *pelagic*, organisms and plankton.

Water cycle The process and path of water transport in its many states of liquid, solid (frozen), and vapor between Earth's lithosphere and *atmosphere*.

Watershed A drainage basin in which rain and snowmelt drains downhill into a shared body of water, such as a river, lake, reservoir, *wetland* or ocean. In some uses, *watershed* refers to the divide between separate drainage areas.

Water surface elevation Under the *NFIP*, the height, in relation to the reference datum, of *floods* of various magnitudes and frequencies in the *floodplains* of coastal or *riverine* areas.

Wave Ridge, deformation, or undulation of the water surface.

Wave height Vertical distance between the wave crest and preceding wave trough.

Weir Low-head dam or wall placed across a canal or river to raise, divert, regulate, or measure the flow of water.

Wetland Defined in the Code of Federal Regulations as "an area inundated or saturated by surface or ground water at a frequency and duration sufficient to support, and that under normal circumstances does support, a prevalence of vegetation typically adapted for life in saturated soil conditions."

Wrack line A string of debris stranded by last high tide; cast-ashore seaweeds, isolated sources of food and shade support an important community of isopods and amphipods as well as providing food for birds.

X zone Under the *NFIP*, areas where *flood* hazard is less than that in the *special flood hazard area (SFHA)*.

Zonation (zonal habitats) Distribution of plants or animals arranged in zones or bands, caused by gradations of biotic factors.

SOURCES FOR DEFINITIONS

American Meteorological Society. *AMS Glossary of Meteorology*, 2nd ed. Boston: Author, 2000, www.ametsoc.org/pubs/glossary_index.htm.

FEMA. *Coastal Construction Manual: Principles and Practices of Planning, Siting, Designing, Constructing, and Maintaining Residential Buildings in Coastal Areas* (FEMA 55), 2005, www.fema.gov/rebuild/mat/fema55.shtm.

Federal Register Code of Federal Regulations. CFR *Title 40—Protection of Environment.* 2009, www.gpoaccess.gov/ECFR/.

IPCC Fourth Assessment Report. *Appendix I: Glossary.* United Nations Framework Convention on Climate Change, ed. A. P. M. Beade, 2007, www.ipcc.ch/ipccreports/tar/wg1/518.htm.

NOAA Coastal Services Center. *Vulnerability Assessment Techniques and Applications (VATA). Glossary,* ed. B. Wayne Blanchard, www.csc.noaa.gov/vata/glossary.html.

U.S. Army Corps of Engineers. *Coastal Engineering Manual Appendix A—Glossary of Coastal Terminology,* ed. Andrew Morang and Andre Szuwalksi, 2003, http://chl.erdc.usace.army.mil/cemglossary.

U.S. Geological Survey National Wetlands Research Center, World Meteorological Organization. *Coastal Terminology.* www.flowmeterdirectory.com/coastal_terminology.html.

AUTHORS AND CONTRIBUTORS

Donald Watson, FAIA, NCARB

Donald Watson is an architect and planner. He was a Rockefeller Foundation Research Fellow in Environmental Affairs (1970–1972), visiting professor and Chair of the Yale School of Architecture Environmental Design Program (1972–1990), and professor and Dean of Architecture at Rensselaer Polytechnic Institute (1990–2001). He received the 2002 ACSA Distinguished Professor Award and AARC 2005 James Haecker Leadership Award for Architectural Research. His publications include *Climatic Building Design* (1984, 1993) coauthored with Kenneth Labs and winner of the AAP Best Book in Architecture and Planning Award. He edited the *AIA Energy Design Handbook 1993* and the John Wiley publication, *Architectural Designs: Classic Pages from Architectural Graphic Standards 1940– 1980.* He is editor of *Time-Saver Standards for Architectural Design* and *Time-Saver Standards for Urban Design.* His architectural designs have received widespread recognition and awards, including AIA COTE Earth Day Top 10 for New Canaan Nature Center 1997. He shared in the 2008 AIA President's Citation and U.S. Green Building Council Leadership Award as a founder of AIA Committee on the Environment (COTE). He serves on the Town of Trumbull Connecticut Conservation Commission, and is a member of the Connecticut Association of Conservation and Inland Wetland Commissions.

Michele Adams, P.E.

Michele Adams, P.E. LEED AP, is Principal Engineer and founder of Meliora Environmental Design LLC, a civil engineering firm specializing in sustainable site design and water resource planning. Building on a multidisciplinary approach, her work includes green infrastructure and low-impact development projects, urban restoration, commercial and residential sustainable water designs, public facilities, and environmental education centers. She was one of the authors of the *Pennsylvania Stormwater Manual* and the NYC Parks "High Performance Landscapes" design guidelines. She is Adjunct Professor at Philadelphia University, a frequent lecturer on the topics of water and sustainability, and serves as a member of the U.S. Green Building Council Sustainable Sites Technical Advisory Committee (SS TAG). Ms. Adams currently chairs the Planning Commission of East Vincent Township, Pennsylvania.

James B. DeStefano, P.E., AIA

Jim DeStefano is a Registered Professional Engineer, a board-certified Structural Engineer, and licensed Architect. He is president of the structural engineering firm of DeStefano & Chamberlain, Inc. Jim has served as the president of the Connecticut Structural Engineers Coalition and director of the National Council of Structural

Engineers Associations (NCSEA). Mr. DeStefano has served on the NCSEA Code Advisory Committee and currently serves on the Structural Engineering Institute (SEI) Sustainability Committee. He is chair of the CASE Fire Protection Committee and past chair of the CASE Special Inspections Committee and the CASE Masterspec Review Committee. Mr. DeStefano is a founder and past chairman of the Timber Frame Engineering Council (TFEC) and co-chairs the TFEC Technical Activities Committee, a member of the American Wood Council (AWC) Task Committee on Timber Framing, and a Director of the Structural Insulated Panel Association (SIPA). He serves on the American Plywood Association (APA) SIP Performance Standard Committee. He has authored numerous technical publications and articles and has served on land use boards and commissions in Westport, Connecticut, including the Planning and Zoning Commission, the Conservation Commission, and the Flood and Erosion Control Board. He was awarded the Engineering Excellence Award from ACEC-Connecticut in 1996 and again in 2008.

Christopher P. Jones, P.E.

Christopher Jones is a consultant specializing in coastal flood hazard analysis and coastal building codes. He has been deployed after major hurricanes since 1995 as part of FEMA's Building Performance Assessment Teams and Mitigation Assessment Teams. He authored the "Flood Resistance" section of the *NIBS Whole Building Design Guide*, was a coauthor for the update of *FEMA's Coastal Construction Manual*, and *FEMA's Home Builder's Guide to Coastal Construction*, and has contributed to numerous other FEMA Building Science publications. He served as principal investigator for an evaluation of NFIP Building Standards. Mr. Jones serves as chair of the ASCE-24 (Flood Resistant Design and Construction) Standards Committee. He has served on the Coastal Committee of the Association of State Floodplain Managers (ASFPM) and the International Code Council, Coastal Inspector Examination Development Committee.

INDEX

Atmosphere, 6, 273

  composition, 6

  dimensions of, 7, C.1

  layers, 8, 274

  moisture, 17, 32

Aquifer, 127, 273. *See also* Groundwater

Base Flood Elevation, 274. *See also* Flood, elevation

Beach. *See* Shore, beach

Beaufort scale, 19, 274, 275

Biodiversity, 36, 40, 275

Bioretention swale, 113–120. *See also* Rain garden

Biosphere, 9, 275

Buffer, 267, 275. *See also* Riparian buffer

Carbon cycle, 31, 32

  sequestraton, 34, 35, 43

Climate:

  change, xviii, xx, 40, 49, 219–222, 260, 264, 266

  definition, 9, 276

  impacts, 63, 226–228

Clouds:

  classification, 13

  formation, 2, 11, 21, 22

  types, 13

Coast, Coastal, Coastline:

  beach types, 154–158

  definitions, 180, 276

  design, 202, 203, 239, 240

  erosion, 158, 159, 166, 167

  flood hazards, 158, 159

  hazard area management, 137, 159, 160–167

  natural habitat, 43, 44

  planned development, 207, 289

  pollution, 60, 231, 260, 285, 286

  regional variations, 35, 36

  sediment budget, 152–153

  transect, 140, 204

Combined Sewer Overflow (CSO), 123, 261, 262, 276

Communities:

  coastal, 63, 199–207

  floodplain, 129, 130

  revitalization, xxi, 207, 272

  visioning workshop (charrette), 198, 209, 216, 240, 243

Coriolis effect, 9–11, 277

Corrosion, 181

Cyclone, Tropical, 9, 14, 23, 57, 260, 291

Cyclogenesis, 20, 21

Deicing chemicals, 112

Dry Floodproofing, 174, 175

Earthquake, 60

Ecological wastewater treatment, 123, 124, 261, 262

Ecosystem services, xvi, 103, 214, 215, 277

    compensation for, 213

    findings of fact, 127–129

Erosion, 147, 152, 278, 289. *See also* **Coast, erosion**

Estuary, xiv, 42, 45, 154

    definition, 40, 278

FEMA (Federal Emergency Management Agency), 130, 137, 169, 261, 278

FIRM (Flood Insurance Rate Map), 138, 141, 148, 279

Floating structures, 244–248

Floods, Flooding, xx, 49–52, 260

    alluvial, 135

    barriers, 164, 175, 251

    costs of, 63, 68, 69, 226–229

    definitions, 135, 279

    design, 135–149, 169, 176-194, 261, 262

    elevation of building, 171–174

    elevation of flood, 138–148, 278, 279, 292

    flash flood, 54

    ice jam, 54

    openings, 147, 182–184, 194 (*See also* **Wet floodprooofing**)

    20th c. U.S. flood history, 50–52

    types of, 54

    zones (NFIP), 139, 144

  Floodplain, 137

    definition, 88, 279

    detention, 98

    disconnected, 95

    management, xvi, 45, 127, 208, 261, 262

Floodway, 141, 142, 279

Forest, 35–37, 87, 110, 111, 128, 267. *See also* **Landscape**

Foundations, 176–184, 246

Franklin, Carol, vii, ix

Freeboard, 146, 279. *See also* **Flood, elevation**

Fujita Scale, 23, 59, 279

Geologic history, 279, 280, C.2

Geologic Hazard Abatement District (GHAD), 214–216

GEOS weather satellite, 12

Geotextile, 161, 162, 279

Gray water, 109, 261, 262

Green infrastructure, 119, 233, 261, 262

Green roof, 105–109, 256, 261, 262

Greenhouse effect, 8, 9, 35, 221, 222

Groundwater, 83, 260, 281

    recharge, 80, 94, 127, 281

    temperatures, 86

Humidity. *See* **Moisture**

Hurricane Katrina, 132, 133, C.16, C.18-C.22

Hurricane. *See* **Storms, hurricane**

Hydrologic cycle, 282, 283. *See also* **Water, water cycle**

Hydrosphere, 9

Impervious surface, 92, 93, 282. *See also* **Permeability**

Innovation, 258, 259, 262, 269

Interpretive exhibits, 125, 126

Japan, 253, 268

Jetty, 161, 163, 282

Jones, Christopher, viii, 147, 149, 294

Kirshen, Paul, 226–228

Land use, 24–36, 93, 260, 265, 284
Landscape,
    altered, 74, 85–87, 91, 93, 100, 176
    natural, 31, 71–73, 85, 91–93, 99, 100
Levees, 143, 236, 237, 249, 250-253, 261, 262, 284
Lower Manhattan, 238–243

MEP (Mechanical / Electrical / Plumbing).
    See Utilities
Meteorology, 10
Metonic cycle, 6, 284
Midnight sun, 5
Moisture, 184–186
Mudflow, Mudslide, 54, 58, 136, 216, 260, 285

Native planting, 102, 111, 261, 262, 285
Natural hazard disaster, 260
    cost of, 61
    probability of occurrence, 141, 287
Nature, lessons of, 258. *See also* Wildlife values
Netherlands, 240, 267, 268
NFIP (National Flood Insurance Program), 136,
    145–147, 285
    regulatory requirements, 191–194
New Orleans Principles, 209–213

Permaculture, 122, 261, 262
Permeability, 94, 285
    paving, 92, 104, 105, 261, 262
pH, 285, 286
Pond, 39, 41
Precautionary principle, xvii, 222
Precipitation, 14, 71

annual, U.S. cities, 76
changes in, 49, 53, 54
convectional, 14
intensity-duration-frequency, 77
interception, 77
orthographic, 14, 16
types, 17

Rain garden, 113, 120, 123, 261, 262
Rainwater collection, 107–109
Regional Plan Association, 240–243
Rio Earth Summit, xvii,
Riparian buffer, 89, 110, 119, 121, 261, 262, 287
    regulated setback, 208
Resilience:
    definition, xv, 287
    design for, xvi, 99, 103, 135, 197, 199–201, 211,
      257, 264, 272
River basins of U.S., C.4–C.13
Roofs, Roofing, 181, 185–187, C.21

Salinity, 260, 288
    gradient, 40
San Francisco Bay Rising Tides Competition, 218,
    229–237, 251–252
Salt marsh, 40, 42, 288
Sea level rise, xviii, 60, 62, 159, 219–222, 287, 288
Seawall, 161
Shore, Shoreline. *See also* Coastline
    beach, 43. 274, 151–158
    cliff, 39, 43, 44, 159
    protection, 160–166
Soils, 78–83, 92, 103, 118,
    carbon sequestration, 35, 36
    cation exchange, 84
    liquefaction, 60, *definition,* 289
    structural capacity, 178, 179. (*See also* Foundations)

Smart Growth, 209, 225, 256

Streams, 84–88, 95–97, 121

   daylighting, 90

Sun-earth geometry, 3, 4, 10

Steep slopes, 128, 159

Storms:

   hailstorm, 22

   hurricane, 25–28, 282, C.3

   ice storm, 25, 112

   landfall impacts, 58

   northeaster, 23, 24, 48

   tropical, 21

   tsunami, 55, 58, 291

Storm surge, 57, 160, 168, 260, 289

Stormwater design, xvi, 63, 91–100

Swamp, 41

   definition, 40, 290

Swimming pools, 190

Symbiosis, 290

Thermohaline circulation, 15, 290

Tornado, 22–24, 59, 291

Tree trench, 114, 116, 117

U.S. Green Building Council, 209, 210

Utilities, 170, 188-190, 193, 201, 211, 262

Vegetation, 78–81, 163, 165. *See also* **Buffer, Landscape**

Vernal pool, 40

   definition, 38

Wastewater, 63, 123

Water, xvii, 3, 31-33, 63, 291

balance, 71–73, 292

global resource, 33

water cycle, 31, 32, 292

Watershed, 38, 230. *See also,* **Web-based planning tools**

   classification, 39

   definition, 37, 292

   planning, xvi, 43, 45, 112, 123–125, 261, 262

Wave, 143, 144, 151, 282, 292

   breaker types, 155

   mechanics, 154

Weather, 3, 8, 45, 59, 17

   global patterns, 15

   on the ground, 14

   U.S. continental, 16

Web-based planning tools:

   FEMA DFIRM, 138, 148

   NOAA Coastal County Snapshots, 62, 65

   NOAA CanVis, 153, 167

Wells, Malcomb, vii, 107

Wet floodproofing, 174, 189

Wetland, 88, 103, 122, 124

   carbon content, 35

   definition, 38, 292

   ecosystem services, 127

   protection, 121, 156, 157, 235

   regulated setback, 208

Williams, Daniel E., vii, xi, 224, 225

Wildlife values, 40–44, 119, 126, 129, 281

Wind, 19, 60, 282

   structural design, 180

   wind speed, 61